Jene M

Computational Organization
Theory

Computational Organization Theory

edited by

Kathleen M. Carley
Michael J. Prietula
Carnegie Mellon University

LEA

LAWRENCE ERLBAUM ASSOCIATES, PUBLISHERS

1994   Hillsdale, New Jersey   Hove, UK

Lawrence Erlbaum Associates, Inc., Publishers
365 Broadway
Hillsdale, New Jersey 07642

Library of Congress Cataloging in Publication Data

Computational organization theory / edited by Kathleen M. Carley,
Michael J. Prietula.
    p. cm.
Includes bibliographical references and index.
ISBN 0-8058-1406-X
    1. Psychology, Industrial—Simulation methods. 2. Organizational
behavior—Simulation methods. 3. Computer simulation. I. Carley,
Kathleen M. II. Prietula, Michael J.
HF5548.8.C583 1994
158.7—dc20   93-39364
                                        CIP

Books published by Lawrence Erlbaum Associates are printed on acid-free
paper, and their bindings are chosen for strength and durability.

Printed in the United States of America
10 9 8 7 6 5 4 3 2 1

Contents

Foreword   **vii**
    Richard M. Cyert

Introduction: Computational Organization Theory   **xi**
    Kathleen M. Carley and Michael J. Prietula

1   The "Virtual Design Team": Simulating How Organization
     Structure and Information Processing Tools Affect Team
     Performance   **1**
     Raymond E. Levitt, Geoffrey P. Cohen, John C. Kunz,
     Clifford I. Nass, Tore Christiansen, and Yan Jin

2   Evolving Novel Organizational Forms   **19**
     Kevin Crowston

3   TASCCS: A Synthesis of Double-AISS and Plural-Soar   **39**
     Harko Verhagen and Michael Masuch

4   ACTS Theory: Extending the Model of Bounded Rationality   **55**
     Kathleen M. Carley and Michael J. Prietula

5   Graph Theoretical Dimensions of Informal Organizations   **89**
     David Krackhardt

 6   A Theoretical Evaluation of Measures of Organizational
      Design: Interrelationship and Performance Predictability   **113**
      Zhiang Lin

 7   Modeling and Computational Analysis of Reactive
      Behavior in Organizations   **161**
      Markku Verkama, Raimo P. Hämäläinen,
      and Harri Ehtamo

 8   Validating an Expert System That Designs Organizations   **179**
      Helmy H. Baligh, Richard M. Burton, and Børge Obel

 9   Computer Simulations of Organizations as Experiential
      Learning Systems: Implications for Organization Theory   **195**
      Theresa K. Lant

10   Social Dilemmas and Fluid Organizations   **217**
      Natalie S. Glance and Bernardo A. Huberman

11   Human and Artificially Intelligent Traders in Computer
      Double Auctions   **241**
      Dhananjay K. Gode and Shyam Sunder

12   Team Coordination Under Individual and Team Goals   **263**
      Ping Shi, Peter B. Luh, and David L. Kleinman

13   A Decision Logic for Operational Risk Management   **289**
      Giampiero E. G. Beroggi and William A. Wallace

Author Index   **309**

Subject Index   **315**

Foreword

Richard M. Cyert
Carnegie Mellon University

Professors Carley and Prietula have done the field of organization theory a great service by putting together this selection of chapters. The book is an excellent summary of the computational approach. Organization theorists have clearly taken a new path methodologically over the last 5 to 10 years. Simulation of organizations goes back at least 30 years, but the current approach has new elements in it.

In the past, simulations have tended to be of actual organizations. They have been built around the study of decision-making processes and have consisted of participants in the organization making decisions in the way that the organization theorists have observed in the real world. There have also been more theoretical approaches where the simulation consisted of participants with particular characteristics doing particular tasks.

In the new approaches as represented by this book, the incentive for the simulations comes to a much greater extent from artificial intelligence and its derivative, expert systems. These new simulations tend to be more complete organizations than the earlier simulations and have been developed as models within which some of the propositions of organization theory can be tested or at least played out for lengths of time that cannot be observed easily in the real world. The development of Soar by Newell and of the social agent by Carley and Newell are representations of the approach that I consider the new approach.

One of the dangers of simulation is that the simulations become so complex that the model is as difficult to analyze as the real world. This defect arises because the creator of the model is trying to encompass too much of the real world. We must always remember that the simulation is a model and is, therefore, a simplified and generalized version of the reality we have observed. The second potential pitfall is that simulations when done frequently enough may begin to appear as though they are the real world to the organization theorist. This perception is, of course, a serious mistake. It is particularly bad if the organization theorist prefers manipulating the model to becoming involved in real problems in real organizations. Social scientists, particularly economists, have a fatal attraction for working on theoretical propositions with mathematical models or simulation models and avoiding the real world. The result becomes a discipline that feeds on itself. Problems that are analyzed become the problems that are in the literature, and there is a tendency to achieve prestige by making a model more complicated than the one in the literature. I do not see any of this happening yet in organization theory, but it is something to be wary of and to guard against.

The big advantage of simulation models over mathematical models is the ability of the simulation to capture more of the real world. There are several chapters using mathematical methods in this book, and they make clear the advantages on the mathematical side (e.g., the chapters by Krackhardt; Shi, Luh, & Kleinman; Glance & Huberman; and Beroggi & Wallace). I would classify the major advantage as increased precision in the definition of terms. Frequently, organization theorists write about propositions in words that are not precise enough to enable the propositions to be tested. The use of mathematics to increase the precision may well be extremely useful. However, for the longer run development of organization theory, I am convinced that simulation is a methodology that will prove to be more fruitful.

The problem of organizational design is attacked in a variety of ways in this book. The design problem is an extremely important one. As one looks over the history of business firms, it is clear that experimentation with different forms of organization is inherent in the process of managing a firm. An important aspect of organizational design relates to specific goals that the designer might want to achieve. Outcomes for particular units can be influenced by the person to whom the unit leader reports. For example, at Carnegie Mellon University when I was president, I wanted the library to move toward the area of automation. This desire developed at a time when few librarians knew anything about computers. We nevertheless changed the organization so that the library reported to the director of the computer center. There was great unhappiness among the librarians over this move, but within a relatively short time the whole atmosphere changed, and the librarians began to realize that computers could be of great aid in making the library run smoothly. The net result over the years has been to make Carnegie Mellon's library a leader in automation.

The usual dimensions of design, however, relate to centralization and decentralization. One of the fallacies of posing the problem in this way is that the question is treated as though there are only two points and as though they are 180 degrees from each other. In fact, the question should be treated in terms of a continuum of points in which there are different degrees of centralization and decentralization. Putting it another way, there are some functions that should be decentralized and some functions that should remain centralized in every organization if one is striving for a maximum amount of efficiency.

Another criterion that can be used in organizational design is that of economizing. This concept brings organization theory closer to economics. The key, however, is using a criterion of economizing without using marginal analysis—in other words, to get a design that economizes with operational criteria. Economizing should be interpreted as actions that maximize the satisfaction of the individual or that produce an output that is desired in the most efficient way. Economists have certain rules of behavior that have been derived using marginal analysis and that ensure the fulfillment of the efficiency criterion. However, in the real world the rules cannot be applied in any precise manner and therefore fail to be useful. The key for organization theory would be to use the concept of economizing with operational rules.

Another methodology that has been used from time to time is experimentation. This book has an excellent chapter on experimental methods to understand market behavior. The chapter by Gode and Sunder simulates competitive markets with the use of artificial intelligence. Experiments have been used in the past, but they have usually been of a simple nature and have focused generally on communication. The possibility of a more complicated simulation in the laboratory might be an effective way for testing out ideas on organization design.

This book is, of course, more than a series of chapters on organizational design. A wide range of topics in organizational theory is considered. The chapter by Lant emphasizes an important topic, organizational learning. This topic is extremely important because it is the key to dynamic behavior in the organization. Basically, the organization sets goals, takes action, and compares the results of the action with the goals. On the basis of its learning from past situations, it then selects some policies to move forward. It may do nothing if the organization's performance is meeting its goals, but it may well take action if the organization is exceeding the goals or if performance is less than the goals. Learning enables the organization to deal with the external world if the learning is effective. Organizations are adaptive, and organization learning is a key to the way in which the adaptations take place.

In conclusion, let me stress again the great contribution that the editors,

Kathleen Carley and Michael Prietula, have made in bringing this collection of articles into print. Organization theory has suffered to some extent from the fact that it has been primarily a broad framework that enables a practitioner to learn about the nature of organizations and provides some keys to the way to design organizations. Computational organization theory brings into play an effort to be more precise and to draw more implications for organization theory from the various simulation models that are conceived and created. These movements are all in the right direction. The important caution, which I repeat, is that all work in computational organization theory must continue to pay attention to the real world. We must not commit the fatal error of taking all of our problems from the literature. Live organizations must be studied, and the results of those studies can then be utilized in simulated models of organizations. If we can proceed along this path, then the future of organization theory as a contributor to the improvement of human welfare is guaranteed.

Computational Organization Theory — An Introduction

Kathleen M. Carley
Michael J. Prietula
Carnegie Mellon University

There is a growing awareness among organizational theorists that people, tasks, and the sociostructural situations defining people's interaction networks matter. Statements such as "organizations don't make decisions, people do," "this is a very complex organizational task," and "it's not what you know but who you know" illustrate the importance of these factors. Research focused on particular constructs regarding people (e.g., psychology, artificial intelligence), tasks (e.g., social psychology, organizational behavior), or social-situational networks (e.g., sociology, anthropology) has, often in exclusion of mutual consideration, generated a fecundity of findings regarding their respective research perspectives.[1]

Two observations relevant to this book can be made regarding these efforts. First, rarely can generalized organizational behavior be explained by examining solely the characteristics of the component agents (e.g., employee's age, gender, race), the tasks (e.g., number of job steps, time to completion), or the situation networks (e.g., formal structure is/not a hierarchy, informal structure is/not dense, communication structure is/not bidirectional or reliable) in isolation. Researchers are beginning to realize that causal explanations and appropriate generalizations of certain organizational phenomena necessarily involve combining perspectives. Thus, we

---

[1]Note that this characterization of perspectives has many forms. For example, Scott (1987) made the basic distinction in terms of social psychology, structural and ecological, and proceeds to elaborate in more detail. The point is that researchers typically align themselves at some perspective, and proceed in relative isolation.

see cross-fertilization of methods and data commencing among psychology, social psychology, and sociology (e.g., Fisk & Taylor, 1984; House, 1977; Taylor & Johnson, 1986).

Second, at "all levels and perspectives" of analysis, the use of formalisms, such as computer simulation, is becoming a more accepted, indeed sometimes indispensable, method for organizational research and theory building; see, for example, the work of Masuch and LaPotin (1989), Harrison and Carroll (1991), and Carley (1992). Computer simulation, a particular interest of this volume, is not new to organizational theorists. Indeed, the history of organizational theory is dotted with use of this approach, often influenced early on by the contributions of the cybernetics, general systems, and systems analysis movements (e.g., Ashby, 1956; Beer, 1964; Haberstroh, 1965); organizational formalisms (e.g., Hage, 1965); and the efforts of systems dynamics (e.g., Forrester, 1961). Perhaps the classic example of simulation is Cyert and March's *A Behavioral Theory of the Firm* (1963), whereas the classic "garbage can model" (Cohen, March, & Olsen, 1972) spawned an entire generation of research (March & Weissinger-Baylon, 1986). However, emerging on the organizational scene is a set of new computational approaches such as expert systems and intelligent agent architectures. Further, there is a renewed and perhaps increased attention to integrating computational and noncomputational techniques. Both of these factors improve our ability to do theory building and are represented by numerous chapters in this volume.

The need to understand organizational behavior is thus moving us as theorists into the realm of detailed computational models of people, tasks, and networks interrelated in complex, dynamic, adaptive ecological systems. New (or sometimes renewed) approaches on how to conduct organizational research from multiple perspectives are appearing; furthermore, there is an increased potential for these approaches, due to theoretical, methodological, and technological progress. Advances in logic, symbolic programming, and network analysis provide important methodologies. Advances in computer technology itself place the requisite modeling tools at the organizational theorists' fingertips. Advances in cognitive science (a strongly interdisciplinary perspective) are revealing fundamental insights into problem solving and decision making through the use of computational models. Similar needs and advances in other disciplines have led to a growth of interest in and recognition of the construction of computational models as a mechanism for theory building and testing, such as computational linguistics, computational physics, and computational economics. For this volume, the area is *computational organization theory*.

Within organization theory, the basic rationale for turning to computational techniques is that, despite their simplified nature, many models of organizations are too complex to be analyzed completely by conventional techniques that lead to closed-form solutions. Thus, many researchers find it necessary to turn to simulation in order to derive predictions. The models of Levitt, Cohen, Kunz, Nass, Christiansen, and Jin (chapter 1), Verhagen and Masuch (chapter 3), Verkama, Hämäläinen, and Ehtamo (chapter 7), and Glance and Huberman (chapter 10), although simplifying away much of what we know to happen in organizations, are nonetheless sufficiently complex to necessitate simulation. There are three basic reasons for such model complexity. First, many models contain nonlinearities that cannot be eliminated through variable transformations. Simply making the models linear often denies the central characteristic of the model that enables it to most closely capture some aspect of reality.

Second, it is often important to deal with difference rather than differential equations. People, facts, and organizations are all discrete items. For example, Krackhardt (chapter 5) is able to develop a series of measures of organizational design that enable researchers to consider how networks affect organizational behavior because he treats agents and the links between them as discrete. Lin (chapter 6) takes measures such as Krackhardt's and, because they are discrete, is able to apply them to a series of artificial organizations and study their relationship to organizational performance. Treating such items as discrete increases the realism of the models but (from a practical standpoint) decreases solvability because fewer analytic solutions are known for difference equations than for differential equations. Translation of difference equations to differential equations also often changes the dynamic properties of the model, as well as the equilibrium solutions.

Third, agents in organizational models tend to act in parallel and to adapt to the behavior of other agents. Behavior of the group is thus recursively defined and self-referential. Controlling the fine order of interaction and enabling adaptive agents are procedures handled most effectively by simulation. Many organizational models could be solved without resorting to computational techniques if we were interested solely in the behavior of two or three agents. However, many individual behaviors are affected by group size, and people behave differently in isolation than in groups. In order to investigate the behavior of groups realistically sized to correspond to organizations, it is necessary to turn to simulation. Such technical considerations address purely how one evaluates a particular functional formulation and locates the predictions that follow from it in the realm of interest.

Aside from the necessity of using simulation to evaluate the specific models proposed in this book, computational techniques offer a variety of advantages to the researcher interested in theory development. This point is made by Lant (chapter 9). The first advantage, theoretical precision, holds both for simulation and for other formal modeling techniques. The process of creating a formal model forces the researcher to be precise about the relationship among entities, to make implicit assumptions explicit, and to describe in detail the mechanisms by which entities and relationships change. In building a simulation model the researcher must make precise choices about how various mechanisms work, such as communication and learning. Although such precision often limits the scope of the model, it also enables the theoretician to locate (and specify) primitive mechanisms that are sufficient to generate complex behavior. The seemingly simple task of converting such eloquent and detailed theories of organizational behavior such as Thompson's (1962) into mathematical equations, logical statements, or code serves to demonstrate how underspecified these theories are and what giant gaps there are in our knowledge of human and social behavior.

The second advantage of computational techniques is predictive accuracy. Dynamic models that contain feedback tend to capture more of the reality of the social situation but often are unsolvable when conventional methods are used. Further, even in the case of models as simple as that described in this volume, it is extremely difficult for the researcher to think them through and derive implications without making mistakes. Even as statistical packages help researchers to derive multiple-regression results without error, computational analysis helps researchers to derive predictions from their models without error.

Another advantage is that the researcher can use computational techniques to examine alternative hypothetical societies in order to learn what alterations in such organizations might be necessary to produce different outcomes. The Organizational Consultant by Baligh, Burton, and Obel (chapter 8) enables this type of analysis. The value of such "what if" exercises is not that they prove why the organization is as it is, but that they provide a way of reasoning about the situation and enable the researcher to create hypotheses that are better informed, which then can be tested empirically.

The final advantage of simulation mentioned here is that it facilitates the development of mechanism-oriented theories. Mechanism-oriented theories, which now dominate cognitive psychology, characterize the individual by a set of mechanisms that process information and perform tasks. Predictions and explanation derive from inferring the behavior these mechanisms would produce. In contrast, variable-oriented theories, which are still the norm in most of sociology, characterize the individual in terms of a set of variables without specifying how these variables arise or change over time. Predictions about the relative effects of these variables and their interactions are posited. In order to model dynamic organizational phenomena at the microlevel we need models of social agents. Although social agents can be characterized as bundles of attributes, as actors they are sets of mechanisms. Thus, mechanism-oriented theories are required as the foundation for dynamic organization theory. This is true whether those actors are individuals operating within organization, as in the work of Verhagen and Masuch (chapter 3), Carley and Prietula (chapter 4), and Lin (chapter 6), or whether they are "organizational agents" operating within a market or in larger environmental settings, as in the work of Gode and Sunder (chapter 11) and Verkama, Hämäläinen, and Ehtamo (chapter 7). In summary, computational techniques are tools for theory construction that help the researcher to increase the specificity of theory, think through the theoretical implications, generate testable predictions, and reason about mechanisms.

The use of computational techniques is not an "all-or-none" proposition. Computational techniques can be fruitfully employed in conjunction with noncomputational models, human experiments, and empirical data to provide a more rich understanding of organizational behavior. For example, Glance and Huberman (chapter 10) use simulation to confirm analytic predictions and illustrate atypical behavior. Similarly, Beroggi and Wallace (chapter 13) combine computational and noncomputational analytic techniques. Baligh, Burton, and Obel (chapter 8) could not have developed the Organizational Consultant without extensive analysis of real organizations and testing of the consultant relative to specific case studies. Shi, Luh, and Kleinman's work (chapter 12) has both empirical and analytic components.

This book brings together a set of researchers working in the area of computational organization theory. Computational organization theory is distributed across many disciplines. Researchers in organizational theory, as well as researchers in distributed artificial intelligence, civil engineering, control theory, electrical engineering, organization economics, social psychology, and organizational sociology, will find familiar themes spread throughout. Nevertheless, several common threads run through these chapters.

First, computational methods are often employed. Second, there is an attention to modeling at least one of the triumvirate: the agents, the tasks, or the networks. Third, cross-cutting the agent–task–network triumvirate is an interest in organizational design, organizational learning, coordination, decision logic, and decision support. Many chapters cross over and are actually in multiple areas. For example, Crowston (chapter 2) employs a learning/adaptive model yet deals with the question of organizational structure. Gode and Sunder (chapter 11), although focusing on the rationality (or in this case nonrationality) of the organizational decision, are nonetheless able to derive implications at the macrolevel for both learning and organizational design. Carley and Prietula (chapter 4) attempt to place agents, tasks, and networks into a unified perspective on organizations.

Beroggi and Wallace (chapter 13) consider how the decision logic employed by agents affects organizational planning, coordination, and effectiveness.

This book grew out of the 1992 TIMS Workshop on Mathematical Organization Theory sponsored by the Institute of Management Science, College on Organizations. The founder of these workshops, Richard Burton of the Fuqua School of Business at Duke University, set the tone of multidisciplinarity, eclectic acceptance of methodologies, and attention to advances in organization theory through understanding process that we followed in future workshops. The intent of the 1992 workshop was to bring together researchers in computational organization theory, to create an awareness of the community, and to provide a forum for intellectual exchange on these topics. Hopefully, this book will further this exchange.

In putting together this volume we have benefited from the support of many individuals, not the least of which are the contributing researchers and their support staffs. We are particularly grateful to Julie Eldridge of TIMS, Mark Kamlet and the Department of Social Decision Science, and Robert Sullivan, Dean of the Graduate School of Industrial Administration at Carnegie Mellon University, for their support of this project and the workshop. Our thanks also to Ruth Silverman for helping to coordinate this project.

REFERENCES

Ashby, W. R. (1956). The effect of experience on a determinant system. *Behavioral Science, 1,* 35–42.

Beer, S. (1964). *Cybernetics and management.* New York: Wiley.

Carley, K. (1992). Organizational learning and personnel turnover. *Organization Science, 3*(1), 20–46.

Cohen, M. D., March, J. G., & Olsen, J. P. (1972). Model of organizational choice. *Administrative Sciences Quarterly, 17*(1), 1–25.

Cyert, R., & March, J. (1963). *A behavioral theory of the firm.* Englewood Cliffs, NJ: Prentice-Hall.

Fisk, S. T., & Taylor, S. E. (1984). *Social cognition.* Reading, MA: Addison-Wesley.

Forrester, J. W. (1962). *Industrial dynamics.* Cambridge, MA: MIT Press.

Haberstroh, C. J. (1965). Organizational design and systems analysis. In J. March (Ed.), *Handbook of organizations.* Chicago: Rand McNally.

Hage, J. (1965). An axiomatic theory of organizations. *Administrative Science Quarterly, 10,* 289–320.

Harrison, J. R., & Carroll, G. R. (1991). Keeping the faith: A model of cultural transmission in formal organizations. *Administrative Science Quarterly, 36,* 552–582.

House, J. S. (1977). The three faces of social psychology. *Sociometry, 40,* 161–177.

March, J., & Weissinger-Baylon, R. (Eds.). (1986). *Ambiguity and command: Organizational perspectives on military decision making.* Boston: Pitman.

Masuch, M., & LaPotin, P. (1989). Beyond garbage cans: An AI model of organizational choice. *Administrative Science Quarterly, 34,* 38–67.

Scott, R. S. (1987). *Organizations: Rational, natural and open systems (2nd ed.).* Englewood Cliffs, NJ: Prentice-Hall.

Taylor, M. C., & Johnson, M. P. (1986). Strategies for linking individual psychology and social structure: Interdisciplinary and cross-disciplinary social psychology. *British Journal of Social Psychology, 25,* 181–192.

Thompson, J. D. (1962). *Organizations in action.* New York: McGraw-Hill.

1

The "Virtual Design Team": Simulating How Organization Structure and Information Processing Tools Affect Team Performance

Raymond E. Levitt, Geoffrey P. Cohen, John C. Kunz,
Clifford I. Nass, Tore Christiansen, Yan Jin
Stanford University

This chapter reports the initial results of research to build and test a computer simulation model of information processing and communication in a multidisciplinary engineering design organization. The Virtual Design Team (VDT) is a computational discrete event simulation model incorporating qualitative reasoning concepts derived from artificial intelligence research. VDT explicitly incorporates information-processing and communication models from organization theory that allow qualitative predictions of organizational performance. The inputs to VDT are a description of the design task and the subtasks that comprise it, including sequential dependencies between subtasks; a description of the actors in the design team and of their organizational structure; and a listing of the communication tools (e.g., facsimile, voice mail, electronic mail, meetings) available to each actor. The output of VDT is a prediction of the total processing time required to complete all subtasks (a surrogate for total labor cost of design), and of the duration to complete the entire design project along the longest or *critical* path through subtasks. VDT's behavior has been validated extensively for internal consistency. Its behavior also compares well with theoretical predictions about, and the observed behavior of, a 120-person team engaged in the design of a large petrochemical refinery. The simulation model can serve as a facility to formulate and test specific conjectures regarding the qualitative effect on project cost and duration of changes in the organization structure of the team, or in the communications tools available to participants. Engineering disciplines have long had mathematical models and, more recently, numerical computational models, to

1

support analysis and optimization of physical systems. This work provides initial evidence that symbolic computer modeling can be used to express and test social science theories applied to real world organizations and the communication tools that they employ.

The goal of the Virtual Design Team research project is to develop computerized analysis tools to support the systematic design of organization structures — including the communication tools that permit data, decisions, and knowledge to be shared within and between organizations — for complex, project-oriented tasks. We begin by sketching out the nature of a systematic design process to show the crucial role of analysis tools in design.

Design of artifacts to meet human needs — whether they be physical artifacts such as buildings, or social artifacts such as business organizations — is a ubiquitous human activity and can be broken down into the following generic steps:

1. Requirements definition — A set of functional, esthetic, and other objectives for the artifact is specified, along with cost, time, regulatory, and other constraints; the required behavior of key subsystems and components can be derived from this set of objectives and constraints for the artifact.

2. Synthesis — A candidate design solution is synthesized, typically by selecting elements from sets of more or less standard primitive components or features, connecting them (to provide load paths, fluid flow channels, information communication channels, etc.), and locating the elements in space.

3. Analysis — The behavior of each candidate solution is predicted by simulating the behavior of the system of connected primitive elements, using cognitive, physical, mathematical, or computational models.

4. Evaluation — The behavior of each candidate solution's subsystems (at whatever level of detail is deemed necessary) is compared against the derived requirements for subsystem behaviors.

5. Acceptance or recycling — Based on the evaluation of performance, a candidate solution is accepted or cycles back to synthesis, with changes guided by the latest evaluation results (Levitt, Jin, & Dym, 1991).

If analysis capabilities are lacking in a given domain, then the relative performance of alternative syntheses cannot be predicted and compared a priori. In this case, evaluation must be based on experience with a given synthesis, so that the design process reverts to adaptation of past experience.

For physical systems such as chemical plants or complex building structures, the behaviors of interest (e.g., reaction products or deflections) can often be predicted by solving sets of equations involving continuous numerical variables. Since the 1960s, the analysis phase of design for many kinds of physical artifacts has been revolutionized by the use of computational analysis tools that have greatly speeded up analysis and have extended its range to situations where closed-form mathematical analysis was previously impossible. Because of this, design has become highly formalized in these engineering domains, and tremendous progress has been made both in understanding the behaviors of interest in each domain and in generating interesting new syntheses, greatly extending the range of artifacts that can be designed and manufactured safely and economically.

In contrast, the use of computers to support analysis in the design of social systems has been very limited. Most organizational behaviors of interest to scientists or managers can only be represented as discrete, nominal, or ordinal variables, leading to a mismatch between these theories and the continuous, quantitative models suited to traditional simulation techniques. Consequently, as Tatum (1984) found, managers of large design and construction projects—like most managers designing large-scale organizations to carry out complex tasks—still rely on adaptation of past organization structures, rather than on systematic generation and evaluation of alternatives, in designing their organization structures.

During the 1980s, artificial intelligence (AI) researchers developed techniques for representing discrete, nonnumerical variables, and for reasoning rigorously about relationships between them (Kunz, Stelzner, & Williams, 1989). These qualitative reasoning techniques provide researchers with a powerful new set of tools to begin developing computational models of problem domains that require qualitative reasoning with discrete, nonnumerical variables (Clancey, 1989). A number of engineering researchers have embraced AI techniques to begin formalizing other phases of design, in particular synthesis of physical artifacts and assembly sequences to manufacture them (Coyne, Rosenman, Radford, Balachandran, & Gero, 1990; Levitt, 1990).

Although others have proposed the use of artificial intelligence modeling ideas to simulate micro-organizational behavior (e.g., Bushnell, Serfarty, & Kleinman, 1988; Carley, Kjaer-Hansen, Newell, & Prietula, 1992; Cohen, 1986; Masuch & LaPotin, 1989), the Virtual Design Team is a pioneering effort to employ ideas from artificial intelligence for modeling the behavior of full-scale organizations (Cohen, 1992; Cohen & Levitt, 1991). Our long-range goal is to develop robust computer simulation models of large-scale, concurrent engineering organizations in order to predict the impact of alternative task definitions, organization structures, and communication tools on the quality, cost, and production time of their products. The VDT model described here is a first step toward that goal: Given detailed descriptions of tasks, actors (individuals and groups), communication tools available to actors, team organizational structure, and a definition of the tasks involved in design of the product, VDT predicts the duration of the design project. The current version of VDT treats the tasks, actors, and product as fixed, and examines the impact of alternative communication tools and organizational structures on the productivity of the design team.

To verify our representation and reasoning framework, we chose to test VDT by observing and modeling a large petrochemical design project. This project was selected as a test case because the engineering design issues were well understood, without significant or novel technical problems.

ORGANIZATION CONCEPTS REPRESENTED IN VDT

The basic premise of the VDT model is that organizations are fundamentally information-processing structures—a view of organizations that dates back to Max Weber's work in the early 1900s, and that is elaborated in the work of March and Simon (1958), Simon (1976), and Galbraith (1977). In this view, an organization is an information-processing and communication system, structured to achieve a specific set of tasks, and comprised of limited information processors (individuals or subteams). These information processors send and receive messages along specific lines of communication (e.g., formal lines of authority) via communication tools with limited capacity (e.g., memos, voice mail, meetings). To capture these characteristics and constraints, VDT employs explicit descriptions of tasks, communications, actors, tools, and structures. Thus, for example, each modeled manager has specific and limited (boundedly rational) information-processing abilities, and managers send and receive messages to and from other actors along prespecified communication channels, choosing from a limited set of communication tools. The view of organizations that we have implemented is presented in Fig 1.1.

Task

Our goal is to analyze engineering design teams carrying out routine designs. We therefore view the task of the design team as the completion of a set of predetermined activities. These activities consist of the design, review, and approval of a series of components or subsystems of the artifact to be designed. For instance, in the case of a refinery, the activities include chemical process design, piping design, and structural design. Each activity involves processing of an amount of information defined as the magnitude of the activity, and communication of information between and among design team participants. These activities are modeled as being sequentially interdependent (Thompson, 1967)—that is, the output of a given task is the

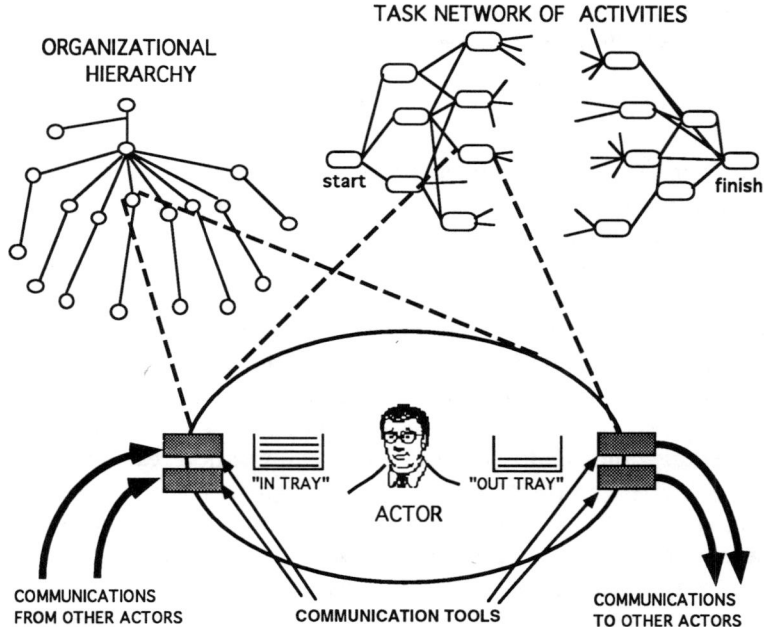

FIG. 1.1. Overview of the virtual design team. VDT models the design task, actors, organization structure, and communication tools. The design task is broken down into a series of activities with precedence relationships and responsible actors. Actors are modeled as information processors with rules for attending to communications waiting for the actor's attention in an "in tray," and rules for deciding which communication tool to employ for sending communications to other actors via an "out tray." The organization structure is defined in terms of communication paths between actors, and the level of the hierarchy at which reviews and approvals can be made. Communication tools, such as meetings, telephones, voice mail, electronic mail, file sharing, and so forth, are modeled in terms of attributes such as synchronicity and bandwidth for communications involving different natural idioms (e.g., text, schematics, three-dimensional geometry). Activities are processed as multiple chunks of information termed *communications* in a stochastic, discrete event simulation.

input for a succeeding task. Thus, the subtasks can be represented in a precedence network.

Because the purpose of VDT is to predict task duration rather than to automate design, we can use an abstracted description of design tasks and the activities that comprise them. Each activity description includes the magnitude of the activity, expressed in terms of the expected number of "communications" needed to satisfy its objectives; precedence constraints with related activities; complexity (high, medium, or low); variability (high, medium, or low); percentage completed; and budgeted duration. In addition, we introduce the notion that both communication and information processing for a given activity will be most effectively performed if the information is represented in an appropriate natural idiom (e.g., text, schematics, three-dimensional geometry). For instance, dimensional coordination is best done with geometric rather than textual representations.

Communications

Activities involve the processing and communication of information. We define a communication to be an elementary packet of information sent from one actor through a specified channel to another actor, using a single communication tool. Completion of each activity involves processing the number of communications specified by the activity's magnitude. Each communication has attributes of time stamp, author, recipient, distribution list, ranking of natural idioms, variability of the associated task, action to be performed on the communication, size, and priority.

VDT represents three basic types of communications: design communications, exceptions, and noise. Design communications carry the information required to perform the specified design activities. Exceptions are generated in VDT to initiate review or approval actions, based on percentage completed (e.g., 30%, 60%, 90%), elapsed time (e.g., weekly, monthly), and task rate of progress versus the planned rate. Exceptions in VDT can thus be viewed as a combination of implicit — but routine — tasks for review and coordination, and truly exceptional remedial actions in the spirit of Galbraith (1977). Exceptions in VDT greatly outnumber specified tasks and produce much of the interesting behavior in the model. Finally, VDT recognizes that some communications received by individuals are irrelevant to accomplishing the task; nevertheless, sorting through and processing these communications, called noise, consumes time of design-team participants.

Each communication is assigned a priority (high, medium, or low) by its sender at the time of transmission. The recipient modifies this priority on receipt of the communication. Priority has an influence on — but does not strictly determine — the order in which actors process communications.

Actors

Actors include managers and design subteams from various disciplines, such as electrical, process, and mechanical engineering. The actor description includes role characteristics, such as position in the team hierarchy; authority for design, approval, and coordination tasks; and allowed communication patterns (either strictly hierarchical or allowing peer-to-peer contact). The actor description also includes individual attributes, such as task experience (high, medium or low) and the natural idioms of communications that the actor processes most effectively (e.g., words, schematics, plans).

Actors execute the following behaviors:

1. Select communications from an "in tray." Managers have limited time and attention to allocate to both routine activities and exceptions, and limited information with which to determine the importance of communications; that is, managers are boundedly rational (Simon, 1976). Managers in the VDT have an in tray—a metaphorical, dynamic queue of communications through which any attempt to communicate with the manager must pass. Managers must decide which communications in the in tray will be addressed immediately, which will be delayed, and which will be discarded. According to our limited field observations, design managers appear to evidence a characteristic pattern in the way that they pay attention to waiting messages and the way they dispatch messages using particular media. Items from each manager's in tray are selected stochastically, based on these criteria, shown in Table 1.1.

2. Process information. The time to process a communication depends (stochastically) on the task attributes, nominal duration, degree of variability, and the match between the capabilities of an actor and the requirements of the design task or exception. Because the content of activities is not modeled in VDT, the system reasons only about the priority of task completion with respect to potential interruptions, and about how rapidly information is processed relative to a nominal information-processing rate. Activities cannot fail explicitly in VDT. Nonconformances in design that result in rework are modeled by extending the activity duration stochastically due to low skill level of the actor, failure to attend coordination meetings, and so forth.

TABLE 1.1
Managers' Attention Rules for Items in the In Tray

Attention Rule	Percentage of Time Used
Sending priority alone	50%
Length of time in in tray, weighted by priority	20%
"The next item noticed"—i.e., the item lying on top of the manager's desk (or on top of the manager's in-tray stack in VDT)	20%
Random selection of items from the in tray	10%

Note. VDT models each manager as stochastically attenidng to communications from the stack of communications in his or her in tray at any given time, using the criteria listed here in decreasing order of likelihood. These attentiond rules were derived from past research and our own limited field observations of design managers, and are used uniformly for all managers as a starting point for initial validation of the model. Attention rules can, if desired, be customized to reflect the attention rules of a given manager more accurately (e.g., VDT could model the attention rule of the first author, who generally reads all electronic mail communications in his in tray before attending to other communications).

3. Send communications to other actors. VDT actors send communications to supervisors, subordinates, managers of predecessor or successor tasks, or others. They use the following criteria for choosing a tool:
• Message priority—Synchronous tools like telephones or face-to-face meetings are used for high-priority communications.
• Primary natural idiom in message—Different tools in VDT have higher or lower bandwidths for different natural idioms; for example, facsimile is more effective than telephone for communicating schematics.
• Proximity of sender to recipient—Face-to-face meetings are more likely to be used for communication between actors in close proximity to one another.
• Cost—The least expensive tool meeting the preceding criteria is used.

If these criteria are in conflict, then the priority of the message is used as the sole basis for choosing a tool stochastically, as shown in Table 1.2.

4. Generate activities to coordinate with other actors, based on the need for approval of completed work, coordination to obtain or share additional information, requirements for periodic or percentage-completion updates, and requirements for milestone review.

Tools

Each communication is transmitted via a tool selected by an actor. There is a literature on individual and organizational choice of technology. In a recent review of this literature, Fulk and Boyd (1991) suggested that selection of communication tools in organizations is influenced both by media richness and by social preferences and norms in organizations.

TABLE 1.2
Probabilities for Stochastic Selection of Communication Tools

| Communication | Message Priority | | |
Tool to be Used	High	Medium	Low
Meeting	35%	15%	10%
Phone	35%	30%	25%
Fax	10%	15%	10%
Mail	15%	35%	53%
E-Mail	3%	3%	2%
Video	2%	2%	0%
Total	100%	100%	100%

Note. If criteria based on message priority, natural idiom in message, proximity of sender to receiver, or cost do not yield a clear choice of a communication tool, then a tool is selected stochastically based solely on message priority, according to the probabilities in this table. These values are based on our limited field observations of design managers, and can easily be modified in VDT.

However, there is no theory that links task characteristics and managers' choice of technologies (Fulk & Steinfeld, 1990). Attempts to analyze these links have been hampered by a holistic or "object-centered" approach to technologies (Nass & Mason, 1990).

Rather than treat each communication tool as analytically indivisible, the VDT framework represents each tool in terms of values on a set of variables that are theorized to affect both the choice of tool and the results of that choice. The adoption and behavior of tools are then defined in terms of the relationships among the tool variables and the characteristics of the task, actors, and organizational structure. In the present version of the VDT, tools are characterized by their *synchronicity* (synchronous, partial, asynchronous), *cost* (low, medium, or high), *recordability* (whether or not a permanent record of the communication is available routinely), *proximity to user* (close or distant), *capacity* (volume of messages that can be transmitted concurrently), and *bandwidth* (low, medium, or high), representing the capability of the tool for communicating information represented in each of the natural idioms supported (i.e., text, schematics, etc.).

For example, voice mail is partially synchronous, low cost, recordable, close proximity, high capacity for concurrent transmission, and high bandwidth for text but low bandwidth for geometry; telephone is similar except that it is synchronous, not recordable, and has low capacity for concurrent transmission; and electronic mail is asynchronous and has high concurrent transmission. Thus, a manager who wants to send a textual communication to a large number of individuals simultaneously will choose a tool such as voice mail or electronic mail rather than telephone. In contrast, the need for synchronous communication (arising from priority) will encourage the use of the telephone as opposed to the other two tools.

Organization Structure

Structure in VDT is defined by a set of organizational relationships among actors, and levels of authority of actors in specific roles. Organizational relationships among actors delimit the channels along which tools can be used to send communications. Relationships modeled in VDT include *supervised-by* to implement hierarchical structure, *coordinates-with* to implement lateral relations among interdependent actors, and *socializes-with* to implement informal structure. A set of project-specific coordination policies assigns decision-making authority to actors in particular roles (e.g., design manager) for reviews and approvals. A centralized structure is implemented by policies that require these exceptions to be resolved by high level-managers (e.g., the design manager); decentralized structures vest this authority in lower level managers (e.g., the subteam managers).

ORGANIZATION THEORY AND VDT

Contingency theory of organizations posits that there is no one best way to organize: The optimum structure for an organization depends on the values of variables describing its task and environment. Jay Galbraith's (1977) formulation of contingency theory proposed that when some of the information required to complete a task is lacking at the responsible node, an *exception* arises—that is, the actor must communicate with a supervisor or peer to obtain the information needed to complete the task. Hierarchical or legitimated lateral relationships define the formal channels that can be used to communicate these exceptions. Organizational performance degrades either when a channel (modeled in VDT as the aggregate capacity of all communication tools available across a given organizational relationship) becomes overloaded with exceptions, or when one or more nodes (modeled as individual or subteam *actors* in VDT) cannot process scheduled tasks and exceptions as rapidly as they arrive. Galbraith's theory made a number of predictions about the effect of task, structure, and tools on the organization's demand and capacity for information processing.

A centralized, hierarchical organization structure, in which the authority to resolve the most frequent types of exceptions is retained by senior managers, can function for routine tasks with little mutual interdependence. However, if the tasks to be performed by the organization are complex, unpredictable, and highly interdependent—as is the case even in routine engineering design—Galbraith predicted that senior managers will become overloaded with exceptions to process.

To bring information-processing capacity in line with demand, Galbraith proposed several remedies. One of these is decentralization of decision-making authority. This structural change reduces the demand for exceptions to be processed by high-level actors in the organization. Alternatively, or simultaneously, information-processing capacity of an organization can be increased by adding communication tools (e.g., voice mail) that enhance channel capacity.

Galbraith's theory was not operationalized, and had to be extended substantially for use in VDT, but it provided the general framework of information-impacted nodes or channels limiting the throughput of information in organizations. The operationalized Galbraith framework in VDT permitted a straightforward testing of his predictions. It simulated the rate at which communications—including exceptions—are transmitted and processed by a team of actors for specified configurations of organizational relationships among actors, decision-making policies, and communication tools.

RELATED WORK

Several researchers have worked in the general area of modeling organization theory (Crowston, 1990; Masuch & LaPotin, 1989; O'Reilly & Chatman, 1987). Malone and Crowston (1990) provided a comprehensive review of research on the use of information technology in organizations and its interaction with organizational structure and performance. The pioneering work of Masuch and LaPotin (1989) resulted in a symbolic simulation model of the commitment, cognitive capacity, and structure of actors performing simple tasks in a hypothetical organization, and contributed the limited blocking test design that we used (Box, Hunter, & Hunter, 1978). Like VDT, Masuch's work built on Simon's bounded rationality theory. However, it does not emphasize information processing, attention rules, or exceptions, and no comparisons were given of the predictions of this model with real organizations.

Carley et al. (1990) discussed the use of an artificial intelligence-based model of a small organization in which intelligent agents communicate and cooperate to perform a distributed decision-making task. This research was quite close in spirit to VDT and focused on examining, at the microlevel, the three-way relationship between individuals' skills, job requirements, and coordination schemes. They modelled tasks with less interdependence but more content than VDT, and they modelled cognitive processes of actors, including some simple kinds of memory and learning, whereas VDT endows actors with almost no ability to reason about the content of their tasks, but incorporates attention rules for actors, and models communication processes in some detail.

Empirical research on the way that new communication tools like electronic mail effect the social structure and performance of organizations (Nass & Mason, 1990; Sproull & Kiesler, 1991) provides background for modeling communication tools in VDT.

HARDWARE AND SOFTWARE IMPLEMENTATION OF VDT

VDT is implemented as a symbolic model using object-oriented programming techniques. It has a set of objects with attributes and behaviors to define the design project and its subtasks, the actors who perform the information-processing tasks that comprise design, and the communication tools available to each actor. Organizational structure emerges from the authority provided to each actor and the channels along which the actor can send and receive communications. The outputs of the model—activity and task durations—are represented in terms of number of clock ticks (see Fig.

1.2). The model is formal in that it includes the basic concepts of, and predicts behavior based on, a set of widely accepted theories. The model was implemented on a Sun Microsystems IPX Sparcstation using the Knowledge Engineering Environment (KEE) and the SimKit discrete event simulation system, both from IntelliCorp.

The model entities all have stochastic behavior. The values of many actor and tool attributes can be one of a set of discrete alternatives or a number from a range. In a given run of the model, these values may be determined by rules (e.g., rules that relate actor attributes to the attributes of a communication), or they may be determined by Monte Carlo simulation, based on a probability distribution set by the user. The discrete attribute alternatives, numeric ranges, and probability distributions used in this initial experiment were all derived from our limited initial field observations of actual engineering design teams.

When a high-level task is initiated in the simulation model, an initial message is sent from the design manager to the various project teams requesting information. Each team then receives an inquiry message, may generate further inquiries while processing this message, and eventually responds. When a task finally completes, the next task in the project can be initiated, either by the manager or by some other actor.

The model computes activity duration numerically in simulation clock units, each of which corresponds to about 1 min of an actor's time. Because each simulation run contains many stochastic "decisions," the durations generated by a set of runs carried out with the same task, actors, organization structure, and communication tools will vary slightly around a mean value. As shown in the following validation section, we found that we could get very close to a converging mean value by averaging the values from three runs of the model for each set of values of the independent variables.

VDT records, and the investigator can inspect, the status of every object throughout the project. We have chosen to focus on one dependent output variable, the overall time for the Virtual Design Team to complete a project. Because many activities are performed concurrently, this overall duration corresponds to the length of the longest or "critical" path through the network of subtasks. The sum of the durations of all subtasks needed to complete the project is also available and can be used as a rough measure of the project's design cost (because the principal element of cost for a design project is the designers' labor).

VALIDATION

In order to validate VDT on a real-world organization, we modeled a routine, 3-year, petroleum refinery design project having a total design/

construction cost of approximately $130 million, a budget duration of 20 months, and, at its peak, approximately 120 managers, engineers, designers, and support staff located in two offices. Because both means and ends are relatively clear and uncontested for actors in this organization—in contrast to organizations like universities or social service agencies—the actors can justifiably be modeled as cooperative and boundedly rational (March, 1988; Simon, 1976).

All actor and task descriptions were derived from this project and held constant. The predefined rules for attending to messages in the in basket and choosing technologies were initially derived from a series of interviews with actors on this project and then compared to observed managerial behavior in a second petrochemical design project. There was enough consistency in managerial behavior across the two projects that the observed values were used as initial settings for these parameters (Cohen, 1992). This is one of several places in which VDT must be refined and calibrated over time for this and other managerial domains.

VDT attributes have discrete qualitative values, such as one of "high," "medium," "low," or one or more of "text," "schematics," or "plans," and so forth. The complete model has over 100 attributes. Because of the size of the attribute space, validation of every possible combination of attribute values is impractical. A principled but limited factorial analysis was used to validate the system's internal consistency. We selected two independent variables—level of centralization of decision making, and presence or absence of voice mail. As explained earlier, the theory predicts that decentralizing decision making and adding voice mail should each decrease the project's duration.

Our candidate organization had a decentralized structure and provided voice mail to its designers. To model different levels of centralization, we changed the level in the hierarchy to which design approval exceptions were routed, from *subteam managers* (decentralized) to *design manager* (centralized). To give actors voice mail capabilities, we reset the synchronicity attribute of the existing telephone tool from "synchronous" to "partially synchronous," the recordability attribute to "recordable," and the capacity attribute to "high capacity." Values of all other variables in the model were set to an average value such as "medium." This form of sensitivity analysis is based on the method of Box et al. (1978), and was also used by Masuch and LaPotin (1989).

Our validation experiment proceeded as follows:

1. Select two relevant variables to test—level of centralization and availablity of voice mail. Set all other variables at average values.

2. Use Galbraith's theory to make a qualitative prediction—that is, predict the direction of change in project duration from the baseline case—when changing each of the two test attributes.
3. Conduct a set of three simulations of VDT for each pair of values of the two independent variables, that is, a total of 12 simulations.
4. Compare the simulated versus theoretically predicted results using standard statistical measures of significance.

By independently varying the level of centralization and the availability of voice mail, we examined the impact of these two variables on the duration of individual tasks and on overall project duration. The results of the simulations are shown in Fig. 1.2, together with predictions from Galbraith's theory (1977). The simulation results are in good agreement with predictions of Galbraith's theory for this project.

- A two-way analysis of variance indicates that, as predicted, centralized decision making leads to longer task duration than does decentralized decision making [mean $= 875$ vs. mean $= 950$; $F(8,1) = 164.11; p < .001$].
- Also as predicted, removing voice mail increases the duration of the project [mean $= 862$ vs. mean $= 888$; $F(8,1) = 32.06; p < .001$].
- The interaction between voice mail and centralization is not significant [$F(8,1) = 1.44; p > .25$].
- For both centralized and decentralized organization structures, voice mail improves performance, as predicted [$t(4) = 3.7, p < .01$, and $t(4) = 5.9, p < .01$, respectively].

Despite the large number of elements in VDT that are operationalized stochastically, the standard deviations for three runs of each of the four scenarios are all relatively small (less than 2% of the means), suggesting that the VDT model is well behaved.

RUNNING TIME OF THE VDT MODEL

A typical case run has 24 activities, 17 actors, about 1 million simulation events, and takes about 90 min to run on a 64-MB Sun IPX workstation. We also conducted several runs with 90 activities; each of these runs required several hours to complete, but produced qualitatively identical results. The 90-activity project is approaching the practical limit of our current hardware and software environment, without optimizing the VDT

Communication Tools

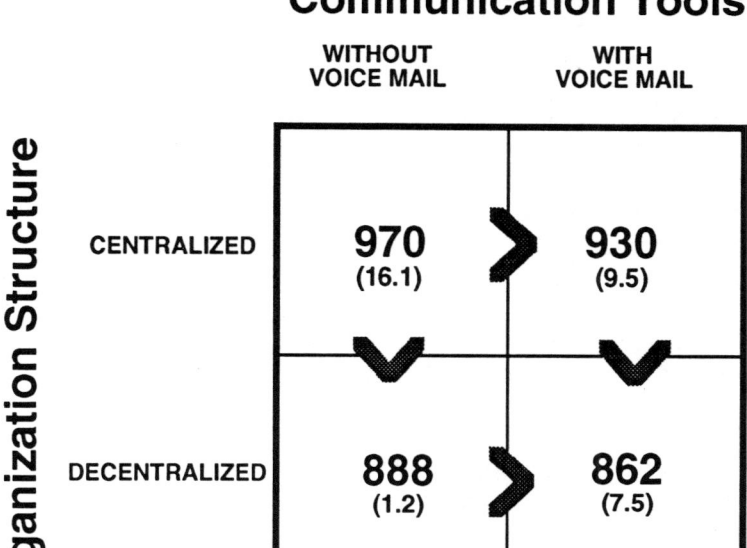

	WITHOUT VOICE MAIL	WITH VOICE MAIL
CENTRALIZED	970 (16.1)	930 (9.5)
DECENTRALIZED	888 (1.2)	862 (7.5)

Organization Structure

Mean Duration and Standard Deviation of Three Simulations, Measured in Work-Hours

FIG. 1.2.   Validation of VDT versus theory for a real project organization. VDT was used to simulate a 120-person team designing a petroleum refinery and to predict the effects of changing decision making from decentralized to centralized, and adding or removing voice mail. The lower right-hand cell represents the base case (decentralized, with voice mail) for the real design team modeled in this experiment. The > signs at cell boundaries represent decreases (or increases in the opposite direction) in project duration between adjacent cells, as predicted by Galbraith's information-processing theory of organizations (Galbraith, 1977). As shown in this figure, VDT's simulated results agree well with the qualitative changes in duration predicted by Galbraith's theory for all four intercell comparisons. The mean duration and standard deviation of the three simulations for each cell are expressed in units that are roughly equivalent to work-hours. VDT has been calibrated so that these predictions of duration are reasonably close to the actual project duration. However, until the model has been further calibrated, we choose to interpret VDT's predictions of duration only in terms of qualitative differences between cells.

system for processing speed. However, we believe that 90 activities is probably close to the optimum level of detail at which to model engineering design tasks, such as refinery design, for the purpose of analyzing their organization structures and information-processing tools.

DISCUSSION

VDT represents an initial, small step toward using computer-based simulation tools to predict the performance of alternative organizational configurations for a set of design actors faced with a routine task. It is currently necessary to extrapolate from synthetic experiments, or to test organization structures and communication tools in costly, natural experiments to determine whether they achieve desired performance objectives. VDT thus allows an investigator to begin exploring fundamental questions of organization science and design that have previously defied systematic analysis.

VDT is explicitly based on information-processing theories of Galbraith (1977), Simon (1973, 1976), and March (March, 1988; March & Simon, 1958), and it incorporates data from observations and interviews of design managers. The objective of this research was to demonstrate that a hybrid symbolic and numerical simulation model could be used to analyze and predict important aspects of the behavior of real organizations. We were confident from the beginning that we could model tasks, actors, organization structures, and communications tools used in routine design tasks. An issue was comparability of results: How could we assess the theoretical and practical validity of model results? Because of the routine nature of the project we modeled and observed, we assumed that we could compare the information-processing patterns in the real project, predictions of classic theory, and results of the simulation model. Our initial results demonstrate that the effects of change in structure and communication tools on organizational output are qualitatively consistent between practice, theory, and the VDT simulation model.

The current model has three significant limitations. First, it can only model routine tasks. We make no claim to be able to model nonroutine or creative design in which the task cannot be specified a priori. Second, VDT's predictions of duration, although quantitative, must be interpreted qualitatively at this stage. With additional empirical testing and refinement, it may be possible to calibrate key elements of the model well enough to begin generating durations that can be viewed as absolute, quantitative predictions of project duration. Finally, decentralization of decision making may compromise the quality of decisions if lower level managers lack the global perspective available at higher levels. Galbraith's theory and the current VDT model are not explicit about issues of decision-making quality, so they cannot model the trade-off between project duration and quality. The next version of VDT (Christiansen, 1992) will extend the current model by explicitly representing and reasoning about the functional requirements of each subtask.

Clearly, this initial demonstration is limited in the type of task, organization, communication tools, and actors it has considered, and further research is needed to explore its limits in these regards. By expanding the theory base of VDT and testing it in other industries, we hope to generalize VDT as an analysis tool that can eventually model and validate a wider range of organization theory in a variety of settings.

ACKNOWLEDGMENTS

The research to develop VDT was initiated by two seed research grants from the Center for Integrated Facility Engineering (CIFE) at Stanford University. The financial support and access to project participants provided by CIFE and its members is gratefully acknowledged. Ongoing research to refine and extend VDT is being supported by grant IRI-9122541 from the National Science Foundation.

We deeply appreciate the enthusiastic participation in this research of Bechtel Corporation, Det Norske Veritas, Digital Equipment Corporation, Fluor Daniel Corporation, Kumagai Gumi (USA), and Pacific Gas and Electric Company.

REFERENCES

Box, G., Hunter, W., & Hunter, J. (1978). *Statistics for experimenters.* New York: Wiley.
Bushnell, L. G., Serfaty, D., & Kleinman, D. L. (1988). Team information processing: A normative-descriptive approach. In S. E. Johnson & A. H. Lewis (Eds.), *Science of command and control: Coping with uncertainty* (pp. 62–72). London: AFCEA International Press.
Carley, K., Kjaer-Hansen, J., Newell, A., & Prietula, M. (1992). Plural-Soar: A prolegomenon to artificial agents and organizational behavior. In M. Masuch & M. Warglien (Eds.), *Artificial organization theory in organization and management theory* (pp. 87–118). Amsterdam: North-Holland.
Christiansen, T. (1992, June). *The virtual design team: Using simulation of information processing to predict the performance of project teams.* CIFE Working Paper 15. Center for Integrated Facility Engineering, Stanford University, Stanford, CA.
Clancey, W. J. (1989, Summer). Viewing knowledge bases as qualitative models. *IEEE EXPERT,* 9–23.
Cohen, G. P. (1992). *The virtual design team: An information processing model of coordination in project design teams.* PhD dissertation, Stanford University Department of Civil Engineering, Stanford, CA.
Cohen, G. P., & Levitt, R. E. (1991). The virtual design team. *Proceedings of the ASCE Construction Congress 91.* Cambridge, MA: American Society of Civil Engineers.
Cohen, M. D. (1986). Artificial intelligence and the dynamic performance of organizational designs. In J. March & R. Weissinger-Baylon (Eds.), *Ambiguity and command: organizational perspectives on military decision making.* Boston, MA: Pittman.
Coyne, R.D., Rosenman, M. A., Radford, A. D., Balachandran, M., & Gero, J. S. (1990). *Knowledge-based design systems.* Reading, MA: Addison-Wesley.
Crowston, K. (1990). *Modeling coordination in organizations.* MIT Sloan School of Management Working Paper No. 3228.

Fulk, J., & Boyd, B. (1991). Emerging theories of communication in organizations. *Journal of Management, (17)*2, 407–446.

Fulk, J., & Steinfeld, C. (Eds.). (1990). *Organizations and communication technology.* Newbury Park, CA: Sage.

Galbraith, J. (1977). *Organization design.* Reading, MA: Addison-Wesley.

Kunz, J. C., Stelzner, M. C., & Williams, M. D. (1989). From classic expert systems to models: Introduction to a methodology for building model-based systems. In G. Guida & C. Tasso (Eds.), *Topics in expert system design* (pp. 87–110). Amsterdam: North-Holland.

Levitt, R. E. (1990, June). Model based planning: An engineering perspective. *Proceedings of IEE Conference on Knowledge-Based Planning,* Brighton, UK.

Levitt, R. E., Jin, Y., & Dym, C. L. (1991). Knowledge-based support for management of concurrent, multidisciplinary design. *Journal of Artificial Intelligence in Engineerng Design, Analysis and Manufacturing, (5)*2, 77–95.

Malone, T. W., & Crowston, K. (1990). What is coordination theory and how can it help design cooperative work systems. *Proceedings of the Conference on Computer Supported Cooperative Work,* Los Angeles, CA.

March, J. G. (1988). *Decisions and organizations.* Oxford: Basil Blackwell.

March, J. G., & Simon, H. A. (1958). *Organizations.* New York: Wiley.

Masuch, M., & LaPotin, P. (1989). Beyond garbage cans: An AI model of organizational choice. *Administrative Science Quarterly, 34,* 38–67.

Nass, C. I., & Mason, L. (1990). On the study of technology and task: A variable-based approach. In J. Fulk & C. Steinfeld (Eds.), *Organizations and communication technology* (pp. 46–67), Newbury Park, CA: Sage.

O'Reilly, C. A., & Chatman, J. A. (1987). Message flow and decision making. In F. M. Jablin, L. L. Putnam, K. H. Roberts, & L. W. Porter (Eds.), *Handbook of organizational communication: An interdisciplinary perspective* (pp. 600–623). Beverly Hills, CA: Sage.

Simon, H. A. (1973). Applying information technology to organization design. *Public Administration Review, 33,* 268–278.

Simon, H. A. (1976). *Administrative behavior: A study of decision-making processes in administrative organization.* New York: Free Press.

Sproull, L., & Kiesler, S. (1991). *Connections: New ways of working in the networked organization.* Cambridge, MA: MIT Press.

Tatum, C. B. (1984). Designing project organizations: How managers decide. *Journal of Construction Engineering and Management, ASCE, 110*(3), 346–358.

Thompson, J. D. (1967). *Organizations in action.* New York: McGraw-Hill.

2

Evolving Novel Organizational Forms

Kevin Crowston
University of Michigan

Organizations appear in many forms. A key problem in organization theory is to explain the distribution of these forms. Why, for example, are manufacturing firms often large integrated corporations rather than the loose alliances of independent contractors often found in the construction industry? Although such questions obviously have many possible answers, organizational ecologists explain the diversity of forms by analogy to biological species (e.g., Singh & Lumsden, 1990). Organizations compete for resources; those with forms more appropriate for the environment are more successful at acquiring resources and thus tend to survive, whereas those with less effective forms tend to fail. Over time, this selection results in an observable match between organizational forms and the environment in which they operate.

A second goal of organization theory is to suggest new organizational forms. I am particularly interested in organizational design for two reasons. First, there is widespread concern that the business environment is changing rapidly, perhaps changing the fitness of organizational forms. In order to design and introduce products more quickly, for example, some manufacturing firms are forging closer ties with third-party suppliers, in some respects moving toward a model more like that of the construction industry. Second, information technology is rapidly changing fundamental constraints on organizations, for example, by making communication and data storage much cheaper or by facilitating previously impractical interactions across time or space. These technical innovations make feasible new organizational forms, some of which may be more effective than existing forms. There are many examples (in the popular business press, at least) of new organizational forms driven by information technology: Batterymarch Investment adopted a novel approach to investment banking, using a computer instead of research staff to identify possible investments (Schmerken, 1987).

These two forces — changes in the environment in which firms operate, and expansion of the space of possible forms — suggest that we may be on the brink of a period of rapid alteration in the punctuated evolution of organizational forms (Stinchcombe, 1965). An important practical question then is how to search this expanded design space for possibly useful forms.

One solution, presumably, is to wait and see. In response to these forces, managers will undoubtedly themselves search for new forms, just as Batterymarch Investments did. As Hannan and Freeman (1986) suggested, "Much entrepreneurial activity involves conscious revision of forms and routines to take advantage of changing opportunities and constraints or to avoid defects in orthodox designs" (p. 63). Although this empirical approach is sure to correctly identify successful forms, it has several drawbacks. First, it is likely to be quite expensive and time-consuming. Second, although the forms that emerge are by definition successful, there is no guarantee that all possibly successful forms will emerge. Finally, it gives managers no advice to help their companies remain viable.

Alternately, we could attempt to predict theoretically what kinds of forms might be successful. Many organizational theories, of course, attempt to do just this. As originally stated, however, theories of organizational ecology say only that if the environment changes, new forms may eventually replace existing ones. These theories describe the processes by which forms emerge, but they provide little insight into what exactly they might be. Indeed, Romanelli (1991) called the question of the origin of new organizational forms "one of the critical unaddressed issues in organizational sociology" (p. 80).

Fortunately there is a third choice, namely computer simulations (Whicker & Sigelman, 1991). Researchers in many disciplines gain insight into complex behaviors by imagining how a computer could be programmed to reproduce them (e.g., Simon, 1981). Simulations have a long history in organizational research; Cyert and March (1963), for example, used this approach. In their analysis of the processes firms use to make pricing decisions, the "process is specified by drawing a flow diagram and executing a computer program that simulates the process in some detail" (p. 2).

In this chapter, I discuss the use of simulations to search for novel organizational forms by reproducing some of the mechanics of organizational evolution. The metaphor of organizations competing and being selected on the basis of their fitness is a compelling one. As it happens, it is also the basis of a computer technique known as the genetic algorithm (Holland, 1992), used to efficiently search large design spaces. If we can more precisely describe the space of organizational forms, we can use this algorithm to search it.

In the rest of this chapter, I describe the genetic algorithm and discuss some issues in applying it to organizational forms. To illustrate the potential of this approach, I then present a simple model of an organization and some preliminary results from using the genetic algorithm. I conclude by discussing possible bases for a more general organizational model and general caveats about the approach.

GENETIC ALGORITHMS

A genetic algorithm works as follows. Given a problem, a random population of possible solutions is generated. Solutions in the population are evaluated and the most promising ones are used in proportion to their fitness as the basis for the next generation of possible solutions. New solutions are created by crossover, that is, by taking two existing solutions, dividing each in two parts, and exchanging parts to create two hybrid solutions. Note that in most genetic algorithms, mutation plays at most a minor role. The process is repeated for some fixed number of generations or until one of the solutions successfully solves the problem.

This technique has been used to evolve solutions to many kinds of problems, including strategic games, optimization problems, mechanical designs, and image classification (Booker et al., 1987). Axelrod (1987), for example, used a genetic algorithm to evolve strategies for playing iterated Prisoner's Dilemma games. Most of these studies represented solutions as strings of bits (zeroes or ones). Axelrod, for example, represented strategies as 64 bits, each bit representing the response of the strategy (defect or cooperate) given the moves of both players in the preceding three rounds of the game. (Note that this representation cannot represent strategies that differentiate on any other criteria — for example, by playing aggressively if they are winning and not otherwise.) The fitness of a strategy is determined by playing it against all other strategies and totaling the payoffs it receives on each round of the game. To create new strategies, two strategies are randomly selected from the population in proportion to their fitness. Both are split at a randomly chosen crossover point (e.g., after the 10th bit); the first half of the first is concatenated with the second half of the second and vice versa to create two new hybrid strategies.

The genetic algorithm has also been applied to objects with complex hierarchical structures such as LISP programs (Koza, 1992). Koza studied a variety of problems that required finding a program that produced some desired output for a particular set of inputs, which he interpreted as a search in the space of possible programs for a most fit program for the problem. Problems studied included planning, symbolic function identification, concept formation, automatic programming, pattern recognition, and strategy formation. A typical pattern recognition problem was, given as input the X and Y coordinates of a point drawn from one of two concentric spirals, to identify the spiral from which the point was drawn.

For each problem, Koza chose a set of operators thought to be useful for solving the problem; for the spiral problem, for example, operators include arithmetic operations, if–then, and sine and cosine. An initial population of LISP programs was generated by randomly picking an operator (addition, subtraction, etc.) or a terminal symbol (either X, Y, or a random constant); if an operator was drawn, the process was repeated to fill in the operands. In each generation, each program was run on the set of input points; a program's fitness was determined by the number of correct outputs. New programs were produced by picking two programs and exchanging randomly chosen subtrees (i.e., entire subexpressions) from each. For the spiral problem, after a large number of generations, the best programs in the population successfully identified all of the given points.

Advantages of Computer Simulations of Organizations

Using computer simulations and the genetic algorithm to search for possible organizational forms has several advantages. First, as Burton and Obel (1980) pointed out, the same experiment can be performed repeatedly under the same conditions, thus providing high internal validity. Second, variations in organizational forms explored in a computer simulation are not restricted by social factors, institutional pressures (DiMaggio & Powell, 1983), or human ingenuity. However, this advantage is simultaneously a major concern about simulations: the potential lack of external validity. Computer models necessarily abstract from real organizations; the features simulated must be chosen carefully to ensure that conclusions drawn from the models can be applied more generally (Burton & Obel, 1980).

Although the genetic algorithm seems random, it turns out to be an effective method for searching a large search space. It can be shown that the individuals in the current population encode large amounts of useful information about combinations of features, called *schemata* (Holland, 1992). These schemata implicitly represent numerous similar individuals not actually present in the population. Furthermore, as the individuals are selected and bred, schemata are also reproduced in the population in proportion to their fitness. In essence, by manipulating a modestly sized population, a genetic algorithm implicitly searches in parallel a much larger portion of the space.

Elements of a Genetic Algorithm

As the preceding examples make clear, there are several issues in applying the genetic algorithm.

Unit of Selection.   First, we must define the individuals that we will be evolving. For the examples discussed earlier, individuals were simply solutions to the given problems, but organizations can be studied and modeled at different levels of analysis.

Representation.   Second, we need a representation of the object to be evolved, general enough to represent any organizational form of interest. Representing only different kinds of hierarchies, for example, would not allow us to consider market mechanisms for the same transactions (Williamson, 1975).

Fitness.   Finally, we need to represent the environment in which the organizations perform and, explicitly or implicitly, a fitness function to identify "good" organizations. By varying the environment, we can look for forms that may be desirable under different conditions.

Unit of Evolution

A first key issue is what to evolve—that is, establishing the level of analysis of the organization. There are two main possibilities: We can represent entire organizations or organizational subunits. The most direct approach is to model entire organizations, for example, by encoding an organization's formal structure. We then use the genetic algorithm to modify these structures, eventually identifying particularly fit organizations.

An alternate approach is to model the competition and cooperation between subunits within an organization to show how these interactions result in a particular organizational form—what Carroll (1984) called the organizational level. For example, Burgelman (1991) examined the ecology of strategies within a company (Intel) to explain changes in overall organizational strategy. Such a simulation models individual subunits (e.g., individual strategies); a population of subunits constitutes a single organization.

To implement such a model in a genetic algorithm, in each generation we distribute the payoff the entire organization receives among the subunits that contributed to the result (e.g., using the bucket brigade mechanism from classifier systems; Holland, 1992). Subunits that contribute more to an organization's success are selected and used to breed the next generation of organizational subunits, thus changing and hopefully improving the entire organization. This approach could also be used to explore the emergence of organizations by modeling interactions between independent actors; however, in this case we would need to develop criteria for when an organization has emerged and which subunits are included.

Representation of Organizations

A second question is, how should organizations be represented, or alternately, what constitutes an organizational form? Romanelli (1991) noted that researchers have proposed several approaches to this question but concluded that there is no general agreement. Obviously this question is governed primarily by researchers' theoretical commitments and the kind of research questions they hope to investigate. For example, an interest in the use of information technology suggests a focus on factors that are directly influenced by such systems, such as communication patterns, costs, or capabilities.

The use of the genetic algorithm does place some constraints on the representation, however. First, we require a representation of an organization (or a subunit) in which crossovers between individuals make sense. This requirement requires viewing an organization as a collection of traits that can be combined and recombined in various ways—what Romanelli (1991) and Hannan and Freeman (1986) described as organizational genetics. Most models of organizations do not have this property. For example, Hannan and Freeman (1986) noted that much of organizational research has used conventional classifications of types of organizations: "We routinely distinguish hospitals, prisons, political parties, universities, stock exchanges, coal mines and fast-food chains" (p. 54), but it is unclear what a cross between a hospital and a coal mine is (for example) or how it could be represented.

Furthermore, we would prefer that the space of possible organizations be *dense*—that is, modifications to the representation of one organization should usually result in another viable organization. Simply representing the formal structure of an organization might be unsatisfactory, for example, because the effects of replacing one department (marketing, say) with another (manufacturing) will usually be a nonfunctioning organization (one with two manufacturing divisions but no marketing). Density of viable forms is not an absolute requirement; a population in which most crosses failed could still evolve, but it would do so much more slowly. Michalewicz (1992) suggests that it is necessary to include "more problem-specific knowledge in the chromosomes' data structures" to perform better (p. 6).

Hannan and Freeman (1986) and Romanelli (1991) reviewed several candidates for these traits, including organizational building instructions, transactions, and routines. Hannan and Freeman (1977) defined an organizational form as "instructions for building organizations and conducting collective action"; presumably these instructions could be combined in different ways, thus giving rise to different organizational forms. They noted, however, that these instructions are not directly observable. Furthermore, the link between these instructions and performance is not specified.

Williamson (1975) viewed an organizational form as sets of transactions and argued that transactions are bundled together to minimize transaction costs. Given a set of transactions to be performed, then, the total cost of various bundles of these transactions (i.e., different organizational arrangements) could be compared.

Finally, Nelson and Winter (1982) suggested viewing an organization as a collection of routines or *memes*. Similarly, McKelvey (1982) described an organization as a collection of *comps,* the "base units of knowledge and skill that make up what the organization knows how to do" (Romanelli, 1991, p. 85). Different organizations have different collections of these routines or comps and will therefore perform differently. However, identifying routines may be problematic; as Romanelli (1991) pointed out, routines are "empirically elusive" (p. 87).

Hannan and Freeman (1986) pointed out that organizations also have higher order coordinating routines. They noted it would be difficult to distinguish (for example) a public and private university without considering such routines, because the skills and activities of individual faculty would be similar or even indistinguishable. To be useful, therefore, an organizational model will have to include both kinds of routines. Later in this chapter I briefly discuss how routines might be used to model an organization.

Given a set of features, organizations can be represented using simple bit strings to encode the presence or absence of a feature. Such a representation has the advantage that it can be easily manipulated by the genetic algorithm. A significant disadvantage is that this representation often determines in advance the size and shape of the final solution, that is, it is not sufficiently dynamic (Koza, 1992). More complex representations, similar to the hierarchical LISP programs used by Koza, could allow for a wide variety of forms, including forms with complex internal structures, such as organizations.

Fitness

Finally, we need a mechanism to assess the fitness of individual organizations. Koza (1992), for example, determined the fitness of individual programs by counting how often they produced the correct answer to the problem; Axelrod (1987) counted a strategy's total winnings. The most straightforward approach to this problem is to choose a task and measure the success of the organization at performing it (e.g., the time required to perform the task, number of tasks performed in unit time, total cost, etc.). Picking a good task is key—it must be abstract enough to simulate but have clear application to a real situation. Better yet, it should be one that could be done in many ways, with no clear dominant best form, and for which the features of the organization of theoretical interest are thought to make a difference in performance. For example, if we chose to model communication patterns within an organization, then the task evaluated should be one for which theory suggests how those patterns affect the outcome (e.g., by affecting how long it takes to perform the task).

Features of the environment also determine in part the fitness of organizations. As with organizational forms, there are many features of the environment that could be represented. Freeman and Hannan (1983), for example, examined the effects of environmental variability and patchiness. The features of the environment modeled are those that are presumed to affect the performance of the organization on the task. In the model of communication patterns discussed earlier, likely environmental variables include the cost or speed of communication.

The environment may also include the other individuals in the population, as in Axelrod's (1987) study, making the success of a particular individual dependent on the behavior of the other individuals. Such a model can exhibit behaviors that depend on the interaction between individuals, such as symbiosis or parasitism. In such a model, an individual's fitness may be defined only implicitly by its relative success in acquiring resources, as in Holland's Eco models (1992). A particularly interesting example of this final case is a system known as the Turing Gas (Fontana, 1991), which models catalysts in chemistry as self-applicable functions (i.e., functions that can be applied to functions to produce new functions). In each generation, new functions are created by randomly selecting pairs of functions and applying the first to the second. To keep the population size constant, whenever a new function is created, an existing function is removed. A function is successful if it appears frequently in the resulting population of functions (i.e., if it is frequently created).

EXAMPLE: ASSIGNMENT OF OVERLAPPING TASKS TO ACTORS

I summarize the previous discussion with an example of this simulation approach. At this initial stage of research, I believe it is most useful to address questions for which there is already some theoretical agreement. This replication allows us to develop some confidence in the technique before applying it to novel problems. Also, a theoretical base is necessary to suggest what features of organizations and the environment should be modeled. The experiment presented here was developed to explore how actors should be assigned to interdependent tasks. It was expected to produce results consistent with Thompson's (1967) suggestions about clustering-related tasks.

The simulation is characterized by a number of parameters, as shown in Table 2.1, but for the experiments reported here, most were held constant. The number of generations and the size of the population were chosen to be large enough to include substantial variance, although the total number of organizations examined, 10^6, is still much smaller than the size of the search space. Two parameters were varied and form the experimental conditions for the experiments: the overlap between tasks, and the coordination penalty actors pay for performing multiple tasks. These parameters are discussed in more detail later. The simulation described here was written in C and run on a Sun 4 workstation. Each run took approximately 30 min, depending on the overlap between tasks.

The Experimental Setup

Representation of Organizations. In this model, an organization is a set of N actors that perform M tasks and is represented as an *NM*-bit string encoding the assignment of actors to tasks (1 if the task is assigned to the actor, 0 otherwise). In these experiments there were 10 actors and 10 tasks, so each organization was represented by a string of 100 bits, for a total of 2^{100} or approximately 1.3×10^{30} possible organizations. There were no limits on how many actors could be assigned to a task or vice versa.

Environment. To model economies of scope, tasks may overlap each other (i.e., the effort required to perform two tasks together may be less

TABLE 2.1
Parameters of the Simulation and Settings in the Reported Experiments

Parameter	Setting in Reported Experiments
Generations	1000
Population	1000
Number of actors	10
Number of tasks	10
Number of subtasks/tasks	10 selected (see text)
Overlap between tasks	0, 1, 3, 5, 7, 10 of the subtasks were assigned (see text)
Penalty (benefit) for an actor performing multiple tasks	(0.5), 0.0, 0.5, 1.0, 2.0
Penalty (benefit) for a task being performed by multiple actors	0.0
Minimum normalized fitness	0.1

than the sum of the effort to perform the tasks separately). This overlap was modeled by representing each task as a set of subtasks (10 in these experiments), where subtasks could be part of multiple tasks. An actor assigned to a task performs the component subtasks. In these experiments the degree of overlap was varied from none (subtasks are part of only one task) to total (all tasks include the same subtasks).

Overlapping tasks were created by assigning some number of subtasks to each task and randomly selecting the remainder. For example, if 5 subtasks were assigned, there would be 50 subtasks in total. Task 0 would include subtasks 0 through 4 plus 5 randomly chosen subtasks; task 1 would include subtasks 5 through 9, plus 5 randomly chosen subtasks; and so on. This would result in tasks randomly overlapping approximately 50% of their subtasks with other tasks. If all 10 subtasks were assigned, then each subtasks would be assigned to only 1 task and there would be no overlap; for the case of 0 unique subtasks, there were 10 subtasks and each task was simply assigned all 10.

In these experiments, the additional subtasks were chosen randomly with replacement from the entire set of subtasks; as a result, a task may actually have fewer than 10 subtasks if the same subtask is chosen more than once. A typical set of tasks is shown in Table 2.2. Table 2.3 shows the overlap between these tasks, calculated as the number of shared subtasks divided by the total number of subtasks; note that because tasks may have different numbers of subtasks, the matrix is not symmetrical.

Calculation of Fitness. In this model an organization's performance is calculated as the inverse of the sum of the times required to perform the subtasks. If some subtasks are not performed by any actor, then the

TABLE 2.2
Example of Tasks and Component Subtasks with Five Subtasks Assigned

```
                                  Component Subtasks

          1111111111222222222233333333334444444444
Task    01234567890123456789012345678901234567890123456789

0       11111             1       1                     1   1
1        1   111111               1       1             1
2            11111    1                            1     1
3             1   1 11111              11
4                   111111              1 1       1
5          1         1    11111111
6          1     1          1 11111                   1
7              1            11   11111       11
8             1       1           1       11111
9          1     1            1       1       1       11111
```

TABLE 2.3
Overlap Between Tasks (Number of Shared Subtasks/Total Number of Subtasks) for Tasks
in Table 2.2

| Task | Task | | | | | | | | | |
	0	1	2	3	4	5	6	7	8	9
0	1.00	0.11	0.00	0.11	0.22	0.22	0.11	0.11	0.11	0.33
1	0.10	1.00	0.20	0.10	0.10	0.10	0.20	0.20	0.10	0.30
2	0.00	0.25	1.00	0.25	0.00	0.12	0.12	0.25	0.00	0.12
3	0.11	0.11	0.22	1.00	0.00	0.00	0.00	0.22	0.11	0.00
4	0.22	0.11	0.00	0.00	1.00	0.33	0.00	0.22	0.11	0.33
5	0.20	0.10	0.10	0.00	0.30	1.00	0.20	0.10	0.00	0.00
6	0.11	0.22	0.11	0.00	0.00	0.22	1.00	0.22	0.11	0.22
7	0.10	0.20	0.20	0.20	0.20	0.10	0.20	1.00	0.00	0.50
8	0.12	0.12	0.00	0.12	0.12	0.00	0.12	0.00	1.00	0.00
9	0.30	0.30	0.10	0.00	0.30	0.00	0.20	0.50	0.00	1.00

organization is not viable and its fitness is zero. (Note that because of the overlap, not all tasks may have to be assigned to an actor for all subtasks to be performed.) The total number of subtasks an organization had to perform varied from 10 (when all 10 tasks share the same 10 subtasks) to 100 (when each task has 10 unique subtasks). As a result, the performance of organizations cannot be compared between overlap conditions. Within each overlap condition, however, the same set of tasks was generated for each coordination penalty condition.

The time required to perform a single subtask is the inverse of the effort actors devote to it. Actors are assumed to divide their effort equally between the subtasks that are assigned to them, so, for example, an actor assigned 3 tasks with a total of 21 distinct subtasks would devote $\frac{1}{21}$ of its total effort to each (and those subtasks would therefore take 21 time units to complete). Because tasks overlap, the number of distinct subtasks an actor must perform may be less than the total of the number of subtasks in the tasks. If multiple actors are assigned the same subtask, then the total effort expended on that subtask is the sum of the efforts of each actor (i.e., for these experiments, I assumed that subtasks were perfectly and costlessly divisible).

Actors all initially have one unit of effort available, but an actor's actual effort may be adversely or positively affected by the number of tasks it is assigned. The coordination penalty (or benefit) was defined as the number of tasks assigned multiplied by a coordination penalty parameter. Actors assigned one task were not penalized (or benefited); actors assigned all 10 tasks had their effort reduced (or increased) by the full penalty factor. For actors assigned an intermediate numbers of tasks, the penalty (or benefit) was proportionally adjusted. In these experiments, four coordination penalty conditions were run: no effect (the total effort was constant), 50% penalty (working on all 10 tasks decreased the total effort to 50%), 200% penalty (working on 10 tasks resulted in a 200% penalty, i.e., working on 5 tasks or more was impossible) and 50% benefit (working on all 10 tasks increased the total effort by 50%). The final condition was primarily intended as a sanity check on the operation of the algorithm (discussed later).

In each generation of the genetic algorithm, the fitnesses of the members of the population were normalized: the best performing organization was given a score of 1, and the worst, a variable parameter set to .1 in these experiments to prevent them from being eliminated completely. As a result, the best performing organizations were selected to be bred 10 times as often as the weakest performers.

Each case was run with a population of 1,000 organizations for 1,000 generations. Every 100 generations the best performing organization of the generation was printed and the entire population of organizations was saved to disk for additional analysis. In addition, the overall best performing organization was printed at the end of the run. The results presented here are for the best performing organization in the final generation.

Hypotheses

Organizations in this model are subject to two countervailing forces: As actors are assigned more tasks, they can take better advantage of the synergies between tasks (depending on the overlap between tasks), but may suffer a reduction in the total effort available (depending on the coordination penalty for performing multiple tasks).

Overlap. For conditions with low overlap, there is no benefit to assigning multiple tasks to an actor, because there is no synergy between tasks. When tasks overlap completely, there is again no benefit in having actors perform multiple tasks, because every task already includes all subtasks. Therefore, this force should have no effect for both low and high values of overlap and should favor assigning related tasks to actors for intermediate values of overlap.

Coordination Penalty. When the coordination penalty is zero or negative (i.e., actors receive no penalty or a benefit for working on multiple tasks), actors should again be assigned multiple tasks. For other values, the coordination penalty will favor designs in which actors are assigned fewer tasks. These forces are summarized in Table 2.4; in the optimal form, the tasks assigned to each actor will be such to balance these forces. Accordingly, the following hypotheses were proposed.

TABLE 2.4
Summary of Conditions, Hypothesized Forces, and Expected Organizational Forms

		Coordination Penalty		
		Negative (Benefit)	Neutral	Positive
Task Overlap	Favored Result	Multiple Tasks per Actor	No Preference	Fewer Tasks per Actor
Low or high	No preference	All tasks assigned to all actors (H1)	Intermediate number of tasks (H2a)	One task per actor (H3a)
Intermediate	Assign related tasks to same actor	All tasks assigned to all actors (H1)	All tasks assigned to all actors (H2b)	Few related tasks per actor (H3b)

Hypothesis 1. When the coordination penalty is negative, both forces are working in the same direction, which will favor an extreme point in the design space, namely, assigning all tasks to all actors.

Hypothesis 2a. When the coordination cost is zero, then there is no force to limit the number of tasks assigned to each actor. For low and high amounts of overlap, however, there is no particular preference for multiple tasks per actor. For these cases, the number of tasks per actor will be an intermediate value.

Hypothesis 2b. For intermediate conditions of overlap, where there is a force to favor assigning multiple tasks, the organizational form will again be an extreme point in the design space.

Hypothesis 3a. When the coordination cost is a penalty, the two forces are in opposition. For low and high amounts of overlap, where there is no preference for multiple tasks per actor, it is hypothesized that actors will be assigned one task each. For low amounts of overlap between tasks, this result requires that each task be assigned to one actor in order for the organization to be viable.

Hypothesis 3b. For intermediate amount of overlap, the organization will balance the cost and benefit of assigning multiple tasks to actors. It is therefore hypothesized that each actor will be assigned a few tasks, and that the tasks each actor is assigned will have a high number of overlapping subtasks.

RESULTS

An example of a final organizational form is shown in Table 2.5. This organization happens to be the result for a run with no overlap between

TABLE 2.5
Example Final Organization Form (No Overlap,
2.0 Penalty Factor)

Actor	Assigned Tasks						
0	1				6		
1		2					9
2	0					7	
3	0						8
4			3	5			
5				4			9
6	1				6		
7		2		5			
8			3				8
9				4		7	

tasks and with a 200% coordination penalty factor. The results of one run of the genetic algorithm for each condition are shown in Table 2.6. The results given are the average number of tasks assigned to each actor (or equivalently, the number of actors assigned to each task). For example, the organization in Table 2.5 has two actors for each task and two tasks for each actor.

Discussion

Hypothesis 1, for the coordination benefit case, was supported; all actors are assigned to work on all tasks.

Hypothesis 2a predicted that for low and high amounts of overlap and no coordination penalty, the preferred form would assign an intermediate number of tasks per actor. However, the actual number of tasks assigned

TABLE 2.6
Average Number of Tasks Assigned to Each Actor by Overlap and Coordination Penalty

	Coodination Penalty (Benefit)			
Assigned Tasks	Benefit for Many Tasks (50%)	No Effect (0%)	Penalty for Many Tasks (50%)	High Penalty (200%)
0^a	10	5.9	1	1
1	10	6.3	1	1
3	10	8.5	2.4	1.5
5	10	10	3.4	1.7
7	10	10	2.9	2
10	10	9.4	2.1	2

[a]Zero assigned tasks means total overlap between tasks; 10 assigned tasks means no overlap between tasks.

was high. Upon examination, this outcome results from the design of this experiment favoring organizational forms with actors performing many tasks. The organization is attempting to minimize $\Sigma\ 1/x_i$ (the total time to do all the subtasks) subject to $\Sigma\ x_i = N$ (the total effort assigned to all subtasks is the sum of the efforts of the actors), where x_i is the total effort assigned to subtask i. This sum is minimized when all the x_i terms are equal, which is most easily achieved, given the random overlap between tasks, by having each actor perform the same set of tasks (i.e., all of them).

Hypothesis 2b—that for intermediate values of overlap and no coordination penalty, all actors would do all tasks—is supported.

Hypothesis 3a predicted that when there are coordination penalties and no force for multiple tasks per actor, the best form would assign one task per actor. This result was obtained for cases with high overlap between tasks. However, as Table 2.6 shows, for low overlap on average actors do two tasks. This result may reflect the high vulnerability of forms with only one actor per task in an environment with many unique subtasks. Recall that a form is viable only if all subtasks are assigned to some actor. If only one actor is assigned to a subtask, then the organization will become nonviable if something happens to that actor. Such a form might evolve, but it is very likely that when it is crossed with another organization, the offspring will be nonviable.

Hypothesis 3b, that intermediate amounts of overlap and a coordination penalty should favor organizations that assign a few related tasks to each actor, seems partially confirmed. The average number of tasks assigned per actor does indeed follow the predicted pattern. Unfortunately, a closer examination of the specific forms reveals that tasks assigned to a particular agent are not particularly closely related; in fact, there seems to be no relationship at all between the degree of overlap of two tasks and their pattern of assignment. This finding suggests that the model of overlap did not accurately capture synergies between tasks, even though it did reproduce other expected behaviors.

Although this model is simple, it is not simplistic. This example does illustrate the possible utility of genetic algorithms (reflecting a complex evolutionary simulation) for studying organizational questions, as well as their ability to produce unexpected results. The model has several possible extensions. First, the current model implicitly has a single product with a fixed payoff; it could easily be extended to multiple products with different payoffs. In such an environment, organizations might specialize by focusing on products with the higher payoffs. In the simplest form, each organization would be modeled independently and face set prices (i.e., perfect competition). A more complex simulation would permit direct competition between organizations, in which case the payoff for a product might depend on how much of that product was produced in total.

One significant limitation of the representation used for these experiments is that it can only represent the assignment of tasks to actors. A major extension would be to model hierarchical structures. Such a model could cluster tasks at various levels of the hierarchy, depending on their interdependencies, as suggested by Thompson (1967). A second limitation is the examination of the possible variance in the outcomes. In particular, each condition should be run multiple times to determine the distribution of these results. In the current implementation each run takes about 30 min to complete, which limits the number of runs possible. Experiments that evaluate fitness by simulating the performance of an organization will be even more computationally intensive. However, genetic algorithms are inherently parallelizable, so moving to a parallel architecture should make it feasible to perform the runs necessary.

FUTURE WORK

To apply the technique described in this chapter more broadly, a general model of what organizations do is necessary. For this purpose, it is interesting to examine how an organization can be represented as a collection of comps (McKelvey, 1982) or memes (Nelson & Winter, 1982). These routines can be modeled as rules or productions indicating the appropriate action to be taken in a situation. For example, a meme could be represented as a production in a classifier system; such systems have already been successfully used with the genetic algorithm (Holland, 1992). Such a representation seems particularly appropriate for use with the genetic algorithm because of the claimed robustness of a rule base to additions or deletions of individual rules.

To illustrate the possible applications of these ideas, I briefly discuss how routines could be used to represent an organizational model such as Malone's (1987) hierarchies and markets. (Again, it seems useful initially to attempt to reproduce findings for which there is some theoretical prediction.) In Malone's model, the problem faced by an organization is processing tasks (e.g., building cars). Tasks are assumed to arrive at some point in the organization but must be decomposed into subtasks to be processed by specialized processors. As in the previous example, we may assume that the environment provides some payoff for successfully completed tasks. Malone compared the performance of four pure forms, namely, functional and product hierarchies and centralized and decentralized markets, each composed of a number of actors of different types.

Each type of actor behaves in a characteristic fashion. Although Malone did not describe them in this way, we can analyze each actor's behavior as a set of routines for primitive operations and for interacting with other actors, as summarized in Table 2.7. Malone's analysis considered only pure organizational forms and therefore only a limited variety of organizational actors; by mixing these basic capabilities we may be able to generate a wide variety of intermediate forms.

The units to be evolved in this model are the individual actors — a population of interacting actors compose an organization. Each actor starts with a random selection of routines and connections to other actors. In each generation, the behavior of the actors is simulated and their interactions determine the performance of the organization. Actors that contribute to the success of the organization, weighted perhaps by some measure of their cost to the organization, are then selected and bred to form the next generation of actors.

Using such a model, the effect of changes in underlying parameters could be assessed. For example, Malone's models included parameters for various

TABLE 2.7

Capabilities of Different Actor Types in Malone's (1987) Model Organizations

Actor Type	Capabilities and Knowledge
Processor	Perform assigned subtasks Respond to bids in a market
Product managers	Decompose tasks into subtasks Know one processor for each type of subtask Communicate with processors to assign subtasks Integrate results of subtasks
Functional manager	Know multiple processors for one type of subtask Pick best processor for a given subtask Communicate with processors to assign subtasks
General manager	Decompose tasks into subtasks Know one functional manager for each type of subtask Communicate with functional manager to assign subtasks Integrate results of subtasks
Buyers in a decentralized market	Decompose tasks into subtasks Know multiple processors for each type of subtask Request bids for each type of subtask Evaluate bids to pick best processor for a given subtask Communicate with processors to assign subtasks Integrate results of subtasks
Buyers in a centralized market	Decompose tasks into subtasks Know one middleman for each type of subtask Communicate with middlemen to assign subtasks Integrate results of subtasks
Middlemen in a centralized market	Know multiple processors for one type of subtask Request bids for one type of subtask Evaluate bids to pick best processor for a given subtask Communicate with processors to assign subtasks

costs, such as performing a subtask, maintaining a unit of production capacity, and sending a message. By substituting a different set of routines, entirely different types of organizations can be modeled. For example, Crowston (1991) modeled the activities performed by participants in engineering change processes and Pentland (1992) modeled the moves made by software support hotline specialists.

CONCLUSIONS

I conclude by briefly discussing two objections that may be raised to this approach to the study of organizations. The first objection argues that patterns of task assignment (as in the example) are a rather impoverished view of an organization. This is undeniable. Identifying appropriate tasks and organizational features is key to the utility of any kind of model. It should be noted, however, that these choices are not determined by the use of the genetic algorithm, but rather depend on the organizational theories of interest. In principle, any set of interesting features could be used, although the genetic algorithm does require that they be recombinable in various ways.

The second objection states that even if we did successfully identify factors that contributed to the performance of an organizational form, it may be that the performance per se is only part of the reason for a form's success. For example, based on simulations of the evolution of competing forms, Carroll and Harrison (1992) suggested that long-term success of a form may be due as much to chance as actual fitness, because of the path-dependent nature of the competition. They therefore cautioned against applying retrospective economic rationality to explain the prevalence of organizational forms.

Hannan and Freeman (1986) argued that institutionalization is important for the success of a form. When other powerful actors endorse a particular form's claims for resources or when it becomes unquestioned that one form is the right one to use, the difficulty of starting an organization and mobilizing resources is greatly reduced. These arguments suggest that the organizations may adopt forms without regard to their inherent performance; indeed, as Stinchcombe (1965) noted, "forms tend to incorporate and retain packages of characteristics that were fashionable or legitimate in the period when the form takes shape" (p. 53). Furthermore, organizational forms may differ in ways beyond those used to calculate fitness, for example, in the quality of work life they provide for their employees.

Even if a new form were preferred, organizational ecologists suggest that constraints exist in changing organizational arrangements. They point out that organizations must behave consistently in order to be successful and that this consistency results in organizational inertia, and therefore argue that most changes in populations occur through selection of organizations, not adaptation of individual organizations (Hannan & Freeman, 1977; Singh & Lumsden, 1990).

These caveats are certainly significant for empirical studies that attempt to explain an observed distribution of forms, and such factors may affect the final implementation of novel designs. For the task of suggesting new forms, however, these objections are far less critical. Indeed, computerized implementations of organizational evolution are best seen as powerful tools for the imagination. Used in this way, this novel use of computers may suggest others, embodied perhaps in novel organizational forms.

ACKNOWLEDGMENTS

This chapter is a revision of a paper presented at the 1992 TIMS Workshop on Mathematical Organization Theory held in Orlando, FL, April 25–26. It has benefited from discussions with Michael Gordon, Helen Klein, Michael Cohen, Brian Pentland, Martha Feldman, Tom Finholt, and Ojelanki Ngwenyama.

The author acknowledges the support of the Ameritech Foundation, through the Information and Organizations Program of the University of Michigan Institute for Public Policy Studies.

REFERENCES

Axelrod, R. (1987). The evolution of strategies in the iterated prisoner's dilemma. In L. Davis (Ed.), *Genetic algorithms and simulated annealing*. London: Pitman.

Booker, L. B., Goldberg, D. E., & Holland, J. H. (1987). *Classifier systems and genetic algorithms* (Tech. Rep. No. 8). Ann Arbor, MI: CSMIL, University of Michigan.

Burgelman, R. A. (1991). Intraorganizational ecology of strategy making and organizational adaptation: Theory and field research. *Organization Science, 2*(3), 239–262.

Burton, R. M., & Obel, B. (1980). A computer simulation test of the M-form hypothesis. *Administrative Science Quarterly, 25*, 457–466.

Carroll, G. R. (1984). Organizational ecology. *Annual Review of Sociology, 10*, 71–93.

Carroll, G. R., & Harrison, J. R. (1992). *Chance and rationality in organizational evolution*. Unpublished manuscript, University of California at Berkeley.

Crowston, K. (1991). *Towards a coordination cookbook: Recipes for multi-agent action*. Unpublished doctoral dissertation, MIT Sloan School of Management.

Cyert, R. M., & March, J. G. (1963). *A behavioral theory of the firm*. Englewood Cliffs, NJ: Prentice-Hall.

DiMaggio, P., & Powell, W. (1983). Institutional isomorphism. *American Sociological Review, 48*, 147–60.

Fontana, W. (1991). Algorithmic chemistry. In C. G. Langton, C. Taylor, J. D. Farmer, & S. Rasmussen (Eds.), *Artificial life II, SFI studies in the sciences of complexity* (Vol. X). Reading, MA: Addison-Wesley.

Freeman, J., & Hannan, M. T. (1983). Niche width and the dynamics of organizational change. *American Journal of Sociology, 88*, 116–145.

Hannan, M. T., & Freeman, J. (1977). The population ecology of organizations. *American Journal of Sociology, 82*, 929–964.

Hannan, M. T., & Freeman, J. (1986). Where do organizational forms come from? *Sociological Forum, 1*(1), 50–72.

Holland, J. H. (1992). *Adaptation in natural and artificial systems* (2nd ed.). Ann Arbor: University of Michigan.

Koza, J. R. (1992). *Genetic programming.* Cambridge, MA: MIT Press.

Malone, T. W. (1987). Modeling coordination in organizations and markets. *Management Science, 33*, 1317–1332.

McKelvey, B. (1982). *Organizational systematics: Taxonomy, evolution, classification.* Berkeley: University of California.

Michalewicz, Z. (1992). *Genetic algorithms + Data structures = Evolution programs.* New York: Springer-Verlag.

Nelson, R. R., & Winter, S. G. (1982). *An evolutionary theory of economic change.* Cambridge, MA: Harvard University Press.

Pentland, B. T. (1992). Organizing moves in software support hotlines. *Administrative Science Quarterly, 37*, 527–548.

Romanelli, E. (1991). The evolution of new organizational forms. *Annual Review of Sociology, 17*, 79–103.

Schmerken, I. (1987). Expert system churns many happy returns. *Wall Street Computer Review, 5*(3), 14–17.

Simon, H. A. (1981). Studying human intelligence by creating artificial intelligence. *American Scientist, 69*(3), 300–309.

Singh, J. V., & Lumsden, C. J. (1990). Theory and research in organizational ecology. *Annual Review of Sociology, 17*, 161–193.

Stinchcombe, A. L. (1965). Social structure and organizations. In J. G. March (Ed.), *Handbook of organizations* (pp. 153–193). Chicago: Rand McNally.

Thompson, J. D. (1967). *Organizations in action: Social science bases of administrative theory.* New York: McGraw-Hill.

Whicker, M. L., & Sigelman, L. (1991). *Computer simulation applications.* Newbury Park, CA: Sage.

Williamson, O. E. (1975). *Markets and hierarchies.* New York: Free Press.

3

TASCCS: A Synthesis of Double-AISS and Plural-Soar

Harko Verhagen
Michael Masuch
University of Amsterdam

Double-AISS (Masuch & LaPotin, 1989) was possibly the first completed effort to build an artificial intelligence (AI) based model of organizational decision making. Intended as a follow-up study of the garbage can model of organizational decision making (Cohen, March, & Olsen, 1972), Double-AISS examined the influence of various organizational parameters on the problem-solving behavior in organizations. In 1990, the Soar architecture (Laird, Newell, & Rosenbloom, 1987) was adapted to build another AI-based model of organizations, called Plural-Soar (Carley, Kjaer-Hansen, Newell, & Prietula, 1991). Plural-Soar examined the influence of communication and learning capabilities on the problem solving behavior of independent actors working on a simple task. The model reported in this chapter, TASCCS, provides—in a sense—a synthesis of Double-AISS and Plural-Soar.

DOUBLE-AISS

Double-AISS (Masuch & Lapotin, 1989) provides a generalization of the *garbage can theory* of decision making (Cohen et al., 1972). "Garbage can" is a metaphor used to characterize loosely coupled decision processes: Preferences are unstable, the technology is unclear, and participation is fluid. In the garbage can model, a decision is an outcome of several relatively independent processes within an organization. Double-AISS tries to overcome the drawbacks of earlier renderings of the garbage can model

(Anderson & Fischer, 1986; Carley, 1986; Padgett, 1980) by using AI techniques rather than numerical equations. The core of the model is formed by the *actors.* They make the decisions in the model. Actors are embedded in an organizational *structure,* which maps the communication possibilities onto the actors. The content of the communication is an *issue.* What actors can do with issues is defined by their *skills* and *actions.* The acronym Double-AISS is derived from these five building blocks.

The Model of an Actor in Double-AISS

In Double-AISS, the rationality of actors is bounded (Simon, 1955). They:

- Do not know all decision alternatives in advance.
- Do not anticipate all consequences of their actions.
- Do not try to optimize but rather to satisfice (that is, try to meet some aspiration level, which depends on prior experience).
- Do not have completely ordered preferences (whereas their commitment to each other or to the organization may be limited).

The organizational structure is implemented as a communication network, which defines which actors can communicate with each other. The *content* of the communication is an issue. Issues are multidimensional sets of interrelated subtasks. In Double-AISS, the categorical task is the production of a memo. This task consists of six subtasks: writing, drafting, typing, editing, approving, and copying. Every subtask is a *dimension* of the memo task. Each issue belongs to one actor at a time.

Skills are the qualifications of an actor. Skills are "applied" to problems, so if an actor can draft a memo and has an issue that contains the need for drafting, then the actor can draft the issue; with the drafting task completed, the issue's subtasks are reduced to five. An actor can choose between several strategies to solve the memo task. The possible actions are reducing an issue, moving an issue to another actor, attracting an issue from another actor, combining two issues into one new issue (which has less dimensions than the two old issues had together), splitting one issue into two new issues (which have more dimensions together than the old one had), or doing nothing.

The Search Space of an Actor in Double-AISS

Double-AISS's organization consists of 10 actors. They make their decision as a function of search through their own problem space. The path of the search depends on seven factors: (a) the search strategy, (b) cognitive capacity, (c) aspirations, (d) preferences, (e) organizational work load, (f) commitment, and (g) organizational structure.

1. The search strategy can be either of the following two: (time-related) depth-first search or (time-related) breadth-first search. In depth-first search, an actor tries to anticipate the future by conceiving sequences of activities. In the process, the actor may try to imagine what another actor would do, given that the alternative under consideration is chosen. In breadth-first search, an actor tries all possible alternatives in turn. Both search modes search until either a satisficing alternative is reached, or the cognitive capacity of an actor is exhausted. The choice for a search alternative is made according to a preference for one of the search modes. If the preferred search strategy gives no result, then the other strategy is given a try. If no satisficing alternative is found, then the last-found tolerable alternative is chosen. If there also is no tolerable alternative, then the action "do nothing" is chosen.

2. The cognitive capacity of an actor is the number of search steps an actor can make per decision cycle.

3. The aspiration level of an actor is the number of tasks an actor expects to complete ("reduce") in one decision cycle. An actor also has a tolerance level. If the aspiration level is not met when the time has come to make a decision, but the tolerance level is met, the corresponding action is chosen.

4. The preferences of an actor concern various parts of the decision process. There are preferences for subtasks, skills, actions, other actors, search strategy, and decision outcome (whether or not to reduce one's own work load at the expense of other actors' work load). Preferences are implemented via the probability with which an alternative is chosen.

5. The work load of the organization is the number of issues that come into the organization at one decision cycle, multiplied with the number of tasks per issue. The work load of an actor is its part of the total work load of the organization.

6. The commitment of an actor to the organization can be one of the following two alternatives: The actor is concerned with only its own work load, or it is concerned with the work load of the organization as a whole (also called individualistic versus cooperative actors, Baron, 1983). The commitment of an actor determines the ordering of the action alternatives. An egotistic actor (concerned only with its own work load) conceives of moving an issue to another actor as a solution, because its own work load decreases. Conversely, attracting an issue from another actor is a nonsolution for it. Altruistic actors think of both moving and attracting as a nonsolution because the overall work load is not reduced.

7. The structure of the organization determines the communication possibilities of an actor. Communication is effected via the exchange of issues.

The Behavior of Double-AISS

The behavior of the organization in Double-AISS results from the interactive effect of individual decisions. The canonical simulation experiment with Double-AISS (Masuch & LaPotin, 1989) examined the impact of various parameters on several measures of organizational performance. The experiment was done as a block design with two variables per block. The independent variables were cognitive capacity, work load, structure, aspiration level, adaptation period, the strength of various preferences, and the maximum depth of the search. The dependent variables were productivity, the number of solutions, nonsolutions, nondecisions, and the organizational climate.

Cognitive capacity and commitment (egotistic/altruistic) turned out to dominate the behavior of the model. Most other independent variables played a significant role as well, but their influence was of secondary importance.

Critique on Double-AISS

Subsequent work on Double-AISS indicated several points of possible improvement, such as (a) the implementation of subtasks and skills, (b) the reduce calculus, (c) the communication structure, and (d) foresight.

1. Both subtasks and skills in Double-AISS are implemented as characters, which serve as abbreviations of the task itself. For example, a stands for "approve," which is both a subtask (as dimension of an issue) and a skill (as a qualification of an actor). This representation may give rise to confusion. Also, subtasks are not related to a subject—for example, one cannot know if a stands for "approve memo X" or "approve memo Y." Therefore, it is not possible to control the order in which subtasks are carried out, although this order might be important. Approving memo X and typing memo Y do not have to be carried out in a specific order, but approving and typing memo X do.

2. The "reduce" calculus used in Double-AISS is idiosyncratic. In the garbage can theory, the role of an issue (problem or solution) depends on the context. In Double-AISS, this context dependency is implemented by means of symbolic valencies (minus signs): A minus sign in front of a subtask indicates a solution; a subtask without the minus sign indicates a problem. For example, it is difficult to grasp what it means to have the skill a (which stands for a memo that needs approving). The reduce action effects the combination of a problem and a corresponding solution, with $-a$ as a skill and a as the subtask for an issue. The same context dependency could better be conceptualized via preferences. For example, the preference to "approve," if strong enough, would put a strain on the decision-making process, leaving other tasks "on hold." This way, skills could represent solutions and issues could represent problems.

3. The communication in Double-AISS is not communication in the ordinary sense, that is flow of information. Instead, communication is effected via the flow of issues.

4. Foresight in Double-AISS is one-sided. The actor who is trying to conceive the future visualizes the possible reaction of other actors by "stepping into their shoes," and not communicating directly with them. And when stepping into another actor's shoes it has a perfect model of that other actor, which is not realistic.

PLURAL-SOAR

Soar (Laird et al., 1987) is an implementation of an elaboration of the human problem-solving paradigm (Newell & Simon, 1972). It is a system capable of general intelligent behavior and can perform the full range of cognitive tasks, employ the full range of problem-solving methods, and learn about all aspects of the tasks and its performance on them. Plural-Soar (Carley et al., 1991) is a model of a small organization implemented in Soar. As in Double-AISS, the model's core is formed by actors (*agents* in Soar terminology). The name Plural-Soar is derived from the contraction of plural agents and Soar.

The Model of an Actor in Plural-Soar

The organization structure is flat — all actors are on the same hierarchical level. Actors have the ability to communicate and to pose questions to all other actors concerning the location of items. The original actor continues searching, whereas the other agents may respond at a later date (if they encounter the item), so one could say a particular problem is solved in parallel mode by the organization, once it is communicated to others. Once the answer is found, it is communicated to the original actor.

The task performed in Plural-Soar is a warehouse task: The warehouse receives orders, and the actors have to take an order, find the ordered item in the warehouse, and put it on a conveyer belt. Every actor can work autonomously; that is, it can perform all actions to complete the warehouse task. These actions are:

1. Move to the left.
2. Move to the right.
3. Move item to left stack.
4. Move item to right stack.
5. Move item to conveyer belt.
6. Ask order.
7. Ask question.

8. Answer question.
9. Wait.

The choice of any of these actions depends on the state of the actor. For instance, in order to put an item onto the conveyer belt, the actor must be in front of a stack and the top item of the stack must be the ordered item. If there is more than one applicable action, preferences determine the choice of the action alternative. The physical properties of the warehouse or the actions of other actors may cause actors to wait for their turn. Only one actor can access a particular stack at a time.

The Actor's Search Space in Plural-Soar

The organization consists of (at most) five actors. Implemented as a separate Soar program, every actor is autonomous in its choice of action alternatives. Every actor has a mental model of the warehouse and knows the number of stacks, their location, and the location of the conveyer belt. The search through the problem space is influenced by the behavior of other actors only when they have to wait at a queue or when there is a question pending. When an actor has filled its order, it goes to the order stack to get a new one. Every item is unique, is ordered only once, and is only once available in the warehouse. The warehouse itself (Fig. 3.1) contains 10 item stacks (each containing 3 items) and 1 order stack plus a conveyer belt (facing the stacks).

The Behavior of Plural-Soar

The canonical simulation of Plural-Soar (Carley et al., 1991) studied the influence of two cognitive capabilities on organizational performance, that is, the ability to memorize a stack and the ability to communicate. The impact of the number of actors was also studied.

Interestingly, increasing the number of actors does not always mean quicker results for the organization. However, more actors does mean less working time per actor. Communication also reduces the working time per actor, provided that there are enough actors with whom to communicate. Waiting time increases when the number of actors increases, but this effect is reduced by communication and memory skills. Because communication is preferred over search, communicating actors have to wait more than noncommunicating ones. Too many actors also reduce the number of answers given, because the waiting time per answer increases.

Critique of Plural-Soar

Plural-Soar, just like Double-AISS, has its drawbacks. Problematic are (a) the cooperation in Plural-Soar, (b) the autonomy of the actors in Plural-Soar, and (c) the implementation of the warehouse task:

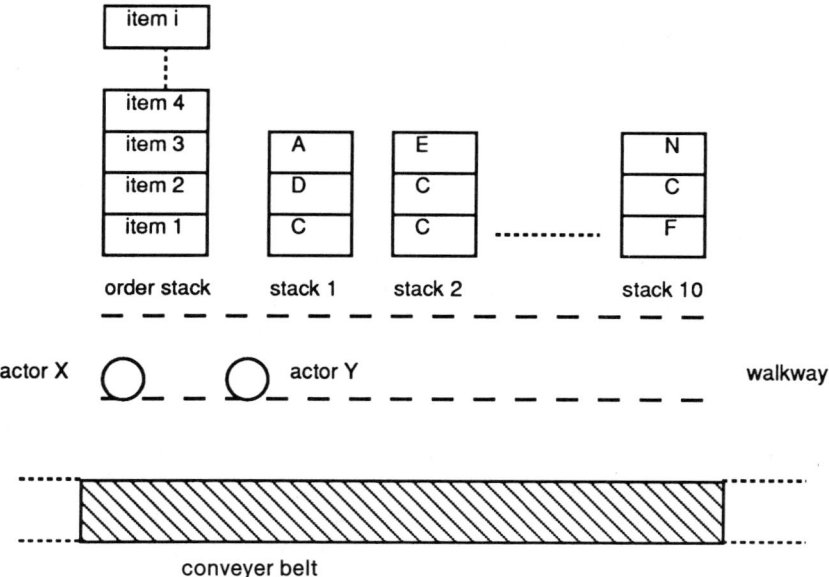

FIG. 3.1.   The warehouse.

1. In Plural-Soar, cooperation consists of posing questions about the location of an item and responding truthfully to questions. Whether an actor's search behavior changes depends on whether it receives an answer (if no answer is received, it engages in exhaustive search). Nevertheless, many of the more elaborate forms of cooperation (such as exchanging tasks) do not occur because agents cannot exchange goals.

2. Actors in Plural-Soar are too autonomous. Each actor can perform the whole warehouse task by itself, so there is no real need for cooperation. A more realistic model would limit the actor's competence, so that actors come to depend on each other; each actor's skills should be limited.

3. Some actions remain implicit in the Plural-Soar model. For instance, the model assumes that an agent perceives the complete content of a stack, once it is in front of it.

MERGING OF DOUBLE-AISS AND PLURAL-SOAR: TASCCS

TASCCS has been built to combine the strong points of both Double-AISS and Plural-Soar. TASCCS's starting point was the code of Plural-Soar, to which several additions were made (Verhagen, 1992). Added were skills, problem-solving strategies, and organizational structure (implemented as a communication network). Also, evaluation of cooperation requests was made to depend on the commitment of the receiving actor. However, preferences were absolute, and bounded rationality has not yet been implemented. Also, there are no specific models of other actors to guide communication. TASCCS is an acronym for tasks, actors, structure, commitment, communication, and skills.

The Model of an Actor in TASCCS

As in Double-AISS and Plural-Soar, problem solving is conducted by actors, with every actor being implemented as a separate Soar program. The actors are characterized by their skills, their place in the organizational hierarchy, and their commitment to the organization. As in Double-AISS, a skill is the ability to perform a (sub)task. An actor's hierarchical position is determined by its place in a communication network. Two communication modes are possible: horizontal and vertical. The actor's commitment is either altruistic or egotistic. The commitment of an actor determines its preference order with regard to problem-solving strategies and its reaction to received requests. Three problem-solving strategies are available: (a) reduce (that is, solve) subtasks, (b) move subtasks to another actor, and (c) attract subtasks from another actor. Commitment is defined as in Double-AISS: Altruistic actors take the work load of the whole organization into account when deciding on a problem-solving strategy, so altruists prefer "reduce" over "move" and "attract" (because these do not solve (sub)problems, as we know). Egotistic actors take only their own work load into account, and prefer "move" to "reduce" to "attract."

The communication modes and problem solving strategies can be combined into five different alternatives: (a) reduce, (b) a request to move, (c) a command to move, (d) a request to attract, and (e) a command to attract. A request to move can be read as: "Can you do <subtask> for me concerning item <item>?" and a command to attract can be read "I want to do <subtask> for you!" In general, commands are not negotiable, and the only condition under which a command is not obeyed is when it cannot be executed. Requests, in contrast, are evaluated by the receiving actor, according to its preferences. Altruistic actors will accept a move request, but egotistic actors will turn it down. Egotistic actors will accept attract requests (it lowers their work load), and altruistic actors turn them down (they prefer to do things themselves).

The ordering of alternatives also depends on the commitment of the actors. Altruistic actors have the following preference order: reduce >attract command >attract request >move request >move command. The egotistic actors have the order: move command >move request >reduce >attract request >attract command. The command mode is chosen when a negative answer is not wanted, and the request mode is chosen when a negative answer is hoped for. Thus, an egotistic actor tries to move a subtask, at first using the command mode, and, if that fails, using the request mode, and turning to less preferred alternatives if that fails, too. Altruistic actors prefer reducing an item to attracting an item, and prefer commands over requests, to increase the chance of a successful attraction.

"Move" and "attract" apply to subtasks of items. When moving a subtask to another actor, the sending actor decides which subtask is moved. One instance of a subtask is "find," so an actor may send the message "Can you find item A for me?" When attracting, the sending actor chooses the subtask, but the receiving actor chooses the item. The message being sent has the form: "Can I find an item for you?"

The warehouse task is split recursively into subtasks (Fig. 3.2). At the top level, the subtasks are take order and fill order. Filling of the order is again split into subtasks, which are finding an item (in the warehouse), and getting the item (getting an item from the stack and putting it on the conveyer belt). In the current model, the skills of the actor are not ordered by preferences, so no skill is preferred over other skills.

To implement the warehouse tasks, both "looking at a stack" and "putting an item on the conveyer belt" were made explicit. "Finding an item" consists of moving through the warehouse and examining the stacks. When an item is found, its location is remembered. "Getting hold of an item" consists of going to the item location, manipulating the stack, and taking the item from the stack. This is signaled by the completion marker "in possession." An item can be put on the conveyer belt by an actor when it is in possession of that actor. The item location has to be communicated when the "get" subtask is moved to (or attracted from) another actor. Also,

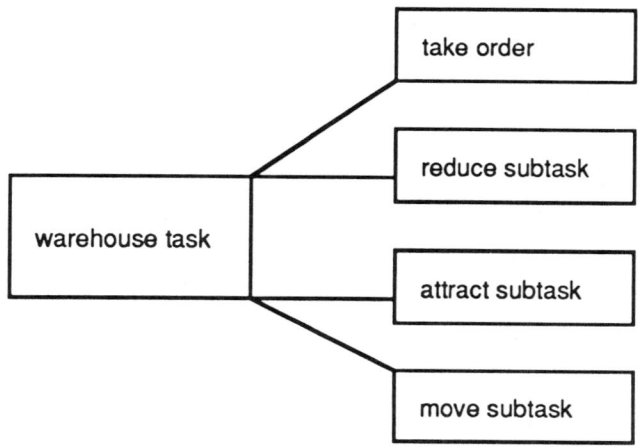

FIG. 3.2.   Subtasks.

once the subtask "get" is reduced by another actor, the item has to be handed over to the original subtask owner. The same holds for the moving or attracting the "put" subtask.

The Search Space of an Actor in TASCCS

The search space of an actor in TASCCS consists of several layers. The top layer is the main decision cycle, illustrated in Fig. 3.3 First, the actor tries to obtain an order. Then the actor decides whether to reduce the first subtask or to move it. This, of course, depends on the actor's commitment. When "reduce" is chosen, the skill to perform that subtask is needed in order to be able to complete the reduction of the subtask (Fig. 3.4). When "move" is chosen, the actor to move the subtask to has to be decided on. This is illustrated in Fig. 3.5.

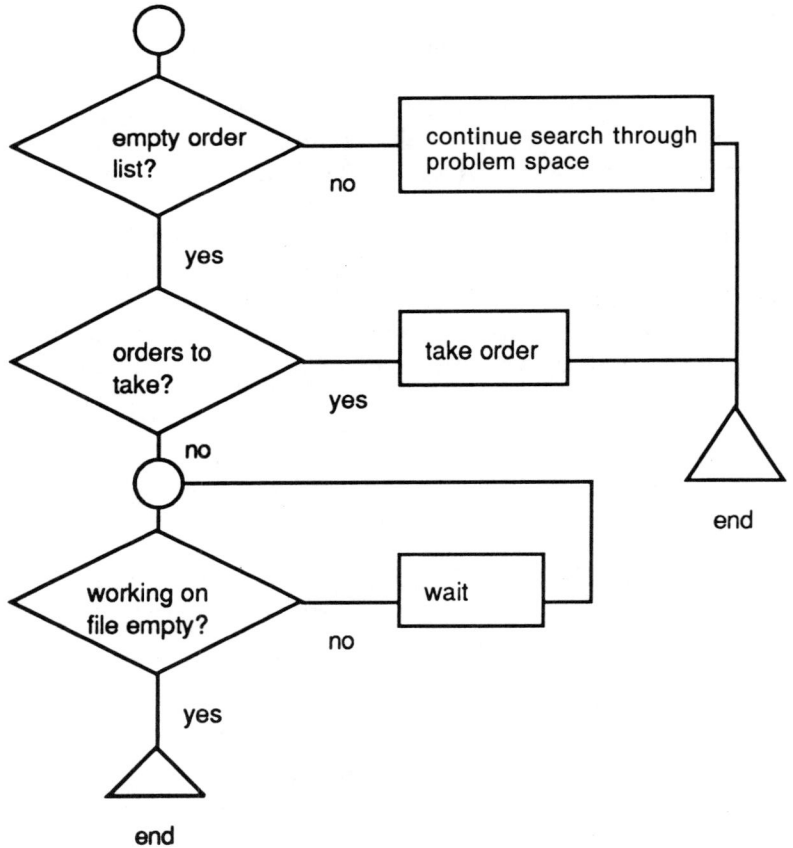

FIG. 3.3. The main cycle of TASCCS.

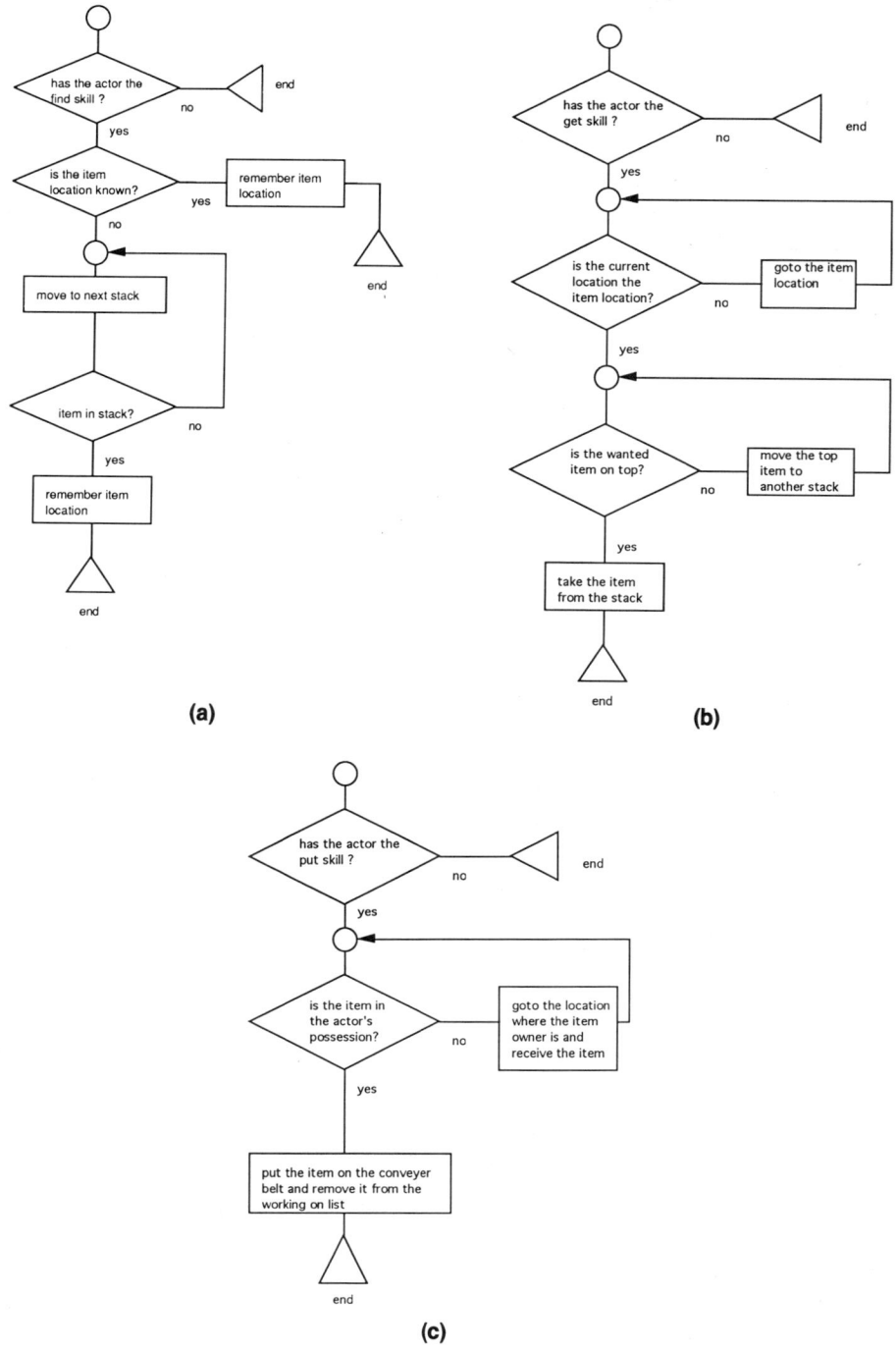

(a)

(b)

(c)

FIG. 3.4.   (a) Find; (b) Get; (c) Put.

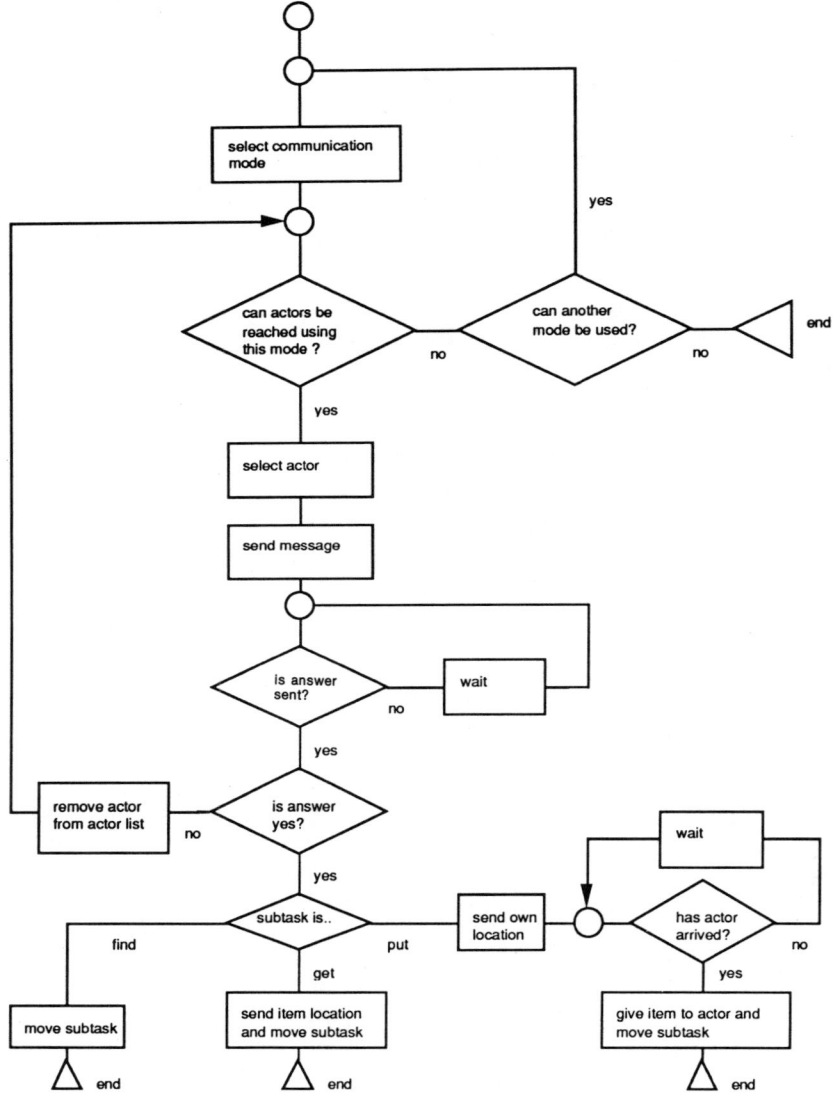

FIG. 3.5.   The move problem space.

Once the actor to communicate with is known, the information exchange can begin. When all the subtasks have been dealt with, the actor has to decide whether to try to attract a subtask from another actor or take an order. An actor receiving a subtask via a move or attract message has to evaluate that message (see Fig. 3.6). Once the actor agrees on the request, the item location has to be exchanged or the item has to be handed over,

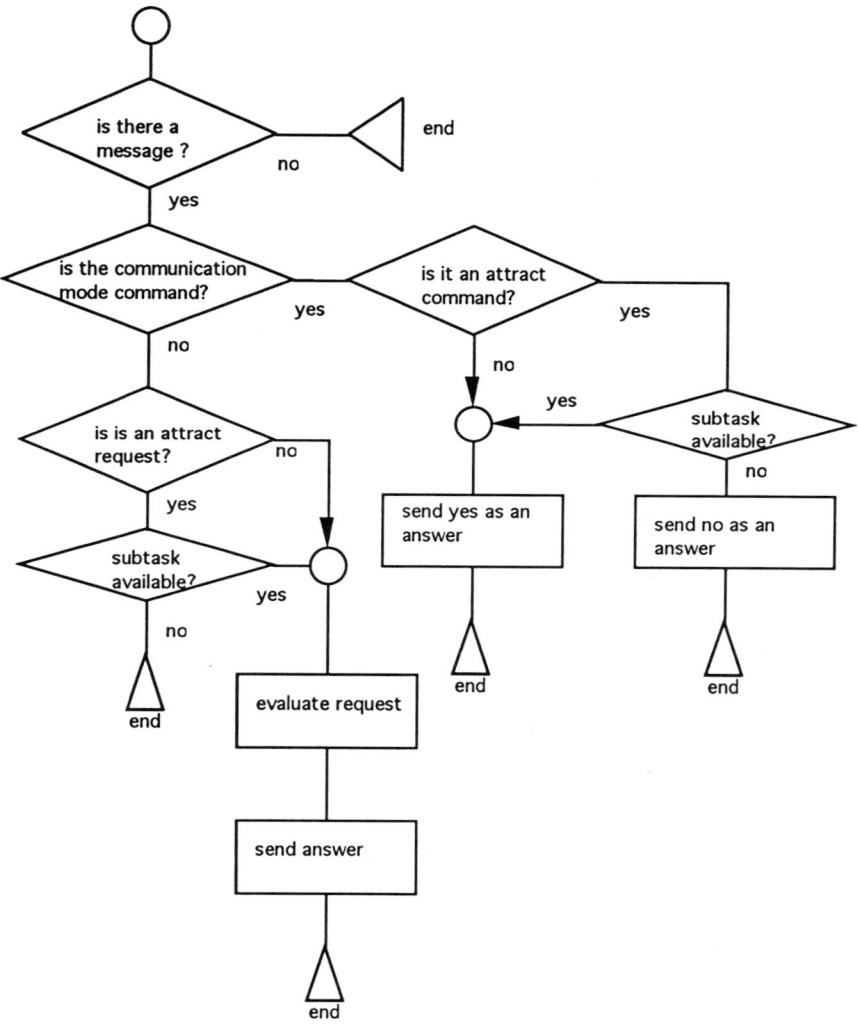

FIG. 3.6.   Evaluating a message.

depending on the subtask involved. When this is done, the receiving actor has to go through the same cycle itself. Shall I reduce it or move it? If an actor has reduced a received subtask, the necessary information has to be fed back to the actor who sent the subtask.

The Behavior of TASCCS

Due to limitations in the computer facilities, the organization of the simulation experiment was set to only two actors, with one actor located

TABLE 3.1
Summary of the Results of TASCCS

	Model Using Communication			Model Without Communication		
	Actor 1	Actor 2	Σ	Actor 1	Actor 2	Σ
Actor moves	0	158	158	88	70	158
Item moves	0	50	50	26	19	45
Waited cycles	1621	577	2198	10	62	72

above the other actor in the organization. The top-level actor is egotistic and the bottom-level actor altruistic. With this organization, the influence of communication on the problem-solving process of the organization was studied. The dependent variables studied were the amount of cycles waited by an actor, the number of times an actor moves to another stack, and the number of items that is moved to another stack.

Results of TASCCS

The results of TASCCS are summarized in Table 3.1. The results for the same model using Plural-Soar are summarized in Table 3.2.

The main difference between our results and the results from Plural-Soar is that the waiting time increases when actors communicate. In Plural-Soar, the waiting time decreases when communication takes place. This is due to the fact that subtasks are solved sequentially in TASCCS. In Plural-Soar, the actor who asks a question waits one cycle for a response. If no response is forthcoming, the agent begins to search for the item. The first actor who asks for an item will search and not wait, as the other actor has not been out to the stacks and so has no information to impart. But the time the first gets his second order and asks for information, the second actor has information that can be imparted. These factors reduce the wait time in Plural-Soar when there are two actors. When there are more than two actors, the actors get in each other's way, so with communication the wait time increases (Carley et al., 1991). Whether the wait time for TASCCS would change for

TABLE 3.2
Summary of the Results of Plural-Soar

	Model with Communication			Model Without Communication		
	Actor 1	Actor 2	Σ	Actor 1	Actor 2	Σ
Actor moves	746	82	158	79	81	160
Item moves	20	15	35	17	19	36
Waited cycles	11	18	29	5	32	37

more than two actors is a point for future research. If an answer arrives before the actor has found the item, the speed of problem solving is increased. Waiting in TASCCS is caused both by the communication pattern and the physical properties of the warehouse (i.e., only one actor can look at a stack at one point in time). In Plural-Soar, the physical properties of the warehouse, the number of actors, and the actors' preferences cause the actors to wait.

The number of moves of an actor is not influenced by changes in communication and cooperation patterns (of the organization as a whole, that is). The only exception is the Plural-Soar case without communication, where the number of actors's moves is slightly higher than in the other simulations.

The increase of the waiting time in the TASCCS model with communication is in accordance with the theory that well-structured problems need specialization in order to make cooperation useful. Cooperation makes the actors dependent on each other—they have to wait for the other actor to perform a subtask or to give an answer. With specialization, the problem-solving process is less tedious. However, specialization also calls for another approach to the communication of subtasks. Subproblems have to be processed in parallel, so that the moving of the "find" subtask allows an actor to take other orders in the meantime. A different implementation of the actions following the completion of the "get" subtask and the moving of the "put" subtask could also speed up the problem-solving process. Not having the original subtask owner as an intermediary item owner but only as a communication manager could be useful, so that after the completion of the "get" subtask, the item does not have to be handed over to the original subtask owner. Instead, the completion can be communicated, after which the communication manager (i.e., the original subtask owner) can send a message, indicating to whom the item should be handed (the actor who accepts the moving of the "put" subtask).

Another important improvement would be to let the actors decide when they take an order. Orders can be distributed by an order manager, like the inflow of items in Double-AISS. In this way, the attract strategy is not an alternative for the taking of an order, but one of the three possible action strategies.

CONCLUSIONS

TASCCS was designed to overcome some shortcomings of its predecessors Double-AISS and Plural-Soar. The results are in accordance with theoretical predictions about the efficiency of cooperation when solving well-structured problems. To make full use of the benefits of the TASCCS, more work is necessary, however. Future work should focus on the implementation of bounded rationality, the use of revisable belief models of other actors to serve as a guideline for communication, and better evaluation of communication (e.g., based on skills, work load, and preferences, instead of only based on commitment). Labor specialization should be added and subtask reduction done in parallel mode to make the advantages of communication and cooperation more clear. Less physical movement and more use of communication will make the problem solving of the organization more effective, from the viewpoint of both physical resources used by actors and a better use of the possibilities communication offers an organization. This can be accomplished by allowing the subtask reduction in parallel mode and by replacing the handing over of items after a moved or attracted "get" subtask to the original subtask owner by the handing over of the item to the actor who reduces the "put" subtask.

REFERENCES

Anderson, P. A., & Fischer, G. W. (1986). A Monte Carlo model of a garbage can decision process. In J. G. March & R. Weisinger-Byron (Eds.), *Ambiguity and command* (pp. 140–164). Marschfield, MA: Pitman.

Baron, R. A. (1983). *Behavior in organizations: understanding and managing the human side of work.* Boston: Allyn & Bacon.

Carley, K. (1986). Efficiency in a garbage can: Implications for crisis management. In J. G. March & R. Weisinger-Byron (Eds.), *Ambiguity and command* (pp. 165–194). Marschfield, MA: Pitman.

Carley, K., Kjaer-Hansen, J., Newell, A., & Prietula, M. (1992). Plural-Soar: Capabilities and coordination of multiple agents. In M. Masuch & M. Warglien (Eds.), *Artificial intelligence in organization and management theory: Models of distributed intelligence* (pp. 87–118). New York: Elsevier Science.

Cohen, M. D., March, J. G., & Olsen, J. P. (1972). A garbage can model of organizational choice. *Administrative Science Quarterly, 17,* 1–25.

Laird, J. E., Newell, A., & Rosenbloom, P. S. (1987). SOAR: An architecture for general intelligence. *Artificial Intelligence, 33,* 1–64.

Masuch, M. (Ed.). (1990). *Organization, management, and expert systems.* New York: Walter de Gruyter.

Masuch, M., & LaPotin, P. (1989). Beyond garbage cans: An AI model of organizational choice. *Administrative Science Quarterly, 34,* 38–67.

Newell, A., & Simon, H. A. (1972). *Human problem solving.* Englewood Cliffs, NJ: Prentice-Hall.

Padgett, J. F. (1980). Managing garbage can hierarchies. *Administrative Science Quarterly, 25,* 583–604.

Simon, H. A. (1955). A behavioral model of organizational choice. *Quarterly Journal of Economics, 69,* 99–118.

Verhagen, H. (1992). *TASCCS: A computer simulation model for simulating organizational behavior.* CCSOM Report 92-78, University of Amsterdam.

4

ACTS Theory: Extending the Model of Bounded Rationality

Kathleen M. Carley
Michael J. Prietula
Carnegie Mellon University

The model of bounded rationality asserts that agents in an organization may be rational in intent, but less than rational in execution because functional limits on cognition severely restrict their ability to achieve optimality in the pursuit of their goals (Simon, 1976). The original purpose of the model was to characterize the effects of a restricted rational agent on the assumptions (and conclusions) of economic and administrative (i.e., organization) theory (Simon, 1979). This model and its variants have significantly influenced, directly and indirectly, theories of organizations, as well as explanations of organizational behavior, to include restrictions on rationality and optimal choice (e.g., Charnes & Cooper, 1963; Cyert & March, 1956, 1963; Glazer, Steckel & Winer, 1992; Huber, 1990; Lord & Maher, 1990; March, 1978; March & Shapira, 1987; Radner, 1975; Simon, 1976; Sims, Gioia, & Associates, 1986; Stinchcombe, 1990; Williamson, 1975). We suggest that advances in organizational theory can be achieved by extending the model of bounded rationality by moving beyond general principles to specific detailed models realized as computer programs. In this chapter, we propose such an extension, and illustrate its role in defining and interpreting two computational theories of organizational behavior.

Bounded rationality was to replace the fundamental model of the agent on which theories of economics and organizations were based with a model that better approximated the actual capacities, and therefore the behavior, of a human decision maker. The natural source of such a "more human model" would be those models proposed by psychology. One part of bounded rationality was that the agent itself was boundedly rational (Simon, 1955), whereas another part was that the environment, and the interrelations between the environment and the agent, set bounds on and therefore constrained the agent (Simon, 1956). As Simon noted (1956), the agent's mental models that enable decisions to be made employ simplifications of reality that "may depend not only on the characteristics — sensory, neural, and other — of the organism, but equally upon the structure of the environment" (p. 130).

In this chapter, we extend the original model of bounded rationality and incorporate the extended model within a general process theory of organizations. We refer to the theory as ACTS theory — organizations are viewed as collections of intelligent agents who are cognitively restricted, task oriented, and socially situated. ACTS theory embodies the two fundamental foci of the original model of bounded rationality: the limited delibrative power of the agent and the constraints of the environment. The extension occurs by (a) replacing the general principles of the boundedly rational agent with a broader, more encompassing perspective of a cognitive agent, and (b) replacing general notions of environmental constraints with two specific environmental perspectives, the task and the organizational social situation within which the task and agent are situated.

The main theme of this chapter is that organization theory may benefit by taking balanced, multiple perspectives of the agent, the task, and the (social) situation in which both the agent's perspective of the task and situation and the reality of such situations are jointly considered. Such a multiple perspective is an instance of what are now called meso-theories, where the term *meso* describes midlevel theories that link microlevel mechanisms to macrolevel phenomena — in our case the physical and social to the cognitive. Because we take this meso-theoretical approach, we are in effect combining the sociology of organizations and the psychology of organizations into a single perspective (cf. Daft, 1989).

In this chapter we present the assumptions of ACTS theory axiomatically. We also illustrate the role of the multiple perspective on the agents' internal representation of this world (agent cognition) and the physical and social world (task and social situation) with a slightly more unified theory of organizations by examining two computational models of organizations — Plural-Soar (Carley, Kjaer-Hansen, Newell, & Prietula, 1992) and an organizational Experiential Learning Model (ELM; Carley, 1990, 1991b, 1992). We demonstrate the use of the ACTS perspective by comparing the extent to which both computational models satisfy the underlying axioms, and examine the results of simulation experiments from these two computational models.

ACTS THEORY

ACTS theory is a theory of constraints and opportunities. Within ACTS, the actions of agents (the composite of which are organizational acts) are constrained by the immutable aspects of the human cognitive architecture, the characteristics of the task, and the nontask characteristics of the organizational environment in which the agents are situated (the social situation). The agent's knowledge, which is continually changing, mediates the effect of the task and social situation on individual and organizational behaviors and performance (Simon, 1976). The task and social situation can be highly volatile and may be immutable only in the short term (Cohen, March, & Olsen, 1972; March & Romelaer, 1976). The volatility creates further constraints on, and opportunities for, action (Carley, 1986; Cohen et al., 1972). Furthermore, this volatility encourages the use of actions whose only value is symbolic (Feldman & March, 1981). ACTS theory seeks to explain such organizational behaviors and performance by supporting the development of a set of computational models interlinked through an organizational design.[1] This set would include a model of the cognitive agent (including knowledge), a model of the task, and a model of the social situation.

At the microlevel, ACTS theory focuses on explicating how a given organizational design will affect the behavior and performance of individual agents as they communicate and reason within a social situation while trying to accomplish a task. At the macrolevel, ACTS theory focuses on explicating the behavior and performance of groups and organizations with different organizational designs, given that the group or organization is comprised of intelligent agents who are socially situated and task oriented. Thus, ACTS theory addresses those research questions in which individual and group decision making play a key role; therefore, what an agent knows and to whom an agent communicates are important components of ACTS theory. As ACTS theory jointly considers multiple (level) perspectives, individual cognition (and hence agents' representation of the task and social situation, which includes other agents) is as key to ACTS theory as are the task and the social situation. The task and social situation constrain behavior by limiting opportunities for action and by setting limits on what the agent knows, does, and therefore can know. ACTS theory is consistent with the tenets of bounded rationality (March & Simon, 1958; Simon, 1976; Simon & Baylor, 1966), but adds precision, prediction, and testability through the specification of the component models.

The general stance taken in this chapter vis-à-vis the actions and decisions of intelligent agents follows from that suggested by Carley and Newell (1990). An agent's actions are a function of the agent's cognitive architec-

---

[1]We view organizational design as including the set of rules of operations or procedures, institutional norms, databases, task decomposition scheme, and the formal and informal organizational structure (Lin & Carley, 1992). Thus, organizational design is present in and affects agents (through their knowledge bases), tasks (through their decomposition), and situations.

ture and knowledge. The cognitive architecture is immutable over time and constant across agents. The mechanisms by which an agent processes information, makes decisions, and learns are a function of the agent's cognitive architecture. The agent's knowledge changes over time as the agent learns (and perhaps forgets). This knowledge is a function of the agent's position within the organization (which is defined from a socio-cultural-historical standpoint), the task in which the agent is engaged (and the associated goals), and the problem or problems that are currently interrupting the organization's "normal," or perhaps ideal, operating conditions.[2] The information processed, the decisions made, and the knowledge learned are all heavily influenced by (a) the knowledge that is currently salient, (b) the knowledge available to the agent by virtue of the agent's social position, (c) the task in which the agent is engaged, and (d) knowledge limitations due to the current difficulties besetting the organization.

The agent's cognitive architecture defines what the agent can possibly do with that knowledge. The agent's position, task, and the current set of difficulties, by affecting what known information is salient and what new knowledge is available, constrain these possibilities and provide opportunities. ACTS theory is thus consistent with Simon's (1981) observation that the apparent complexity of human behavior lies not with the mechanisms of reasoning, but with the task environment. ACTS theory is also consistent with Carley and Newell's (1990) extension of Simon's argument, in which they argue that the vast complexity of the task and social situation is necessary for many characteristically human (social) behaviors to emerge. Thus, ACTS theory refocuses the attention of the researcher interested in organizations on the details through which task and social environment (interaction and communication with other agents) influence agent and group adaptation (including socialization and enculturation) and performance.

ACTS theory focuses on articulating collective organizational constraints and opportunities—as defined by the individual agents, the task(s) being performed by the agents, and the specific social situation (and its ramifications) within which the agents are situated—and how these constraints and opportunities serve to restrict and enable individual and hence emergent collective (i.e., organizational) phenomena in a dynamic and often volatile organizational setting.

ACTS theory is an extensible, deductive theory, embodied in a fundamental set of propositions functioning as axioms and an expandable set of testable propositions functioning as theorems deduced from the axioms (Blalock, 1969). Ideally, the fundamental set of axioms should serve as the

---

[2]These problems may be part of the general difficulties faced by the organization that make organizational life anarchical at times (Cohen et al., 1972) or they may be more catastrophic in nature, like those occurring when high-risk technology is employed (Perrow, 1984).

presumably true (or, perhaps, untestable but plausible) propositions from which a set of theorems can be deduced to explain and predict observed phenomena. These axioms reflect the primary components and sources of constraints and opportunities in ACTS theory. They reflect the agent, task, and social situation, and the interrelation between these constructs, and are shown in Tables 4.1 and 4.2.

Collectively, these axioms provide an image of organizations as both dynamic and historically bound, constrained by and constraining human action, purposive and reactionary, restricted by and capable of generating organizational culture. From this perspective, organizations are collections of tasks and situated intelligent agents engaged in performing tasks. The agents are generally intelligent agents that cooperate and coordinate (to varying degrees) with each other, from socially situated positions within organizational structures (which embody previous interactions and decisions and are continually reconstructed) through the exchange of information and resources, in order to perform tasks (which accomplish goals that are more or less articulated) despite the obstacles or problems that make organizational life less than predictively certain.

These axioms assert that organizational agents are generally intelligent

TABLE 4.1
Agent, Task, and Social Situation Axioms of ACTS Theory

Agent Axioms:

Axiom 1.   Organizations are composed of goal-directed, intelligent agents (decision makers) who can learn, communicate, and take action in pursuit of goals.

Axiom 2.   All goal-directed cognitive deliberation, perception, and communication by agents occurs within a physical symbol system architecture that is functionally constrained by natural physical laws.

Axiom 3.   Symbolic cognitive architectures and their derivative forms, such as Soar and the Problem Space Computational Models of Newell (Newell et al., 1990; Yost & Newell, 1989), sufficiently describe the mechanisms by which a goal-directed agent exhibits intelligence, communication, and learning within the constraints of Axiom 2. Such goals need not be articulated or be articulable by the agent. Further, the goals can be automatically generated or selected by the agent as deliberation ensues.

Task Axiom:

Axiom 4.   An organizational agent performs one or more tasks in an organization in order to achieve specific personal, task, and/or social (group and organizational) goals, several of which may simultaneously arise and, perhaps, conflict with each other.

Social Axiom:

Axiom 5.   An organizational agent occupies a position (formal and informal) in the organization that is a socio-cultural-historical artifact involving one (or more) socially situated roles.

TABLE 4.2
Interlink Axioms of ACTS Theory

Axiom 6.	The agent's current task and social situation define a limited set of knowledge, opportunities, and consequent constraints on action and learning. Individual deliberation and choice are restricted by the constraints of architecture and knowledge (the latter of which is affected by personal history, current task, and current social situation).
Axiom 7.	An organizational agent will select goals and actions enabled by the current task and social situation as perceived (and represented) by the agent.
Axiom 8.	Organizations are faced with dynamic environments that can alter the characteristics of the task or social situation temporarily or permanently. Difficulties can and frequently do arise, upsetting the normal or standard operating conditions in the organization. These difficulties can be with the agents (e.g., lack of experience or poor motivation), the tasks (e.g., change in design specifications), or the social situation (e.g., turnover level or broken communication channels).
Axiom 9.	The social situation is continually constructed as individuals engage in concurrent actions (Carley, 1991a). The existence of socially situated positions and all their attendant characteristics (opportunities for interaction and mobility, relative power, links with other positions, status, associated procedures, etc.) is the result of previous interactions among individuals and their decisions and actions. Further interaction and decision making by individuals will alter the social situation and these positions.

agents and that computational models, such as the problem space computational model articulated by Newell, Yost, Laird, Rosenbloom, and Altman (1990), are sufficient (if properly specified) for modeling such agents. The problem space computational model is one articulation based on a symbolic architecture of cognition, which, in general, has the potential for having the necessary and sufficient conditions for intelligent behavior (Newell & Simon, 1976; Newell, 1990). The particular selection in Axiom 4 was chosen as there exists a well-defined instantiation of the symbolic cognitive architecture in the form of a computer program, Soar (Newell, Rosenbloom, & Laird, 1989), that would enable a firm theoretical infrastructure for simulations (i.e., computational organizational models) requiring strong models of individual intelligence and cognition.

Computational models, by their very nature, move beyond the principles of bounded rationality to specific details of the cognitive architecture. The nature of the organizational agent is central to ACTS theory and should figure prominently in the computational model. Within ACTS theory, the more generally intelligent the agents, the more capable they are of learning, the greater the number of organizational behaviors that will be explainable with the same formal model (other things being equal), given the constraints imposed by the task and social situation. Similarly, the more complex the socio-cultural-historical situation, the more detailed the organizational designs and the tasks being engaged in, the greater the number of organizational behaviors that will be explainable with the same formal model. Yet, the task and social situation are as key to ACTS theory as individual cognition, for it is through an examination of the interaction between the physical and social world and the cognitive world that we can begin to craft an accurate theory of how decisions are made in organizations. In fact, the complexity of a computational model required to represent the critical decision-making properties of an organizational agent may be much less than the general capability of an intelligent agent, if the task, knowledge, and organizational situation collectively restrict and constrain the optional behaviors, knowledge, goals, and communication of the agents. Thus, a specific organizational situation may so attenuate the degrees of intellectual freedom brought to bear on a task that far simpler agent models may effectively achieve the level of sophistication required for a computational organizational model. In Table 4.3, some typical individual and organizational behaviors explainable with a detailed model of cognition, task, or social situation are listed.

Although ACTS theory, like open systems theory (Scott, 1987), recognizes that the environment is dynamic, it suggests that there may be immutable and fundamental principles on which a theory of organizations can be developed, but that such principles can only be observed by examining human reasoning and interaction under both optimal and less than optimal conditions. Further, to the extent to which there are such immutable principles, they will arise from the physical constraints inherent in the human cognitive architecture, the properties of the task, and the design of the organization. Accordingly, we illustrate each of the three components (agent cognition, task, and social situation), using two computational models: Plural-Soar and ELM. Figure 4.1 shows the interrelation of these three components and the position of Plural-Soar and ELM in this trinity.

Plural-Soar and ELM may be considered as partially sufficient from an

TABLE 4.3
Agent Model Components and Associated Individual/Organizational Actions

Agent Component of Actions		
Cognitively Restricted	Task Oriented	Socially Situated
Reasoning	Scheduling	Norms
Adaptation	Coordination	Coordination
Planning	Negotiation	Culture
Error	Performance	Communication
Compulsiveness	Goal specification	Procedures
Choice/judgment	Goal selection	Trust

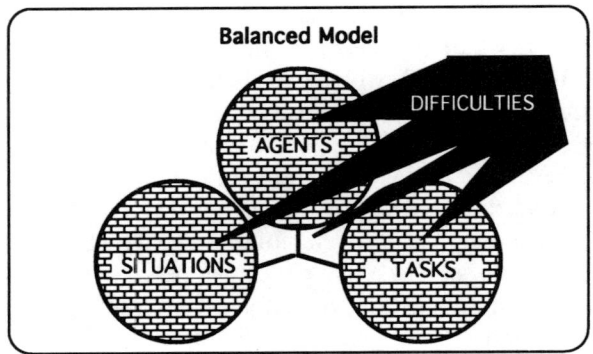

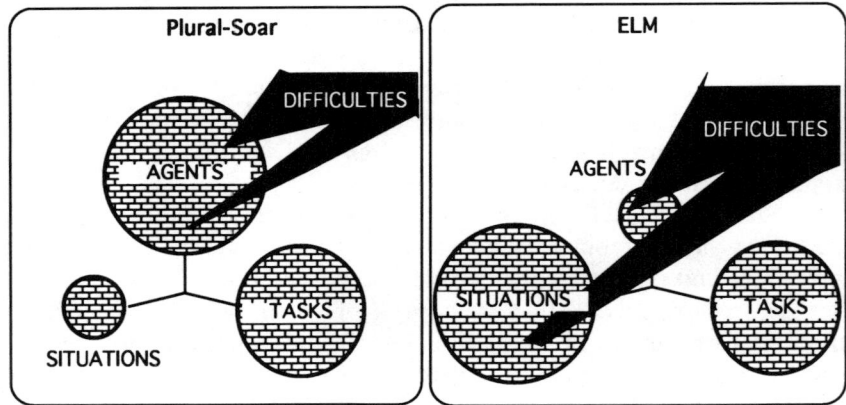

FIG. 4.1.   Relative sophistication of ACTS components realized in Plural-Soar and ELM.

ACTS point of view, as neither completely embodies the full multiple perspectives of agent cognition, task, and social situation. However, the point must again be made regarding the distinction between the individual complexity of an agent model *qua* agent, and the actual complexity required (or permitted) as afforded by the multiple perspectives considered jointly. Thus, the collective perspectives may coconstrain each other such that most of the variance in behavior (individual or collective) is accounted for by a disproportionate subset of either the task, situation, or agent. For example, a highly constrained task and social situation may afford a highly constrained (and restricted) cognitive agent, where differences in organizational (i.e., collective) behavior are accounted for by variations in task parameters, and not by differences in agent cognition (e.g., knowledge, learning, richness of the model). On the other hand, unconstrained task situations may have much of the variance accounted for by differences in agent parameters (e.g., agents with more knowledge make better choices, agents that can learn reduce collective errors, agents that can communicate reduce collective effort). Consequently, stronger (i.e., more detailed) models (of a perspective) may be traded off against weaker models, depending on the particular setting. But that setting is strictly determined by the specification of the three components (i.e., task, agent, situation) and how they coconstrain each other.

Both Plural-Soar and ELM have strong task models. Plural-Soar focuses on the cognitive world at the expense of the social; ELM focuses on the social at the expense of the cognitive. Plural-Soar couples a weaker model of social situation with a stronger model of cognition to examine organizational performance for organizations facing a task that requires filling customer orders from stocks in a warehouse. Plural-Soar employs a model of distributed organizational decision making and action in which each agent is modeled using a general model of intelligence. Using Plural-Soar, the performance of organizations with essentially uncoordinated agents can be examined.

In contrast, ELM couples a stronger model of a social situation with a weaker model of an agent. Within ELM, organizational performance is examined for organizations facing a simple binary choice task. ELM employs a model of distributed organizational decision making and action in which each agent is modeled as being boundedly rational and learning through individual experience. The performance of multiple organizations (within which the agents can be placed in a large number of different social situations) can be contrasted.

Our purpose in presenting Plural-Soar and ELM is twofold: (a) to illustrate the relationship between ACTS theory axioms and actual computational organizational models, and (b) to suggest the type of minimally sufficient models of the task, social, and cognitive perspectives necessary to formulate an instantiation of ACTS theory. We advance Plural-Soar as a candidate for a strong agent model, ELM as an example of a social situation model, and both the warehouse and binary-choice tasks as examples of minimally sufficient task models.

ACTS theory, as articulated by the axioms in prior Tables 4.1 and 4.2, serves as a common reference permitting multiple models of organizations to be compared to each other. The extent to which a given computational model directly addresses (or should address) an axiom depends on the extent to which the constructs under investigation are salient to the axiom. This, in turn, determines the nature of the inferences that can be made from the computational model. How Plural-Soar and ELM relate to the axioms of ACTS theory is summarized in Table 4.4.

PLURAL-SOAR: A STRONG AGENT MODEL

Plural-Soar is an exploratory computational organizational model used to examine how a set of agents, predicated on a strong model of a generally

TABLE 4.4
Extent to Which Plural-Soar and ELM Address ACTS Axioms

Axioms	Plural-Soar	ELM
Agent:		
1	met	met
2	met	met
3	met	not met
Task:		
4	not met	not met
Social:		
5	minimal	mostly met
Interlink:		
6	met	met
7	met	met
8	minimal	met
9	not met	minimal

intelligent agent, can be combined into a functioning organization (Carley et al., 1992; Prietula & Carley, 1992). The Plural-Soar system can be used to address questions regarding the impact of individual learning, rationality, norm violation, and knowledge differences on organizational performance and disfunctionality. Plural-Soar is a collection of agents interlinked into an organizational design and working collectively to perform a task, each Plural-Soar agent runs on a separate workstation, and all workstations are interconnected. Plural-Soar is designed to operate in effective real time; that is, there is a set of problems available (orders to be filled in a warehouse), and each agent acts on a problem (searches the warehouse to fill the order). By specifying the social situation (the number of agents and the communication scheme) and each agent's knowledge and set of available actions (including preferences for particular actions and task standard operating procedures), a unique type of organizational design is identified (e.g., a five-person warehouse team with no communication capabilities). The system is nonstochastic, so each organizational type need only be simulated once to determine its performance (see Carley et al., 1992).

Each Plural-Soar agent has an equivalent cognitive architecture, Soar, so all agents have the same set of architectural capabilities and constraints. Soar (Laird, Newell, & Rosenbloom, 1987) is a symbolic cognitive architecture capable of exhibiting general learning and intelligence through goal-oriented, flexible behavior. Initially, all agents have equivalent task knowledge (e.g., where to pick up orders to fill), task preferences (e.g., preferring to search the warehouse in a particular fashion), social knowledge (e.g., other agents may have information relevant for the search), and social preferences (e.g., preferring to ask other agents for information rather than perform an uninformed search). Furthermore, each agent constructs a mental model of the task and updates it based on experience as the ask unfolds. An agent only has access to its personal knowledge and mental model (interagent communication is one of the social properties manipulated).

The overall task goal for each agent is quite simple — fill available orders. The general components of the task are shown in Figure 4.2. To achieve the goal, an agent must proceed to, and select an order from, a particular location (the order stack), locate the locations in the warehouse (item stacks) of the item(s) listed on the order (either through search or by asking other other agents), and move the item(s) necessary to fill the order (once located) to a specific location (conveyer belt). Each order contains a list of items requested by a customer, but no information about where the requested items are in the warehouse.

Each agent occupies a specific social (but completely undifferentiated) position in an organization. Agents differ initially only in the physical order (queue) in which they are standing in front of the order stack at the begining of the simulation. As the agents perform the task, different experiences with the environment (i.e., orders, warehouse locations, other agents) cause agents to accumulate different knowledge. Over time, different agents will evolve different mental models of the task and social situation. Further, a

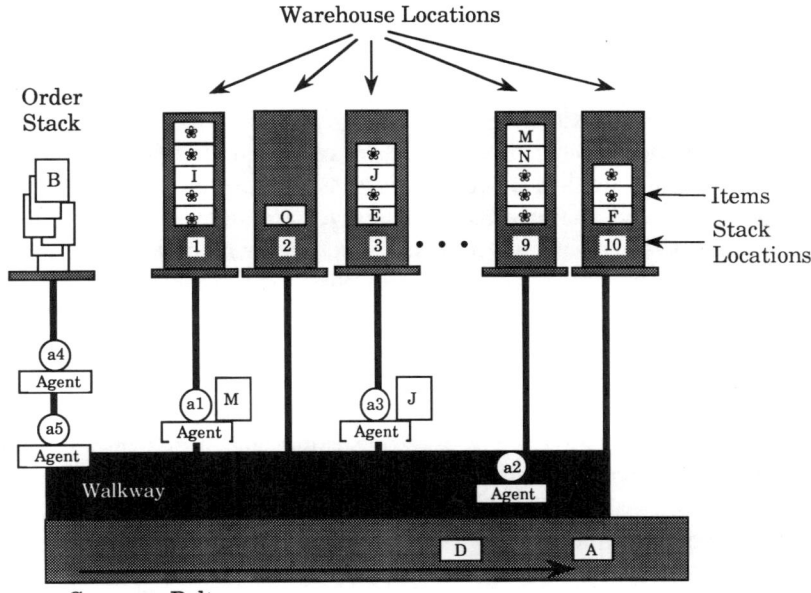

FIG. 4.2. Figural representation of warehouse components and agents.

given agent's mental model of task and social situation may differ from reality due to cognitive limitations (i.e., restricted perception of other agents' behaviors) as well as task and social opportunities for gathering knowledge (e.g., by restricting agent communication). The capabilities of an agent can be altered by manipulating components of the agent model.

An agent can directly perceive the items at an order stack only when the agent is situated at the particular stack location. Agents proceed to locations along the walkway, but there are no physical constraints for agents moving along the walkway, which means that agents can "pass each other" on the walkway and proceed to the same location. However, two or more agents at the same location cannot manipulate items or orders at the same time. When agents are at the same location they form a first-in, first-out queue, allowing the first arriving agent to manipulate the stack. Although agents at the same location cannot manipulate a stack at the same time (i.e., remove items on top of the desired item), an agent at an immediately adjacent location can move items to this stack and vice versa (i.e., placing removed interfering items out of the way).

An agent can locate a specified item in the warehouse by conducting an exhaustive search (i.e., moving to each stack and examining the contents), retrieving the item–location association from its memory (only if the agent has previously perceived the item at some location), or by asking other agents. Agents are inherently "lazy" and prefer to use either information in memory or information gathered by asking others, avoiding exhaustive search. Agents also trust themselves more than others and prefer to use information from their own memory rather than information gathered by asking others. Agents will respond to questions (of item locations) only if they have encountered the questioned item in a stack. All agents operate on an effectively one-to-many broadcast form of communication.

There are no hierarchical authority relations among these agents — all have equal rights to select and process an order. Nor are there any implicit social status relations — all agents are indifferent between which other agents they ask for information or to whom they provide information. The only authority structure is task-opportunism — the particular job an agent attempts to carry out is simply the next available order on the order stack. Furthermore, one agent cannot usurp or stop a job from another agent. Thus, assignments (of jobs to agents) are not planned, but emerge opportunistically as collective problem solving ensues. Apparent social differences are a consequence of the agents' and the organizations' task history.

ACTS Axioms and Plural-Soar

Plural-Soar automatically meets Axioms 1, 2, 3, 6, and 7, as it uses Soar agents. Plural-Soar does not meet Axiom 4, as personal, task, and organizational goals are largely equivalent. To meet this axiom the agents would need to be extended so that they had models of other agents and could consider the differential benefits of filling their own orders versus helping others so that the organization as a whole filled all orders more effectively. In terms of Axiom 5, as previously noted, the Plural-Soar agents occupy positions that are undifferentiated (at least initially).

Axiom 8 is only minimally met, as the orders do get filled, thus leading to a redistribution of items in the stacks, and the items do get moved from the locations in which they are expected. In one sense, Plural-Soar deals only with stable situations; that is, all orders are available, all agents are available, no external crises are occurring that distract agents from the task at hand, and there is no time pressure. In this sense, it does not meet the spirit of Axiom 8. Problems could be easily added to the situation within this framework. In another sense, for those things that can go wrong, the agent already has procedures or answers. Agents clearly do not have complete information, but they have the ability to ask questions and search. Agents may be unable to perform their assigned task because another agent is in front of them, or because the item they desire is at the bottom of the stack. In this case, predefined preferences make these difficulties nonproblems by providing a solution. However, there are relatively few items and few stacks so such difficulties, although inevitable, are not catastrophic.

Finally, Axiom 9 is not met. The agents do not alter their position within the organization on the basis of previous interactions. Developing agents with such social construction abilities would require the agents to have models of other agents. This, however, is not a restriction on Plural-Soar, but simply a limit on this particular agent model defined in Plural-Soar.

It is important to differentiate between the fundamental adequacy of Soar as a plausible model of a generally intelligent agent and Plural-Soar as a model of an intelligent agent situated within a particular organizational context. The former addresses the extent to which Soar is psychologically valid as a theory of cognition, whereas the latter addresses the extent to which an agent modeled in Soar possesses the necessary and sufficient mechanisms to model the form and substance of reasoning within a particular organizational context.

The Soar model is one of the most elaborate cognitive simulations in existence. Plural-Soar is simply the first tentative step in placing Soar agents in an organizational setting and so determining the extent to which it makes possible a socially valid organizational simulation. With Plural-Soar, explorations can begin to examine how much context knowledge is necessary given Soar to sufficiently model the social agent. This first step, however, begins to reveal both the adequacies and inadequacies of Soar. SOAR is adequate in the sense that behavioral (i.e., knowledge-based) differences across agents can be represented. Plural-Soar agents were given preferences, such as, prefer to ask rather than search. These preferences serve, in a way, as an encoding of organizational norms and behavioral (perhaps even emotional) traits. Agents with different characteristics can thus be easily modeled by giving them not only different knowledge, but also different preferences. Plural-Soar is seen as sufficient to generate some important expected organizational behaviors — for example, economies of scale and individual rationality resulting in social dysfunctionality (and organizational suboptimality).

The architecture presented in this chapter permits models of an autonomous agent performing self-contained tasks. This allows a team of agents to be defined, where each agent is performing a subtask of processing orders in the warehouse. This is accomplished without adding any further control knowledge to the "team" (individually or collectively) apart from what is already present in the individual agents. Because the tasks are self-contained, little cooperation or coordination between agents is required to do the task. Cooperation among the agents (in the form of communication) affects the efficiency with which tasks are done.

Thus the team is made up of a set of agents with totally distributed decision making. Each agent decides at any time what to try to do. There is no overarching organizational structure and, consequently, no particular limitations on knowledge due to the agent's role in the organization. The coordination between agents in performing the task is a function of the physical constraints on, and capabilities of, the agents. No negotiation, planning, or communication related to coordinating the task takes place. Therefore, despite a sophisticated model of the agent, Plural-SOAR is not adequate to model organizations in general due to the lack of social situations and the subsequent constraints and opportunities they afford to the agents who occupy the associated positions. No coordination, negotiation, planning, or mobility takes place and no organizational design issues can be addressed (such as power exchanges and turnover).

The knowledge held by each agent is very episodic and task specific. To the extent that the environment is volatile (i.e., the composition of the warehouse changes rapidly with respect to memory), the agents' knowledge of the warehouse structure is fragile. In the current system, an agent simply ignores environmental changes unless they prevent the agent from doing the task.

Exploring Agent, Task, and Organizational Properties

To illustrate how Plural-Soar is used to investigate organizational issues, we examined the effects of agent communication, organizational size, and task arrangement on organizational performance. One might expect with the warehouse task that allowing agents to communicate should improve organizational performance — agents should be able to decrease their search of the stacks (and hence physical agent movements) by simply asking other agents for the location of the needed item. When an agent makes decisions based on answers from other agents, it upgrades its knowledge (mental model) of the task and social situation on the basis of the other agents' knowledge of the task and social situation. Transferring knowledge between agents (updating each agent's model of the task) should decrease the need to move or physically manipulate the environment. Similarly, increasing the size of the organization (i.e., the number of agents) should result in decreasing organizational effort, as more knowledge is distributed and therefore sharable.

To examine this question within Plural-Soar, organizations comprised of one to five Plural-Soar agents were simulated under four conditions. The four conditions consisted of crossing two levels of order size (15 orders with one item per order, or 5 orders with three items per order) with two levels of communication (whether or not all agents could communicate with each other). The results are shown in Fig. 4.3.

Communication does not always decrease effort. Specifically, agents that are able to alter their knowledge of the task and social situation on the basis of others' knowledge may not decrease their physical effort. This is in part,

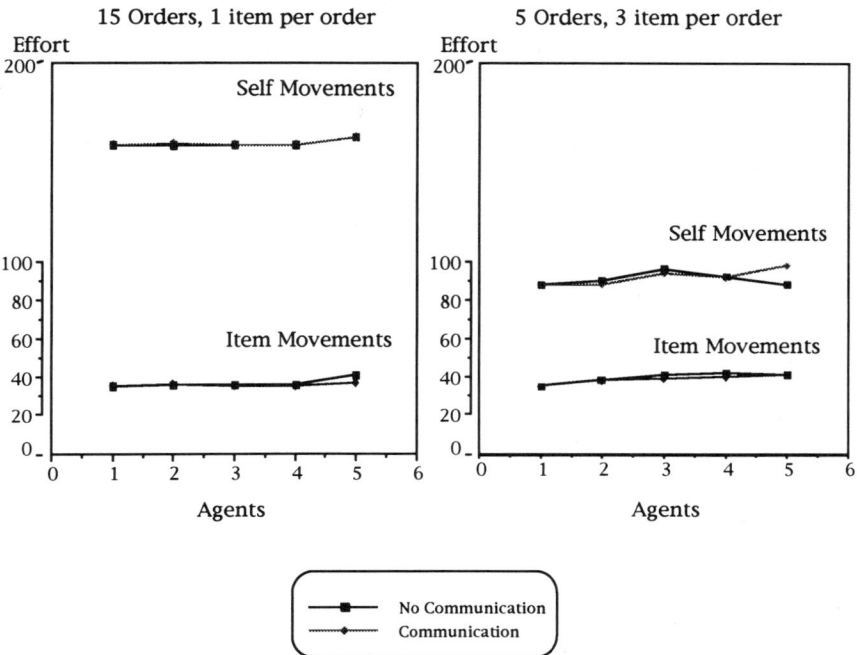

FIG. 4.3.   Effect of order size and communication on organizational effort.

because there is a minimum amount of physical effort to do the task and in part because the agents' mental models do not match the physical reality. An agent may get information from another agent on the location of an item, only to discover that the item has been moved. These two causal factors result in an interaction between task and communication. With 15 orders and one item per order, communication decreases effort and so improves organizational performance, not because it decreases the agents' physical movements (which remain almost constant) but because it decreases the number of times agents move items. In contrast, communication may increase, decrease, or have no effect on agent movements when there are 5 orders and three items per order. The ability to examine the subtleties of the interaction between task and communication is a direct result of having a multiple perspective on the cognition, task, and social situation.

A second important point about the Plural-Soar investigation is that it demonstrated that, at least for this version of the warehouse task, the major determinant of the organizational outcome was neither the fact that human rationality is bounded, nor the specific architecture of human cognition (as embodied by Soar). Rather, it was the way in which rationality was bounded in terms of the specific knowledge on which the architecture operated that effected certain outcomes. In other words, although the agent's cognition (Soar) allowed it to do the task, the agent's preferences (as knowledge) controlled how it did that task. For example, the agents had a preference to move items that were stacked on top of an item they were seeking onto an adjacent stack to their left rather than onto a stack to their right. Agents also preferred to ask other agents where items were located, rather than perform an uninformed search. When organizational agents are presented with a task, it is necessary to explicate when the immutable aspects of agent cognition (the architecture) and not the knowledge/preferences dictate the organizational outcome. Replacing principles of bounded rationality with specific cognitive models and replacing generic task descriptions with specific task models enable analysis at this level.

ELM: A STRONG SOCIAL SITUATION MODEL

The organizational experiential learning model (ELM) is a simulation testbed that has been used to examine the relative performance of organizations that vary in their design and where agents act on the basis of their personal (organizational) experience. Previous studies using ELM have examined the impact of personnel turnover on organizational performance for different organizational coordination schemes (Carley, 1992), the relationship between information redundancy and personnel turnover (Carley, 1990), and the impact of various crises on organizational performance

(Carley, 1991b). ELM employs a simple situated-cognition model of individual action in which agents learn from their individual experience. What information agents have access to, what they know, and what actions they can take are dependent on their social situation in the organization and the specific task assigned to them. In ELM, the social situation is defined by the agent's position in the particular organizational design.

Unlike Plural-Soar, where the agents operate in real time and so may be doing different tasks in parallel, in ELM the agents are forced to act in parallel doing exactly the same type of task. The testbed is designed so that in each time period the organization is faced with a new task, similar, but not identical, to previous tasks. The task the organization must accomplish is to determine whether a given binary "word" of length n has more ones than zeroes (e.g., 1101101). The organizational problem is a word of length 2^n. Each time period, every agent acquires new information on some portion of the task (i.e., a subset of the binary word, such as 1101 of the prior example), decides whether there are more ones than zeroes in the full task (based on current data and the results of prior decisions), and communicates this decision (not the information used to make the decision) to the proper agent(s) in the particular organizational structure simulated.

Agents may differ in their mental model of the task (i.e., the likelihood of ones and zeroes) as they are seeing different subtasks or experiencing different aspects of the full task. By specifying a particular organizational design, a unique organizational type can be simulated (e.g., a hierarchy with low turnover and a completely segregated task decomposition scheme). The particular organizational design potentially affects the agents' mental model of the task, as it determines what information is available to the agents. In making its decision, each agent brings all of the knowledge that it has to bear, based on the new data and historical experience. Thus, each agent's decision reflects not only on its representation of the current task but its historical knowledge accumulated by working on previous organizational tasks.

Once all of the agents have made their decisions, the organization makes an organizational decision, either through the actions of the chief executive officer (CEO; a top-level decision-making agent in a hierarchical structure integrates information across agents) or through the voting of all agents (as in a team structure). For each task (i.e., each time period) there is a correct decision based on the actual features of the task. Organizational performance is measured by examining whether the organization's decision is the correct decision. Finally, every agent receives feedback on its decision — new knowledge on what was the correct organizational response in the situation. Monte Carlo simulation is used to estimate average performance across a large number of tasks.

All agents, regardless of their position in the organization, are boundedly rational and make decisions solely on the basis of their personal experience. Each agent has a hierarchically organized knowledge base containing a cumulative record of the subtasks that it receives, its decisions, and the true decisions for the associated full tasks. As the agent encounters subtasks, it learns rules for how to respond to the specific situation. However, these agents are not constructed from detailed, general cognitive models; rather, they are specificially crafted for this type of task and thus represent a restricted cognitive, task-oriented model.

The social situation is defined by the organizational design, which includes the following features: the composite organizational structure, task-decomposition scheme, associated order of processing, and rules for processing information and communication. The organizational design is viewed as a tacit coordination scheme. Both the organizational structure and the task decomposition scheme can be defined in network terms.

Using ELM, a variety of organizational structures can be examined, such as, the centralized hierarchy, the dual-command hierarchy, and the team (see Figs. 4.4, 4.5, and 4.6). In these illustrative structures, three types of agent roles are defined: the analyst (A), the assistant executive officer (AEO), and the chief executive officer (CEO). In these figures, analysts are represented as circles, AEOs as lightly shaded circles, and a CEO as a black circle. For the organizational structures shown, only the analysts have access to the "raw data" (the ones and zeroes) of the task. The task decomposition scheme is a *blocked structure;* that is, in all organizations each analyst sees only a portion of the task (i.e., a subset of the full binary

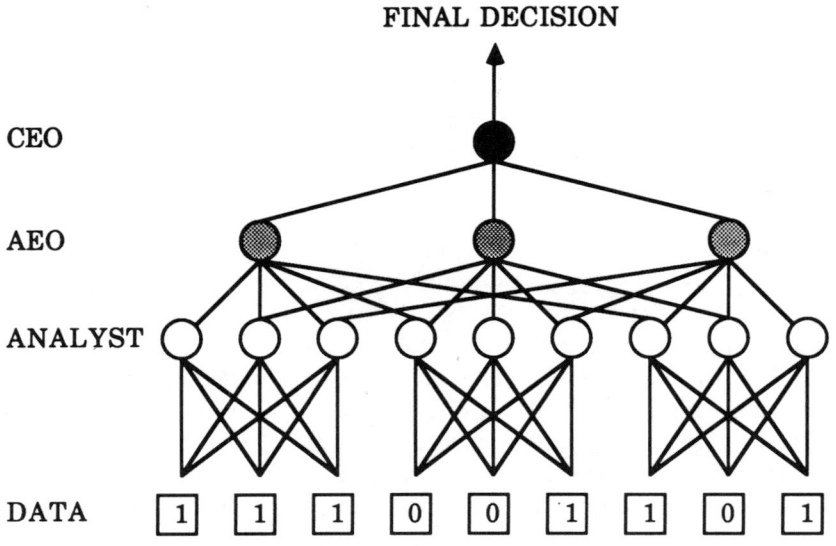

FIG. 4.4.   Centralized hierarchy structure used in ELM.

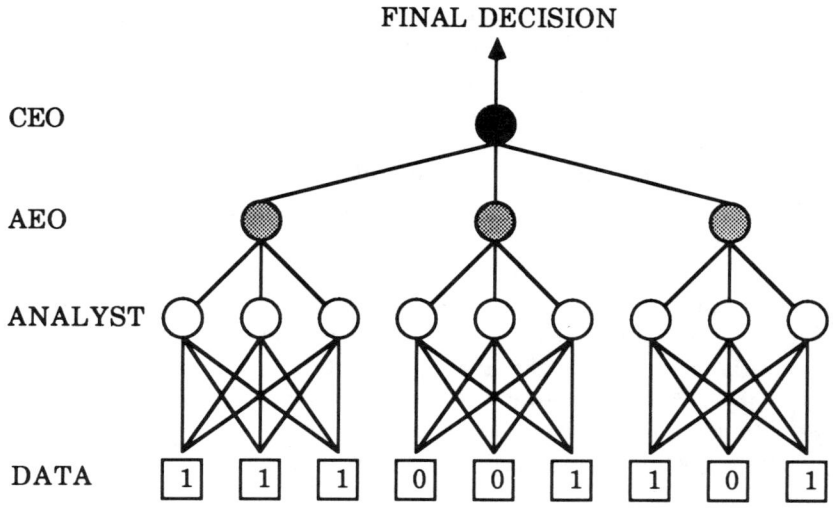

FIG. 4.5. Dual-command structure used in ELM.

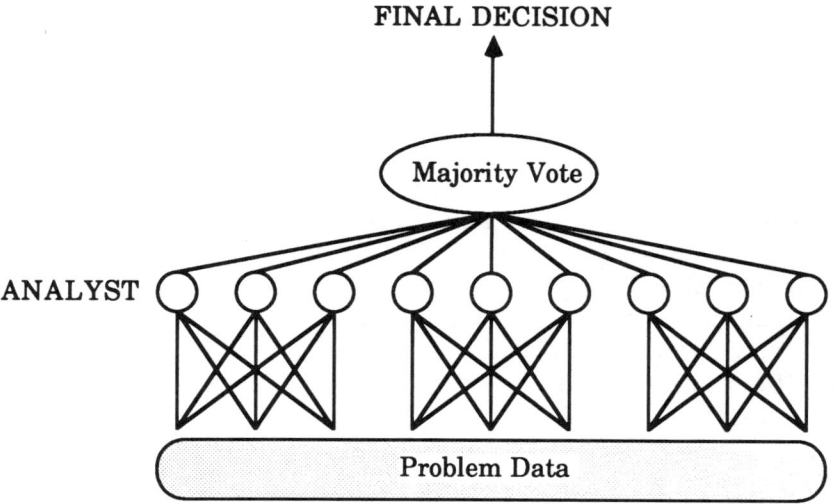

FIG. 4.6. Team structure used in ELM.

word) as defined by the particular task decomposition scheme. In hierarchies, institutional memory is centralized in the upper management, albeit in a reduced-information form. In team structures, institutional memory is completely distributed to the component agents. The presence of upper level management, by mediating the decisions made by lower level agents (analysts), can reduce the impact of various debilitations, such as turnover or unavailability, thus affecting the level of information redundancy needed for equivalent performance (Carley, 1990, 1992). Information loss is higher the more complex the task faced by the agents and the greater the number of levels in the organizational structure.

The distribution of subtasks (i.e., which agent receives which subset of of the binary word) defines the amount of redundancy at the lowest level and is referred to as the *task decomposition scheme*. Figure 4.7 illustrates three task decomposition schemes that have been examined using ELM. In Fig. 4.7, each square at the bottom of the structure represents the bit of information (1 or 0), with the total (organizational) problem being comprised (in this case) of nine total bits (word length). To illustrate the potential interaction between the task decomposition scheme and the organizational structure, the analysts are shown as though they are reporting to an AEO. The level of information redundancy is defined as the average number of analysts who know each piece of information (indicated by links to specific bit positions in the word). When the redundancy level equals the number of analysts, we have a situation in which all analysts have access to all information, which corresponds to the case of complete information/complete overlap discussed in other studies (Carley, 1986; Cohen et al., 1972). As the level of redundancy increases relative to the number of analysts, the complexity of the subtasks faced by the analysts increases.

Within ELM the organization's performance can be examined both under normal operating conditions and under substandard operating conditions. Within this framework, difficulties are typically modeled as disruptions in what information is available to whom. Difficulties degrade organizational performance because they decrease the degree to which the agents' mental model of the task matches the task. The impacts of various difficulties on organizational performance have been examined: turnover (Carley, 1990, 1992), incorrect information, communication breakdowns, and agent unavailability (Carley, 1991a). Thus, this framework can be used to examine organizational performance under both standard/optimal and substandard/ crisis conditions.

ACTS Axioms and ELM

The primary advantage of the ELM system is that it can be used as a generic testbed for examining the performance of a large number of organizational designs under either standard or substandard conditions (as when difficulties occur) for different classes of tasks. Using this testbed, insight into the effect of social situation on performance may be gained. In particular, this approach could be used to explore limits on performance due to structural properties. From the perspective of ACTS, the importance of ELM is that it specifies the minimum model of the social situation, and it specifies that

Blocked Decomposition Scheme

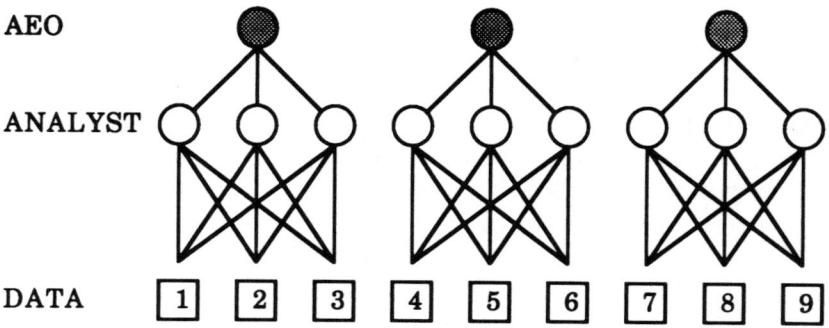

Segregated Decomposition Scheme

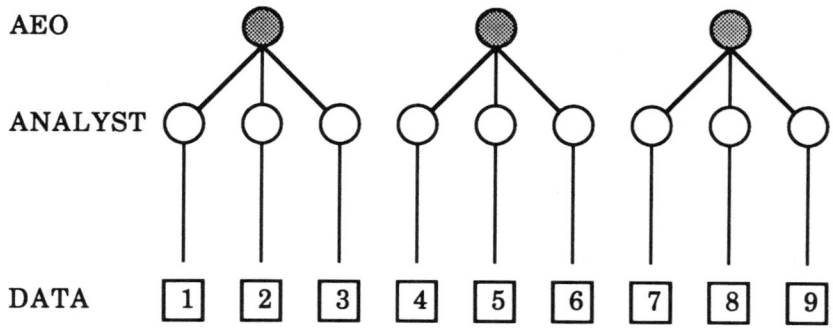

Distributed Decomposition Scheme

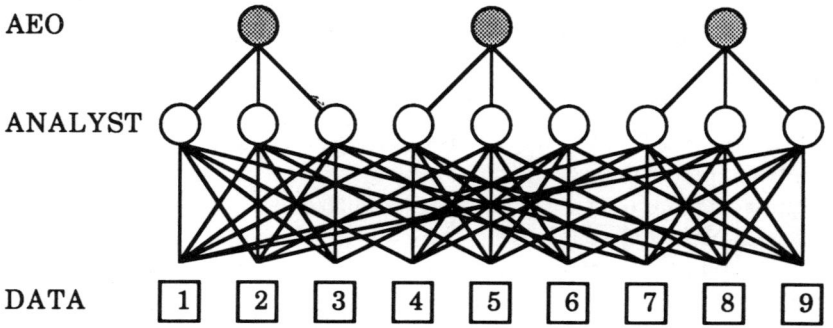

FIG. 4.7. Example task decomposition schemes used in ELM.

the organization's design can be characterized by detailing the network of relations between personnel and information, and the procedures for moving or altering personnel or information. It is in this sense that ELM better fulfills Axiom 5 than does Plural-Soar (see Table 4.2). Another advantage of ELM, from the ACTS perspective, is that it can be used to examine whether and to what extent organizational performance is affected as various difficulties and crises arise. In this way, Axiom 8 is fulfilled.

In contrast to Plural-Soar, the individual ELM agents are quite simple. Nevertheless, they do meet Axioms 1, 2, 6, and 7, but do not meet Axiom 3. These agents do not have a general capability to learn, but rather learn information about predefined categories given this type of binary task. Even though the ELM agents engage in one-trial learning (like the Plural-Soar agents), they may not perform correctly in subsequent trials as their predefined categories (their predefined way of representing the task) may prevent them from utilizing the information they have learned relative to a specific task. Further, like Plural-Soar, ELM does not meet the spirit of Axiom 4 as personal, task, and organizational goals are largely equivalent. Within the ELM system, issues such as negotiation and group-think cannot be addressed due to the inadequate model of the agent. In Plural-Soar, these issues cannot be addressed due to the inadequate model of the social situation. Some of the ELM agents, the managers, unlike Plural-Soar agents, do have (simple) models of other agents. These managers, within the constraint that they must remain managers, do adjust their interaction with other agents in a fashion consistent with that suggested in Axiom 9. To more fully approximate the intent of Axiom 9, all agents should be provided with models of other agents, and should be allowed to change positions in the organization. To more fully approximate Axiom 9, ELM agents would need to have specific mental models of the situation and the task.

Exploring Crises, Tasks, and Organizational Structures

The set of organizational structures in Figs. 4.4, 4.5, and 4.6 and the set of task decomposition schemes in Fig. 4.7 define nine types of organizational designs. Each of these types was simulated 200 times for 100,000 time periods. After 100,000 time periods a crisis occurred (explained later). In each case, there was no turnover. Thus, we can interpret these results as the expected behavior of organizations of highly trained agents. Performance is measured using ensemble averaging—the percentage of correct decisions made during 100 time periods as averaged across 200 simulation runs of organizations with that particular type of design. Each time period, the organization works on a different problem. Performance under optimal conditions was measured for the 100 time periods immediately preceding the crisis. Performance under crisis conditions was measured for the 100 time periods at the end of the crisis period. The crisis lasted for 300 time periods. Each crisis is characterized by type (the incoming information was incorrect, there was a communication breakdown, or an analyst was unavailable), strength (the number of simultaneous problems, one, two, or three), and duration (10, 20, or 50 time periods).

The results are shown in Fig. 4.8. In this discussion we are not concerned with the specific and differential effects of the different characteristics of crises. Thus, the performance during crisis shown is the average performance across all 27 crisis conditions for that organizational design.

Studies of organizational design often focus on the structure of the organization, describing why some structures should outperform other structures. For example, hierarchies are expected to exhibit lower performance than teams due, to uncertainty absorption (March & Simon, 1958), information condensation (Downs, 1967), and information distortion (Jablin, Putnam, Roberts, & Porter, 1986). These arguments lead one to expect that dual-command structures should lie somewhere between hierarchies and teams in terms of performance. However, these arguments provide no guidance as to either the impact of crisis or the relationship between task decomposition scheme and performance.

In Fig. 4.8 performance under optimal and crisis conditions is shown. Contrary to the expectations, dual-command structures do not exhibit performance between that of hierarchies and teams. Similar to several earlier simulation studies, unsegmented structures (such as teams) often outperform more centralized structures (such as hierarchies; see, for

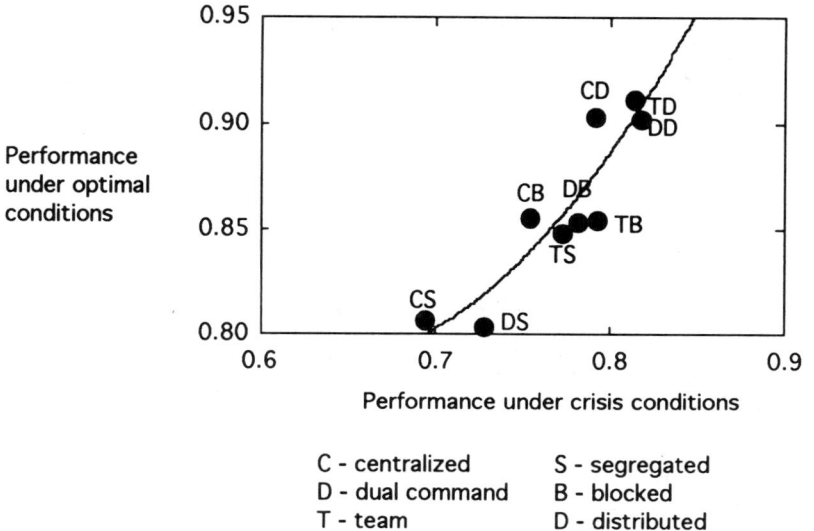

FIG. 4.8.   Effect of task decomposition, structure, and crisis events on performance.

example, Anderson & Fischer, 1986; Cohen et al., 1972). However, unlike these earlier studies, the analysis in this chapter suggests that whether teams outperform hierarchies depends on the extent to which the agents have different mental models of the task. In Fig. 4.8 the line indicates that the relationship is nonlinear, such that organizations with a blocked structure are the least affected by the stress of crisis (i.e., they show less of a drop in performance during crises than do other organizational designs). Similar to Cohen et al. (1972), this study suggests that segregated task decomposition schemes (decision structure) lead to lower performance. In addition, we see that decomposing the task in a distributed fashion such that there is redundancy, but not total equivalence or overlap in task information, leads to the highest performance both under optimal and crisis conditions. For any particular type of organizational structure, in terms of performance under either optimal or crises conditions, a segregated structure performs the worst and the distributed structure performs the best, with the blocked structure situated between the two performance extremes. These results suggest that the decomposition scheme has a more regular impact on performance than does the organizational structure.

These results are not directly comparable with much previous simulation research on organizational design, in large part because this study, unlike most others, uses a distributed task in which all agents must always be involved and in which different agents work on different parts of the task. Further, many other studies conflate the task decomposition scheme and the organizational structure, in large part because they do not look at specific tasks. Within ELM, the task and the social situation are clearly separated; thus, agents' mental models of task and social situation emerge as separate factors affecting organizational performance. Thus, this study addresses issues of how similar agents' mental models of the task need to be and how accurate the agents' mental models of the task need to be, and at the same time addresses issues of organizational design.

DISCUSSION

In this chapter we have proposed a general theory of organizational behavior based on an extended model of bounded rationality of the agents comprising an organization. We have also argued that a unified theory of organizations (linking organizational/group phenomena with individual agent models) might be developed if we consider organizations as collections of tasks and agents engaged in performing tasks, such that both agents and tasks are situated within a specific organizational structure. Organizational (i.e., collective) behavior is viewed as emergent behavior from groups of deliberating agents interacting to perform these˜ tasks within that organizational context. This theory embodies four important beliefs, which are critical for the evolution of a theory of organizations: the need to move organizational theory to a meso-level, the need to replace the principles of bounded rationality with extended and specific models of cognitive agents (which exist as computational theories), the need to replace general notions of environmental constraints with specific characterizations of tasks and social situations, and the corresponding need to move to broader and more encompassing theories of organizations expressed and tested as computational models to unify component organizational findings.

This view suggests that if organizational studies cannot account for a sufficient characterization of the critical properties of the participant agents (e.g., ones that are knowledge-based, adaptable, but cognitively restricted), the task, or the socia -situation and how they interact and coconstrain each other, the quality and generalizability of the results may be limited. The proposed ACTS theory may serve as the foundation for a theory of organizations that exhibits this multiple perspective. We illustrated the use of ACTS theory in comparing two computational models, Plural-Soar and ELM, each of which is partially sufficient with respect to ACTS axioms and each of which exhibits the level of detail needed to begin to make progress in models of this type. Moving toward such a theory will bring up new research concerns, such as the following:

- What can one expect from a computational theory of organizations predicated on a computational theory of agents?
- What are some of the research issues that arise when the researcher takes on a multiple-perspective agenda?
- What type of tasks should be considered?

Expectations for a Computational Organization Theory

Within cognitive science, the search for a general theory of cognition has led to the development of computational models that embody substantial cognitive theory. In essence, these computational models perform the task they seek to describe and become both the instrumentation of and the tool for developing the theory. Such models encompass, and extend (to greater and lesser degrees), the principles of bounded rationality and focus research attention on the fundamental mechanisms underlying behavior.

Because organizations are collections of tasks and intelligent agents, it is empirically consistent to construct organizational models by weaving into an organizational design models of individual agents, tasks, and social situations. Even as progress in cognitive science has been facilitated by replacing the premises of bounded rationality with computational theories of cognition,[3] progress in organizational science may be facilitated by replacing models of organizations as collections of boundedly rational agents with models of organizations as collections of cognitive agents, when the phenomena under investigation require it. This suggests that within organization science, the search for a general theory of organizations may also lead to the development of computational models that embody organizational theory. In fact, organizational theorists are attempting to reconcile macro-organizational activity with the behavior of individuals (e.g., Staw, 1991), and recent research on organizational design is moving in precisely this direction (Baligh, Burton, & Obel, 1992; Carley, 1992; Lin & Carley, 1992). If the analogy with cognitive science holds, such a movement to computational approaches within organization science should refocus the attention of researchers on the mechanisms underlying organizational behavior, a proposal that has not gone unnoticed by organization theorists (Stinchcombe, 1991). Computational research that examines the kinds of mechanisms that work together focuses on both process and product of behavior, enforces rigor and uniformity in descriptions of mechanism and process, and admits systematic testing of the theoretical components and their contribution to behavior (Prietula & Weingart, 1991).

If models of individual cognition are sufficient models of an agent's social and organizational behavior, then a computational model of an organization composed of a collection of such agent models, in addition to a model of the physical and social world, should account for the major forms of organizational goal-oriented deliberation that underlie organizational and group phenomena, such as organizational learning, group communication, group goal setting, negotiation, and group-think.[4] Such a computational organization model should generate a robust characterization of group behavior and a strong theoretical basis for exploring substantive issues of organizational design, strategy and behavior. A major research question then is whether, in fact, these models of the cognitive agent are sufficient as a model of the social/organizational agent. Carley and Newell (1990) argued that they are very near to the social agent, limited mainly by a lack of attendance to emotions. Consequently, there is still a question of whether a full ACTS model will be sufficient to characterize all relevant aspects of organizational life. Despite the insight that ACTS theory

---

[3]The use of cognitive simulations as psychological models has been demonstrated in several domains — extensively in medicine (e.g., Clancey & Shortliffe, 1986) and to a lesser extent in business (e.g., Bouwman, 1983), as well as in planning (Wilensky, 1983), particular models of skill acquisition (Neves & Anderson, 1981), and even scientific discovery (Langley, Simon, Bradshaw, & Zytkow, 1987).

[4]For an extended discussion of this point and an analysis of which organizational and social behaviors should be observable given such models, see Carley and Newell (1990).

may potentially provide, we may still find that there are organizational behaviors, particularly those that are intimately tied to emotions such as behavior under stress, that are not entirely articulable in an ACTS model. Elaboration of the theory would then be necessary.

Nevertheless, even an "emotionally restricted" ACTS model, such as that achieved by combining Plural-Soar and ELM, could advance our understanding of organizations. Indeed, the growing body of research in human organizations suggesting that the psychological processes and strategies of managers (particularly CEOs) have profound organizational and even industry-level reverberations (e.g., Bateman & Zeithaml, 1989a, 1989b; Chandler, 1990; Donaldson & Lorsch, 1983; Mintzberg, 1973, 1978; Snyder & Glueck, 1980) argues that much insight can be gained by systematically examining a cognitively predicated model of artificial organizations.

Research Implications of Engaging Multiple Perspectives

Constructing ACTS models requires addressing a number of issues that arise when a multiple perspective is taken on the agent, task, and situation. For example, in modeling the organization it will be necessary to simultaneously model important components of the "real" organization and task, as well as the organization and task as "perceived" by each agent, necessitating a more precise model of enactment (Weick, 1969). A consequence is that it will be possible to examine issues of social cognition, such as the extent to which agents need to share their mental models of the task or the cognitive social structure (Krackhardt, 1987) in order to work effectively together. As another example, in modeling an organization it will often be necessary to model the implicit links to the external world based on the ties that the agents have outside of the organization. This goes beyond a simple enumeration of interaction-based ties. The deeper cognitive issue entails identifying what knowledge passes outside of the workplace that affects actions within the workplace and when external/nonwork knowledge becomes salient in doing tasks within the organization. The deeper social issue involves examining how changes in the sociodemographic distribution of individuals in society affect the perception of, and changes in, demographic-related culture and concerns within the organization.

The representation of organizations as collections of tasks and individuals performing those tasks brings to the forefront the issue of representing organizational as well as individual task-related knowledge. It will thus be necessary to represent not only the procedures (which can be thought of as heuristics and methods shared across individuals) but also the external sources of information and agents' knowledge about these sources. Even those models of organizations that consider the role of agents in making organizational decisions rarely allow those agents to access sources beyond their own historical knowledge (see, for example, Marschak, 1955; McGuire & Radner, 1986; Tang, Pattipati, & Kleinman, 1991). Yet in real organizations there are many alternate information sources available for the agent to accomplish tasks, such as documents (static data), live data feeds (text, video), computer-based information systems (procedurally flexible), or other (intelligent) agents.[5]

The Study of Tasks

Both Plural-Soar and ELM employ abstracted models of real tasks. Both the warehouse task and the binary-choice task are rudimentary; nevertheless, they contain many of the properties and complexities generally attributable to distributed decision making tasks: Agents work cooperatively, agents may not be engaged in face-to-face discussion, each agent has its own task, the organizational goal requires all agents to perform their tasks, issues of effort allocation and distributed skills arise, the task is not solved by all agents reaching consensus, the task has several parameters that can be manipulated to adjust difficulty, and so forth. Using such tasks, questions can be addressed that center on economies of scale, and the impact of information sharing, task decomposition, and communication on organizational performance.

Meaningful research in coordination and communication requires surprisingly simple tasks (Weingart, 1989). Indeed, the simplicity of the task can be advantageous, because it clarifies the relationship between organizational and individual goals and problem-solving constraints. Both the warehouse and the binary-choice tasks can be expanded in ways that realistically represent manipulations in cognitive, as well as social and organizational, perspectives. In many disciplines, attention by multiple researchers to a small number of tasks that can be performed by humans, but also modeled computationally, has admitted the accumulation of scientific information. For example, "Drosophila tasks" are used in cognitive psychology (e.g., the Tower of Hanoi), as well as in political science (e.g., the Prisoner's Dilemma). Perhaps organizational science can also benefit from the development of a small set of characteristic modelable tasks that, when held constant, can be used to investigate the implications of various theories. The warehouse task and binary-choice task are possible candidates.

By appreciating the influence of the task and social situation, organizational models will be able to address issues such as the interrelationship

---

[5]For a perspective that considers both individual cognition and organizational design, see Huber (1990).

between organizational designs and tasks, the role that information sharing plays in organizational performance, and the interrelationship between norms and technology. It is beyond the scope of this chapter (or current knowledge) to put forward a full theory of task influence or to define influential task dimensions from the multiple perspective on agent, task, and situation. Such a theory can be elaborated through many studies that examine significant tasks in a systematic fashion. We do note, however, that a minimally adequate model of task must specify actions that can and cannot be taken in pursuit of the task, the constraints that denote task decomposability and component interrelatedness, and the knowledge needed to perform the task.

CONCLUSION

The search for a fundamental theory of organizations of any consequence or explanatory power requires going beyond a theory of the task or a theory of the organizational situation, but requires in addition a general theory of the intelligent agent that expands the model of bounded rationality. Such a theory must encompass:

1. The physical world where agents are engaged in specific tasks, and are barraged by both information and difficulties that require continual adaptation by the agent (and subsequently the organization) to achieve goals.
2. The cognitive world where the agents' knowledge of their self, their social situation, the task, and the extant difficulties determine what actions they take, what they learn, and what goals they pursue.
3. The social world where agents and task are situated within and across specific organizational positions.

ACTS theory is a first step toward the articulation of a theory that addresses these perspectives.

ACTS models (as instantiations of theory) can, if sufficiently specified, provide a perspective on organizational behavior and performance that goes beyond the rhetoric of bounded rationality to the specific details of how constraints and opportunities afforded by cognition, task, and situation determine organizational behavior. ACTS models can provide a perspective on organizational design that goes beyond the rhetoric that effective organizational design is contingent on the task (Lawrence & Lorsch, 1967) and the environment by providing a detailed prescription as to what are the systematic relationships between performance, design, task, and environment. Detailed ACTS models can be used to generate a series of propositions about organizational life that could not be generated with taskless models and/or models of the organization as collections of boundedly rational agents. ACTS models can make it possible to address a variety of topics central to organizational theory, ranging from the impact of new technology to the evolution of organizational norms within a systemic framework in which the dynamic behavior of actual individuals and groups can be examined simultaneously. By combining models of the agent, task, and situation, ACTS models can provide an integrated theoretical platform with sufficient detail to facilitate simultaneous attention to both theory and policy issues. However, saying that such computational models can forward theoretical development is one thing — crafting and evaluating such models is quite another thing, for simulation in organizational science should be expected to be no less complex than in physical science. Small, incremental steps may be needed to understand the level of complexity in fluid, highly symbolic, social aggregations of intelligent agents. Ideally, an encompassing, unifying theoretical perspective may facilitate the search for answers. We have argued that the search for unifying theories of organizations is a realistic, plausible, albeit difficult, goal for organizational science. ACTS theory is an incremental step toward that goal.

ACKNOWLEDGMENTS

Support was provided by the National Science Foundation under grants from Social and Economic Sciences (SES, 8707005) and Information, Robotics and Intelligent Systems (IR, 9111804).

REFERENCES

Anderson, P. A., & Fischer, G. W. (1986). A Monte Carlo model of a garbage can decision process. In J. Marsh & R. Weissinger-Baylon (Eds.), *Ambiguity and command: Organizational perspectives on military decision making* (pp. 140–163). Boston, MA: Pitman.

Baligh, H. H., Burton, R. M., & Obel, B. (1992, April). *Validating the organizational consultant on the fly*. Paper presented at the TIMS Workshop on Mathematical Organization Theory, Orlando, FL.

Bateman, T., & Zeithaml, C. (1989a). The psychological context of strategic decisions: A test of relevance to practitioners. *Strategic Management Journal, 10,* 587–592.

Bateman, T., & Zeithaml, C. (1989b). The psychological context of strategic decisions: A model and convergent experimental findings. *Strategic Management Journal, 10,* 59–74.

Blalock, H. (1969). *Theory construction*. Englewood Cliffs, NJ: Prentice-Hall.

Bouwman, M. (1983). Human diagnostic reasoning by computer: An illustration from financial analysis. *Management Science, 29*(6), 653–672.

Carley, K. (1986). Efficiency in a garbage can: Implications for crisis management. In J. Marsh & R. Weissinger-Baylon (Eds.), *Ambiguity and command: Organizational perspectives on military decision making* (pp. 195–231). Boston, MA: Pitman.

Carley, K. (1990). Trading information redundancy for task simplicity. *Proceedings of the 23rd Annual Hawaii International Conference on System Sciences.* New York: IEEE Press.

Carley, K. (1991a). A theory of group stability. *American Sociological Review, 56,* 331–354.

Carley, K. (1991b). Designing organizational structures to cope with communication breakdowns: A simulation model. *Industrial Crisis Quarterly, 5,* 19–57.

Carley, K. (1992). Organizational learning and personnel turnover. *Organization Science, 3*(1), 20–46.

Carley, K., Kjaer-Hansen, J., Newell, A., & Prietula, A. (1992). Plural-Soar: A prolegomenon to artificial agents and organizational behavior. In M. Masuch & G. Massimo (Eds.), *Distributed intelligence: Applications in human organizations* (pp. 87–118). Amsterdam: North-Holland.

Carley, K., & Newell, A. (1990, August). *On the nature of the social agent.* Paper presented at the American Sociological Association Annual Meeting, Washington, DC.

Chandler, A. (1990). *Scale and scope: The dynamics of industrial capitalism.* Cambridge, MA: Belknap Press.

Charnes, A., & Cooper, W. (1963). Deterministic equivalents for optimizing and satisficing under chance constraints. *Operations Research, 11,* 18–39.

Clancey, W., & Shortliffe, E. (Eds.). (1986). *Readings in medical artificial intelligence: The first decade.* Reading, MA: Addison-Wesley.

Cohen, M. D., March, J., & Olsen, J. (1972). A model of organizational choice. *Administrative Sciences Quarterly, 17*(1), 1–25.

Cyert, R., & March, J. (1956). Organizational factors in the theory of oligopoly. *Quarterly Journal of Economics, 70,* 44–64.

Cyert, R., & March, J. (1963). *A behavioral theory of the firm.* Englewood Cliffs, NJ: Prentice-Hall.

Daft, R. (1989). *Organizational theory and design.* St. Paul, MN: West.

Donaldson, G., & Lorsch, J. (1983). *Decision making at the top: The shaping of strategic direction.* New York: Basic Books.

Downs, A. (1967). *Inside bureaucracy.* Boston, MA: Little, Brown.

Feldman, M., & March, J. (1981). Information as signal & symbol. *Administration Science Quarterly, 26,* 171–186.

Glazer, R., Steckel, J., & Winer, R. (1992). Locally rational decision making: The distracting effect of information on managerial performance. *Management Science, 38*(2), 212–226.

Huber, G. (1990). A theory of the effects of advanced information technologies on organizational design, intelligence and decision making. *Academy of Management Review, 15*(1), 47–71.

Jablin F. M., Putnam, L. L., Roberts, K. A., & Porter, L. W. (1986). *Handbook of organizational communication: An interdisciplinary perspective.* Beverly Hills, CA: Sage.

Krackhardt, D. (1987). Cognitive social structures. *Social Networks 9,* 109–134.

Laird, J., Newell, A., & Rosenbloom, P. (1987). Soar: An architecture for general intelligence. *Artificial Intelligence 33,* 1–64.

Langley, P., Simon, H., Bradshaw, G., & Zytkow, J. (1987). *Scientific discovery: Computational exploration of the creative processes.* Cambridge, MA: MIT Press.

Lawrence, P., & Lorsch, J. (1967). *Organization and environment: Managing differentiation and integration.* Cambridge, MA: Graduate School of Business Administration, Harvard University.

Lin, Z., & Carley, K. (1992, August). *Maydays and murphies: A study of the effect of organizational design, task, and stress on organizational performance.* Paper presented at the American Sociological Association Annual Meeting, Pittsburgh, PA.

Lord, R., & Maher, K. (1990). Alternative information processing models and their implications for theory, research and practice. *Academy of Management Review, 15*(1), 9–28.

March, J. G. (1978). Bounded rationality, ambiguity, and the engineering of choice. *Bell Journal of Economics, 9*(2), 758–608.

March, J. G., & Romelaer, P. (1976). Position and presence in the drift of decisions. In J. G. March & J. P. Olsen (Eds.), *Ambiguity and choice in organizations* (pp. 251–275). Bergen, Norway: Universitetsforlaget.

March, J. G., & Shapira, Z. (1987). Managerial perspectives on risk and risk taking. *Management Science, 33*(11), 1404–1418.

March, J. G., & Simon, H. (1958). *Organizations.* New York: Wiley.

Marschak, J. (1955). Elements for a theory of teams. *Management Science, 1,* 127–137.

McGuire, C. B., & Radner, R. (1986). *Decision and organization.* Minneapolis: University of Minnesota Press.

Mintzberg, H. (1973). *The nature of managerial work.* New York: Harper & Row.

Mintzberg, H. (1978). Patterns in strategy formulation. *Management Science, 24,* 934–949.

Neves, D., & Anderson, J. (1981). Knowledge compilation: Mechanisms for the automatization of cognitive skills. In J. R. Anderson (Ed.), *Cognitive skills and their acquisition* (pp. 57–84). Hillsdale, NJ: Lawrence Erlbaum Associates.

Newell, A. (1980). Physical symbol systems. *Cognitive Science, 4,* 135–183.

Newell, A. (1990). *Unified theories of cognition.* Cambridge, MA: Harvard University Press.

Newell, A., Rosenbloom, P., & Laird, J. (1989). Symbolic architectures for cognition. In M. Posner (Ed.), *Foundations of cognitive science* (pp. 93–131). Cambridge, MA: MIT Press.

Newell, A., & Simon, H. (1976). Computer science as empirical inquiry: Symbols and search. *Communications of the ACM, 19,* 113–126.

Newell, A., Yost, G., Laird, J., Rosenbloom, P., & Altman, E. (1990, September). *Formulating the problem space computational model.* Paper presented at the 25th Anniversary Symposium, School of Computer Science, Carnegie Mellon University.

Perrow, C. (1984). *Normal accidents: Living with high risk technologies.* New York: Basic Books.

Prietula, M., & Carley, K. (forthcoming). *Computational organization theory: Autonomous agents and emergent behavior.* The Journal of Organizational Computing.

Prietula, M., & Weingart, L. (1991, August). *Cognition in naive negotiation: A knowledge-based approach.* Workshop on Methods in Cognitive Research, Academy of Management Conference, Miami.

Radner, R. (1975). Satisficing. *Journal of Mathematical Economics, 2,* 253–262.

Scott, W. R. (1987). *Organization: Rational, natural, and open systems.* Englewood Cliffs, NJ: Prentice-Hall.

Simon, H. (1955). A behavioral model of rational choice. *Quarterly Journal of Economics, 69,* 99–118.

Simon, H. (1956). Rational choice and the structure of the environment. *Psychological Review, 63,* 129–138.

Simon, H. (1976). *Administrative behavior* (3rd ed.). New York: Free Press.

Simon, H. (1979). Rational decision making in business organizations. *American Economic Review, 69*(4), 493–513.

Simon, H. (1981). *The sciences of the artificial* (2nd ed.). Cambridge, MA: MIT Press.

Simon, H., & Baylor, G. (1966). *A chess mating program.* Proceedings of the 1966 Spring Joint Computer Conference, Boston.

Sims, H., Gioia, D., & Associates. (1986). *The thinking organization.* San Francisco: Jossey-Bass.

Snyder, N., & Glueck, W. (1980). How managers plan: The analysis of managers' activities. *Long Range Planning, 13,* 70–76.

Staw, B. (1991). Dressing up like an organization: When psychological theories can explain organizational action. *Journal of Management, 17*(4), 805–819.

Stinchcombe, A. (1990). *Information and organizations.* Berkeley: University of California Press.

Stinchcombe, A. (1991). The conditions of fruitfulness of theorizing about mechanisms in social science. *Philosophy of the Social Sciences, 21*(3), 367–388.

Tang, Z., Pattipati, K., & Kleinman, D. (1991). An algorithm for determining the decision thresholds in a distributed detection problem. *IEEE Transactions on Systems, Man and Cybernetics, 21*(1), 231–237.

Weingart, L. (1989). *Group goals, effort, planning and group performance.* Unpublished doctoral dissertation, Northwestern University, Chicago.

Weick, K. (1969). *The social psychology of organizing.* Reading, MA: Addison-Wesley.

Wilensky, R. (1983). *Planning and understanding: A computational approach to human reasoning.* Reading, MA: Addison-Wesley.

Williamson, O. (1975). *Markets and hierarchies: Analysis and antitrust implications.* New York: Free Press.

Yost, G., & Newell, A. (1989). A problem space approach to expert systems specification. In *Proceedings of the 11th International Joint Conference on Artificial Intelligence* (Vol. 1, pp. 621–627). San Mateo, CA: Morgan Kaufmann.

5

Graph Theoretical Dimensions of Informal Organizations

David Krackhardt
Carnegie Mellon University

In his classic work on the architecture of complexity, Simon (1981) noted the uncanny presence of hierarchy in virtually all complex systems. He further argued that there was a universal function to such hierarchical forms: They are efficient and robust against disruptions that might threaten the cybernetic goals of the system. And although formal organizational charts are obviously hierarchical, he argued that informal organizations also would be found to be hierarchically structured: "If we make a chart of social interactions, of who talks to whom, the clusters of dense interaction in the chart will identify a rather well-defined hierarchic structure. The groupings in this structure may be defined operationally by some measure of frequency of interaction in this sociometric matrix" (Simon, 1981, p. 197).

This idea that informal organizations will naturally evolve into a hierarchical structure is intriguing and has intuitive appeal. The theme can be found with empirical support elsewhere. For example, Michels (1915) noted that even democratically based voluntary organizations evolve toward a centralized, hierarchical structure as they grow. Guetzkow and Simon (1955) discovered that small groups that are allowed unlimited choice of communication channels tend to centralize their communication flows into a hierarchical "wheel" structure.

The normative part of Simon's claim, that hierarchy exists because it allows the system to operate more efficiently and survive outside disturbances, is also appealing. From this, we may deduce a hypothesis about the structure of informal organizations and performance.

Simon's model of hierarchy raises three unresolved issues, two theoretical and one methodological. First, as Simon admitted himself (1981, p. 213), people do communicate outside the preferred boundaries defined by the formal hierarchy of the organization. That is, perfectly hierarchical informal organizations are rare. Nonetheless, he argued, these exceptional communication links are relatively limited and not consequential to the overall pattern of hierarchy in the organization.

The second theoretical problem with Simon's model is that it flies in the face of several normative theories of organizational structure that emphasize the value of communication and information flows outside the normal, hierarchical boundaries. Burns and Stalker (1961) argued that when an organization is faced with a dynamic environment, an organic, nonhierarchical, informal structure is more appropriate for organizational effectiveness and survival. Allen (1977) demonstrated that research and development organizations can enhance their effectiveness by promoting communication outside the formal, hierarchical boundaries:

> Increased communication between R&D projects and other elements of the laboratory staff were in every case strongly related to project performance. Moreover, it appears that interaction outside the project is most important. On complex projects, the inner team cannot sustain itself and work effectively without constantly importing new information from the outside world. (pp. 122–123)

And Krackhardt and Stern (1988) presented experimental evidence that under some conditions organizations are better off if they maximize strong cross-departmental relationships.

The third problem with Simon's model is one of measurement and consequent testability. Given that pure hierarchies do not exist, we must somehow differentiate between structures as being more or less hierarchical. Otherwise, we have no way of confirming or disconfirming his predictions. He offered no specifics for measuring the degree of hierarchy in social systems. In fact, systems whose elements appear to have no hierarchical structure (systems he calls *flat* hierarchies), he argued, are still hierarchical with an indefinitely large "span."

The purpose of this chapter is to broaden Simon's ideas of hierarchical structures as they pertain to informal organizations. First, I dispense with the assertion that informal organizations are necessarily hierarchical. Instead, I argue that this is an empirical question and an appropriate object of research. Second, I propose that hierarchical forms will have implications for organizations, but that some of the implications may not necessarily enhance the organization's efficiency or ability to survive (i.e., they are not necessarily functional). Finally, I specify a method for measuring the degree to which the informal organization is structured in a way that Simon would call hierarchical. Because the ability to answer the former research questions depends on this last measurement issue, I begin with the development of measures of informal structure.

GRAPH THEORY AND MEASURES OF STRUCTURE

Graph theory (Harary, 1969) provides us with a precise language for representing structures of all forms, including the structures Simon referred to as hierarchical. Because I draw on graph theory in this chapter, I provide definitions as necessary for clarity. A *graph* (G) is defined as a set of N points $P = \{P_i\}$ and a set of unordered pairs of those points $L = \{P_i, P_j\}$; these latter elements are often referred to as lines connecting those points. In the immediate context, these points represent people in the organization, and the pairs of points represent relationships (such as interaction, communication) between those organizational members. For example, if person i interacts with person j, then the ordered pair (P_i, P_j) is included in set L that defines the relationship *interaction*.

A directed graph, or *digraph* (D), is defined as a set of points $P = \{P_i\}$ and a set of *ordered* pairs of points $L = \{P_i, P_j\}$. A digraph is used to represent relations that are potentially asymmetric, such as authority or giving advice. For example, if i is the immediate supervisor to j, and L is defined as the set of formal authority relationships, then L would contain the ordered pair (P_i, P_j) but would not contain the ordered pair (P_j, P_i).

Graph theory definitions are often easier to convey by example. Figure 5.1 provides an example of two graphs and one digraph. Graphs are represented with points and lines connecting the points. Digraphs are represented by points and lines with arrowheads on them to indicate the order of the pair of points being connected. The graph in Fig. 5.1c represents a special function. It is the *underlying graph* of the digraph in Fig. 5.lb. The underlying graph of a digraph is the graph obtained by "removing the arrows" from the digraph. That is, if digraph D contains either the ordered pair (P_i, P_j) or (P_j, P_i), then the underlying graph G will include the unordered pair (P_i, P_j).

A point and a line are *incident* with one another if the line contains the point in its pair. In Fig. 5.1a, P_2 is incident with line (P_1, P_2). A *walk* is an ordered sequence of alternating points and lines, starting and ending with points, such that each line is incident with the point that precedes it and with the point that follows it. A path is a walk with no repeating points. In Fig. 5.1c, the sequence P_3, (P_3, P_5), R_5, (P_5, P_4), P_4 constitutes a path from P_3 to P_4. One point is said to be able to reach another if there exists a path that

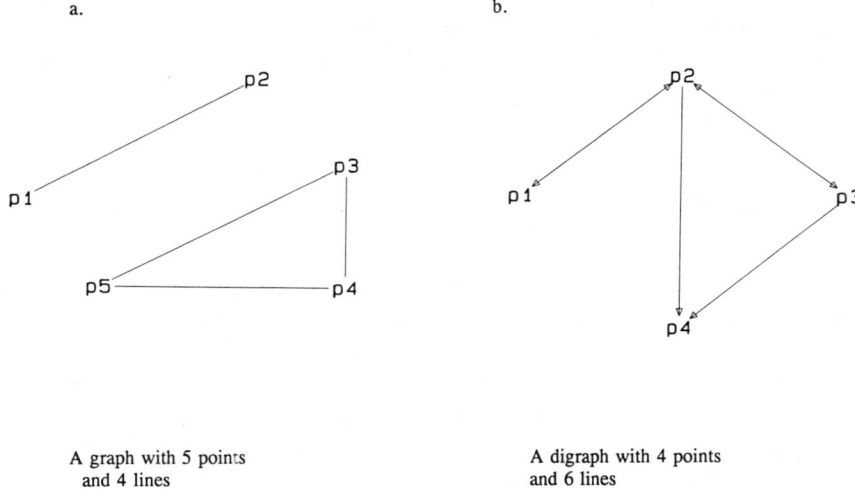

a.

A graph with 5 points
and 4 lines

b.

A digraph with 4 points
and 6 lines

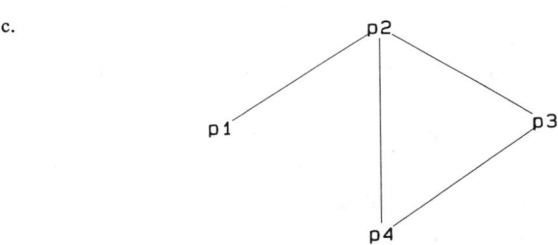

c.

The underlying graph of digraph b
has 4 points and 4 lines.

FIG. 5.1.   Examples of graphs and digraphs.

starts at the first point and ends at the second. All pairs of points in the graph in Fig. 5.lc are mutually reachable.

With a small restriction in the definition of incidence of points and lines, these same definitions apply to digraphs as well. In an ordered point-line pair, $[P_i, (P_j, P_k)]$, the point and line are incident with each other if $P_j = P_i$. In an ordered line-point pair, $[(P_j, P_k), P_i]$, the line and point are incident with each other if $P_k = P_i$. The definitions of paths and reachability are identical to those in graphs. In the digraph represented in Fig. 5.1b, a path exists from P_1 to P_4 but not from P_4 to P_1. Therefore, P_1

can reach P_4 but not vice versa. In fact, P_4 cannot reach any other point, but each other point can reach P_4.

A *connected graph* is a graph in which each point can reach every other point. Figure 5.1c is connected; Fig. 5.1a is not. A subgraph (S) of graph (G) is a graph whose points and lines are also in G. A component (C) of graph (G) is a connected subgraph of G with two characteristics: (a) All the lines in G incident to every point in C are included in C, and (b) there is no point in G not included in C that, in G, can reach a point included in C. Figure 5.1c has one only component; Fig. 5.1a has two components.

A *connected digraph* is a digraph in which each point can reach every other point in the underlying graph of the digraph. Each point in the digraph of Fig. 5.1b is reachable from every other point in the underlying graph Fig. 5.1c. Thus, the digraph in Fig. 5.1b is connected. A *component* (C) of a digraph (D) is a connected subgraph of D with the following characteristics: (a) All the lines in D incident to every point in C are included in C, and (b) there is no point in D not included in C that, in the underlying graph of D, can reach a point included in C. The digraph in Fig. 5.1b has one component only.

With these tools and definitions developed so far, it is possible to represent the informal structure of any organization. But to fully explore Simon's notions of hierarchical structure, it will be necessary to develop some additional operations. From these, one can determine the extent to which an informal structure approximates a pure hierarchical structure.

PURE HIERARCHICAL STRUCTURES: THE OUTTREE

The first task before us is to establish a pure structure as a standard against which other structures can be compared. For the purposes of this analysis, the ideal candidate for such a structure is, in graph theory terms, the *outtree*. Before a formal definition is presented, an intuition of what constitutes an outtree is provided for the reader in Fig. 5.2, which contains four examples. First, it should be noted that outtrees are digraphs. Second, every point, with the exception of the one point at the "top" of the outtree, has exactly one arrow pointing to it, although the points may have several arrows emanating from them. If these arrows represented authority relationships, then we might interpret this statement as noting that each point has one and only one "boss," but each point may have any number of subordinates. In fact, it should be immediately apparent to the reader that each of these figures could be examples of organizational charts—the *archetypical formal hierarchy,* as Simon termed it (1981, p. 197).

There are several reasons that the outtree serves as a reference base for

a.   b.

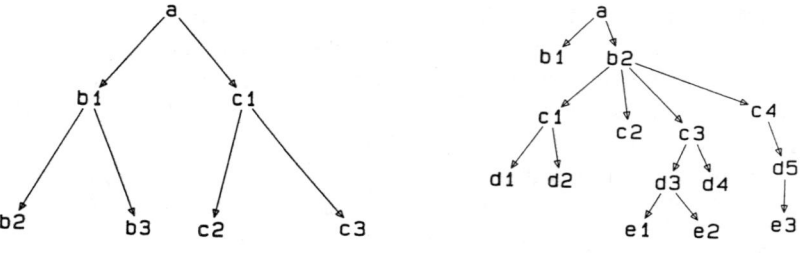

c.   d.

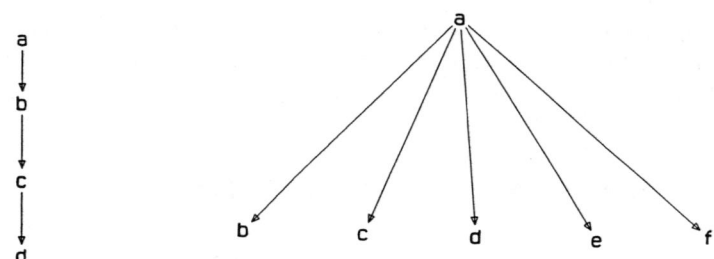

FIG. 5.2.   Examples of outtrees.

the study of informal structures. First, all of Simon's hierarchical systems can be represented as an outtree.[1] Second, as mentioned earlier, they correspond to our intuition of the archetypical hierarchy, the formal organization. Third, they preserve several fundamental principles of classic organizational structure, including unity of command, unambiguous chain of command, and the scalar principle.

But this graph theory concept provides more than an archetype. It provides a basis for describing observed organizational structures and measuring their deviance from this archetype. To pursue this, it is first

---

[1]It is worth noting at this point that most of Simon's hierarchical systems are represented by an inclusion relation, rather than the type of interpersonal relations used throughout this chapter.

necessary to formally define an outtree using more graph theory. There are many ways to so define an outtree (e.g., Wilson, 1979, p. 45). For reasons that become clear shortly, I use the following four conditions of a digraph as a definition of an outtree. These conditions are both necessary and sufficient for the digraph to be an outtree:

1. The digraph is connected.
2. The digraph is graph hierarchic.
3. The digraph is graph efficient.
4. Every pair of points in the digraph has a least upper bound.

If a graph violates any of these four conditions, then it is not an outtree. Moreover, we can count the number of violations in each of the dimensions to give us a measure of distance from the archetypal structure. Because these violations are based on independent criteria, the picture of the structure described by each dimension differs considerably. Figure 5.3 displays some examples of these differences. In the center of the figure is an outtree. Each of the other four figures surrounding the outtree represents an extreme case where one (and only one) of each of the four conditions is violated to the maximum extent possible. It is useful to refer to this figure as each of the four dimensions is defined next.

Each of the four measures of degree of structure is based on the number of outtree violations that exist in any particular structural arrangement. As such, each condition becomes a *dimension* of structure, continuously varying in value from 0 to 1. That a graph has a value of 1.0 on all four dimensions is equivalent to stating that a graph is an outtree. Also, each of the four dimensions has different implications for the organization. Each of these dimensions and its implications for the organization is next described in turn.

1. Connectedness. The definition of connectedness was already provided earlier: A digraph is connected if each point can reach every other point in the underlying graph. To say that a digraph is *disconnected* implies that there are at least two components in the digraph. The degree to which the digraph is disconnected is a function of the number of violations of the connectedness condition. A violation is defined as a point being unable to reach another point in the underlying graph. If we divide the number of violations by the maximum number of possible violations (i.e., in the case where no point can reach any other point), we have a continuum representing the degree to which the graph is disconnected. Subtracting this ratio from 1 gives us the degree of connectedness in the structure. The *degree of connectedness* is then defined as:

Connectivity = 0   Hierarchy = 0

a

f   b

g

e   c

d

a ←——→ b ←——→ c ←——→ d ←——→ e ←——→ f

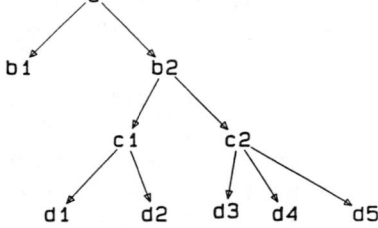

Outtree:
    Connectivity = 1.0
    Hierarchy = 1.0
    Graph efficiency = 1.0
    Least-upper-boundedness = 1.0

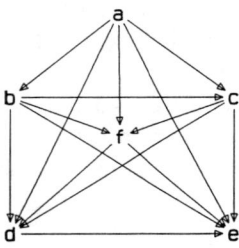

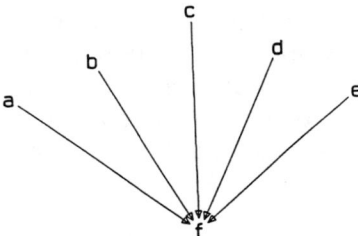

Graph efficiency = 0   Least-upper-boundedness = 0

FIG. 5.3.   The four dimensions of structure.

$$\text{Connectedness} = 1 - \left[\frac{V}{N(N-1)/2} \right]$$

where V is the number of pairs of points that are not mutually reachable, and the maximum number of violations is the total number of pairs of points $= N(N-1)/2$.

The degree of connectedness in a set of social relations is the simplest of the measures. At one end of the spectrum, an outtree is completely connected. A disconnected graph represents a division in the social system. The more people are separated from each other, the more difficult it is to organize them through the network. At the extreme, no one is connected to anyone (connectedness = 0); everyone is an independent actor.

If the task facing the organization is routine, and the environment does not change, then connectedness may not be essential to the performance of the organization in its task. But if the organization has many exceptions that require consultation, a set of established communication and advice relations that incorporates all actors, at least indirectly, would be essential. Also, lack of connectedness may be a reflection of a major political division, such that one side does not talk to the other side(s).

2. Graph Hierarchy.[2] The *graph hierarchy* condition states that in a digraph D, for each pair of points where one (P_i) can reach another (P_j), the second (P_j) cannot reach the first (P_i). For example, in a formal organizational chart, a high-level employee can "reach" through the chain of command her subordinate's subordinate. If the formal organization is working properly, this lower level employee cannot simultaneously "reach" (i.e., cannot be the boss of a boss of) the higher level employee.

To measure the degree of hierarchy of digraph D, a new digraph D_r must be created. D_r is defined as the *reachability digraph* of D. Each point in D exists in D_r; moreover, the line (P_i, P_j) exists in D_r if and only if P_i can reach P_j in D. If D is graph hierarchic, then D_r will have no symmetric lines in it. That is, if the line (P_i, P_j) exists in D_r then the line (P_j, P_i) does not. A violation to this condition exists every time a symmetric line exists in D_r. The degree of hierarchy, then, is defined as:

$$\text{Graph hierarchy} = 1 - \left[\frac{V}{\text{Max}\,V} \right]$$

where V is the number of unordered pairs of points in D_r that are symmetrically linked (that is, where P_i is linked to P_j and P_j is linked to P_i), and Max$V$ is the number of unordered pairs of points in D_r where P_i is linked to P_j or P_j is linked to P_i.

Graph hierarchy exists to the extent that the relations are strictly ordered. For example, hierarchy occurs if relations are determined by status, prestige, or formal authority. Informal relations, such as advice relations, can be ordered, but are not necessarily so. An outtree (such as the organizational chart) is perfectly hierarchical. At the other extreme, if there

---

[2]The term *hierarchy* is used differently here than by Simon. Nothing in Simon's work specifies asymmetry of relations. However, the term's use in this chapter corresponds more closely to the common use of the word. From here on, I will use the term *hierarchy* to refer to graph hierarchy rather than Simon's definition.

is no status in a system, then no graph hierarchy is likely to emerge in the informal relations.

A mechanistic organization is likely to be very status ridden (Shrader, Lincoln, & Hoffman, 1989). Members are likely to go up the organization for advice. To the extent that this is true, a mechanistic organization will be characterized by a high degree of hierarchy in advice relations. In an organic organization, on the other hand, status is more diffuse, and project leaders may not hesitate to seek advice from subordinates or someone from a different group in the organization. In such an environment, advice relations might not be hierarchically arranged at all.

3. Graph Efficiency. One of the conditions of an outtree is that the underlying graph is connected and contains exactly $N-1$ lines. Fewer lines than that and the digraph disconnects into components. More lines than that creates multiple paths and cycles between points. In a sense, these multiple paths are redundant in graph-theory terms, and they disrupt the stoic, bare-bones nature of the pure outtree structure.

The technical definition of the *graph efficiency* condition is: In the underlying graph (G_1, G_2, etc.) of each component (D_1, D_2, etc.) of digraph D, there are exactly N_n-1 links, where N_n is the number of nodes in the corresponding component D_n. Because fewer than N_n-1 links is not possible (because that would break the component into subcomponents), violations occur to the extent that more than this minimum number of links is present. The degree of graph efficiency is defined as:

$$\text{Graph efficiency} = 1 - \left[\frac{V}{\text{Max}V} \right]$$

where V is the number of links in excess of N_n-1, summed over all components, and Max$V$ is the maximum number of links in excess of N_n-1 possible, summed over all components.

Links are not without costs in a social system. They take time and resources to maintain. Thus, the concept of graph efficiency characterizes how dense the network is beyond that barely needed to keep the social group even indirectly connected to one another.

Graph inefficiency should not be confused with social inefficiency or economic inefficiency. To say that a group is graph inefficient simply implies it has more than the $N-1$ links required to remain connected. In fact, in a high-tech, organic organization faced with a dynamic and unpredictable environment, graph inefficiencies may be called for to facilitate the quick cross-fertilization of innovative ideas (Shrader et al., 1989). Thus, graph efficiency reflects the cost of a dense network; it avoids answering the question about the benefits of such a network.

Nonetheless, some conjectures could be made about the relationship between graph efficiency and organizational efficiency. An organization that is so bare bones in its informal structure that it is perfectly graph efficient is also fragile. It is vulnerable to the arbitrary deletion of a link or point (for example, through attrition). Some redundancies (graph inefficiencies) in the informal network also help to short-circuit long communication paths and thus that may slow down information flow. Thus, very high values of graph efficiency are likely to be associated with less than optimal organizational performance.

On the other hand, extremely dense informal networks that would characterize very low efficiency scores are likely to be overburdened with networking. Employees cannot be expected to relate to everyone else in the organization. People would spend all their time interacting and have little left over for getting their work done. Thus, we expect a curvilinear relationship between graph efficiency and organizational effectiveness, with the optimum graph efficiency value to lie between 0 and 1.

4. Least Upper Boundedness. In order for a pair of actors to have a *least upper bound* (LUB), they each must have access to a common third person in the organization to whom they both can "appeal" (through the network). This third person (called an *upper bound*) must be someone to whom they both defer (either directly or indirectly) in the network. A given pair of actors may have many upper bounds. In such cases, a least upper bound is a member of that set of upper bounds who in turn can appeal to or defer to the remaining upper bounds. In a formal organization chart, the LUB of two employees is the closest boss who has formal authority over both of them.

The technical definition of the least upper bound condition is given as follows: Within each component (D_1, D_2, etc.) of digraph D, each pair of points (P_i and P_j) has at least one least upper bound (LUB). An upper bound for a pair of points (P_i and P_j) is a third point (P_k) from which there is a path to each of the pair; a least upper bound is an upper bound (P_k) that is included in at least one directed path from each other upper bound (P_l, P_m, . . .) to each of the pair (P_i, P_j). Violations to this condition occur whenever a (P_i, P_j) pair of points in D_n has no LUB. The degree of LUBedness is defined as:

$$\text{LUB} = 1 - \left[\frac{V}{\text{Max}V} \right]$$

where V is the number of pairs of points that have no LUB in each component summed across all components, and Max$V$ is the maximum number of pairs of points that could possibly have no LUB. It should be noted that point k may be equal to point i or j. That is, two points (P_i and P_j) that are connected always have as a LUB one of the two points (P_i or P_j or both). Because a component C_n must have at least $N_n - 1$ lines, every component has by definition at least $N_n - 1$ pairs of points that do have LUBs. Therefore, the maximum number of violations for a component of a digraph is:

$$\text{Max} V = \frac{(N_n - 1)(N_n - 2)}{2}$$

This is the most complex measure of the four measures of structure. It has interesting implications for structures, however. First, it is the only condition of the four that is sensitive to the direction of the arrows in the digraph. It is possible to change the LUB score from 0.0 to 1.0 (or vice versa) simply by changing the direction of all of the arrows in a digraph. Thus, the meaning of the direction of a relationship becomes important here. It is assumed that all relationships are defined in a way that suggests that an arrow from P_i to P_j implies that P_j defers to P_i, or that P_i has more status than P_j.

The LUB condition preserves the unity-of-command principle in formal organizations. It also ensures that there is only one "chief executive" at the top. Violations of the condition are an indication that there may be too many informal cooks spoiling the pot. For example, in Fig. 5.3, the digraph in the lower right corner has a LUB score of 0, indicating that the number of violations is at a maximum. If the relationship represented by the arrows happened to be authority, the lower point in the digraph would be subject to the orders of five different "top dogs."

It has been suggested elsewhere (Doreian, 1971; Friedell, 1967) that a LUB condition in an informal network is an indication of how differences or conflict might be managed within the organization. If a LUB exists for a pair of actors, then that LUB person has a potential position for settling or dealing with the conflict. When relatively few of the pairs of actors have a LUB, then conflict would be predicted to be difficult to resolve in the organization.

BEHAVIOR OF THE FOUR DIMENSIONS IN RANDOM DIGRAPHS

Thus far, four measures of structure have been proposed along with tentative relationships to organizational phenomena. We are left with the empirical question, what do organizations look like in the real world? But before that question is pursued, there is another empirical question worth exploring: How do these measures behave in structures that are truly random rather than ordered, as the word structure implies? The answer to this question provides the empiricist with a type of null hypothesis against which he or she can compare real-world observations.

To study this question, random structures were generated. Two parameters were manipulated in these random digraphs, the number of points in the digraph ($= N$) and the probability that any two points are connected to each other with a line ($= P$). Four different sized digraphs were created: $N = 5, 10, 20,$ and 50. The value of P, which virtually determines the number of lines in the digraph, varied from .01 to .10 in increments of .01, and then from .15 to .9 in increments of .05. For each combination of N and P, 500 digraphs were generated, for a total of 52,000 digraphs. For each digraph generated, the degree of connectedness, graph hierarchy, graph efficiency, and least-upper-boundedness was calculated.

The results of these simulations are depicted in the Appendix. In each graph the mean value, the 95th percentile value, and the 5th percentile value of one of the four structure measures are plotted as a function of P for the given N.

These plots provide ranges of values one would expect if the lines of the digraphs were randomly drawn. Two general conclusions are evident from these simulations. First, the range of probable structure values for a given P is greatly reduced as N increases. Second, the relationship between P and each of the specific measures is very strong in random graphs when N is large ($= 50$).

The fact that P, and by implication the density of the relations, is so closely correlated with these graph values in large digraphs is not a surprise. For example, perfect connectedness is impossible until the digraph has at least $N-1$ lines. Beyond that, it is expected that the more lines there are the easier it would be to randomly create a connected digraph. And graph efficiency is easily construed as a surrogate for density; thus, the near linear relationship between P and efficiency when $N = 50$ is no surprise.

Two points are worth underscoring in relation to these simulation results. First, just because values of these structural dimensions in random digraphs seem heavily constrained by P and N does not mean that real-world digraphs cannot be found outside these values. For example, the digraph in the lower left corner of Fig. 5.3 (with a graph efficiency of 0) is a kind of structure that has $P = .5$ and a hierarchy of 1.0. This structural pattern could exist for any N size. If the graph were size $N = 10$, the simulation results indicate that the graph hierarchy of 1.0 would be incredible, if not virtually impossible. Of course, this case is quite possible in the real world, where status often aligns such deference relations just as a magnet aligns free-floating iron particles in its field. Observing such a structure, we would conclude that there was such a force aligning these relations, because we would never expect to see such a structure by chance. These simulation results, then provide a reference point for comparison as real-world data are collected.

The second point is a cautionary note. These four structural measures are sensitive to densities. And densities in relations are very sensitive to how the relation is measured. We often collect such data by asking employees directly whom they talk to, whom they go to for advice, whom they seek out in the case of problems, and so forth. Sometimes we modify these questions with temporal ranges, such as ". . . at least every day," ". . . at least once a week." Such modifications can greatly affect densities. Even when the same question is consistently asked, the researcher can affect the density of the relation by insisting on various levels of confirmation of the relation (e.g., both actors must agree that P_i goes to P_j for advice before the P_i, P_j line is drawn). These simulations suggest that researchers wishing to make cross-organizational comparisons along these four dimensions must pay particular attention to how the method of data collection could affect the variance in density among the organizations studied.

CONCLUSION

In this chapter I have argued that graph theory provides a rich descriptive language for assessing organizational structure. With few exceptions (e.g., Mackenzie, 1986; Shrader et al., 1989), little research has taken advantage of this natural link between mathematics and organizational theory.

But not only does graph theory describe, it permits us to measure the degree of structure in organizations in more precise terms than is ordinarily done in field research. Moreover, by dividing the ultimate structure, the outtree, into its four constituent parts, different qualities of lack of structure can be measured. It is suggested that these four dimensions are each related to different organizational phenomena:

1. Connectedness is associated with the ease with which the organization can deal with and implement change.
2. Graph hierarchy is associated with the degree to which the organization is dominated by status in its informal relations.
3. Graph efficiency has a curvilinear relationship to organizational effectiveness.
4. Least-upper-boundedness is associated with organizational conflict.

Empirical evidence in support of these conjectures awaits us. In due course, I expect these predictions to be modified, conditioned, and perhaps even discarded and replaced with more accurate theories. In the meantime, using these graph-theoretic concepts to build on Simon's original idea of hierarchy should allow us to better grasp the role of organizational structure as an independent variable in organizational theory.

APPENDIX
STRUCTURE OF RANDOM GRAPHS BY *P*

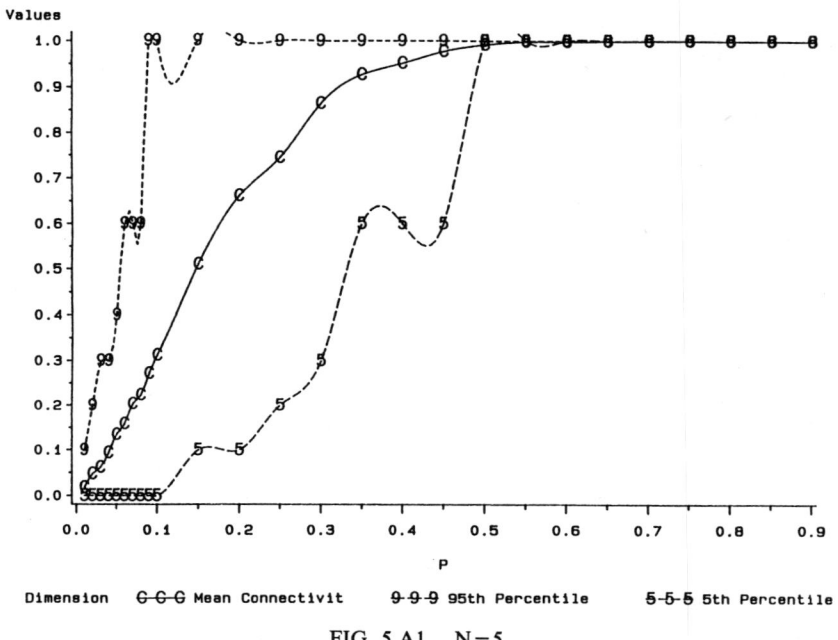

FIG. 5.A1.   N=5.

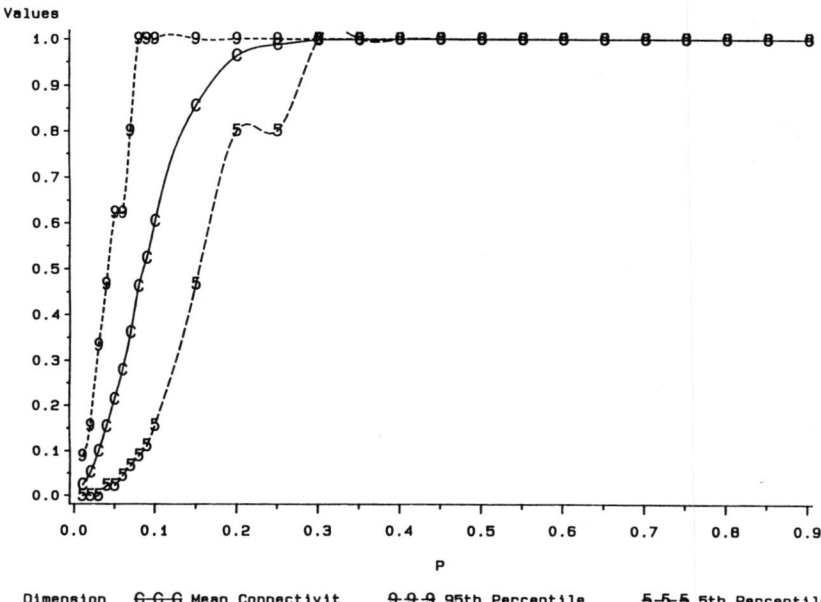

FIG. 5.A2.   N=10.

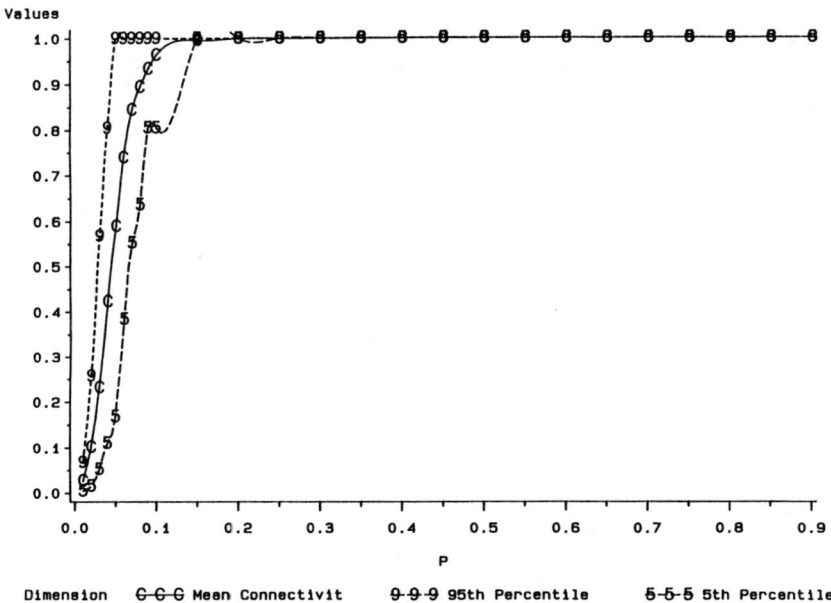

FIG. 5.A3.   N=20.

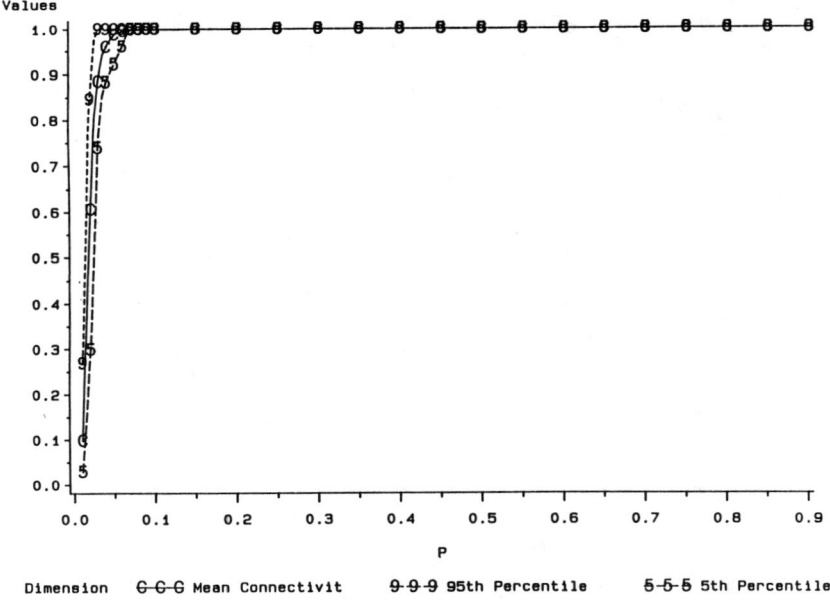

FIG. 5.A4.   N=50.

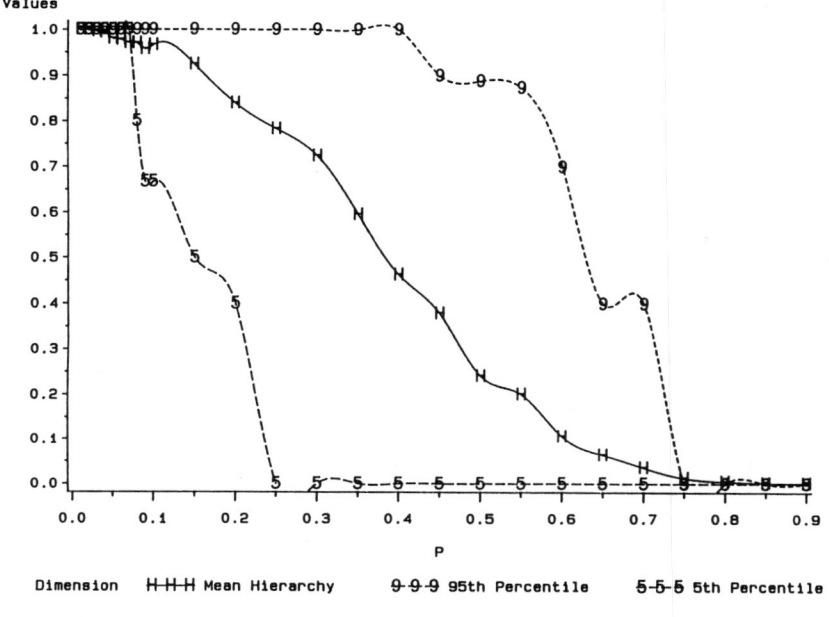

FIG. 5.A5. N=5.

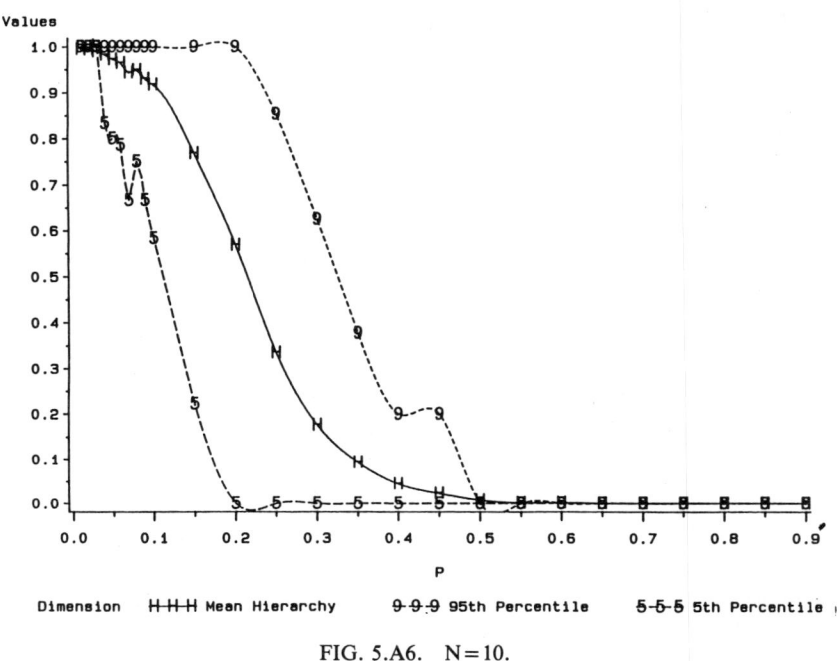

FIG. 5.A6. N=10.

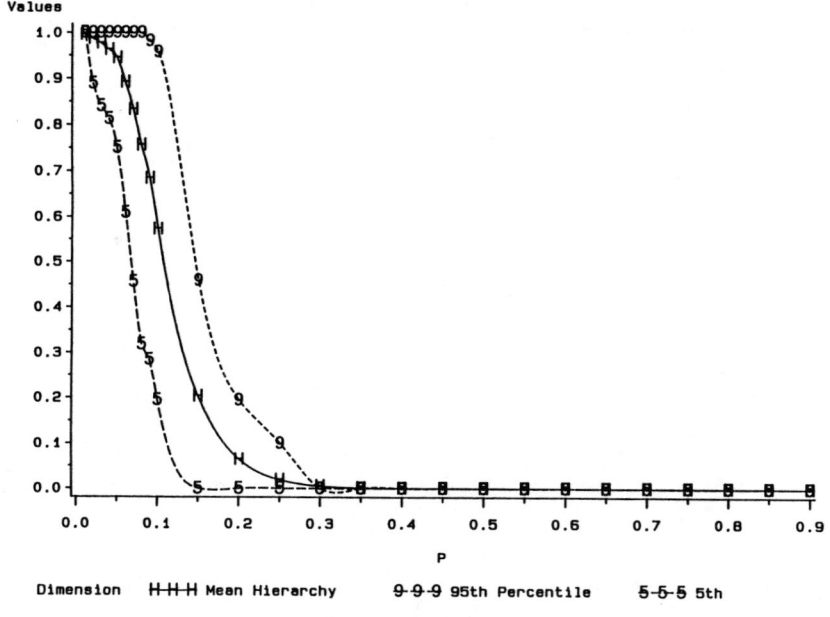

FIG. 5.A7.   N=20.

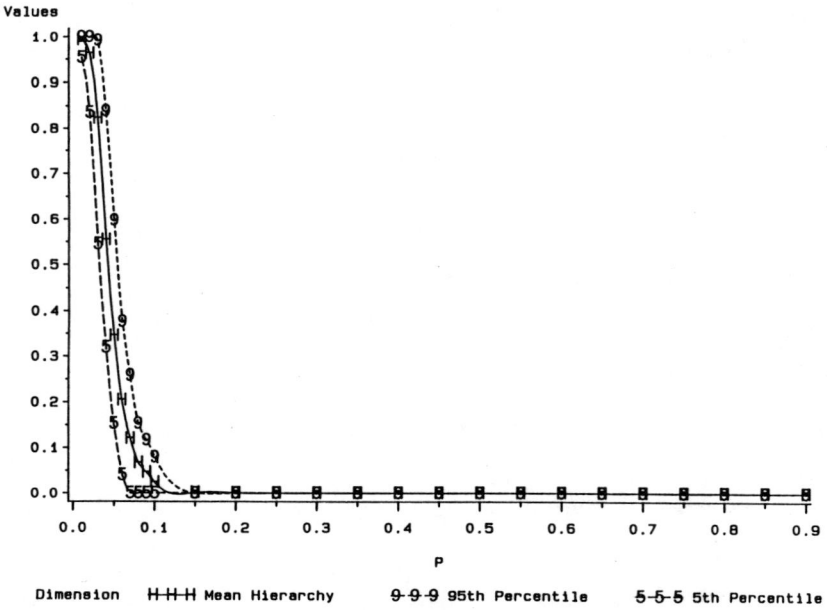

FIG. 5.A8.   N=50.

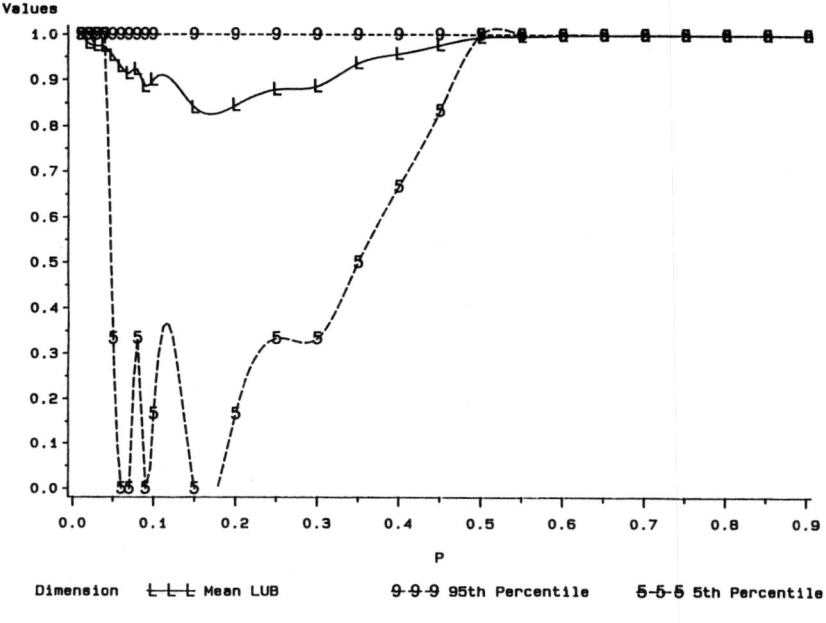

FIG. 5.A9. N=5.

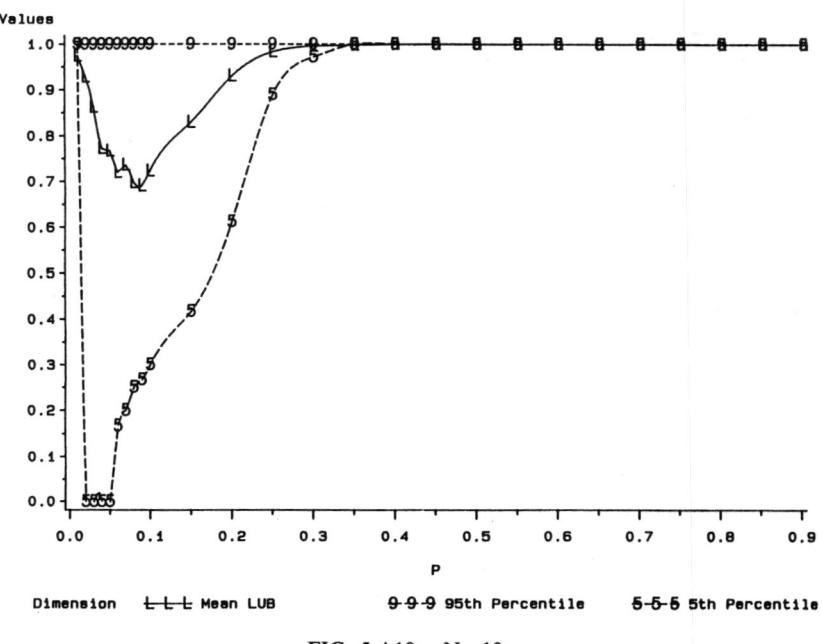

FIG. 5.A10. N=10.

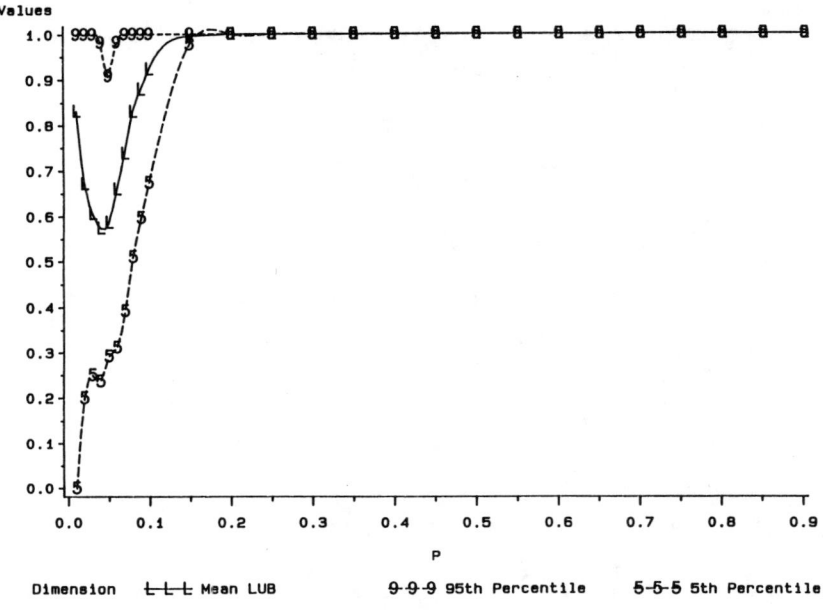

FIG. 5.A11. N=20.

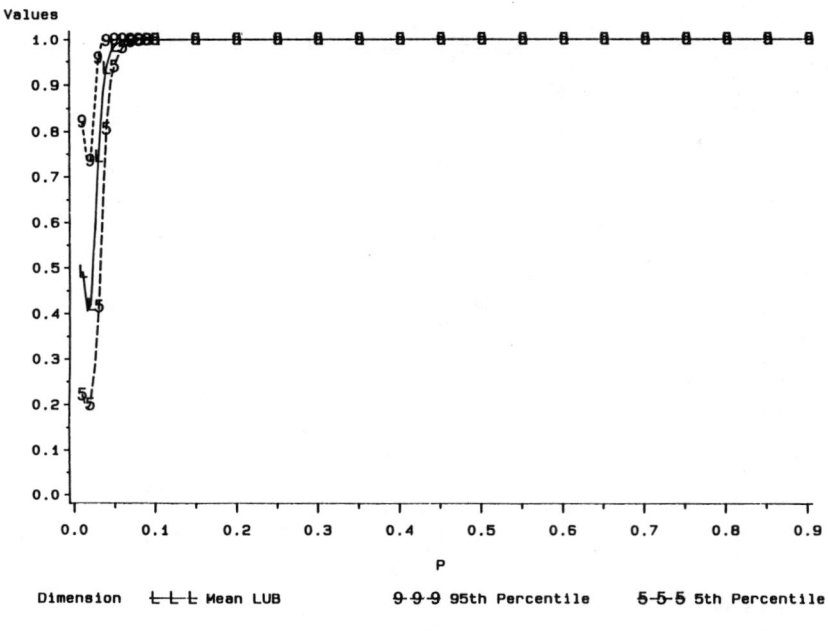

FIG. 5.A12. N=50.

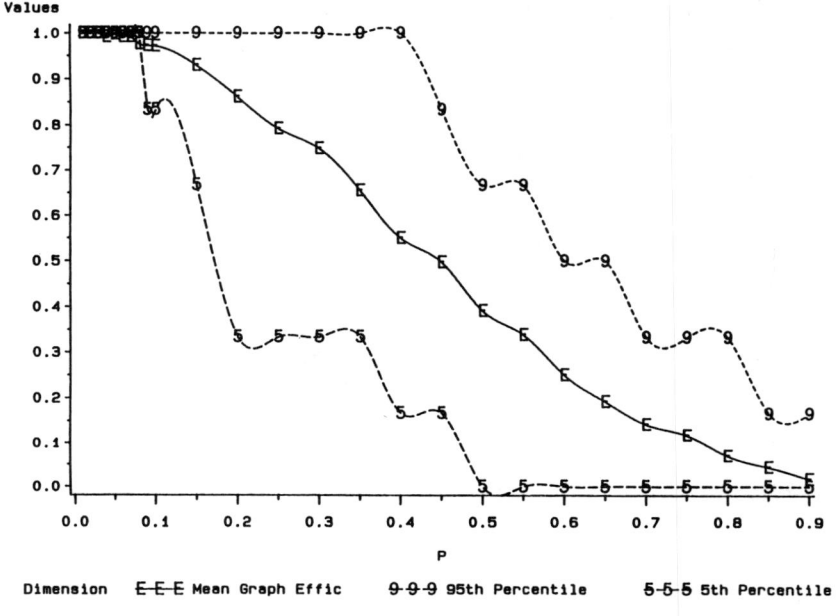

FIG. 5.A13.   N=5.

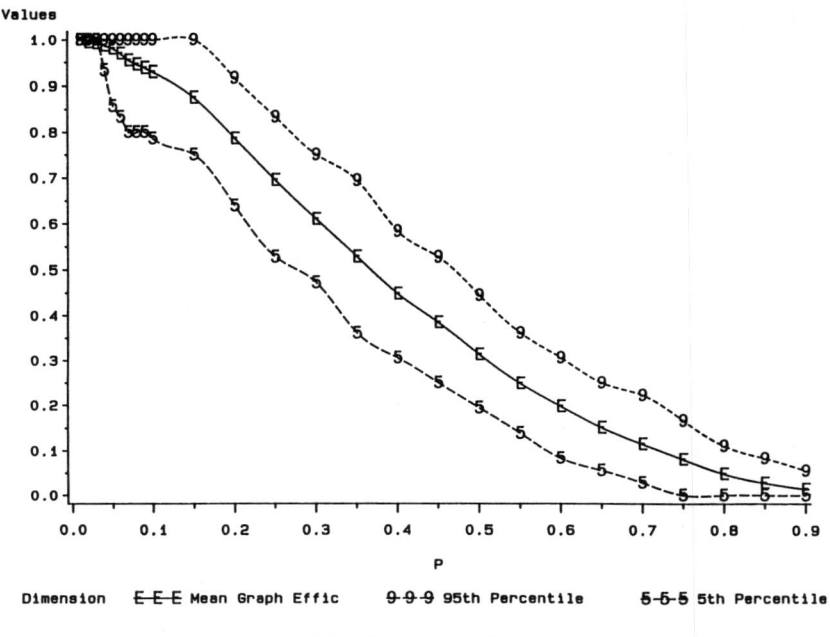

FIG. 5.A14.   N=10.

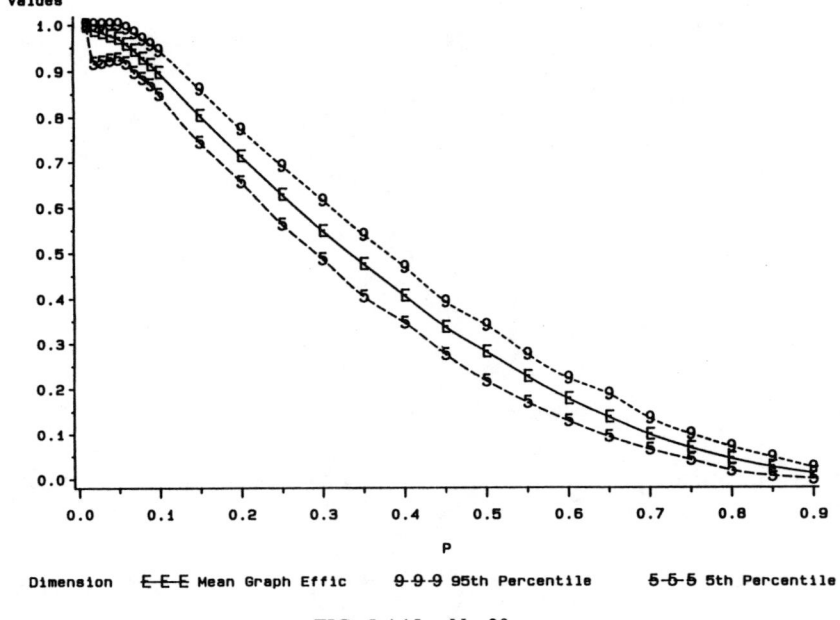

FIG. 5.A15. N=20.

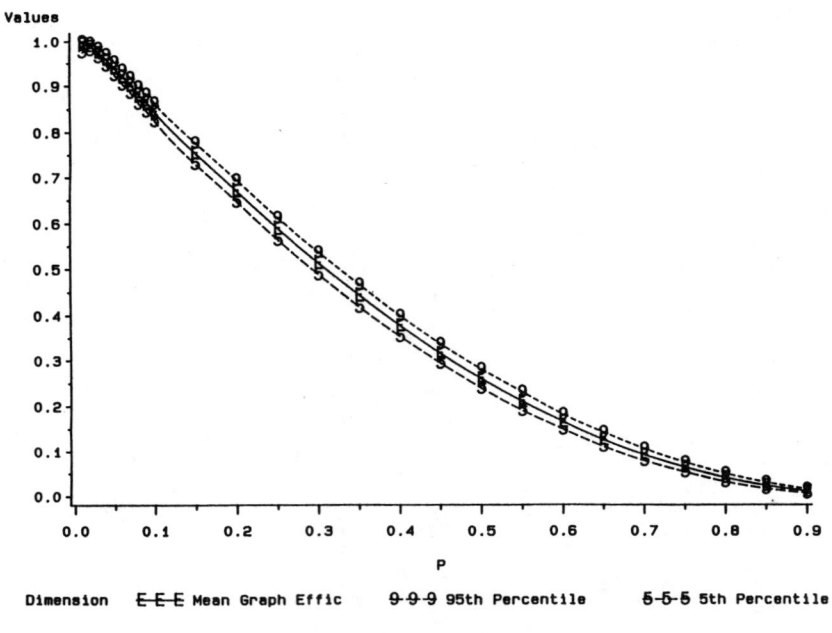

FIG. 5.A16. N=50.

REFERENCES

Allen, T. J. (1977). *Managing the flow of technology*. Cambridge, MA: MIT Press.

Burns, T., & Stalker, G. M. (1961). *The management of innovation*. London: Tavistock.

Doreian, P. (1971). *Mathematics and the study of social relations*. New York: Schocken Books.

Friedell, M. F. (1967). Organisations as semilattices. *American Sociological Review, 32*(February), 46–54.

Guetzkow, H., & Simon, H. (1955). The impact of certain communication nets upon organization and performance in task-oriented groups. *Management Science, 1,* 233–250.

Harary, F. (1969). *Graph theory*. Reading, MA: Addison-Wesley.

Krackhardt, D., & Stern, R. N. (1988). Informal networks and organizational crises: An experimental simulation. *Social Psychology Quarterly, 51*(2), 123–140.

Mackenzie, K. D. (1986). *Organizational design: The organizational audit and analysis technology*. Norwood, NJ: Ablex.

Michels, R. (1915). *Political parties*. Glencoe, IL: The Free Press.

Shrader, C. B., Lincoln, J. R., & Hoffman, A. N. (1989). The network structures of organizations: Effects of task contingencies and distributional form. *Human Relations, 42,* 43–66.

Simon, H. A. (1981). *The sciences of the artificial* (2nd ed.). Cambridge, MA: MIT Press.

Wilson, R. J. (1979). *Introduction to graph theory* (2nd ed.). London: Longman.

6

A Theoretical Evaluation of Measures of Organizational Design: Interrelationship and Performance Predictability

Zhiang Lin
Carnegie Mellon University

Various mathematical measures of organizational design have been suggested in the literature on organizations. These include structural indicators (Krackhardt, this volume; Krackhardt & Stern, 1988; Seashore, 1962) and process indicators (Carley, 1991; Mackenzie, 1978; Malone, 1986; Tancredi & Woods, 1972). Presumably, the value of these measures is not simply that they characterize organizational design, but that they should provide insight into organizational performance (Mackenzie, 1978; Scott, 1987), although sometimes from different perspectives (such as efficiency and cost). Mackenzie, for example, demonstrated in certain cases that a high degree of hierarchy will enhance the effectiveness and the efficiency of the organization. Lincoln, Hanada, and McBride (1986) also argued in their comparative study of Japanese and American firms that a higher level of hierarchy in the formal structure leads to better performance of the Japanese firms.

These measures have rarely been contrasted against each other relative to their ability to predict organizational performance. Rather, researchers often develop new measures with little attention to the value of previous measures. Krackhardt (this volume), for example, developed several interesting measures of organizational design from a graph theoretical perspective and argued their expected relevance to performance, but did not contrast this with Mackenzie's measure of hierarchy and efficiency. Similarly, Malone (1986) took a coordination perspective and developed a reasonable measure of design in terms of cost, suggested its relevance to performance, but did not contrast the work with Mackenzie's measures. In essence, the interrelationships among these mathematical measures have not been systematically examined. A systematic evaluation of these measures clarifies the relations among them, tests their potential to predict performance, and possibly suggests constraints on measures of organizational design. In this chapter, I conduct a systematic evaluation of these measures using computer simulations of organizations.

There are several reasons for evaluating organizational design measures using simulated organizations. First, in practice there is little consensus on what constitutes organizational performance. Research has shown that it is impossible to obtain the best or sufficient indicator of organizational performance, and that whether an organization is said to perform well depends on "the purposes and constraints" placed on the organizational performance measure (Cameron, 1986). Performance has been viewed from a variety of perspectives, such as productivity (Argote & Epple, 1990), profitability (Lawrence & Lorsch, 1967), and reliability (Roberts, 1989). Although such measures may indicate what the organization is doing, they do not necessary suggest how well it is doing it.

Second, assuming that we find a reasonable indicator of organizational performance that lets us gauge action against an objective indicator, it is virtually impossible to obtain sufficient data for comparing organizations with a range of designs under both normal and stressful situations. The difficulty of getting such data includes time limits on data acquisition, confidentiality, insufficient information on specific operating conditions within organizations, and lack of comparability across industries. Such difficulties tend to result in an imbalanced design from an analysis standpoint and so call into question the generalizability of the results. A related difficulty with field studies of performance is that they typically focus on successful firms (Child, 1974; Drazin & Van de Ven, 1985; Lawrence & Lorsch, 1967; Long, 1980). As such, they provide little insight from a design perspective as to whether "failed" firms differ in design from "successful" firms.

Third, evaluation of organizational measures by simulation has the following advantages:

1. Using simulation, we can fully explore various aspects of organizations and their performance, thus providing a basis for a systematic evaluation of organizational measures.

2. We can conduct balanced simulation experiments, and control certain factors to examine the effect of other factors.

3. We can consider both successful and failed firms. Thus results will not be biased by looking only at successes.

4. Simulated organizations have been shown to resemble the real-world organizations in an idealized way (Lin & Carley, 1993). The performance characteristics of simulated organizations are under certain conditions

comparable to the performance characteristics observed in the real world (Lin & Carley, 1993).

5. Researchers have also shown that organizational performance is affected by factors such as organizational design (Houskisson & Galbraith, 1985; Kumar, Ow, & Prietula, 1993; Lawrence & Lorsch, 1967), task environment (Drazin & Van de Ven, 1985), and stress (Anderson, 1977). Only a systematic examination of these factors on organizations can address the issue of what really constitutes organizational performance. By using simulation, we can get insight into these important factors with less cost than conducting human experiments or field studies. Once the dominant factors are examined, human experiments or field studies can be done to test the theoretical results.

The measures of organizational design evaluated in this chapter are listed in Table 6.1. The theoretical evaluation will be carried out by examining the interrelationships among these measures given a set of stylized organizational designs, and by examining the ability of these measures to predict the performance of computer-simulated organizations (Lin & Carley, 1992).

This chapter is organized as follows. First, I briefly describe the stylized organizational designs that are of great interest to researchers in organizational study. Next, I interpret the definitions of organizational measures given by their authors, and calculate these measures given the stylized designs. I then examine the interrelationship among these measures. Following that, I evaluate the ability of these measures to predict organi-

TABLE 6.1
Existing Organizational Measures

Name of Measure	Abbreviation	Author
Organizational cost[a]	Cost	Malone (1986)
Organizational cost[a]	Cost	Carley (1991)
Organizational task process efficiency[b]	Effm	Mackenzie (1978)
Graph efficiency[b]	Effk[d]	Krackhardt (this volume)
Organizational hierarchy[c]	Hiem	Mackenzie (1978)
Graph hierarchy[c]	Hiek[d]	Krackhardt (this volume)
Graph connectivity[c]	Conk[d]	Krackhardt (this volume)
Graph least-upper-boundedness[c]	Lubk[d]	Krackhardt (this volume)
Graph E-I index[c]	Eiks[d]	Krackhardt and Stern (1988)
Organizational communication level[c]	Coml	Lin (1994)
Organizational anti-blocking level[c]	Antl	Lin (1994)

[a]The measure is in the category of cost measures.
[b]The measure is in the category of efficiency measures.
[c]The measure is in the category of structure measures.
[d]For the measure, there also exists an adjusted version indicated by applying an "a" to the end of the original abbreviation.

zational performance as given by the simulations. Finally, I discuss the theoretical implications of these results.

ORGANIZATIONAL DESIGN

Measures of organizational design typically focus on either the organizational structure and/or the task decomposition scheme. Some measures, such as those developed by Krackhardt (this volume) and Krackhardt and Stern (1988), focus exclusively on who communicates to, or commands, whom. Following Carley (1991), I refer to this as *organizational structure.* Other measures, such as those developed by Malone (1986), Carley (1991), and Lin and Carley (1992), consider who has access to what resources and what new data, has responsibility for what portion or aspect of the task. Again, following Carley (1991), I refer to this as the *task decomposition scheme.* Clearly, organizational design involves both the organizational structure and the task decomposition scheme. Indeed, it has been argued that the organizational structure and the task decomposition scheme must be codesigned. That is, some organizational structures are incompatible with some task decomposition schemes (Mackenzie, 1978). Clearly, organizational structure and task decomposition scheme may work together to affect performance (Mackenzie, 1978). Nevertheless, from a purely structural perspective, organizational structures and task decomposition schemes can be measured separately. From a graphical vantage, organizational structure is simply the set of decision-making units (people or groups) represented as circles and the lines (of communication or commands) between them. The task decomposition scheme is simply the set of decision-making units (represented as circles), the set of resources/tasks-/raw information (represented as boxes), and the lines (of control) between decision-making units and resources.

A set of organizational structures is defined. At least five stylized organizational structures exist in the literature:

1. Team with voting—a totally decentralized structure in which organizational decision is through majority voting of each member of the organization.

2. Team with a manager—basically a flat hierarchy such that although each analyst examines information and makes a recommendation, the ultimate organizational decision is made by the manager (or team leader).

3. Hierarchy—a multilevel communication structure in which each baseline agent examines information and makes a recommendation to his or her immediate supervisor, who in turn makes a recommendation to the top-level manager, who makes the ultimate organizational decision.

4. Matrix-1—like the hierarchy, a multilevel communication structure, except that some baseline agents can have communication with two managers across divisions (although when the structure is team with voting or team with a manager, there is only one large division) in the organization.

5. Matrix-2[1]—like matrix-1, except that each baseline agent has two communication links with two middle managers across divisions.

A detailed description of these organizational structures can be found in Lin and Carley (1992).

Similarly, a set of task decomposition schemes can be defined. At least six stylized task decomposition schemes have appeared in the literature:

1. Segregated-1[2]—each baseline agent has access to one task component.
2. Segregated-2—similar to segregated-1; the only difference is that each baseline agent now has access to a different task component usually not within own division.
3. Overlapped-1—each baseline agent has access to two task components, with one task components being overlapped with another baseline agent.
4. Overlapped-2—each baseline agent has access to three task components, with two task components being overlapped with another baseline agent.
5. Blocked—each baseline agent has access to three task components, but usually each three agents within the same division have the same three task components.
6. Distributed—each baseline agent has access to three task components, usually across different divisions.

A detailed description of these task decomposition schemes can be found in Lin and Carley (1992).

I created a set of organizational designs by combining all five structures with all six task decomposition schemes. This resulted in 30 organizational designs (Figs. 6.1–6.5).

Clearly, there are aspects of organizational design that are not captured by these organizational designs, nor are they captured by most mathematical measures. Many of these factors, such as organizational culture, attitude of personnel, rules, and procedures, although appearing to affect

---

[1]Matrix-2 structure is the same as matrix structure in Lin and Carley (1992).

[2]Segregated-1 is the same as segregated, and overlapped-1 is the same as overlapped in Lin and Carley (1992).

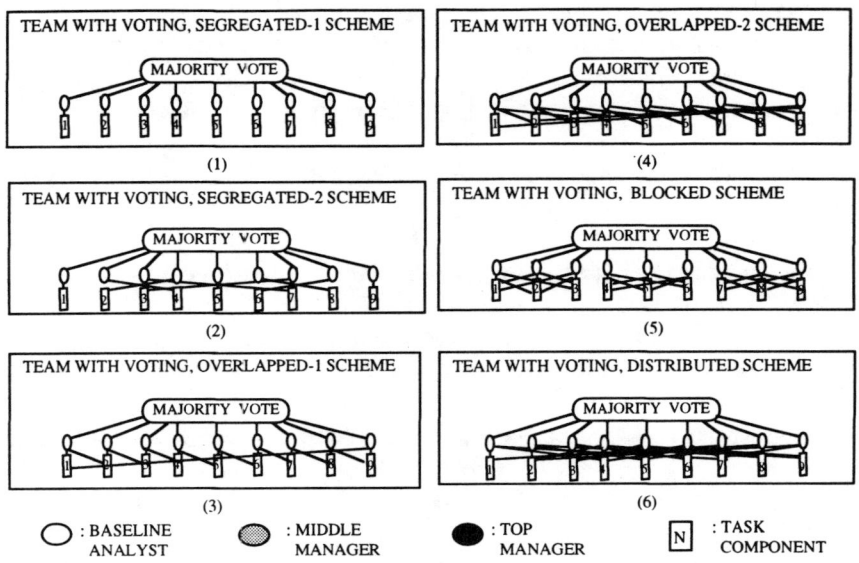

FIG. 6.1. Organizational forms related with team with voting structure.

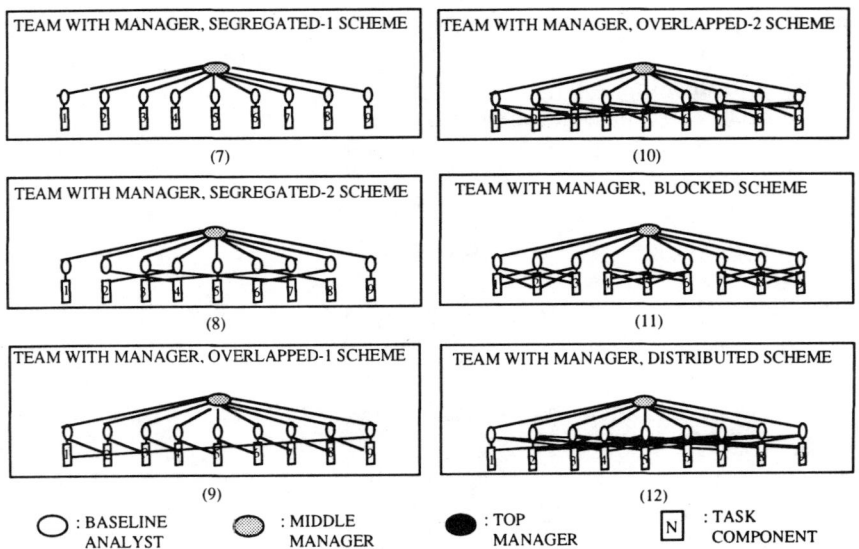

FIG. 6.2. Organizational forms related with team with a manager structure.

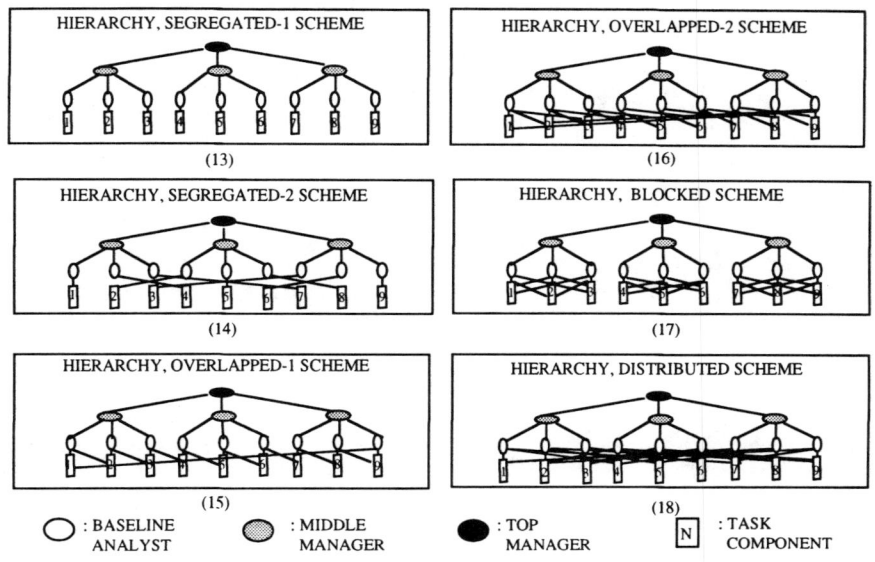

FIG. 6.3. Organizational forms related with hierarchy structure.

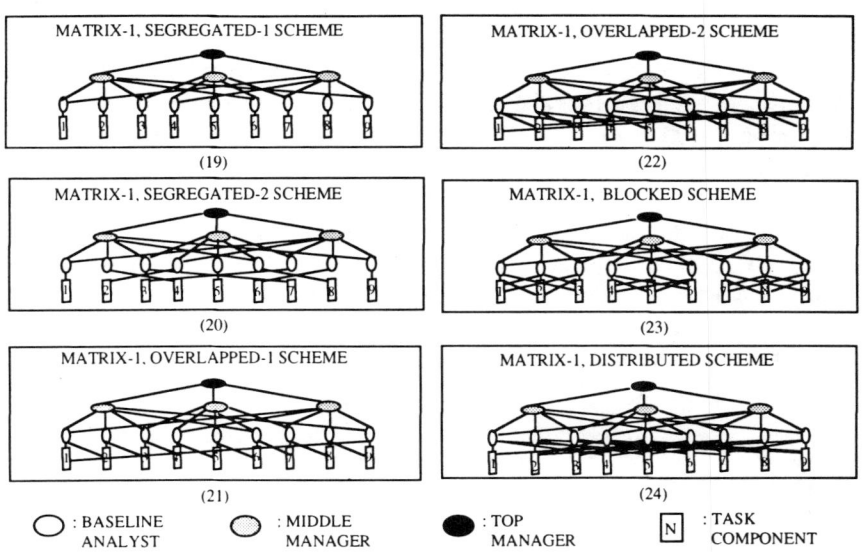

FIG. 6.4. Organizational forms related with matrix-1 structure.

119

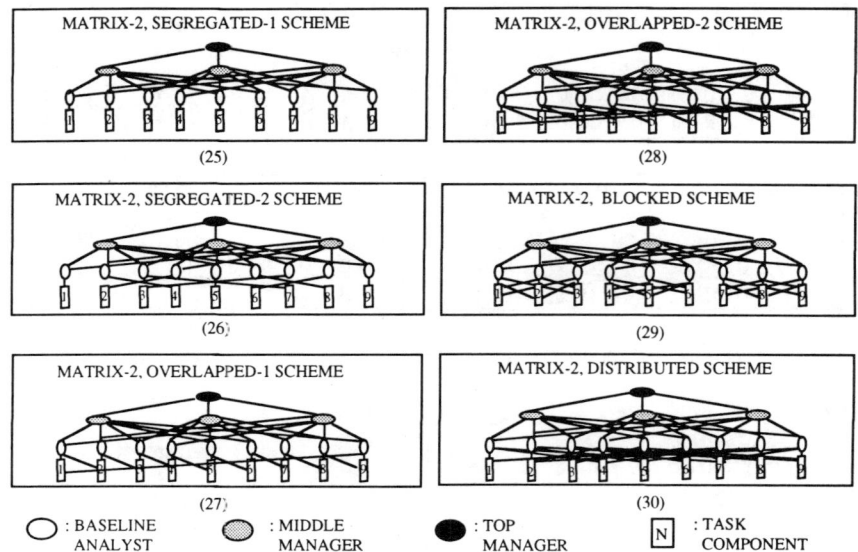

FIG. 6.5.   Organizational forms related with matrix-2 structure.

performance, are also highly related to the organizational structure and the task decomposition. Thus, the source of relationship between these factors and performance is unclear. More to the point for this analysis, such factors are not considered by the measures we wish to contrast. One such factor that has been shown to have a major impact on performance is training (Hammond, 1973; Perrow, 1984; Shrivastava, 1987). In my analysis, I examine three training scenarios:

1. Untrained—each agent in the organization makes decisions by basically guessing.
2. Experientially trained—each agent in the organization makes decisions by referring to historical experience.
3. Operationally trained—each agent in the organization makes decisions by using standard operating procedure.

A detailed description of these training scenarios can be found in Lin and Carley (1992).

MEASURES OF ORGANIZATIONAL DESIGN: DEFINITIONS AND CALCULATIONS

The measures I evaluate can be categorized into three categories: cost measures, efficiency measures, and structure measures (see Table 6.1). Cost measures include organizational cost (Carley, 1991; Malone, 1986); efficiency measures include organizational task process efficiency (Mackenzie, 1978) and graph efficiency (Krackhardt, this volume and); structure measures include organizational hierarchy (Mackenzie, 1978), graph hierarchy, graph connectivity, graph least-Upper-boundness (Krackhardt, this volume), graph E-I index (Krackhardt & Stern, 1988), organizational communication level (Lin, 1994), and organizational anti-blocking level (Lin, 1994). Note that these measures are only about structures and task decomposition scheme of organizational design. The definitions and calculations of the above measures are described according to their categories as follows.

Cost Measures

The organizational cost measure (cost) created by Carley is defined as the summation of information processing cost (pieces of information being processed and reported) and communication cost (Carley, 1991), which is shown as:

$$O_C = I_C + C_C \qquad (1)$$

where O_C is the organizational cost, I_C is the information-processing cost, which can be thought of as total number of pieces of information being processed by the organization, and C_C is the communication cost, which can be thought of as total number of communication links installed in the organization.

Malone (1986) defined organizational cost measure (cost) as the summation of production cost, coordination cost, and vulnerability cost, with the last meaning the cost due to failures at certain positions in the organization:

$$O_C = P_C + C_C + V_C \qquad (2)$$

where O_C is the organizational cost, P_C is the total production processing cost, C_C is the total coordination interaction cost, and V_C is the total loss due to failure.

As vulnerability cost is measured in terms of the expectation of such failure, it is not feasible here. With vulnerability cost being discarded, Malone's cost measure is the same as Carley's cost measure.

To illustrate how cost measure is calculated, I list two examples:

1. For an organization with matrix-1 structure and distributed task decomposition scheme [(24) in Fig. 6.4], there are 13 agents in the organization, including 9 baseline analysts, with 6 of them having two communication links with middle managers. Each baseline analyst has access to three pieces of information and reports one decision, with six of

them reporting to two managers, each middle processes five pieces of information and reports one decision, and the top manager processes three pieces of information and reports one decision. So, the total information processing cost is $I_c = 9 \times (3 + 1) + 6 + 3 \times (5 + 1) + 1 \times (3 + 1) = 64$. As 6 of the baseline analysts have two communication links with middle managers, the total communication cost is $C_c = 9 + 6 + 3 = 18$. Thus the organizational cost is $O_c = I_c + C_c = 64 + 18 = 82$.

2. For an organization with matrix-2 structure and overlapped-1 task decomposition scheme [(27) in Fig. 6.5], there are 13 agents in the organization, including 9 baseline analysts, each having two communication links with middle managers. Each baseline analyst has access to two pieces of information and reports decision to two managers, each middle manager processes six pieces of information and report one decision, and the top manager processes three pieces of information and report one decision. So the total information cost is $I_c = 9 \times (2 + 2) + 3 \times (6 + 1) + 1 \times (3 + 1) = 61$. As each baseline analyst has two communication links with middle managers, the total communication cost is $C_c = 9 + 9 + 3 = 21$. Thus, the organizational cost is $O_c = I_c + C_c = 61 + 21 = 82$.

Efficiency Measures

There are two approaches in defining efficiency measures. One is Mackenzie's (1978) and the other is Krackhardt's (this volume). The major difference between the two is that Mackenzie treats efficiency as the percentage of necessary behavior over actual behavior, whereas Krackhardt treats efficiency as the percentage of nonredundant graph connections over maximum nonredundant connections. As Krackhardt's original measures do not consider task decomposition scheme as part of the organization, expansions were made to let the measures be more representative of organizational designs that also include task decomposition schemes.

Mackenzie's organizational task process efficiency measure (Effm) is defined as follows:

$$E_T = m_T / n_T \tag{3}$$

where E_T is the degree of task process efficiency, m_T is the minimum number of interactions necessary to reach the end in the task process, and n_T is the actual number of interactions taken to reach the end of the task process.

The following two examples show how this measure is calculated:

1. For an organization with matrix-2 structure and overlapped-1 task decomposition scheme [(27 in Fig. 6.5], there are 13 agents in the organi-

zation, including 9 baseline analysts, each having two communication links with middle managers. Each baseline analyst has access to two pieces of information and reports one decision to two managers, each middle manager processes six pieces of information and reports one decision, and the top manager processes three pieces of information and reports one decision. So, the actual number of interaction is $n_T = 9 \times (2 + 2) + 3 \times (6 + 1) + 1 \times (3 + 1) = 61$, whereas the minimum number of interactions needed is without the additional interactions by baseline analysts to middle managers and additional access to task information. So, the minimum number of interaction is $m_T = 9 \times (1 + 1) + 3 \times (3 + 1) + 1) + 1 \times (3 + 1) = 34$. Thus, the task process efficiency is $E_T = m_T / n_T = 34/61 = 55.74\%$.

2. For an organization with team with voting structure and overlapped-1 task decomposition scheme [(3) in Fig. 6.1], there are 9 agents in the organization with all of them being baseline analysts, each having access to two pieces of task information and reporting one decision. Thus the actual number of interaction is $n_T = 9 \times (2 + 1) = 27$, and the minimum number of interaction is with the redundant access to the task information by baseline analysts, so $m_T = 9 \times (1 + 1) = 18$. Thus, the degree of task process efficiency is $E_T = m_T / n_T = 18/27 = 66.67\%$.

Krackhardt's original definition of graph efficiency measure (Effk) is given as:

$$G_E = 1 - V / \text{Max} V \tag{4}$$

where G_E is the graph efficiency, N_n is the total number of nodes, V is the number of links in excess of the $N_n - 1$, summed over all components, and $\text{Max} V$ is the maximum number of links in excess of $N_n - 1$ possible, summed over all components.

The following are two examples illustrating the calculation of this measures given stylized designs:

1. For an organization with team with voting structure and any task decomposition scheme [(1)–(6) in Fig. 6.1], there are 9 agents in the organization with all of them being baseline analysts, thus there are $N_n = 9$ nodes. There is no link in access of $N_n - 1 = 8$ nodes, so $V = 0$, with $\text{Max} V = 9 \times 8 - 8 = 64$. Thus the graph efficiency is $G_E = 1 - V / \text{Max} V = 1 - 0 = 100.00\%$.

2. For an organization with hierarchy structure and any task decomposition scheme [(13)–(18) in Fig. 6.3], there are 13 agents in the organization with 9 baseline analysts; thus there are $N_n = 13$ nodes. The number of links in access of $N_n - 1 = 12$ is 0, so $V = 0$, the maximum number of links in

access of $N_n - 1$ or Max$V$ is $9 \times 8 - 8 = 64$. Thus, the graph efficiency is $G_E = 1 - V/\text{Max}V = 1 - 0/64 = 100.00\%$.

As mentioned before, Krackhardt's original definition of graph efficiency measure needs to be expanded to include the aspect of task decomposition scheme. This following is the adjusted Krackhardt's definition of graph efficiency measure (Effka):

$$G_E = 1 - V/\text{Max}V \qquad (5)$$

where G_E is the graph efficiency, N_n is the total number of nodes (including task information), V is the number of links in excess of the $N_n - 1$, summed over all components and Max$V$ is the maximum number of links in excess of $N_n - 1$ possible, summed over all components [i.e., Max$V = (N_a - 1)^2 + N_i \times (N_b - 1)$, where N_a is the number of agents, N_i is the number of pieces of information, and N_b is the number of baseline analysts, $N_n = N_a + N_i$].

The following two examples show how this measure is calculated:

1. For an organization with matrix-1 structure and overlapped-1 task decomposition scheme [(21) in Fig. 6.4], there are $N_a = 13$ agents in the organization with 6 of them having two communication links with middle managers. Of the 13 agents, there are $N_b = 9$ baseline analysts. There are $N_i = 9$ pieces of task information. Each baseline analyst has access to three pieces of information, each middle processes five pieces of information, and the top manager processes three pieces of information. As the number of links in access of $N_n - 1 = N_a + N_i - 1 = 21$ is $V = 12 + 6 + 9 + 9 - 21 = 15$, and the maximum number of links in access of 21 is Max$V = 12 \times 12 + 9 \times 8 = 144 + 72 = 216$. Thus the graph efficiency is $G_E = 1 - V/\text{Max}V = 1 - 15/216 = 201/216 = 93.06\%$.

2. For an organization with team with manager structure and overlapped-2 task decomposition scheme [(10) in Fig. 6.2], there are $N_a = 10$ agents in the organization, of them one manager and $N_b = 9$ baseline analysts. Each baseline analyst has access to three pieces of task information. As the number of links in access of $N_n - 1 = N_a + N_i - 1 = 18$ is $V = 9 + 9 + 9 + 9 - 18 = 18$, and the maximum number of links in access of 21 is Max$V = 9 \times 9 + 9 \times 8 = 153$. Thus the graph efficiency is $G_E = 1 - V/\text{Max}V = 1 - 18/153 = 135/153 = 88.23\%$.

Structure Measures

Organizational structure is measured by features such as organizational degree of hierarchy, organizational connectivity, organizational least-upper-boundedness, and organizational communication level. There are three main methods in defining these measures: Mackenzie's (1978), Krack-hardt's (this volume, Krackhardt & Stern, 1988), and Lin's (1994). They include measures such as Mackenzie's degree of hierarchy (Hiem), Krack-hardt's degree of graph hierarchy (Hiek), Krackhardt's graph connectivity (Conk), Krackhardt's graph least-upper-boundedness (Lubk), Krackhardt and Stern's Graph E-I index (Eiks), Lin's communication level (Coml), and Lin's anti-blocking level (Antl). As Krackhardt's original measures do not consider task decomposition scheme as part of the organization, I expanded the definitions to include task decomposition schemes so that these measures are more meaningful for organizational designs that also include task decomposition schemes.

Mackenzie's degree of hierarchy measure (Hiem) looks at the redundancy of organizational structure and is defined as follows:

$$H = 1 - (U_T + C + U) / (T + U_T) \tag{6}$$

where H is degree of hierarchy, T is total number of non-untimely behaviors, C is number of cousin behavior, which is represented by the relationship between two agents of the same level, U is number of uncle-nephew behaviors, which is represented by the relationship of two agents of different levels across different divisions, and U_T is number of behaviors that are redundant or untimely.

The following two examples show the calculation of this measure:

1. For an organization with team with voting structure and distributed task decomposition scheme [(6) in Fig. 6.1], there is no cousin relationship, nor uncle–nephew behavior, so $C = 0$ and $U = 0$. The number of behaviors that are redundant is the redundant information access behavior, so $U_t = 9 \times 2 = 18$. The total number of nonredundant behavior is $T = 9 \times (1 + 1)$, with each agent reporting one decision. Thus the degree of hierarchy is $H = 1 - (0 + 0 + 18) / (18 + 18) = 1 - 1/2 = 50\%$.

2. For an organization with matrix-2 structure and overlapped-2 task decomposition scheme [(28) in Fig. 6.5], there are 9 uncle–nephew relationships but no cousin relationship, so, $U = 9$, $C = 0$. The number of behaviors that are redundant is the redundant information access behavior and uncle–nephew behavior, so $U_t = 9 \times 2 + 9 \times 1 + 3 \times 3 = 36$. And the total number of nonredundant behavior includes minimum necessary information access and reporting, so $T = 9 \times (1 + 1) + 3 \times (3 + 1) + 1 \times (3 + 1) = 34$. Thus, degree of hierarchy is $H = 1 - (9 + 36) / (34 + 36) = 35.71\%$.

Krackhardt's original definition of graph hierarchy measure (Hiek) focused on the density of reciprocal links in a graph setting and is:

$$G_H = 1 - V / \text{Max}V \qquad (7)$$

where G_H is the degree of graph hierarchy, V is the number of pairs of points in D_r (reachability of graph D) where P_i is linked to P_j and P_j is linked to P_i, Max$V$ is the number of pairs of points in D_r where P_i is linked to P_j or P_j is linked to P_i, and Max$V = N \times (N - 1) / 2$, where N is the number of agents.

The following two examples show the calculation of this measure:

1. For an organization with team with voting structure and any task decomposition scheme [(1)–(6) in Fig. 6.1], there are 9 agents of which there are no two linked, so $V = 0$ and Max$V = 9 \times 8/2 = 36$. The degree of hierarchy is $G_h = 1 - V / \text{Max}V = 1 - 0/36 = 100.00\%$.

2. For an organization with hierarchy structure and any task decomposition scheme [(13)–(18) in Fig. 6.3], there are 13 agents, of which there are $V = 12$ links and Max$V = 13 \times 12/2 = 78$. The degree of hierarchy is $G_h = 1 - V/\text{Max}V = 1 - 12/78 = 66/78 = 84.61\%$.

Krackhardt's original definition of graph connectivity measure (Conk) looked at the density of connections among organizational nodes in a graph setting and is defined as follows:

$$G_C = 1 - V / \text{Max}V \qquad (8)$$

where G_C is the graph connectivity, V is the number of pairs of points that are not mutually reachable, and Max$V$ is the maximum number of violations of the total number of pairs of points.

Two examples show the calculation of this measure:

1. For an organization with team with voting structure and any task decomposition scheme [(1)–(6) in Fig. 6.1], there are 9 agents of which the number of pairs that are mutually reachable is 0, so $V = 9 \times 8 / 2 = 36$ and Max$V = 9 \times 8 / 2 = 36$. Thus the graph connectivity is $G_c = 1 - V / \text{Max}V = 1 - 1 = 0.00\%$.

2. For an organization with team with manager structure and any task decomposition scheme [(7)–(12) in Fig. 6.2], there are 10 agents, of which all pairs are mutually reachable, so $V = 0$ and Max$V = 10 \times 9 / 2 = 45$. The graph connectivity is $G_c = 1 - V / \text{Max}V = 1 - 0/45 = 100.00\%$.

Krackhardt's original definition of graph least-upper-boundedness measure (Lubk) also looks at the connections among organizational nodes in a graph setting but with emphasis on least upper bound and is defined as follows:

$$\text{LUB} = 1 - V / \text{Max}V \qquad (9)$$

where LUB is the degree of least-upper-boundedness, V is the number of pairs of points that have no least upper bound in each component summed across all components, and $\text{Max}V$ is the maximum number of pairs of points that could possibly have no LUB for each component summed across all components; $\text{Max}V = (N - 1) \times (N - 2) / 2$, where N is the number of agents.

The following are two examples of how this measure is calculated:

1. For an organization with team with manager structure and any task decomposition scheme [(7)–(12) in Fig. 6.2], there are 10 agents. The number of pairs that have no least upper bound is $V = 36 - 9 = 27$; $\text{Max}V = (10 - 1) \times (9 - 1) / 2 = 36$. The degree of least-upper-boundedness is $\text{LUB} = 1 - V / \text{Max}V = 9 / 36 = 25.00\%$.

2. For an organization with matrix-1 structure and any task decomposition scheme [(19)–(24) in Fig. 6.4], there are 13 agents. The number of pairs of agents that have no least upper bound is $V = (13 - 1) \times (12 - 1) / 2 - 12 - 6 = 48$, and $\text{Max}V = (13 - 1) \times (12 - 1) / 2 = 66$. Thus, $\text{LUB} = 1 - V / \text{Max}V = 1 - 48 / 66 = 18 / 66 = 27.27\%$.

Krackhardt and Stern's original definition of graph E-I index (Eiks) looks at the ratio of interdivisional connections over intradivisional connections and is defined as follows:

$$E-I = (EL - IL) / (EL + IL) \tag{10}$$

where E-I is the E-I index of the organization, EL is the number of external communication links, which is across divisions, and IL is the number of internal communication links, which does not cross divisions.

I list two examples showing the calculation of this measure:

1. For an organization with matrix-2 structure and any task decomposition scheme [(24)–(30) in Fig. 6.5], there are $EL = 9$ external communication links and $IL = 12$ internal links. Thus $E-I = (9 - 12) / (9 + 12) = -1 / 4 = -0.25$.

2. For an organization with team with voting structure and any task decomposition scheme [(1)–(6) in Fig. 6.1], $EL = 0$ and $IL = 9$. Thus $E-I = (0 - 9) / (0 + 9) = -1.00$.

As previously mentioned, Krackhardt's measures also need expansions to be suitable for organizational designs that include task decomposition scheme. The adjusted definition of Krackhardt's graph hierarchy measure (Hieka) is defined as follows:

$$G_{\text{H}} = 1 - V / \text{Max}V \tag{11}$$

where G_H is the degree of graph hierarchy, V is the number of pairs of points in D_r (reachability of graph D) where P_i is linked to P_j and P_j is linked to P_i, and $Max V$ is the number of pairs of points in D_r where P_i is linked to P_j or P_j is linked to P_i. The calculation is $Max V = N_a \times (N_a - 1) / 2$, where N_a is the number of agents.

The following two examples illustrate how this measure is calculated, given the stylized designs:

1. For an organization with team with voting structure and distributed task decomposition scheme [(6) in Fig. 6.1], there are 9 agents plus 9 pieces of task information, of which there is no pair that is reciprocally linked, so $V = 0$, and $Max V = 10 \times 9 / 2 = 45$. Thus, the degree of hierarchy is $G_H = 1 - V / Max V = 1 - 0 / 45 = 100.00\%$.

2. For an organization with hierarchy structure and blocked task decomposition scheme [(17) in Fig. 6.3], there are 13 agents, and 9 pieces of task information, of which there are $V = 12$ reciprocal links. And $Msx V = 13 \times 12 / 2 = 78$. The degree of hierarchy is $G_H = 1 - V / Max V = 1 - 12 \ 78 = 84.61\%$.

The adjusted definition of Krackhardt's graph connectivity measure (Conka) is defined as follows:

$$G_C = 1 - V / Max V \tag{12}$$

where G_C is graph connectivity, V is the number of pairs of points that are not mutually reachable, and $Max V$ is the the maximum number of violations of the total number of pairs of points, which is calculated as $Max V = N_a \times (N_a - 1) / 2 + N_i \times N_b$, where N_a is the number of agents, N_i is the number of pieces of information, and N_b is the number of baseline agents, or analysts.

The following two examples illustrate the calculation of this measure:

1. For an organization with team with voting structure and blocked task decomposition scheme [(5) in Fig. 6.1], there are 9 agents and 10 pieces of information, of which the number of pairs that are mutually reachable is 9. Also, $Max V = 9 \times 8 / 2 + 9 \times 9 = 117$, so $V = 117 - 9 = 108$. Thus the graph connectivity is $G_c = 1 - V / Max V = 1 - 108 \ / 117 = 9 / 117 = 7.69\%$.

2. For an organization with team with manager structure and segregated-1 task decomposition scheme [(7) in Fig. 6.2], there are 10 agents and 9 pieces of task information, of which all are mutually reachable, so $V = 0$ and $Max V = 10 \times 9 / 2 + 9 \times 9 = 126$. Thus the graph connectivity is $G_c = 1 - V / Max V = 1 - 0 \ / 126 = 100.00\%$.

The adjusted definition of Krackhardt's graph least-upper-boundedness measure (Lubka) is as follows:

$$LUB = 1 - V / \text{Max}V \qquad (13)$$

where LUB is the degree of least-upper-boundedness, V is the number of pairs of points that have no least upper bound in each component summed across all components, and $\text{Max}V$ is the maximum number of pairs of points that could possibly have no LUB for each component summed across all components; $\text{Max}V = (N_a - 1)(N_a - 2) / 2 + N_i \times N_b$, where N_a, N_i, and N_b are defined as previously in Equation 9.

Two examples are listed as follows to illustrate the calculation of this measure:

1. For an organization with team with manager structure and overlapped-2 task decomposition scheme [(10) in Fig. 6.2], there are 10 agents and 9 pieces of task information. The number of pairs that have least upper   bound   is $9 + 9 \times 3 = 36$,   and $\text{Max}V = 9 \times 8 / 2 + 9 \times 9 = 117$. So $V = \text{Max}V - 36 = 81$. Thus, the degree of least-upper-boundedness is LUB $= 1 - V / \text{Max}V = 1 - 81 / 117 = 36 / 117 = 30.77\%$.

2. For an organization with matrix-1 structure and overlapped-1 task decomposition scheme [(21) in Fig. 6.4], there are 13 agents and 9 pieces of task information. The number of pairs that have least upper bound is $12 + 6 + 18 = 36$,   and $\text{Max}V = 12 \times 11 / 2 + 9 \times 9 = 147$.   So $V = 147 - 36 = 111$.   Thus,   LUB $= 1 - V / \text{Max}V = 1 - 111 / 147 = 36 / 147 = 24.49\%$.

The adjusted definition of Krackhardt and Stern's definition of graph E-I index (Eiksa) is listed as follows:

$$E\text{-}I = (EL - IL) / (EL + IL) \qquad (14)$$

where E-I is the E-I index of the organization, EL is the number of external links, across divisions, and IL is the number of internal links, which does not cross divisions.

The following two examples show the calculation of this measure:

1. For an organization with matrix-2 structure and blocked task decomposition   scheme   [(29)   in   Fig.   6.5],   there   are EL $= 9 + 0 = 9$ external links and IL $= 12 + 27 = 39$ internal links. Thus E-I $= (9 - 39) / (9 + 39) = -30 / 48 = -0.63$.
2. For an organization with team with voting structure and overlapped-1 task decomposition scheme [(3) in Fig. 6.1],

EL = 0 + 3 = 3 and IL = 9 + 15. Thus E-I = (3 − 15) / (3 + 15) = − 12 / 18 = − 0.67.

The definition of Lin's organizational communication level measure (Coml) focuses on the density of communication links within an organization and is:

$$COML = CL / MCL \tag{15}$$

where COML is the communication level, CL is the actual communication links in the organization, and MCL is the maximum possible communication links in the organization; $MCL = N_a \times (N_a - 1) / 2$, where N_a is the number of agents in the organization.

The following two examples show how this measure is calculated, given the stylized designs:

1. For an organization with hierarchy structure and segregated-2 task decomposition scheme [(14) in Fig. 6.3], there are total CL = 12 communication links, and the maximum number of possible communication links is MCL = 13 × 12 / 2 = 78. Thus, the communication level COML = CL / MCL = 12 / 78 = 15.38%.

2. For an organization with team with voting structure and overlapped-1 task decomposition scheme [(3) in Fig. 6.1], there are CL = 0 communication links, and the maximum number of possible communication links is MCL = 9 × 8 / 2 = 36. Thus the communication level COML = CL / MCL = 0.00%.

The definition of Lin's organizational anti-blocking level measure (Antl) looks at the density of information access linkages across divisions within the organization and is:

$$ABLL = N_t \times N_d / MN_t \times MN_b \tag{16}$$

where ABLL is the anti-blocking level of task decomposition scheme, N_t is the number of access links to task from each analyst, N_d is the average number of division accessed by each analyst, MN_t is the maximum possible number of access links to task from each analyst (as 3 here), and MN_b is the maximum average number of division accessed by each analyst (as 3 here).

The following two examples illustrate the calculation of this measure:

1. For an organization with matrix-1 structure and blocked task decomposition scheme [(23) in Fig. 6.4], each baseline analyst has access to three pieces of task information, but all within division, so $N_t = 3$ and $N_d = 1$. Thus ABLL = 3 × 1 / (3 × 3) = 1 / 3 = 33.33%.

2. For an organization with matrix-1 structure and distributed task decomposition scheme [(24) in Fig. 6.4], each baseline analyst has access to three pieces of task information, and each analyst has access across three divisions, so $N_t = 3$ and $N_d = 3$. Thus, ABLL = $3 \times 3 / (3 \times 3)$ = 100.00%.

INTERRELATIONSHIP: AN ANALYSIS

Each of these measures captures a different aspect of organizational design. To examine the interrelationship of these measures, I did a Pearson correlation analysis. The correlations are in Table 6.2. In Table 6.2, we see that many of the organizational measures are highly correlated. This suggests that these measures of organizational design, despite being derived from different perspectives, are strongly interrelated.

The fact that these measures of organizational design are highly interrelated suggests that the different perspectives are similar and that we may only need to consider a few of them for theoretical evaluation. The following step is to categorize these measures into several major groups.

Using cluster analysis on the Pearson correlations, these measures are categorized (Fig. 6.6). At the 0.75 level, seven major categories appear. One measure was chosen as a representative of each group. The seven groups are:

1. Cost — organizational cost (Carley, Malone), representing also Eiks (graph E-I index by Krackhardt and Stern), Coml (communication level by Lin), Lubk (graph least-upper-boundedness by Krackhardt), Conk (graph connectivity by Krackhardt), and Conka (graph connectivity by Krackhardt, adjusted).
2. Effk — graph efficiency (Krackhardt).
3. Hiem — organizational hierarchy (Mackenzie), representing also Effka (graph efficiency by Krackhardt, adjusted) and Effm (organizational efficiency by Mackenzie).
4. Hieka — graph hierarchy (Krackhardt, adjusted), representing also Hiek (graph hierarchy by Krackhardt).
5. Lubka — graph least-upper-boundedness (Krackhardt, adjusted).
6. Eiksa — graph E-I index (Krackhardt and Stern, adjusted).
7. Antl — organizational anti-blocking level (Lin).

The representative measures were chosen without particular order. In the remaining analysis, I focus on these seven measures.

TABLE 6.2
Pearson Correlation Between Organizational Measures

	Cost	Effm	Ettk	Ettka	Hiem	Hiek	Hieka	Conk	Conka	Lubk	Lubka	Eiks	Eiksa	Coml
Cost	1.00													
Effm	−0.61	1.00												
Effk	−0.82	0.53	1.00											
Effka	−0.32	0.91	0.27	1.00										
Hiem	−0.76	0.92	0.70	0.71	1.00									
Hiek	−0.84	0.22	0.65	−0.08	0.41	1.00								
Hieka	−0.84	0.22	0.65	−0.08	0.41	1.00	1.00							
Conk	0.70	−0.03	−0.35	0.20	−0.16	−0.91	−0.91	1.00						
Conka	0.71	−0.08	−0.35	0.14	−0.20	−0.91	−0.91	0.99	1.00					
Lubk	0.82	−0.21	−0.62	0.08	−0.39	−0.99	−0.99	0.92	0.92	1.00				
Lubka	0.73	−0.87	−0.51	−0.81	−0.77	−0.47	−0.47	0.39	0.43	0.47	1.00			
Eiks	0.82	−0.46	−0.88	−0.12	−0.75	−0.70	−0.70	0.41	0.41	0.67	0.37	1.00		
Eiksa	0.24	−0.23	−0.31	−0.14	−0.30	−0.10	−0.10	−0.05	−0.05	0.09	0.13	0.32	1.00	
Coml	0.84	−0.22	−0.65	0.08	−0.41	−1.00	−1.00	0.91	0.91	0.99	0.47	0.70	0.10	1.00
Antl	0.30	−0.64	−0.16	−0.72	−0.46	−0.00	−0.00	0.00	0.03	0.00	0.69	0.00	0.48	0.00

Note: n (number of pairs) = 30 in each cell.

TREE DIAGRAM

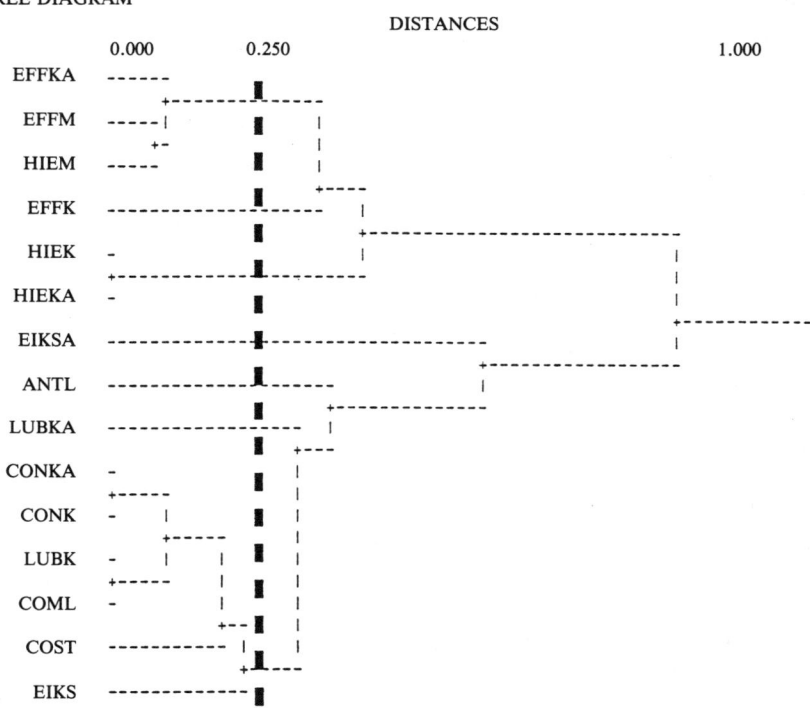

FIG. 6.6. Cluster analysis of all organizational measures based on their definitions. Distance metric is 1-Pearson correlation coefficient single linkage method (nearest neighbor). Number of observations is 30.

PERFORMANCE PREDICTING

Model Description

The organizations simulated by Lin and Carley (1992) were faced with a limited-choice task in which they made decision choices under stress from limited alternatives, according to information they had through organizational communication processes. Choice tasks were selected, as they are very common in situations such as policymaking, price setting, planning, and a host of other similar things (Allison, 1971; March & Olsen, 1976; Shull, Delbecq, & Cummings, 1970).

The performances of organizations were measures of how well the organizations' decision choices match the true state of the task environment. In the organizational literature, organizational performance has also been measured by organizational effectiveness (Mackenzie, 1978; Pfeffer & Salancik, 1978) and organizational efficiency (Mackenzie, 1978; Scott, 1987). In most cases, those three measures can be defined in terms of each other.

Organizations are often affected by stresses. In examining organizational performance it is important to consider two sources of stress: external hostile conditions (or maydays, caused by hostile task environment) and internal suboptimal operating conditions (or murphies, caused by suboptimal operating condition within organizational design). I treat type I errors (make decisions that the aircraft is hostile but in fact it is friendly) and type II errors (make decisions that the aircraft is friendly but in fact it is hostile) with equal weight; thus a study of a friendly external situation would be symmetrical to the study of a hostile external situation. I studied five types of murphies:

1. Missing information—a piece of incoming information for a particular problem was not available.
2. Incorrect information—a piece of incoming information was erroneous.
3. Agent unavailability—an analyst was not available to help the organization solve the problem and so did not report his or her decision to the manager.
4. Communication channel breakdown—an analyst was unable to report to a superior because the communication channel was unavailable.
5. Agent turnover—an analyst left the organization and was replaced by a new analyst.

For each type of murphy, the number of simultaneous murphies ranged from zero to three.

The task environment was defined as the collection of all problems that the organization could face. It can vary on a large number of dimensions (in this model, the number of task components was fixed at nine). Two aspects of task environment that have received little attention are decomposability and biasness. *Task decomposability* measures the interrelationships among components of task environment. A task environment is decomposable if there are no complex interactions among components that need to be understood in order to solve a problem, and nondecomposable if otherwise. *Task environment biasness* measures the distribution of all possible outcomes. A task environment is unbiased if all the possible outcomes are equally likely to occur, and biased if otherwise. Based on these two manipulations, I examined four different task environments. They are: (a) biased decomposable, (b) unbiased decomposable, (c) biased nondecomposable, and (d) unbiased nondecomposable. A detailed description of the task environment characteristics can be found in Lin and Carley (1992).

Another important aspect of the model, the organizational design, included five organizational structures, six task decomposition schemes, and three training scenarios, as previously described.

Method

The organizations were simulated using a computer simulation testbed built in C within the VAX/VMS computer system. Using this testbed, it was possible to systematically alter task environments (four types), organizational structures (five types), task decomposition schemes (six types), and training scenarios (three types). A total of 360 organizational types was examined (Table 6.3). The performance of each organizational type was calculated as the percentage of correct decisions made by the organization over 19,683 problems, which was the number of problems that the organizations could face. Each type was simulated under optimal operating conditions (no murphies), and under each of the internal suboptimal conditions (one or more murphies). There were 20 situations (four levels of severity, including "no" murphies, and five types of murphies). Altogether, I examined 360 organizational types by 20 situations, for a total of $360 \times 20 = 7,200$ cases.

This simulation experiment is a combination of numerical estimation (as I consider all possible problems the organization can face—all 19,683) and Monte Carlo analysis (as for each organization, the location of each murphy is randomly chosen in each problem).

Performance Prediction: Correlation Analysis

The predictability of measures of organizational design is tested by contrasting how well the seven representative measures (see Fig. 6.6) predict organizational performance. Using both correlation analysis and stepwise regression analysis, the relation between measure's value for each organization and the performance of each organization across all 7,200 organizational cases was examined. These analyses are done both overall and

TABLE 6.3
Summary of the Factors Examined in the Computer Simulation Model

Major Factor	Subcomponent
Organizational design (90 types)	5 Structures 6 Task decomposition schemes 3 Training Scenarios
Task environments (4 types)	4 Task environments
Internal situations (20 situations)	5 Internal stress (murphy) types 4 Levels of severity
	7,200 total cases[a]

[a]A case is a combination of each aspect of all subcomponents.

controlling for task environments, training scenarios, external conditions, and internal operating conditions.

In the correlation analysis, I examined the magnitude and direction aspects of the Pearson correlations (between predicted performance by measures and performance from simulations).

Across All Task Environments

The correlation across all task environments is shown in Table 6.4. The result shows that no measure of organizational design is a good indicator of organizational performance across different training scenarios, external conditions, and internal conditions, when considering the magnitudes and directions of correlations, (*good indicator* means that the absolute values of the Pearson correlations are consistently greater than .100 and that the signs of the Pearson correlations are consistently of the same direction across specified conditions). However, this pattern changes under different training scenarios.

Experientially Trained. Under experiential training, still no measure of organizational design seems to be a good indicator of performance across different external conditions and internal conditions, when considering the magnitudes and directions of correlations. However, under average external conditions, Hieka becomes a fairly good indicator of performance across different internal conditions. Under hostile external condition, Cost, Effk, Hiem, and Eiksa become good indicators of performance across different internal conditions, when considering the magnitudes and directions of correlations.

Operationally Trained. Under operational training, no measure of organizational design seems to be a good indicator of performance across different external conditions and internal conditions, when considering the magnitudes and directions of correlations. Under average external condition, still no measure is a good indicator of performance across different internal conditions. However, under hostile external conditions, all measures of organizational design—Cost, Effk, Hiem, Lubka, Eiksa, and Antl—become good indicators of performance across different internal conditions, when considering the magnitudes and directions of correlations.

Biased Decomposable Task Environment

The correlation when facing a biased decomposable task environment is shown in Table 6.5. The results show that no measure of organizational design seems to be a good indicator of organizational performance across different training scenarios, external conditions, and internal conditions,

TABLE 6.4
Correlation of Major Organizational Measures with Organizational Performance Across All Task Environments

| | Experientially Trained | | | | | | Operationally Trained | | | | | |
| | Average | | | Hostile | | | Average | | | Hostile | | |
	All	Opt	Sub	All	Opt	Sub	All	Opt	Sub	All	Opt	Sub
Cost	-0.096	-0.147	-0.079	0.149	0.266	0.137	0.035	-0.013	0.057	0.163	0.157	0.167
Effk	0.032	0.048	0.026	-0.114	-0.219	-0.101	-0.043	-0.012	-0.058	-0.155	-0.151	-0.158
Hiem	-0.024	0.008	-0.036	-0.126	-0.216	-0.117	-0.054	0.010	-0.085	-0.194	-0.168	-0.205
Hieka	0.191	0.239	0.176	-0.048	-0.087	-0.044	-0.016	0.003	-0.024	-0.099	-0.107	-0.097
Lubka	0.007	-0.027	0.019	0.049	0.140	0.035	0.054	-0.016	0.088	0.172	0.137	0.188
Eiksa	0.016	0.009	0.018	0.124	0.162	0.125	0.060	0.052	0.065	0.134	0.142	0.132
Antl	0.081	0.059	0.089	0.085	0.140	0.080	0.075	0.022	0.101	0.170	0.144	0.182

Note. Average—average (across all) external condition; Hostile—hostile external condition (maydays); All—all internal condition; Opt—optimal internal condition; Sub—suboptimal internal condition (murphies); n—number of pairs of cases for correlation, with $n = 2,400$ under all internal condition, $n = 600$ under optimal internal condition, $n = 1,800$ under suboptimal internal condition.

TABLE 6.5
Correlation of Major Organizational Measures with Organizational Performance When Facing Biased Decomposable Task Environment

	Experientially Trained						Operationally Trained					
	Average			Hostile			Average			Hostile		
	All	Opt	Sub	All	Opt	Sub	All	Opt	Sub	All	Opt	Sub
Cost	0.271	0.532	0.218	-0.133	0.193	-0.162	0.228	0.808	0.098	0.511	0.778	0.446
Effk	-0.178	-0.380	-0.136	0.075	-0.183	0.093	-0.199	-0.676	-0.092	-0.458	-0.661	-0.410
Hiem	-0.274	-0.438	-0.243	0.042	-0.364	0.060	-0.276	-0.816	-0.145	-0.587	-0.816	-0.535
Hieka	-0.091	-0.376	-0.028	0.189	0.236	0.217	-0.134	-0.565	-0.037	-0.304	-0.498	-0.255
Lubka	0.378	0.679	0.318	-0.132	0.242	-0.162	0.242	0.624	0.158	0.539	0.712	0.502
Eiksa	0.248	0.335	0.233	0.007	0.036	0.008	0.185	0.471	0.122	0.334	0.476	0.301
Antl	0.272	0.736	0.470	0.170	0.259	-0.058	0.326	0.503	0.213	0.348	0.620	0.461

Note. Average—average (across all) external condition; Hostile—hostile external condition (maydays); All—all internal condition; Opt—optimal internal condition; Sub—suboptimal internal condition (murphies); n—number of pairs of cases for correlation, with $n = 600$ under all internal condition, $n = 150$ under optimal internal condition, $n = 450$ under suboptimal internal condition.

when considering the magnitudes and directions of correlations. Again, this pattern changes under different training scenarios.

Experientially Trained. Under experiential training, still no measure of organizational design seems to be a good indicator of performance across different external conditions and internal conditions, when considering the magnitudes and directions of correlations. However, under average external conditions, all measures of organizational design—Cost, Effk, Hiem, Hieka, Lubka, Eiksa, and Lubka—become good indicators of performance across different internal conditions. Under hostile external conditions, only Hieka becomes a good indicator of performance across different internal conditions, when considering the magnitudes and directions of correlations.

Operationally Trained. Under operational training, all measures of organizational design—Cost, Effk, Hieka, Lubka, Eiksa, and Antl—seem to be fairly good indicators of performance across different external conditions and internal conditions, when considering the magnitudes and directions of correlations. This patterns remains the same under average external condition or hostile external condition.

Unbiased Decomposable Task Environment

The Pearson correlation when facing an unbiased decomposable task environment is shown in Table 6.6. The results show that no measure is a good indicator of organizational performance across different training scenarios, external conditions, and internal conditions, when considering the magnitudes and directions of correlations. Again, this pattern changes under different training scenarios.

Experientially Trained. Under experiential training, still no measure of organizational design seems to be a good indicator of performance across different external conditions and internal conditions, when considering the magnitudes and directions of correlations. However, under average external conditions, Cost, Effk, Hiem, Hieka, and Lubka become good indicators of performance across different internal conditions. Under hostile external conditions, Cost, Effk, Hiem, Lubka, Eiksa, and Antl become good indicators of performance across different internal conditions, when considering the magnitudes and directions of correlations.

Operationally Trained. Under operational training, no measure of organizational design seems to be a good indicator of performance across different external conditions and internal conditions, when considering the magnitudes and directions of correlations. Under average external condition, Cost, Effk, Hiem, and Hieka become good indicators of performance across

TABLE 6.6
Correlation of Major Organizational Measures with Organizational Performance When Facing Unbiased Decomposable Task Environment

| | Experientially Trained | | | | | | Operationally Trained | | | | | |
| | Average | | | Hostile | | | Average | | | Hostile | | |
	All	Opt	Sub	All	Opt	Sub	All	Opt	Sub	All	Opt	Sub
Cost	-0.626	-0.707	-0.627	0.382	0.356	0.406	-0.294	-0.744	-0.192	0.121	-0.121	0.172
Effk	0.298	0.319	0.309	-0.277	-0.337	-0.273	0.217	0.508	0.156	-0.146	-0.121	-0.174
Hiem	0.237	0.321	0.207	-0.327	-0.344	-0.337	0.279	0.760	0.165	-0.176	0.109	-0.242
Hieka	0.772	0.828	0.799	-0.164	-0.014	-0.209	0.209	0.468	0.157	-0.052	0.057	-0.074
Lubka	-0.412	-0.530	-0.377	0.193	0.153	0.212	-0.211	-0.665	-0.096	0.189	-0.101	0.258
Eiksa	0.085	0.095	0.086	0.216	0.254	0.215	-0.061	-0.137	-0.046	0.167	0.439	0.161
Antl	-0.003	-0.092	0.048	0.181	0.177	0.190	-0.084	-0.362	-0.007	0.240	0.251	0.279

Note. Average—average (across all) external condition; Hostile—hostile external condition (maydays); All—all internal condition; Opt—optimal internal condition; Sub—suboptimal internal condition (murphies); n—number of pairs of cases for correlation, with $n = 600$ under all internal condition, $n = 150$ under optimal internal condition, $n = 450$ under suboptimal internal condition.

140

different internal conditions. Under hostile external condition, Effk, Eiksa, and Antl become good indicators of performance across different internal conditions, when considering the magnitudes and directions of correlations.

Biased Nondecomposable Task Environment

The correlation when facing a biased nondecomposable task environment is shown in Table 6.7. The result shows that no measure is a good indicator of organizational performance across different training scenarios, external conditions, and internal conditions, when considering the magnitudes and directions of correlations. This pattern changes slightly under different training scenarios.

Experientially Trained.   Under experiential training, still no measure of organizational design seems to be a good indicator of performance across different external conditions and internal conditions, when considering the magnitudes and directions of correlations. This pattern remains the same under average external condition or hostile external conditions.

Operationally Trained.   Under operational training, all measures of organizational design — Cost, Effk, Hiem, Hieka, Lubka, Eiksa, and Antl — seem to be fairly good indicators of performance across different external conditions and internal conditions, when considering the magnitudes and directions of correlations. This pattern remains the same under average external conditions or hostile external conditions.

Unbiased Nondecomposable Task Environment

The correlation when facing an unbiased nondecomposable task environment is shown in Table 6.8. The result shows that measures of organizational design Hiem, Lubka, and Antl are good indicators of organizational performance across different training scenarios, external conditions, and internal conditions, when considering the magnitudes and directions of correlations. However, this pattern changes slightly under different training scenarios.

Experientially Trained.   Under experiential training, measures of organizational design Hiem, Lubka, and Antl are still fairly good indicators of performance across different external conditions and internal conditions, when considering the magnitudes and directions of correlations. However, under average external conditions, Cost, Hiem, Hieka, Lubka, Eiksa, and Antl become good indicators of performance across different internal conditions. Under hostile external conditions, all measures of organizational design — Cost, Effk, Hiem, Hieka, Lubka, Eiksa, and Antl — become good indicators of performance across different internal conditions, when considering the magnitudes and directions of correlations.

TABLE 6.7

Correlation of Major Organizational Measures with Organizational Performance When Facing Biased Nondecomposable Task Environment

	Experientially Trained						Operationally Trained					
	Average			Hostile			Average			Hostile		
	All	Opt	Sub.	All	Opt	Sub	All	Opt	Sub	All	Opt	Sub
Cost	0.046	0.438	0.018	−0.047	−0.079	−0.054	0.671	0.797	0.625	0.676	0.793	0.634
Effk	−0.072	−0.288	−0.062	−0.021	−0.110	−0.022	−0.614	−0.686	−0.588	−0.624	−0.692	−0.600
Hiem	−0.096	−0.333	−0.086	−0.029	−0.006	−0.034	−0.733	−0.811	−0.705	−0.739	−0.808	−0.714
Hieka	0.058	−0.290	0.094	0.118	−0.015	0.139	−0.438	−0.526	−0.405	−0.442	−0.526	−0.412
Lubka	0.048	0.587	0.008	−0.080	−0.120	−0.091	0.622	0.689	0.598	0.625	0.683	0.605
Eiksa	0.019	−0.286	0.046	0.085	0.055	0.099	0.444	0.472	0.434	0.447	0.479	0.436
Antl	0.040	0.101	0.470	0.015	−0.144	−0.058	0.533	0.569	0.213	0.533	0.566	0.461

Note. Average—average (across all) external condition; Hostile—hostile external condition (maydays); All—all internal condition; Opt—optimal internal condition; Sub—suboptimal internal condition (murphies); n—number of paris of cases for correlation, with $n = 600$ under all internal condition, $n = 150$ under optimal internal condition, $n = 450$ under suboptimal internal condition.

TABLE 6.8
Correlation of Major Organizational Measures with Organizational Performance When Facing Unbiased Nondecomposable Task Environment

	Experientially Trained						Operationally Trained					
	Average			Hostile			Average			Hostile		
	All	Opt	Sub	All	Opt	Sub	All	Opt	Sub	All	Opt	Sub
Cost	−0.102	−0.152	−0.086	0.331	0.534	0.321	0.327	0.685	0.307	0.333	0.567	0.314
Effk	0.009	0.013	0.008	−0.205	−0.348	−0.195	−0.295	−0.613	−0.279	−0.315	−0.536	−0.298
Hiem	−0.249	−0.230	−0.263	−0.164	−0.301	−0.153	−0.402	−0.770	−0.389	−0.413	−0.652	−0.400
Hieka	0.438	0.502	0.426	−0.268	−0.388	−0.266	−0.195	−0.463	−0.176	−0.217	−0.418	−0.196
Lubka	0.313	0.300	0.325	0.159	0.318	0.144	0.353	0.609	0.352	0.328	0.445	0.332
Eiksa	−0.142	−0.173	−0.135	0.195	0.265	0.196	0.245	0.556	0.224	0.330	0.622	0.300
Antl	0.272	0.246	0.289	0.170	0.279	0.164	0.326	0.577	0.323	0.348	0.510	0.344

Note. Average—(across all) external condition; Hostile—hostile external condition (maydays); All—all internal condition; Opt—optimal internal condition; Sub—suboptimal internal condition (murphies); n—number of pairs of cases for correlation, with $n = 600$ under all internal condition, $n = 150$ under optimal internal condition, $n = 450$ under suboptimal internal condition.

Operationally Trained. Under operational training, all measures of organizational design—Cost, Effk, Hiem, Hieka, Lubka, Eiksa, and Antl—seem to be fairly good indicators of performance across different external conditions and internal conditions, when considering the magnitudes and directions of correlations. Under average external condition or hostile external conditions, this pattern remains the same.

Performance Prediction: Stepwise Regression Analysis

In the prior analysis, no measure was consistently a good indicator of performance. These results may be a function of not having considered interaction effects among these measures. Using stepwise regression, I examined whether interaction accounts for this previous result. A series of stepwise regressions was run such that all seven measures and their two-way interactions were the possible independent variables and the simulated performance was the dependent variable, with the entry level set at .500. These regression models were run overall and under different task environments, training scenarios, external conditions, and internal conditions.

The results show that there is still no measure or set of measures that consistently predict organizational performance across all task environments. Regressions goodness of fit (R^2) values are constantly below .300, regardless of training scenarios, external conditions, and internal conditions. Further, if the internal organizational condition is suboptimal, then regardless of task environments or training scenarios, the R^2 values are low (refer to the Appendix, Tables 6.A1–6.A5, for details). This finding indicates that in general, these measures do not, either singularly or in combination, predict performance.

Under optimal internal conditions, however, almost all measures of organizational design and their two-way interactions become good (significant) predictors of organizational performance, with the goodness of fit of the regressions being constantly above .900, regardless of task environments, training scenarios, and external conditions (Tables 6.9 and 6.10). This shows that existing organizational measures and their two-way interactions can only predict performance if the internal condition of the organization is stress free. However, which measure (or set of measures) does best depends on task environment, training scenario, and external conditions.

Summary

The analyses show that there is no universally good single indicator of organizational performance across all situations. However, some measures, such as Cost, Effk, Hiem, and Hieka, appear more frequently to be good predictors under particular situations. There are also interaction effects between measures of organizational design, but such effects typically exist when the organization is not stressed internally. Further, which measure (or

TABLE 6.9
Regressions for Predicting Performance of Experientially Trained Organizations Under Optimal Internal Conditions

	Across All External Conditions				Hostile External Conditions (Maydays)			
	BD	UD	BN	UN	BD	UD	BN	UN
Intercept	(−)***	(−)***	(+)***	(+)***			(−)***	(+)***
Cost	(+)***	(+)***	(−)***	(−)***		(+)*	(+)***	
Effk	(−)***	(−)***		(−)***			(+)***	
Hiem	(+)***	(+)***	(+)***	(−)***			(+)***	(+)***
Hieka	(+)***	(+)***	(−)***	(−)***		(+)*	(+)***	
Lubka	(+)***	(+)***	(+)***	(−)***	(+)***			
Eiksa	(+)***	(+)***	(−)***	(−)***	(+)**		(+)***	(+)***
Antl	(−)***	(−)***	(−)***	(+)***	(−)***		(−)***	(+)***
Cost × Effk	(+)***	(+)***			(−)**			
Cost × Hiem	(−)***	(−)***		(+)***	(−)***		(−)***	
Cost × Hieka	(−)***	(−)***	(+)***	(+)***	(+)***	(−)***	(−)***	
Cost × Lubka	(−)***	(−)***	(−)***	(+)***	(−)***		(−)***	
Cost × Eiksa	(−)***	(−)***		(+)***			(−)***	
Cost × Antl	(+)***	(+)***	(+)***	(−)***	(+)***	(−)***	(+)***	(−)***
Effk × Hiem	(−)***	(−)***	(−)***	(+)***			(−)***	
Effk × Hieka			(+)***	(+)***	(+)***	(−)*	(−)***	
Effk × Lubka	(−)***	(−)***	(−)***	(+)***			(−)***	
Effk × Eiksa				(+)***	(−)***	(−)*	(−)***	
Effk × Antl	(+)***	(+)***	(+)*	(−)***	(+)***	(−)*	(+)***	(−)***
Hiem × Hieka	(−)***	(−)***		(+)***	(−)**		(−)***	(−)***
Hiem × Lubka	(+)***	(+)***	(−)*	(−)***			(+)***	
Hiem × Eiksa	(−)***	(−)***			(+)***	(+)*	(+)***	
Hiem × Antl	(+)***	(+)***		(−)***	(+)***	(−)***	(+)***	
Hieka × Lubka	(+)***	(+)***	(−)***	(−)***	(−)***		(+)***	(−)**
Hieka × Eiksa	(−)***	(−)***	(+)***	(+)***			(−)***	(−)***
Hieka × Antl	(+)***	(+)***		(−)***	(+)***	(+)***	(+)***	
Lubka × Eiksa	(−)***	(−)**	(+)***	(+)***	(+)***		(+)***	(−)***
Lubka × Antl	(+)***	(+)***		(−)***	(+)***		(+)***	
Eiksa × Antl	(+)***	(+)***	(−)***	(−)***			(+)***	(+)***
R^2	0.998	0.999	0.960	0.973	0.998	0.976	0.998	0.638

Note. BD—biased decomposable; UD—unbiased decomposable; BN—biased nondecomposable; UN—unbiased nondecomposable. Number of pairs of cases for correlation is 600 in each regression (column). Significance level is .5000 for entry into the model; *$p < .01$, **$p < .005$, ***$p < .001$.

set of measures) predicts well depends on the environment, training scenario, and external condition the organization faces.

The fact that some two-way interactions also show their significant effects in predicting performance even when single measures are not significant suggests that new measures that catch the interaction effect of individual measures may be better indicators of organizational performance than existing single measures.

TABLE 6.10
Regressions for Predicting Performance of Operationally Trained Organizations Under
Optimal Internal Conditions

	Across All External Conditions				Hostile External Conditions (Maydays)			
	BD	UD	BN	UN	BD	UD	BN	UN
Intercept	(−)***	(+)*	(+)***	(−)***	(+)**	(−)***	(−)***	(+)***
Cost	(+)***		(−)***	(+)*	(−)***	(+)***	(+)***	(−)***
Effk	(+)***			(+)***		(+)***	(+)***	(+)***
Hiem	(+)***		(−)***	(−)***	(−)**	(+)***		(−)***
Hieka	(+)***		(−)***		(−)***	(+)***		(−)***
Lubka		(−)***	(−)***	(−)***				(−)***
Eiksa	(+)***	(−)***	(−)***	(−)***				(−)***
Antl	(−)***	(+)***		(+)***		(+)***	(−)***	(+)***
Cost × Effk	(−)***		(−)***	(−)***	(−)***		(−)***	(−)***
Cost × Hiem	(−)***	(+)***	(+)***				(+)***	
Cost × Hieka			(+)***	(+)***	(+)***	(−)***		(+)***
Cost × Lubka	(−)***	(+)***	(+)***	(+)***		(+)***	(−)***	(+)***
Cost × Eiksa	(−)***		(+)***	(+)***	(+)***	(+)***		(+)***
Cost × Antl	(+)***	(−)***		(−)***		(−)***	(+)*	(−)***
Effk × Hiem			(+)***	(+)***	(+)***	(−)***		(+)***
Effk × Hieka	(−)***		(+)***	(−)***	(+)***	(−)***		
Effk × Lubka			(+)***	(+)***	(+)***	(−)***	(+)*	(+)***
Effk × Eiksa		(−)***				(−)***	(−)*	
Effk × Antl	(+)***				(+)**	(+)***	(+)***	
Hiem × Hieka	(−)***	(+)*	(+)***	(+)***		(−)***		(+)***
Hiem × Lubka	(+)***	(−)***	(−)***	(−)***	(−)**		(−)***	(−)***
Hiem × Eiksa	(−)***	(−)***	(+)*	(+)***				(+)***
Hiem × Antl	(+)***	(−)***	(−)***	(−)***		(−)***	(−)***	(−)***
Hieka × Lubka		(+)***	(−)***	(−)***	(−)***	(+)***		(−)***
Hieka × Eiksa	(−)***		(+)***	(+)***		(+)***	(+)*	(+)***
Hieka × Antl	(+)***	(−)***		(−)***		(−)***		(−)***
Lubka × Eiksa	(−)***	(−)***	(+)***		(−)***	(−)***		
Lubka × Antl	(+)***	(−)***		(−)***		(−)***		(−)***
Eiksa × Antl	(+)***	(−)***	(−)***	(−)***	(−)***	(−)***	(−)***	(−)***
R^2	0.995	0.986	0.996	0.987	0.976	0.984	0.987	0.986

Note. BD—biased decomposable, UD—unbiased decomposable, BN—biased nondecomposable, UN—unbiased nondecomposable. Number of pairs of cases for correlation is 600 in each regression (column). Significance level is .5000 for entry into the model; $*p < .01$, $**p < .005$, $***p < .001$.

DISCUSSION AND CONCLUSION

There is no measure (or set of measures) consistently good at predicting organizational performance. The reason for the lack of a universally good indicator of organizational performance can be traced to the definitions of these measures. Each measure only encompasses part of organizational design: either the structure or the task decomposition scheme. Performance is a function of design (including training), task environment, and stress (Lin & Carley, 1992). These measures, therefore, all fall short of capturing the effect of multiple factors on organizational performance.

Simulation has enabled a systematic, economic evaluation of these measures of organizational design across numerous factors that are of interest to researchers in organizations. In fact, to examine these same factors using human experimental subjects would have taken at least 10 years and cost at least 2 million dollars.[3] Computer simulation is a powerful extension of human cognition. As pointed out by Ostrom (1988), computer simulation offers a third symbol system in studying social science, besides natural language and mathematics, because "computer simulation offers a substantial advantage to social psychologists attempting to develop formal theories of complex and interdependent social phenomena." Fararo (1989) also regarded computational process as one of the three processes (the other two are theoretical and empirical processes) necessary to the development of any discipline.

This chapter demonstrates the usefulness of simulation to advance theory by providing, for the first time, a systematic test of the power of measures suggested by different theories. Through simulation, one can test and discard measures, thus avoiding costly mistakes in data collection during human experimental or real-world conditions. Nevertheless, these results must be viewed with caution. The simulated organizations in this research are in a static environment. Further, factors such as timing and agent styles are not considered in this research. These factors may limit our ability to generalize some of the reported results. Future research should consider evaluating organizational measures against simulated organizations in a dynamic environment with individual agent preferences.

In conclusion, this chapter offers a theoretical evaluation of existing measures of organizational design regarding their predictability and has found that without considerations of specific factors (such as task environment, stress, and organizational design), these measures do not predict performance. This exercise is very important as it clarifies the confusions among, tests the predictability of, and provides new insights into the existing measures of organizational design.

ACKNOWLEDGMENT

The author is grateful to Kathleen Carley and Michael Prietula for their careful and constructive editing on an earlier version of this manuscript.

---

[3]In the summer of 1992, the author assisted with a series of human experiments (12 groups) examining the performance of one of the 7,200 organizational cases. Each group consisted of four subjects and took 1 hour and $30 to run. Thus to examine all the 7,200 organizational cases without any break, it would have taken $12 \times 7,200 = 86,400$ hours (3,600 days, or 120 months, or 10 years), and $30 \times 12 \times 7,200 = \$2,592,000$.

TABLE 6.A1

Regressions for Organizational Performance Across All Task Environments

	Experientially Trained						Operationally Trained					
	Average			Hostile			Average			Hostile		
	All	Opt	Sub	All	Opt	Sub	All	Opt	Sub	All	Opt	Sub
Intercept					(−)***		(+)***	(+)***	(+)***	(+)***	(+)***	(+)***
Cost	(+)***											
Effk												
Hiem												
Hieka			(+)***		(+)***							
Lubka					(+)***	(+)***						
Eiksa												
Antl					(−)***							
Cost × Effk												
Cost × Hiem	(−)*	(−)***										
Cost × Hieka					(+)***							
Cost × Lubka	(+)***	(+)***	(+)***	(−)**	(−)***	(−)**						
Cost × Eiksa		(−)***										
Cost × Antl												
Cost × Hiem										(−)***	(−)***	(−)***

Effk × Hieka											
Effk × Lubka											
Effk × Eiksa											
Effk × Antl											
Hiem × Hieka											
Hiem × Lubka											
Hiem × Eiksa											
Hiem × Antl											
Hieka × Lubka					(−)***	(−)*					
Hieka × Eiksa											
Hieka × Antl					(+)***						
Lubka × Eiksa										(+)*	
Lubka × Antl					(+)***						
Eiksa lmu Antl											
R^2	0.060	0.097	0.052	0.117	0.355	0.106	0.010	0.004	0.015	0.055	0.047	0.060

Note. Average—average (across all) external condition; Hostile—hostile external condition (maydays); All—all internal condition; Opt—optimal internal condition; Sub—suboptimal internal condition (murphies); n—number of pairs of cases for correlation, with n = 2,400 under all internal condition, n = 600 under optimal internal condition, n = 1,800 under suboptimal internal condition. Significance level is .5000 for entry into the model; *$p < .01$, **$p < .005$, ***$p < .001$.

TABLE 6.A2
Regressions for Organizational Performance Under Biased Decomposable Task Environment

	Experientially Trained						Operationally Trained					
	Average			Hostile			Average			Hostile		
	All	Opt	Sub	All	Opt	Sub	All	Opt	Sub	All	Opt	Sub
Intercept		(−)***	(−)**			(−)***		(−)***		(+)***	(+)**	(+)***
Cost		(+)***				(+)***		(+)***			(−)***	(+)***
Effk		(−)***	(+)***					(+)***				
Hiem		(+)***	(−)**			(+)**		(+)***				
Hieka		(+)***	(+)***		(+)***	(+)***		(+)***				
Lubka		(+)***	(−)**		(+)***	(+)***				(−)*	(−)**	
Eiksa		(+)***			(+)**						(−)***	
Antl	(−)***	(−)***			(−)***			(+)***				
Cost × Effk		(+)***			(+)***			(−)***				
Cost × Hiem		(−)***	(−)**		(−)**	(+)**		(−)***			(−)***	
Cost × Hieka		(−)***	(+)***		(−)***			(−)***	(−)**	(−)**		
Cost × Lubka	(−)***	(−)***	(+)***		(+)***	(−)**		(−)***			(+)***	
Cost × Eiksa		(−)***	(−)***		(−)***	(−)***		(−)***				
Cost × Antl	(+)***	(+)***	(+)***		(+)***			(+)***			(+)***	

	0.783	0.998	0.833	0.470	0.998	0.454	0.156	0.995	0.077	0.094	0.976	0.112
Effk × Hiem								(−)***				(+)***
Effk × Hieka			(−)***		(+)***							(+)***
Effk × Lubka			(+)**									(+)***
Effk × Eiksa					(−)***							
Effk × Antl		(+)***	(+)**		(+)***			(+)***				(+)**
Hiem × Hieka		(−)***	(−)***		(−)***			(−)***				
Hiem × Lubka		(+)***				(−)**		(+)***				(−)**
Hiem × Eiksa		(−)***			(+)***		(−)**	(−)***				
Hiem × Antl		(+)***			(+)***	(−)***	(−)**	(+)***				
Hieka × Lubka	(−)*	(+)***			(−)***			(−)***				(−)***
Hieka × Eiksa	(+)***	(−)***		(+)*	(+)***			(+)***				
Hieka × Antl	(−)***	(+)***		(+)**	(+)***	(+)**		(−)***				
Lubka × Eiksa	(+)***	(−)***			(+)***			(+)***				(−)***
Lubka × Antl	(+)***	(+)***						(+)***				
Eiksa × Antl		(+)***						(+)***				(−)***
R^2	0.783	0.998	0.833	0.470	0.998	0.454	0.156	0.995	0.077	0.094	0.976	0.112

Note. Average—average (across all) external condition; Hostile—hostile external condition (maydays); All—all internal condition; Opt—optimal internal condition; Sub—suboptimal internal condition (murphies); n—number of pairs of cases for correlation, with $n = 600$ under all internal condition, $n = 150$ under optimal internal condition, $n = 450$ under suboptimal internal condition. Significance level is .5000 for entry into the model; $*p < .01$, $**p < .005$, $***p < .001$.

151

TABLE 6.A3
Regressions for Organizational Performance Under Unbiased Decomposable Task Environment

	Experientially Trained						Operationally Trained					
	Average			Hostile			Average			Hostile		
	All	Opt	Sub	All	Opt	Sub	All	Opt	Sub	All	Opt	Sub
Intercept	(−)**	(−)***					(+)***	(+)*		(+)***	(−)***	(+)***
Cost	(+)**	(+)***									(+)***	
Effk	(+)**	(−)***			(+)*						(+)***	
Hiem	(+)***	(+)***									(+)***	
Hieka	(+)**	(+)***			(+)*						(+)***	(−)**
Lubka		(+)***		(+)***				(−)***				
Eiksa	(+)***	(+)***						(−)***				
Antl		(−)***						(+)***			(+)***	
Cost × Effk		(+)***		(+)***								
Cost × Hiem	(−)**	(−)***	(+)*					(+)***				
Cost × Hieka	(−)***	(−)***		(−)***	(−)***						(−)***	
Cost × Lubka	(−)**	(−)***	(+)***					(+)***			(+)***	
Cost × Eiksa	(−)**	(−)***									(+)***	
Cost × Antl		(+)***	(−)**		(−)***			(−)***			(−)***	

	0.760	0.999	0.713	0.306	0.976	0.281	0.223	0.986	0.203	0.298	0.984	0.258
Effk × Hiem	(−)***	(−)***		(−)***							(−)***	(−)**
Effk × Hieka	(−)**				(−)*						(−)***	
Effk × Lubka	(−)*	(−)***		(−)***							(−)***	
Effk × Eiksa					(−)*			(−)***			(−)***	
Effk × Antl		(+)***			(−)*						(+)***	
Hiem × Hieka	(−)**	(−)***		(+)***				(+)*			(−)***	
Hiem × Lubka	(+)**	(+)***						(−)***				
Hiem × Eiksa		(−)***			(+)*			(−)***				
Hiem × Antl		(+)***	(−)*		(−)***			(−)***			(−)***	
Hieka × Lubka	(+)**	(+)***	(−)***					(+)***			(+)***	
Hieka lmu Eiksa	(−)***	(−)***(									(+)***	
Hieka × Antl	(+)*	(+)***	(+)**		(+)***			(−)***			(−)***	
Lubka × Eiksa	(−)*	(−)**						(−)***			(−)***	
Lubka × Antl	(+)*	(+)***						(−)***			(−)***	
Eiksa × Antl	(+)***	(+)***						(−)***		(−)***	(−)***	(−)**
R^2	0.760	0.999	0.713	0.306	0.976	0.281	0.223	0.986	0.203	0.298	0.984	0.258

Note. Average—average (across all) external condition; Hostile—hostile external condition (maydays); All—all internal condition; Opt—optimal internal condition; Sub—suboptimal internal condition (murphies); n—number of pairs of cases for correlation, with $n = 600$ under all internal condition, $n = 150$ under optimal internal condition, $n = 450$ under suboptimal internal condition. Significance level is .5000 for entry into the model; *$p < .01$, **$p < .005$, ***$p < .001$.

153

TABLE 6.A4
Regressions for Organizational Performance Under Biased Nondecomposable Task Environment

| | Experientially Trained | | | | | | Operationally Trained | | | | | |
| | Average | | | Hostile | | | Average | | | Hostile | | |
	All	Opt	Sub	All	Opt	Sub	All	Opt	Sub	All	Opt	Sub
Intercept		(+)***		(+)***	(−)***	(+)***	(+)***	(+)***	(+)***	(−)*	(−)***	(+)***
Cost		(−)***	(+)***		(+)***			(−)***		(+)***	(+)***	
Effk					(+)***					(+)**	(+)***	(−)**
Hiem		(+)***			(+)***			(−)***				
Hieka		(−)***			(+)***	(+)**		(−)***				(−)**
Lubka		(+)***						(−)***				
Eiksa	(−)**	(−)***			(+)***			(−)***				
Antl	(−)**	(−)***			(−)***				(+)***		(−)***	
Cost × Effk								(−)***		(−)***	(−)***	
Cost × Hiem					(−)***	(+)*		(+)***		(+)***		
Cost × Hieka		(+)***			(−)***			(+)***				
Cost × Lubka		(−)***			(−)***			(+)***			(−)***	
Cost × Eiksa					(−)***			(+)***				
Cost × Antl	(+)***	(+)***	(−)***		(+)***						(+)*	

	0.372	0.960	0.303	0.061	0.998	0.077	0.120	0.996	0.061	0.482	0.987	0.398
Effk × Hiem		(−)***			(−)***			(+)***				(+)**
Effk × Hieka		(+)***			(−)***			(+)***				
Effk × Lubka		(−)***			(−)***			(+)***			(+)*	
Effk × Eiksa		(+)*			(−)***					(+)*	(−)*	
Effk × Antl					(+)***						(+)***	
Hiem × Hieka					(−)***			(+)***				
Hiem × Lubka		(−)*			(+)***			(−)***			(−)***	
Hiem × Eiksa					(+)***			(+)*				
Hiem × Antl					(+)***			(−)***		(−)**	(−)***	
Hieka × Lubka	(+)**	(−)***			(+)***			(−)***		(−)**		
Hieka × Eiksa		(+)***			(−)***			(+)***			(+)*	
Hieka × Antl					(+)***							
Lubka × Eiksa	(+)**	(+)***			(+)***			(+)***				
Lubka × Antl					(+)***							
Eiksa × Antl	(−)***	(−)***	(−)*		(+)***			(−)***			(−)***	
R^2	0.372	0.960	0.303	0.061	0.998	0.077	0.120	0.996	0.061	0.482	0.987	0.398

Note. Average—average (across all) external condition; Hostile—hostile external condition (maydays); All—all internal condition; Opt—optimal internal condition; Sub—suboptimal internal condition (murphies); n—number of pairs of cases for correlation, with $n = 600$ under all internal condition, $n = 150$ under optimal internal condition, $n = 450$ under suboptimal internal condition. Significance level is .5000 for entry into the model; *$p < .01$, **$p < .005$, ***$p < .001$.

TABLE 6.A5
Regressions for Organizational Performance Under Unbiased Nondecomposable Task Environment

	Experientially Trained						Operationally Trained					
	Average			Hostile			Average			Hostile		
	All	Opt	Sub	All	Opt	Sub	All	Opt	Sub	All	Opt	Sub
Intercept	(+)***	(+)***	(+)**	(+)***	(+)***	(+)***		(−)***	(−)***		(+)***	(−)***
Cost		(−)***					(+)***	(+)*	(+)***		(−)***	(+)***
Effk		(−)***						(+)***	(+)***		(+)***	(+)***
Hiem	(−)***	(−)***			(+)***			(−)***			(−)***	
Hieka		(−)***	(+)*	(+)***				(−)***			(−)***	
Lubka		(−)***						(−)***			(−)***	
Eiksa		(−)***			(+)***			(+)***			(+)***	
Antl		(+)***			(+)***			(−)***		(−)***	(−)***	
Cost × Effk												
Cost × Hiem		(+)***						(+)***	(−)***		(+)***	(−)***
Cost × Hieka	(+)**	(+)***					(−)***	(+)***			(+)***	(−)***
Cost × Lubka		(+)***						(+)***		(−)**	(+)***	
Cost × Eiksa		(+)***			(−)***			(+)***			(+)***	
Cost × Antl		(−)***						(−)***	(−)***	(+)***	(−)***	

Predictor												
Effk × Hiem		(+)***						(+)***			(+)***	
Effk × Hieka		(+)***						(−)***				
Effk × Lubka		(+)***						(+)***			(+)***	
Effk × Eiksa		(+)***										
Effk × Antl	(+)***	(−)***				(−)***	(+)***		(+)***			(+)***
Hiem × Hieka		(+)***				(−)***		(+)***	(+)***	(+)***	(+)***	
Hiem × Lubka		(−)***			(−)***			(−)***			(−)***	
Hiem × Eiksa								(+)***			(+)***	
Hiem × Antl		(−)***					(−)***	(−)***	(−)***	(−)***	(−)***	(−)***
Hieka × Lubka		(−)***				(−)**	(+)***	(−)***			(−)***	
Hieka × Eiksa		(+)***				(−)***		(+)***			(+)***	
Hieka × Antl		(−)***					(−)*	(−)***			(−)***	(−)*
Lubka × Eiksa		(+)***				(−)***	(−)**	(−)***	(−)**		(−)***	
Lubka × Antl		(−)***				(−)**	(−)***	(−)***	(−)**	(−)***	(−)***	(−)**
Eiksa × Antl		(−)***				(+)***		(−)***			(−)***	(−)**
R^2	0.040	0.973	0.049	0.068	0.072	0.638	0.762	0.987	0.701	0.776	0.986	0.718

Note. Average—average (across all) external condition; Hostile—hostile external condition; All—all internal condition; Opt—optimal internal condition; Sub—suboptimal internal condition (murphies); n—number of pairs of cases for correlation, with $n = 600$ under all internal condition, $n = 450$ under suboptimal internal condition, $n = 150$ under optimal internal condition. Significance level is .5000 for entry into the model; *$p<.01$, **$p<.005$, ***$p<.001$.

157

REFERENCES

Allison, G. T. (1971). *Essence of decision: Explaining the Cuban Missile Crisis.* Chicago: Scott, Foresman.

Anderson, C. R. (1977). Locus of control coping behavior, and performance in a stress setting: A longitudinal study. *Journal of Applied Psychology, 62*(4), 446–451.

Argote, L., & Epple, D. (1990). Learning curves in manufacturing. *Science, 247,* 920–924.

Cameron, K. S. (1986). Effectiveness as paradox: Consensus and conflict in conceptions of organizational effectiveness. *Management Science, 32*(5), 539–553.

Carley, K. M. (1991). *Coordination for effective performance during crises when training matters. Working Paper, Department of Social and Decision Sciences, Carnegie Mellon University.*

Child, J. (1974). What determines organizational performance? The universal vs. the it-all-depends. *Organizational Dynamics, 3*(1), 2–18.

Drazin, R., & Van de Ven, A. H. (1985). Alternative forms of fit in contingency theory. *Administrative Science Quarterly, 30,* 514–539.

Fararo, T. (1989). *The meaning of general theoretical sociology.* Cambridge: Cambridge University Press.

Hammond, K. R. (1973). Negative effects of outcome-feedback in multiple-cue probability learning. *Organizational Behavior and Human Resources, 9,* 30–34.

Houskisson, R. E., & Galbraith, C. S. (1985). The effect of quantum versus incremental M-form reorganization on performance: A time series exploration of intervention dynamics. *Journal of Management, 11,* 55–70.

Krackhardt, D., & Stern, R. N. (1988). Informal networks and organizational crises: An experimental simulation. *Social Psychology Quarterly, 51*(2), 123–140.

Kumar, A., Ow, P. S., & Prietula, M. J. (1993). Organizational simulation and information systems design: An operations level example. *Management Science, 39*(2), 218–240.

Lawrence, P. R., & Lorsch, J. W. (1967). *Organization and environment: Managing differentiation and integration.* Boston: Graduate School of Business Administration, Harvard University.

Lin, Z. (1994). *Organizational performance—Theory and reality.* Doctoral dissertation, Carnegie Mellon University.

Lin, Z., & Carley, K. M. (1992, August). *Maydays and murphies: A study of the effect of organizational design, task, and stress on organizational performance.* Paper Presented at the 1992 Annual Meeting of the American Sociological Association, Pittsburgh, PA.

Lin, Z., & Carley, K. M. (1993). *Organizational performance responding to crises—Theory and practice.* Working Paper, Carnegie Mellon University.

Lincoln, J. R., Hanada, M., & McBride, K. (1986). Organizational structures in Japanese and U.S. manufacturing. *Administrative Science Quarterly, 31,* 338–364.

Long, R. J. (1980). Job attitude and organizational performance under employee ownership. *Academy of Management Journal, 23,* 726–737.

Mackenzie, K. D. (1978). *Organizational structures.* Arlington Heights, IL: AHM.

Malone, T. W. (1986). Modelling coordination in organizations and markets. *Management Science, 33*(10), 1317–1332.

March, J. G., & Olsen, J. P. (1976). *Ambiguity and choice in organizations.* Bergen: Universitetsforlaget.

Ostrom, T. M. (1988). Computer simulation: The third symbol system. *Journal of Experimental Social Psychology, 24,* 381–392.

Pfeffer, J., & Salancik, G. R. (1978). *The external control of organizations.* New York: Harper & Row.

Perrow, C. (1984). *Normal accidents: Living with high risk technologies.* New York: Basic Books.

Roberts, K. (1989). New challenges to organizational research: High reliability organizations. *Industrial Crisis Quarterly, 3*(3), 111–125.

Scott, W. R. (1987). *Organizations: Rational, natural, and open systems.* Englewood Cliffs, NJ: Prentice-Hall.

Seashore, S. E. (1962). *The assessment of organizational performance.* Ann Arbor: Survey Research Center, University of Michigan.

Shrivastava, P. (1987). *Bhopal: Anatomy of a crisis.* Cambridge, MA: Ballinger.

Shull, F. A., Jr., Delbecq, S. L., & Cummings, L. L. (1970). *Organizational decision making.* New York: McGraw-Hill.

Tancredi, L. R., & Woods, J. (1972). The social control of medical practice: Licensure versus output monitoring. *Milbank Memorial Quarterly, 50*(1), 99–126.

7

Modeling and Computational Analysis of Reactive Behavior in Organizations

Markku Verkama
Raimo P. Hämäläinen
Harri Ehtamo
Helsinki University of Technology

The focus of this chapter is on the modeling and computational analysis of interaction processes in organizations. In particular, we examine dynamic processes resulting from *reactive* behavior, where the agents in an organization react to each others' actions. We develop a framework for the formal analysis of dynamic reactive behavior and carry out simulations to study the effects of different behavioral patterns within this framework.

The computational analysis concentrates on goal-seeking behavior described by utility maximization, which is taken to be myopic in a simple behavioral model. Because of uncertainty about the other agents' reactions, the resulting dynamic interaction process is often unstable. We present ways of modifying the agents' decision rules so as to take into account this uncertainty. Computational analysis shows that the modified decision rules may lead to stable interaction processes so that stationary actions are reached. This is called a *stable organizational structure*. The contributions of the work lie in the modeling effort and especially in the analysis of simple, but efficient and realistic, ways of taking into account uncertainties in the myopic utility maximization model.

As the approach developed here demonstrates the benefits of an interdisciplinary approach to problems of organization theory, it is timely and useful to explore the issue in depth. For example, complex interaction and communication patterns in organizations can be simulated with computational techniques developed in artificial intelligence (AI) . We could, in fact, call this research area the study of artificial organizations. The potential of an interdisciplinary approach to the study of coordination and cooperation has recently attracted growing interest (Malone & Crowston, 1991; Verkama, Hämäläinen, & Ehtamo, 1992). Clearly, coordination and cooperation are important problems in organization theory. New AI techniques are also likely to prove useful in the study of other important issues, such as organizational behavior, learning, and structure of organizations. These new techniques include object-oriented programming, genetic algorithms, learning automata, and neural networks.

We see the simulation analysis of different behavioral phenomena in organizations as a particularly interesting emerging area. In order for such analyses to be useful, one must be able to mimic human decision making artificially. No doubt this is a challenging task; some progress, however, has already been made. For example, Arthur (1991, 1993) has examined a learning automaton in a choice situation where payoffs are stochastic. After calibration the automaton replicates human learning behavior quite well. Arthur's model was developed for studying a particular situation, but computational cognition architectures that model the general mechanisms underlying human rationality have been proposed, too. An example of such an architecture is SOAR, which has also been implemented as software (Laird, Newell, & Rosenbloom, 1987). Why should one go to the trouble of replicating human behavior? Holland and Miller (1991) pointed out that experiments using artificial agents can be controlled carefully, which is difficult with humans, and large-scale experiments can be conducted at low cost. Lane (1993a, 1993b) argued that artificial economies may give insights into economic phenomena that manifest emergence of hierarchical organizations. For discussion on AI and economics see also Moss and Rae (1992).

Another problem area for AI applications is formed by questions related to different organizational structures. For example, genetic algorithms may prove useful in organizational ecology. This research direction examines the effects of environment on organizational structure from a population ecology perspective (Hannan & Freeman, 1977). Incidentally, organization theory itself has a role in AI, especially in distributed artificial intelligence, which studies the collective behavior of intelligent agents (Bond & Gasser, 1988).

Many problems of organization theory concern decision making. This establishes a link to group problem solving and group decision making (e.g., Chatterjee, Kersten, & Shakun, 1991). For instance, advances in information technology have made it possible to develop tools for facilitating group work. Empirical research with such decision aids enhances our understanding of group decision processes and organizational behavior.

Although the techniques that have become available are appealing, the value of the traditional mathematical approach to organizational problems should not be underestimated. The bulk of the mathematically oriented literature has concentrated on various incentive problems and on the efficient use of information in organizations; team theory and game theory have played an important role (e.g., Radner, 1987). Differences between organizational forms have been studied from the point of view of imperfect decision making (Heiner, 1988; Sah & Stiglitz, 1985). But even though important issues such as the incentive problems have been tackled, it is evident that the complexity of real organizations soon makes analytic approaches intractable. Hence the need for new techniques arises. We would like to stress, however, that the use of computational techniques should not mean the rejection of the analytic modeling tradition. Rather, the research ought to build on clearly stated models, no matter what techniques are eventually used to explore the problems posed.

This chapter is organized as follows. We first formalize a general framework for analyzing reactive behavior in organizations. Next we specify the decision rules, which, in the subsequent section, are analyzed computationally.

A FRAMEWORK FOR ANALYZING REACTIVE BEHAVIOR

The model we present for analyzing reactive behavior tries to capture the basic elements of the interaction process. Our ideas are largely motivated by the model formulated by Dow (1990). Dow studied organizations as adaptive networks of information-processing units. The behavior of the agents was described by learning mechanisms, and the organizational structure was regarded as a pattern of interaction among these mechanisms. The learning mechanisms were governed by feedback about past performance. Here our objective is to study interaction among decision rules that depend on past actions.

Roughly speaking, the setup we are interested in is the following. Let there be an organization of agents with each agent having a set of possible actions. The agents make observations about the past actions, and they are assumed to be autonomous in the sense that each agent has its own goals and control over its own actions. What happens when time evolves? What kind of behavioral patterns, both individual and collective, can be observed? The agents here can be, for example, humans, animals, intelligent artificial agents, or organizations such as firms.

Let us now formalize this setup. There are n agents; the set of the agents is denoted by $N = \{1, \ldots, n\}$. We shall assume that n is fixed but this is not necessary. Let $t \in \{0,1,2, \ldots\}$ index time. At time t each agent i chooses an action a_i^t from the set of possible actions A_i^t. The corresponding joint action is

$$a^t = (a_1^t, \ldots, a_n^t) \in A^t = A_1^t \times \cdots \times A_n^t \qquad (1)$$

When the agents choose their actions, the state of their environment changes and the agents observe this change. This *technological* relationship between the actions and the consequent informational feedback to the agents is an important component in the description of interactions in organizations (Dow, 1990). We take the simplest approach in modeling this link by assuming that each agent makes perfect observations about the actions taken by all the other agents and that this information is a sufficient description of the environment's state for the agent to reach its goals. This may seem a rather limiting assumption. Nevertheless, the assumption does not necessitate that the agents' decisions depend solely on the observed actions. The agents can still have beliefs, and they can use private randomization in their decision making. The assumption naturally covers the case where the agents observe other variables but are able to deduce the past actions from these.

The history of the organization at time t is

$$h^t = (a^0, a^1, \ldots, a^{t-1}) \qquad t = 1, 2, \ldots \tag{2}$$

By this assumption, h^t is known to all agents at time t. The set of possible histories is denoted by H^t. Reactive behavior of agent i is described by a *decision rule* d_i^t that links the history h^t to the action at time t. That is, decision rules are mappings of the form $d_i^t \colon H^t \mapsto A_i^t$. Reactive behavior in an organization of agents is thus described by

$$a_i^t = d_i^t(h^t) \qquad i \in N \qquad t = 1, 2, 3, \ldots \tag{3}$$

A decision rule defines the *behavioral* relationship between the informational inputs and the subsequent actions. Note that decision rules may describe complicated decision processes. For instance, if an agent had multiple, possibly conflicting goals, its decision rule would incorporate the procedures needed for solving the conflict. The decision rules studied later in this chapter are relatively simple. One is tempted to call h^t the state of the agent system, but the action history does not generally contain all information about the organization. For example, the randomization processes the agent might use are thought to be contained implicitly in the time evolution of the decision rules. We do not assume that the agents know each others' decision rules.

Our objective is to examine the development of the interaction patterns of decision rules—that is, the time evolution of the system in Equation 3. There are also other research questions that can be analyzed within this framework. One such problem is to compare the relative efficiency of different decision rules, provided that a performance measure is given. This opens the possibility of evolutionary considerations; one could use genetic algorithms for finding the best decision rule with respect to the performance measure. Miller (1989) provided an example of this kind of study in the context of the Prisoner's Dilemma.

One can easily generalize the model by adding a coordinating agent who acts first at each time step. This coordinator could be the leader of the organization, or the coordinator could be used to generate more complex information structures. For example, the coordinator could be the only one to observe all actions; the other agents would only observe information signals from the coordinator. In Dow's (1990) model the agents receive signals that depend on the actions and on the history in a stochastic manner. In our model with a coordinator this corresponds to a situation where the coordinator's signals are randomized. Different variants can also be generated by changing the order in which the agents make decisions. For the purposes of this chapter, the basic model just described is, however, adequate.

MYOPICALLY OPTIMIZING AGENTS

Let us now describe the decision rules to be studied in more detail. First of all, we assume that the agents have stationary preferences over the possible states of their environment. As the agents make observations about the actions, we assume that their preferences have a utility representation over the set of possible joint actions. Because the preferences are stationary, we shall also keep the sets of the possible actions stationary so that $A_i^t = A_i$, $A = A_1 \times \cdots \times A_n$. Hence, each agent has a utility function $U_i(a)$: $A \mapsto R$ and the agents act so as to maximize their utility. This is used to define the decision rules. To avoid ambiguity in the relaxation schemes that follow, we assume that the sets A_i are infinite; that is, the decision variables are continuous. Otherwise, with discrete variables, a more complicated notation would be needed. As the sets A_i are infinite, we also assume that $U_i(a)$ are continuous and bounded in a and strictly quasiconcave with respect to a_i, and that the sets A_i are compact and convex. These technical assumptions are made to ensure the existence of unique maximizing reactions.

The basic type of reactive behavior is the one where the agents act myopically to maximize their individual expected utilities. The agents act under uncertainty if they do not know each others' decision rules—how the others are going to react. The simplest possible guess is that the others will stick to their past actions. This gives rise to the following decision rule:

$$d_i^t(h^t) = \arg\max_{a_i \in A_i} U_i(a_1^{t-1}, \ldots, a_i, \ldots, a_n^{t-1}) \qquad t \geq 1 \qquad (4)$$

The first actions at $t = 0$ are chosen by another mechanism or taken as given. We call the resulting behavior *best-response dynamics* (BRD). Note that d_i^t is now a function of a^{t-1} only. The BRD decision rule can thus be expressed in the form $d_i^t(h^t) = r_i(a^{t-1})$, where $r_i(\cdot)$ is called the *best response*.

Best-response dynamics has been studied previously in game theory and in economics (e.g., Başar, 1987). It has been subject to a lot of criticism especially in economics, where it is considered a possible model of behavior for oligopoly firms (Daughety, 1988). A characteristic feature of BRD is the simplicity of the expectations about the other agents' reactions. Although all agents are going to react, they still expect the others not to do so. Furthermore, the agents do not change their beliefs about the other agents' behavior even though they have observed otherwise during the unfolding of the interaction. Nevertheless, the idea of myopically optimizing agents is intriguing. Even if BRD is one of the simplest goal-driven individual behavioral patterns, it leads to complex collective behavior.

What happens when multiple agents are involved in a BRD process? Mathematically, the BRD interaction

$$a_i^t = r_i(a^{t-1}) \tag{5}$$

describes a discrete-time dynamic system, which can be analyzed with the standard techniques of systems theory. In the long run the system may diverge, oscillate, or converge to a stationary point $\bar{a}$ that satisfies $r_i(\bar{a}) = \bar{a}_i, i \in N$. Chaotic behavior may occur too. The interesting case is the one where the system converges to a stationary point and remains there so that the agents reach stationary decisions. In the sense of Dow (1990), this corresponds to a *stationary organizational structure*. We call diverging, oscillating, or chaotic behavior *unstable;* these do not lead to any fixed organizational structure.

At this point it is appropriate to indicate the connections with game theory. The triplet (N, A, U), $U = (U_1, \ldots, U_n)$, defines a static game in the strategic form (Friedman, 1991). The stationary points of the BRD interaction (Equation 5) are (noncooperative) Nash equilibria of this game, and vice versa. In other words, for each agent i it holds

$$U_i(\bar{a}_1, \ldots, \bar{a}_i, \ldots, \bar{a}_n) \geq U_i(\bar{a}_1, \ldots, a_i, \ldots, \bar{a}_n) \quad a_i \in A_i \tag{6}$$

so that unilateral deviations from $\bar{a}$ are individually unprofitable. This means that no agent has reason to deviate from the stationary organizational structure. The existence of at least one equilibrium is guaranteed under the current assumptions about the action sets and utility functions (Friedman, 1991). Hence, when we study the interaction patterns of the BRD decision rule, we are actually examining whether BRD behavior leads to a Nash equilibrium. Such analysis is rewarding from the viewpoint of game theory not only because of computational aspects, but also because it could provide justification for the use of the Nash equilibrium as a solution concept. This emphasizes the interdisciplinary nature of the problem in hand. Convergence conditions for the BRD process have been derived for games with infinite action sets (e.g., Başar, 1987). The more complex case of games with finite action sets has also been examined (Stahl, 1988).

When myopic utility maximization is considered as a model of behavior, one must pay attention to the uncertainty about the other agents' actions. Intuitively, human decision makers often try to hedge against uncertainties. This is called *risk-averse behavior*. In utility theory, risk-averse behavior means, for example, that a decision maker prefers \$50 to a lottery that gives \$100 or nothing with probabilities .5 for each. The present case is somewhat different, because the outcome is usually uncertain no matter what action the agent takes. One approach would be to devise decision rules that make the best out of the worst possible outcome. The approach we take is to utilize a personal observation about human behavior. It seems that decision makers often stick to a decision already made, even though there might be reasons to revise that decision. One is unwilling to change a course of actions that has been chosen—this can be called prudence, conservatism, or, in organizations, inertia against changes. In other words, new decisions are often made only when there is little or no uncertainty about the need. The spirit is summarized by "OK, I made that decision so I might as well stick to it for some time and see what happens." Yet the agents using BRD rules change their own actions instantly to the best response, which is based on uncertain information. Therefore, it seems justified and realistic to modify BRD so as to take into account the underlying uncertainties by modeling this inertia of behavior. It may be true that inertia is present in decision making even without uncertainties; this question calls for empirical research. For instance, inertia may also result from the costs of decision making or from external legal barriers. We next examine three simple ways of introducing caution, or inertia, into best-response behavior.

One way to be cautious is to compromise: Instead of the best response, the agents choose a compromise between it and the previous action. This can be described mathematically by a weighted average:

$$d_i^t(h^t) = (1 - \lambda_i)\, a_i^{t-1} + \lambda_i r_i(a^{t-1}) \qquad 0 < \lambda_i \le 1 \qquad (7)$$

where λ_i is the relaxation parameter of agent i. The assumptions about the action sets guarantee that the compromise in Equation 7 is a valid action. We shall call the behavior defined by this decision rule *relaxed best-response dynamics* (RBRD). The computational effects of using relaxation in best-response adjustment processes have been analyzed previously (Başar, 1987; Fisher, 1961). Başar gave the interesting interpretation that "the design [relaxation] parameters . . . could be viewed as each player's belief on the accuracy or validity of the policy chosen by the other player" (p. 549). The idea of taking into account uncertainties is the same. Relaxation changes only the dynamic behavior of the BRD process, not the stationary decisions. In other words, the stationary actions are the same in BRD and in RBRD, but the actions may converge to the stationary values in the latter process even if they do not so in the former. Of course, this depends on the system and on the relaxation parameters.

A compromise allows abrupt changes in the actions if the best response deviates a great deal from the previous action. This can be prevented by giving bounds that limit the difference between two consecutive actions, provided that this difference can be measured. Assume that there exists a metric ρ_i that measures the distance between any two elements of A_i. Then the decisions of agent i could be required to satisfy

$$\rho_i(a_i^t, a_i^{t-1}) \leq B_i^t \qquad t = 1, 2, \ldots \tag{8}$$

where $B_i^t > 0$ is the bound for agent i. We call the BRD behavior subject to this constraint *bounded best-response dynamics* (BBRD). The choice of the metric depends on the setup, and general rules cannot be given. The main idea is that the bounds correspond, for example, to common rules of thumb. Bounded reactions have other interpretations, too: They may reflect physical constraints such as technical limitations in implementing new actions. Again, the bounds effect the dynamics of best-response behavior while the stationary points remain the same. These dynamic effects are nonlinear and difficult to analyze analytically.

We argued earlier that sometimes decision makers do not want to change their actions at all, not even if new information is received and a change would seem rational. Rather than capturing this, the two previous modifications, RBRD and BBRD, actually describe smooth adjustment processes. One way to model nonsmooth inertia is to define individual reaction times for each agent. For example, agent 1 might only react at every third step — in the meantime the agent observes what is going on. But these reaction periods are unlikely to remain constant, so we model this phenomenon by letting the agents react asynchronously with random reaction times. We call the associated behavior *asynchronous best-response dynamics* (ABRD) if the actual new reactions are the ordinary best responses at the appropriate times. Hence, in ABRD the agents do not explicitly learn during the waiting periods. The decision rules of the agents now include stochastic processes that select the time steps when the agents take new actions. The ABRD decision rule is thus generally of the form

$$d_i^t(h^t) = \begin{cases} r_i(a^{t-1}) & \text{if } s_i^t = \text{``reaction''} \\ a_i^{t-1} & \text{if } s_i^t = \text{``no reaction''} \end{cases} \qquad t = 1, 2, \ldots \tag{9}$$

where s_i^t is the associated stochastic process with the possible states "reaction" and "no reaction." Asynchronous reactions are also realistic in the sense that in real organizations synchronicity is difficult to manage, so agents are likely to react in an asynchronous manner. How to select the stochastic processes is a modeling issue. In the extreme, the waiting periods would be so long that the other agents reach stable actions, thus seemingly reducing the uncertainty about their future actions to minimum. In other words, waiting periods implicitly model an effort to learn the behavior of the other agents. Asynchronous reactions change the nature of the original system (Equation 5) completely, and the techniques used with the standard BRD process cannot be used to analyze ABRD interactions. Related issues, such as the convergence of asynchronous algorithms, are studied in the field of distributed computing (e.g., Bertsekas & Tsitsiklis, 1991).

The modifications discussed can naturally be mixed with each other. For instance, reactions could be both relaxed and asynchronous. However, we concentrate in this chapter on pure BRD, RBRD, BBRD, and ABRD behavior. A summary of these is given in Table 7.1. One can of course think of more sophisticated ways of hedging against uncertainties, such as learning and prediction mechanisms; the discussion and development of the related analysis techniques are topics of future research.

SIMULATION ANALYSIS

Now that the decision rules of interest have been specified, we turn to the question of their interaction. The nature of BBRD and ABRD behavior calls for computational simulation analysis. Here an object-oriented programming paradigm proves useful. The essence of this approach is that both the data (parameters) and the methods (decision rules) are integrated in the definition of an object. A useful feature is inheritance: New objects can be defined so that they inherit the properties of one or more objects. It is handy to define agents as objects; a more sophisticated agent object can

TABLE 7.1
Summary of the Decision Rules

Decision Rule	Definition
Best-response dynamics (BRD)	Agent maximizes utility myopically; best response is given by $r_i(a^t) = \arg\max_{a_i} U_i(a_1^t, \ldots, a_i, \ldots, a_n^t)$
Relaxed best-response dynamics (RBRD)	Agent uses a weighted average of the previous action and the best response, $(1 - \lambda_i)a_i^t + \lambda_i r_i(a^t)$
Bounded best-response dynamics (BBRD)	Agent uses myopic best responses constrained by $\rho_i(a_i^{t+1}, a_i^t) \le B_i^{t+1}$
Asynchronous best-response dynamics (ABRD)	Agent uses myopic best responses with random reaction times

inherit the properties of a base object and add new features. This makes it easy to create a large number of agents and simulate different interaction phenomena in large scale. Although all this can be accomplished with procedural techniques, the object-oriented paradigm lends a greater degree of versatility with a smaller effort. Our simulation program MART (Multi-Agent Reactions Testbed) was written in C++ that supports object-oriented programming. With the MART prototype one can simulate the interaction of different decision rules and also other phenomena such as entry and exit of agents.

The utility functions and the action sets of the agents must be fixed for each simulation. Here we use utility functions that represent the profit functions of Cournot oligopolists (e.g., Daughety, 1988). The Cournot model describes an oligopoly with n firms that sell a homogeneous good and only make quantity decisions. The behavior of the buyers is described by an inverse demand function $p(\cdot)$: If a_i denotes the supply by firm i, then the price of the good is $p(\Sigma^n_{i=1} a_i)$. The sales revenue of a firm is simply the product of its supply and the price of the good; the production cost is $c_i(a_i)$. The profits of the firms are thus given by

$$U_i(a) = p(\sum_{j=1}^{n} a_j)a_i - c_i(a_i) \tag{10}$$

It is assumed that the outputs are confined to sets $A_i = [0,a_i^{max}]$. The Cournot model is simple, but we expect the simulations to give insights into the dynamics of the different decision rules in more general settings. Note that asynchronous reactions are especially realistic in the market setup.

For simulations with the ABRD decision rule, the randomization in Equation 9 must be characterized. The simplest choice is that at each simulation step an agent using ABRD reacts with probability q; the previous action is repeated with probability $1 - q$. Hence, the time to the next reaction is random and geometrically distributed. The geometric distribution has no memory, and the expected time to the next reaction is always $1/q$.

Next, interactions of the BRD, RBRD, BBRD, and ABRD decision rules are simulated in two different cases. The simulations have been carried out with a linear inverse demand function $p(Q) = \alpha - \beta Q$ and quadratic cost functions $c_i(a_i) = \gamma_i a_i + \delta_i a_i^2$. The parameters in the simulations have been chosen for demonstration purposes only and do not represent any real market data. Some preliminary simulations were already presented by Verkama et al. (1992).

Case 1

Let us examine four agents, or firms, with the parameters in Table 7.2. Verkama et al. (1992) showed that unstable oscillatory behavior results if all

TABLE 7.2
Parameters of Case 1, $\alpha = 20.0$, $\beta = 1.0$

i	γ_i	δ_i	a_i^0
1	1.12	0.20	2.0
2	1.34	0.89	2.0
3	1.27	0.84	2.0
4	2.10	0.21	2.0

agents use BRD; this is depicted in Fig. 7.1. They also showed that stable behavior may occur if all four agents use RBRD, BBRD, or ABRD decision rules.

What will happen if different agents use different decision rules? Simulations show that for convergence to occur, it is in fact enough that one of the agents uses a decision rule other than BRD. With suitable parameter values, the stationary actions are reached whenever at least one agent uses RBRD, BBRD, or ABRD. Convergence turns out to be fast if the RBRD rule is used, and it happens on a wide range of relaxation parameters. With bounded reactions, convergence is usually slower than it is with relaxation. Furthermore, the actions do not necessarily set to the equilibrium values but rather oscillate around them with a small amplitude. This is due to the unstable nature of the BRD behavior at this equilibrium: The actions tend away from the equilibrium, but the bound(s) prevent them from escaping too far away. With ABRD the convergence depends on the reaction probability. For example, with $q = 0.5$ convergence always seems to occur.

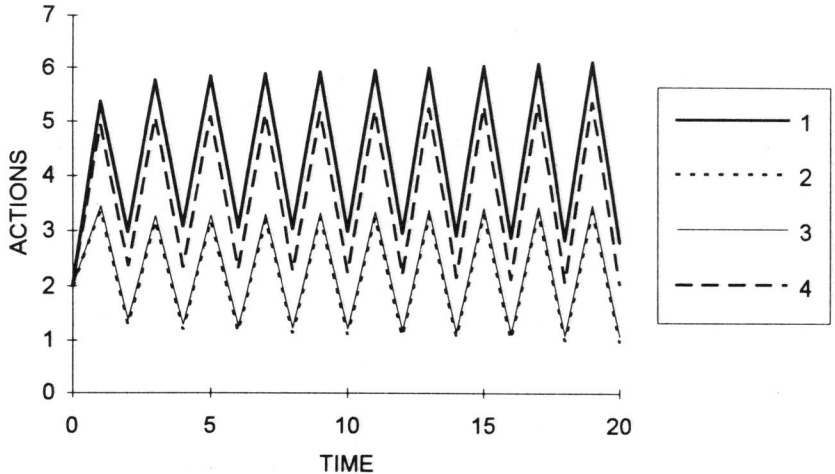

FIG. 7.1.   Unstable BRD behavior with four agents.

TABLE 7.3
Parameters of Case 2, $\alpha = 25.0$, $\beta = 1.5$

i	γ_i	δ_i	a_i^0
1	1.50	0.36	3.53
2	1.16	0.17	2.08
3	1.43	0.84	1.08
4	1.69	0.94	2.14
5	1.28	0.59	3.72

Case 2

Consider five agents with the parameters in Table 7.3. Again, BRD by all agents leads to unstable behavior and a stable organizational structure is not reached. The simulation results are largely similar to those in Case 1 with the exception that now stability seems to require that at least two agents use decision rules other than BRD.

Figure 7.2 shows a simulation where agents 1 and 5 use the RBRD rule with the parameters $\lambda_1 = .4$ and $\lambda_5 = .3$, respectively. Convergence is fast and similar results are obtained with any other pair of agents. Generally we observe that, somewhat counterintuitively, smaller relaxation parameters give better convergence. On the other hand, convergence becomes slow if the relaxation parameters are close to zero. From the viewpoint of conservatism, a small relaxation parameter means that the agent prefers the old action to the best response. Similar results can be reported with the BBRD rule.

Convergence also results whenever any two agents use ABRD with a

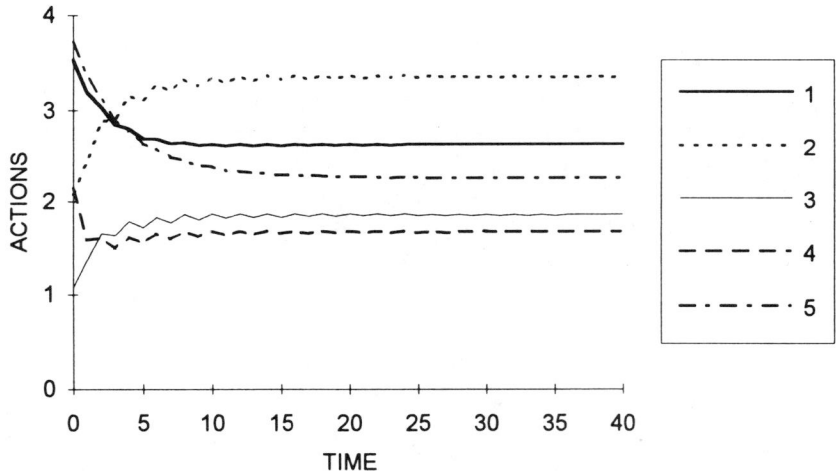

FIG. 7.2.   Relaxation by agents 1 and 5 stabilizes the actions.

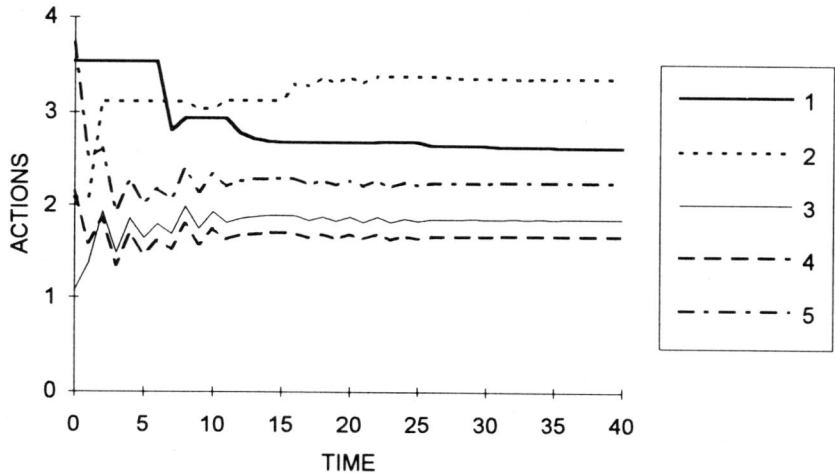

FIG. 7.3.   Stability when agents 1 and 2 react asynchronously.

suitable reaction probability q. Figure 7.3 shows a typical simulation where agents 1 and 2 react with probability $q = .4$. Note that simulation outcomes are now random.

With the ABRD rule the likelihood of convergence depends on q, or more generally on the stochastic process used in Equation 9. To get an idea of how the reaction probability affects convergence in this example, we ran a large number of simulations to estimate convergence probabilities. Figure 7.4 shows the estimated probability of convergence as a function of the reaction probability q of agents 1 and 2. The estimates have been obtained as follows: With each different q we ran 30 simulations of 95 steps and

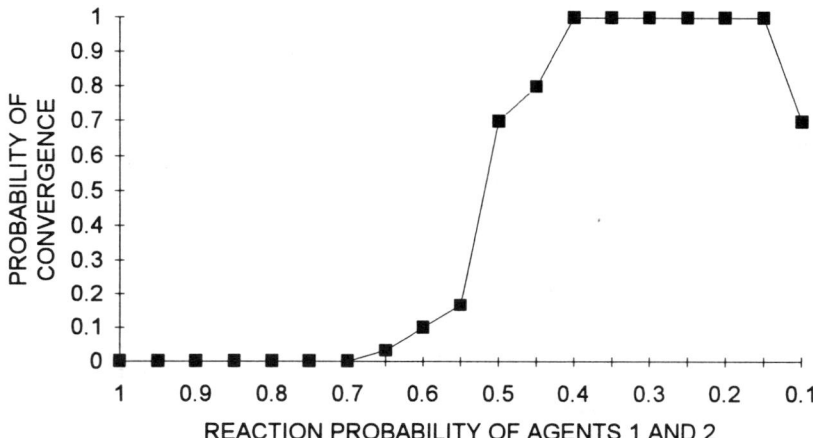

FIG. 7.4.   The estimated probability of convergence as a function of the reaction probabilities of agents 1 and 2.

checked if the process was stable. The inequality $|a_i^{95} - \bar{a}_i| < .005$ was used as a test of stability. If it was true for all i, then the simulation was counted as having converged; otherwise, the process was considered unstable. The probability estimates are simply the relative frequencies of the converged simulations. A sample of 30 runs does not necessarily give accurate statistics, but the estimates give a good idea of how convergence depends on the reaction probabilities in this particular example. The probability of convergence jumps up in the neighborhood of $q = .5$ where the probabilities of reacting and not reacting are even. At this point the expected time to the next reaction exceeds 2 and the waiting effect becomes more tangible. In other words, when $q < .5$ the agents, on the average, actually hold waiting periods to observe the actions of the others. If q is close to zero, convergence becomes slow which explains the transient near $q = .1$ in Fig. 7.4. With the utility functions and the type of asynchronicity used here, a stochastic stability analysis of asymptotic ABRD behavior is also possible.

The simulations confirm the view that BRD behavior is often unstable if practiced by all agents; this is well known in the economic and game-theoretic literature. What is new is that the interaction patterns become stable if some of the agents take into account the uncertainties about the other agents' actions. In other words, myopic utility maximization seems a more plausible behavioral pattern if uncertainties are not ignored. This result is obtained with three simple modifications that introduce caution to best-response reactions. Apart from our preliminary work (Verkama et al., 1992), the observations about the stabilizing effects of the bounded and asynchronous reactions seem to be new. The findings about asynchronicity are significant especially from the viewpoint of economics modeling. In these simulations, prudent or conservative behavior is superior to straight-forward maximizing behavior. One may think that ABRD, BBRD, and RBRD are simplified versions of the best-response behavior, which always calls for exact optimization. The modified rules describe adaptive rather than strictly rational modes of behavior. Naturally, we need to carry out more extensive simulations to make sure that the results do not depend only on the specific utility functions used here.

Interestingly enough, similar results have been obtained in at least two different contexts. Heiner (1989) studied a dynamic setting where a decision maker tries to follow an optimal decision target. He showed that instead of jumping directly to the perceived optimal choice, it pays to adjust gradually toward it; that is, it pays to be cautious. Heiner also cited experiments where this kind of adaptive behavior has actually been observed. In an earlier study Heiner (1988) also showed that, under certain conditions, agents do not necessarily benefit from trying to imitate the behavior of fully optimizing agents. These conditions, however, do not rise from imperfect information but from the agents' imperfect decisions. In the present context the difference between these two is not clearcut. Miller (1989) studied strategies represented by automata in a repeated Prisoner's Dilemma where the past actions were observed imperfectly. He noted that when noise increased, less complex strategies performed better. In other words, even if a sophisticated decision rule is called for under perfect information conditions, this may not be so when there are uncertainties. These results suggest that simple rules of thumb may be efficient in coping with uncertainty, which to some extent is also the interpretation of our results. A related perspective is given by psychologists who have argued that optimality is beyond human capabilities, so that human rationality is bounded and we rely on approximate methods (Simon, 1990).

CONCLUSION

In this chapter we presented a framework for studying behavioral patterns where the agents in an organization react to each other's actions with optimizing decisions. Best-response behavior was analyzed within the framework. In best-response dynamics the agents try to maximize their individual utilities myopically and assume that the other agents will not react. The use of this decision rule can result in different types of collective behavior. In particular, the actions of the agents may converge to stationary decisions. This happens rarely if all agents use the best-response decision rule. One reason for this is that the agents do not take into account uncertainty about the others' actions. We examined three modified decision rules that describe more cautious behavior. Simulations with a market model show that the modifications can render the interaction process stable so that stationary decisions are reached. One may think that the modified decision rules describe a simpler, adaptive behavior as opposed to the complex best-response dynamics that always calls for exact optimization. In this sense our results reinforce earlier results indicating that simple rules of thumb may cope well with uncertainties (Heiner, 1989; Miller, 1989).

The chapter highlights the benefits of an interdisciplinary approach to organizational problems. The development of new computational methods opens up exciting research possibilities. A particularly notable area is the simulation analysis of individual and collective behavior in organizations. Currently, however, realistic simulations await the development of algorithms and models mimicking human behavior. The framework developed here can also be used for studies other than the stability analysis of decision rule interactions. It was mentioned that the fitness of different decision rules could be analyzed. Such analysis could use ideas from evolutionary game theory (Maynard Smith, 1982) and could benefit from techniques such as genetic algorithms. Another interesting question is how the decision rules themselves could adapt. The evolutionary approach may give a new perspective to many questions. For example, Hansen and Samuelson (1988) studied under what conditions evolutionary processes select equilibrium actions of economic agents. Extending this idea, one could carry out simulations to study what evolutionary processes, if any, lead to existing organizational structures and whether they coincide with any kind of equilibrium behavior. The relationship between inertia in individual behavior and structural inertia in organizations is another research problem that could be analyzed with simulations and evolutionary techniques. For example, Hannan and Freeman (1984) argued that evolutionary selection processes favor organizations with rigid structures. All in all, there are numerous challenging research possibilities where emerging computational techniques are likely to be found useful.

ACKNOWLEDGMENTS

Markku Verkama acknowledges the support of the Väinö Tanner Foundation, the Finnish Cultural Foundation, and the Swedish Foundation of Culture in Finland. Raimo P. Hämäläinen acknowledges the support of the Academy of Finland.

REFERENCES

Arthur, W. B. (1991). Designing economic agents that act like human agents: A behavioral approach to bounded rationality. *American Economic Review Papers and Proceedings, 81,* 353–359.
Arthur, W. B. (1993). On designing economic agents that behave like human agents. *Journal of Evolutionary Economics, 3,* 1–22.
Başar, T. (1987). Relaxation techniques and asynchronous algorithms for on-line computation of non-cooperative equilibria. *Journal of Economic Dynamics and Control, 11,* 531–549.
Bertsekas, D. P., & Tsitsiklis, J. N. (1991). Some aspects of parallel and distributed iterative algorithms—A survey. *Automatica, 27,* 3–21.
Bond, A. H., & Gasser, L. (Eds.). (1988). *Readings in distributed artificial intelligence.* San Mateo, CA: Morgan Kaufmann.
Chatterjee, K., Kersten, G., & Shakun, M. F. (Eds.). (1991). Group decision and negotiation [Focused issue]. *Management Science, 37*(10).
Daughety, A. F. (Ed.). (1988). *Cournot oligopoly: Characterization and applications.* Cambridge, UK: Cambridge University Press.
Dow, G. K. (1990). The organization as an adaptive network. *Journal of Economic Behavior and Organization, 14,* 159–185.
Fisher, F. M. (1961). The stability of the Cournot oligopoly solution: The effects of speeds of adjustment and increasing marginal costs. *Review of Economic Studies, 28,* 125–135.
Friedman, J. W. (1991). *Game theory with applications to economics* (2nd ed.). New York: Oxford University Press.
Hannan, M. T., & Freeman, J. (1977). The population ecology of organizations. *American Journal of Sociology, 82,* 929–964.

Hannan, M. T., & Freeman, J. (1984). Structural inertia and organizational change. *American Sociological Review, 49,* 149–164.

Hansen, R. G., & Samuelson, W. F. (1988). Evolution in economic games. *Journal of Economic Behavior and Organization, 10,* 315–338.

Heiner, R. A. (1988). Imperfect decisions in organizations: Toward a theory of internal structure. *Journal of Economic Behavior and Organization, 9,* 25–44.

Heiner, R. A. (1989). The origin of predictable dynamic behavior. *Journal of Economic Behavior and Organization, 12,* 233–257.

Holland, J. H., & Miller, J. H. (1991). Artificial adaptive agents in economic theory. *American Economic Review Papers and Proceedings, 81,* 365–370.

Laird, J. E., Newell, A., & Rosenbloom, P. S. (1987). SOAR: An architecture for general intelligence. *Artificial Intelligence, 33,* 1–64.

Lane, D. A. (1993a). Artificial worlds and economics, part I. *Journal of Evolutionary Economics, 3,* 89–107.

Lane, D. A. (1993b). Artificial worlds and economics, part II. *Journal of Evolutionary Economics, 3,* 177–197.

Malone, T. W., & Crowston, K. (1991). *Toward an interdisciplinary theory of coordination.* Working Paper No. 3294-91-MSA, Massachusetts Institute of Technology, Sloan School of Management.

Maynard Smith, J. (1982). *Evolution and the theory of games.* New York: Cambridge University Press.

Miller, J. H. (1989). *The coevolution of automata in the Prisoner's Dilemma.* Working Paper No. 89-003, Santa Fe Institute.

Moss, S., & Rae, J. (Eds.). (1992). *Artificial intelligence and economic analysis: Prospects and problems.* Hants, UK: Edward Elgar.

Radner, R. (1987). Decentralization and incentives. In T. Groves, R. Radner, & S. Reiter (Eds.), *Information, incentives, and economic mechanisms: Essays in honor of Leonid Hurwicz* (pp. 3–47). Oxford: Basil Blackwell.

Sah, R. K., & Stiglitz, J. E. (1985). Human fallibility and economic organization. *American Economic Review Papers and Proceedings, 75,* 292–297.

Simon, H. A. (1990). Invariants of human behavior. *Annual Review of Psychology, 41,* 1–19.

Stahl, D. O., II. (1988). On the instability of mixed-strategy Nash equilibria. *Journal of Economic Behavior and Organization, 9,* 59–69.

Verkama, M., Hämäläinen, R. P., & Ehtamo, H. (1992). Multi-agent interaction processes: From oligopoly theory to decentralized artificial intelligence. *Group Decision and Negotiation, 2,* 137–159.

8

Validating an Expert System That Designs Organizations

Helmy H. Baligh
Richard M. Burton
Duke University

Børge Obel
Odense University

The Organizational Consultant is a knowledge-base expert system to aid the design of organizations. It is a decision support system that can help in analyzing, diagnosing, and designing organizations. This chapter describes a process that incorporates information obtained from the use of the Organizational Consultant to validate and improve it. As experts get to be experts by doing, so the Organizational Consultant may be improved through a systematic process of use and modification. We discuss how the validation process improves the underlying knowledge and, hence, the system. After we briefly describe the expert system, we review the validation liaterature, and we then present our own process of learning from the use of the system—that is, how to validate and improve the Organizational Consultant.

THE ORGANIZATIONAL CONSULTANT

The Organizational Consultant (Baligh, Burton, & Obel, 1990) specifies approporiate organizational contingencies or structures and properties for given organizational situations, as shown in Fig. 8.1. It determines values for the structure and its properties. The inference engine begins with a list of questions, seeking the needed facts from the user about the organization's situation, the values for the contingent factors. The facts that it needs to know are those of the size, ownership, managerial preferences, environment, strategy, and technology. The system's inference engine begins with a

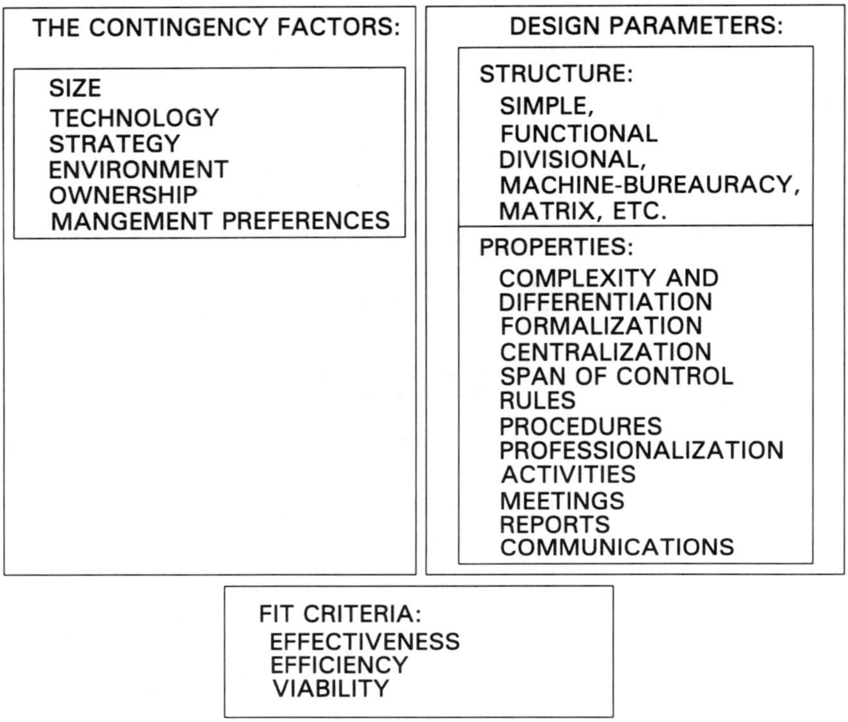

THE CONTINGENCY FACTORS:	DESIGN PARAMETERS:
SIZE TECHNOLOGY STRATEGY ENVIRONMENT OWNERSHIP MANGEMENT PREFERENCES	STRUCTURE: SIMPLE, FUNCTIONAL DIVISIONAL, MACHINE-BUREAURACY, MATRIX, ETC.
	PROPERTIES: COMPLEXITY AND DIFFERENTIATION FORMALIZATION CENTRALIZATION SPAN OF CONTROL RULES PROCEDURES PROFESSIONALIZATION ACTIVITIES MEETINGS REPORTS COMMUNICATIONS

FIT CRITERIA:
EFFECTIVENESS
EFFICIENCY
VIABILITY

FIG. 8.1. Organizational Consultant: Contingency–design relations.

goal, works backward through the knowledge base, using the facts, and recommends a structure and its properties, such as "a functional structure with high formalization and many rules."

The Organizational Consultant analyzes the current organizational structure from the answers it obtains from the user on 27 questions related to the functioning of the organization. The current design of the organization is then described in terms of structure and properties. Next, the Organizational Consultant asks the user for inputs related to 16 major situational variables. The answers are then translated into values for the internal concepts used in the system. Based on these facts, the system recommends the structure and properties that best fit the specified situation. The situation itself is analyzed and possible situational misfits are identified. Finally, the current and prescribed organizational structures are compared and possible changes are recommended. The system also includes a feature that enables the user to change input values and rerun the consultation, thereby providing a mechanism to perform sensitivity analysis.

VALIDATION

The classic work on the validity issue in social science is Campbell and Stanley (1963). Cook and Campbell (1976) later developed four concepts of validity: internal validity, statistical conclusion validity, external validity, and construct validity. The validation of an expert system involves the same general principles of validation, with some differences in detail. The issue is well discussed in a number of works (Berry & Hart, 1990; Blanning, 1981; Preece, 1990).

The principles have been stated in various ways. Feldman and Arnold (1983) defined validity in terms of content, construct, and criterion-related validity. They needed answers to the questions, does it make sense to a group of experts, is it measuring the underlying characteristics, and is it related to the real-world intent? McGraw and Harbison-Briggs (1989) presented a variety of verification and validity techniques. Hayes-Roth, Waterman, and Lenat (1983) considered validation to be a major concern in developing expert systems.

The expert system designs organizations that fit well-defined sets of circumstances. It is a normative model, which shows what a segment of the world ought to be like. The validation process of such a system should be expected to differ from that of a positive model. For example, the correctness of the predictions of the positive model would be replaced by the correctness of the "predictions" of the expert system—whether the design recommendations are reasonable and helpful. Validating the expert system involves showing it to be correct, consistent, comprehensive, relatively complete, and operational.

O'Leary (1988) suggested that there are six possibilities for analyzing an expert system:

> Analyze the knowledge base for accuracy, analyze the knowledge base for completeness, analyze the knowledge base weights, test the inference engine, analyze the condition-decision matches for decision quality, and analyze the condition-decision matches to determine whether the right question was found for the right reasons. (p. 75)

No one of these six possibilities is sufficient to validate the expert system. Yet these questions do address the fundamental validity issues and are related to the social science validity operationalizations (albeit in a somewhat different form). In Table 8.1, these validation criteria are juxtaposed with others developed by Feldman and Arnold (1983) and Cook and Campbell (1976). Each validation approach begins with the model itself and its content, and then considers its relevance within the context of the problem. McGrath, Martin, and Kulka (1982) suggested a triangulation approach: cases, experts,

TABLE 8.1
Comparing Validation Approaches

	A priori	
Content	Internal validity	Analyze the knowledge base for:
		• Accuracy
	Statistical validity	• Completeness
		• Base weights
	In situ	
Construct	External validity	Test the inference engine
Criterion-related	Construct validity	Analyze the condition-decision for decision quality
		Analyze the condition-decision to determine if right answers for right reasons
Feldman and Arnold (1983)	Cook and Campbell (1976)	O'Leary (1988)

and students. Assuring the validity of the Organizational Consultant by using the results of its application in cases and real-world situations is analogous to Davis' (1984) list of expert behaviors: Solve the problem, explain the result, learn, restructure the knowledge, determine relevance, and degrade gracefully. This is learning by doing.

Expert system validation can be considered as a process or a product — that is, how to do validation and the results you obtain. There are at least three ways to discuss validation: (a) an application of validation criteria (e.g., O'Leary's to the expert system), (b) the product of validation (i.e., what changes were made to the expert system), and (c) the process of validation. Our interest in the validation process concerns what to do, why to do it, and what can be learned.

THE FOUNDATION EXPERT SYSTEM

Validation of an expert system is an ongoing, never-ending process that is realized through application and experience. A knowledge-base expert system is validated, and hopefully improved, the same way an individual becomes an expert: through practice and experience. The object is therefore to develop a validation process that specifies what to do, how to learn, and what to learn. The process of validating the Organizational Consultant described here addresses all three aspects. Throughout the process, the expert system continues to offer better organizational design solutions. But however much we improve it, it remains an imperfect "expert system" that requires a skilled and experienced user to apply it in a reasonable fashion.

The model embodied in the system is the result of the synthesis of partial theories in the literature, subsequent theorizing, and the transformation of positive models into normative ones. In earlier research (Baligh & Burton, 1981; Burton & Obel, 1984), it was suggested that decision rules (i.e., if–then conditional imperative statements) could be developed and applied to recommend appropriate organizational designs. The tasks of both developing the requisite number of rules and applying them are involved and laborious. The use of a "logic machine" makes the application much easier, and helps in the process of modifying the set of rules first developed by an expert. Knowledge-base expert systems supply the logic machine needed. Thus, a knowledge base for organizational design could be systematically developed within a number of different logic machines or shells.

The model began with a set of rules we had developed earlier in production rule form (Baligh, Burton, & Obel, 1987). To these we added partial theories from the literature. Sometimes these were normative; sometimes we had to derive normative forms from positive or descriptive ones. An example of a partial theory is Duncan's (1979) decision tree, which specifies appropriate organizational designs for different values of the environmental variable of uncertainty. This model has six if–then rules. But Duncan's rules, as are many others, are very limited and they needed to be connected to other partial theories, for example, Perrow's (1967) theory on technology and structure. The process of combining and fitting these two models required the creation of more theories. This theory-building phase continued until a basic model with an appropriate domain of contingency variables and ranges of design variables was developed. This process was described in Baligh, Burton, and Obel (1993). The model's domain included, among others, size, strategy, technology, environment, and management preferences. Its range had design parameters of centralization, specialization, formalization, and so forth.

Validation and Continued Model Development

The first working expert system was the result of literature models and new theorizing only. Once running, the system produced designs that were used to modify and improve it. The validation process we describe is based on the work of O'Leary (1988). O'Leary's six recommendations are the following:

1. Analyze the knowledge base for accuracy.
2. Analyze the knowledge for completeness.
3. Analyze the knowledge base weights.
4. Test the inference engine.
5. Analyze the condition-decision for decision quality.
6. Analyze the condition–decision matches to determine whether the right answer was found for the right reasons.

We call the first three a priori criteria and last three in situ tests.

The a priori criteria demand that the contingency-design relations (see Fig. 8.1) be stated as accurately as possible in the production rule knowledge-base format. Briefly stated, the basic theory and its rules were developed by the three authors independently, and then they compared their rules. The bases of their efforts were literature models and their own theoretic work and models. The result was a set of prescriptive if–then rules mapping facts into design variables. These rules were reviewed for accuracy, consistency, and completeness by the authors. The creation of design rules is relatively straightforward. Crafting a consistent and coherent set of rules is an ongoing and difficult job. O'Leary's third criterion, analyzing the knowledge base weights, is a formidable task. There are two ways to consider the base weights, or certainty factors, attached to the if–then rules. These factors may refer to the relative strength of the various contingency statements made in the literature and the authors' models. Consider the two statements, "if size is large, then decentralization is high" and "if the strategy is analyzer, then decentralization is medium." The issue is to assign certainty factors to each of these rules to reflect their relative strengths, or importance to the goals of the organization, both separately and collectively. The knowledge base weight may refer to the strengths of the arguments that support the rule, that is, the quality and correctness of the rule. It is this latter component that is the object of an in situ test. (Testing the inference engine was not a major issue.) These issues were considered using cases, working with executives and students (as we discuss later in more detail).

O'Leary's criteria were not applied in strict order; we moved generally from a priori consideration to in situ ones. The modifications were to adjust certainty factors, add rules, and drop rules (Fig. 8.2). We reduced O'Leary's six criteria to a two-step process of (a) "basic theory," or a priori careful specification of the expert system, and (b) in situ experience and modification from use.

A Process of Validation

The validation process used on the Organizational Consultant relies on information obtained from cases, consultation with executives, dialogue with experts, and executive MBA (master's program in business adminis-

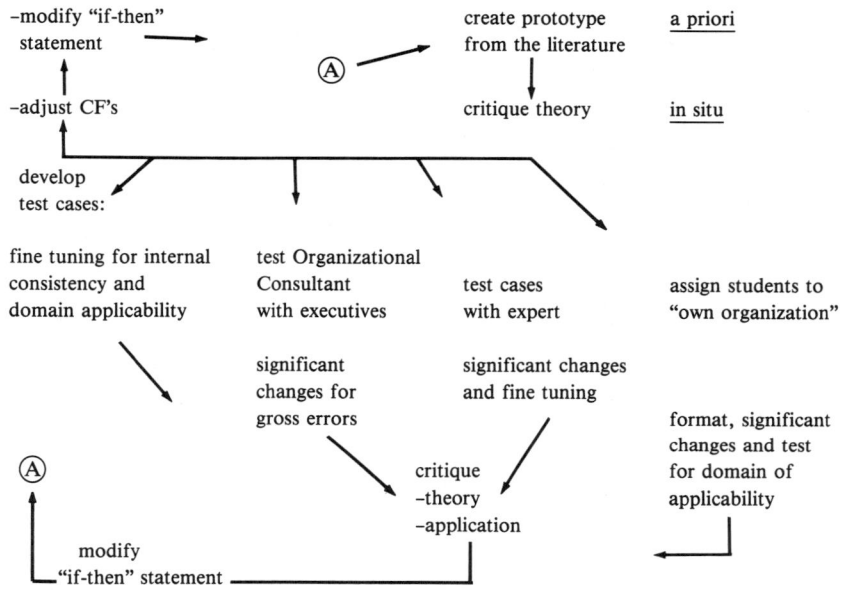

FIG. 8.2. Validation.

tration) student assignments. The order of testing was similar to that previously described, but involved all three sources in no special order.

In the process of validation, we make small and large changes in production rules, in the ease of use, and in the domain of applicability of the Organizational Consultant. As we illustrate, modifying the Organizational Consultant combines theory and application. Through application, issues are raised, but resolution depends on theory and its appropriate incorporation into the Organizational Consultant. It also forces us to reconsider the theory, thus necessitating further theory development. The validation process included three different types of tests: text cases, executives, and executive MBA students.

Text Cases

The first test was based on seven cases selected from textbooks. The cases were chosen to obtain variation across the values of the contingencies, such as large and small firms, manufacturing and service, and so forth, faced by the organizations to be designed (see Table 8.2). The authors, acting as experts, then solved these cases using their own expertise as well as material from instructor's manuals. A major objective of this test was to examine the domain of applicability of the Organizational Consultant, because it is based on theory that is posited to be very general. From these seven cases, it was observed that the Organizational Consultant functioned generally

TABLE 8.2
Characteristics of the Test Cases

	Structure	Formalization	Centralization	Complexity
Textbook	Functional	High	Medium	High
	Functional	Medium	Medium	Medium
	Divisional	High	Low	High
	Adhocracy	Low	Low	High
	Matrix	Low	Low	High
	Machine bureau	Medium	Medium	Medium
	Professional bureau	Medium	Low	High
Executive company	Unknown	Medium	Medium	Medium
	Simple	Medium	Medium	Low
	Simple	Low	High	Low
	Unknown	Medium	Medium	Medium
	Unknown	Medium	Medium	Medium
New cases	Simple	High	High	Low
	Simple	Medium	Medium	Low
	Simple	Low	High	Low
	Functional	High	Low	Medium
	Simple	Low	Low	Low
	Functional	High	Medium	Medium
	Simple	Low	Low	Low
A few executives				
Test 1	Adhocracy	Low	Low	High
Test 2	Matrix	Low	Low	High
Test 3	Machine bureau	Medium	Medium	Medium

very well. In many detailed recommendations, however, it needed to be improved. For example, recommendations on the use of committees and better communications were part of the expert recommendations, but initially were not in the Organizational Consultant recommendations. Based on the results of these cases, the knowledge base was revised with respect to both adding and refining the rules as well as fine-tuning the certainty factors. This process continued until the Organizational Consultant provided acceptable results for each case. The use of cases as the basis for developing a knowledge base is similar to the approach used by Chadha, Mazlack, and Pick (1991).

Executives

The Organizational Consultant was then used by executives in telecommunications, pharmaceutical, manufacturing, and retailing firms, among others. As before, the organizations varied on a number of dimensions. An initial issue concerned the manner in which the Organizational Consultant posed questions to the executives. In the first version, the Organizational Consultant asked very general and abstract questions. Most executives had difficulties answering these questions and preferred questions that were objective and detailed. Consequently, the Organizational Consultant was revised to ask detailed questions and then transform the answers into appropriate internal program inputs. For example, executives were not comfortable with the Miles and Snow (1978) strategy typology: prospectors, analyzers, defenders, and reactors. However, they were very confident in answering more detailed questions about their strategy. The detailed responses were then transformed into one of four strategy types. Similarly, some executives had difficulty with a size measure of small, medium, or large, but they knew their employee count. Further tests showed that these changes made it much easier for the executives to use the program.

In most cases, the Organizatioinal Consultant provided design decisions that the executives deemed to be reasonable and appropriate. In a few cases it provided design decisions that many executives considered to be inappropriate; for example, a simple organization was recommended when the executives argued that a functional, divisional, or matrix organization was more appropriate. As size is a major factor to yield a simple structure, we found our size measure needed to be modified, as we discuss later. Again, the rule set was changed and revised so that the Organizational Consultant would provide correct answers to the companies analyzed. For each change, the original textbook cases were rerun to make sure that within the domain area no inappropriate changes were made that produced inappropriate designs for these cases.

A few more test cases were created from the companies visited and added to the original set of cases. In rerunning the new set of cases, it was found that there were a few deficiencies in the domain of variables of the expert system. These were addressed with appropriate variables, and three additional cases were created so that the Organizational Consultant would cover basic organizational configurations. We now have 22 test cases. The characteristics of these are shown in Table 8.2. Each time the Organizational Consultant is altered, either due to work with executives and experts or by normal development work, these 22 cases are rerun to ensure that no inappropriate behavior ensues.

With the set of 22 cases, the authors again assumed the role of experts and did blind comparisons for the 22 cases. First, the Organizational Consultant was applied to yield recommendations and reasons. Second, and independently, one of us offered analysis, recommendations, and reasons for the same cases. Generally, the results were similar and reconcilable. However, we observed:

- The Organizational Consultant was systematic; the expert jumped to conclusions from time to time.
- The Organizational Consultant infrequently made large "errors"; the expert did not.

In the first situation, the expert was learning and changing recommendations as the reasoning from the expert system produced insight and understanding. Changes in the Organizational Consultant were rarely made on this basis. In the second situation, the Organizational Consultant was changed. Large errors were usually the result of an imbalance of influence among the contingency factors—for example, the Organizational Consultant would base its recommendation primarily on technology and minimize the strategy influence. Adjusting the certainty factors was then required. These results showed us how and where to make appropriate changes in the Organizational Consultant.

Executive MBA Students

Over a 4-year period, approximately 150 executive MBA students in an organizational design course have chosen to apply the Organizational Consultant to their own organization. The executive students represent a broad domain of potential applicability for the Organizational Consultant. The organizations represent the following diverse group:

- Size and scope: large organizations, small organizations; total organization, department in a large organization.
- Industry and business: telecommunications, computers, banking, education, consulting, manufacturing, software development, public utilities, governmental organizations, not-for-profit service.
- Technology: routine and not, divisible and not.
- Strategy: prospector to defender.
- Management preference: strong power desire by top management, to less so.

As with the earlier cases, not all possible combinations (approximately 13 million) of contingency factors were represented, but many real-world combinations were supported.

The executive student assignment was straightforward: Write a narrative describing your organization, and apply the Organizational Consultant to your organization. They were then to give recommended changes for their organizations and show how they were to be realized. Finally, they were to critique the Organizational Consultant, a particularly important source for validation. These criticisms dealt with "user-friendly" issues, as well as with substantive issues of domain variables, design parameters, and rules. Without dwelling on the user-friendliness problems, students were rather clever in finding ways to trash the program—they found various format, grammatical, and spelling errors; they found the data input routine laborious and inflexible, and found the resulting output difficult to operationalize. But they also gave very constructive suggestions to improve these user issues. We have incorporated most of their suggestions.

The criticisms of the Organizational Consultant's recommendations were most helpful. For example, the domain variable of the organization's size caused much confusion. Using the theory in the literature as a guide, we initially had measured size in terms of the number of employees (Robbins, 1990). In applying the Organizational Consultant at the departmental level, a number of students (and executives) found that the recommendation from the rule "if the organization is small, then the structure is simple" was different from what they had observed. More importantly, their conclusions were different from what we reasoned to be the appropriate structure. As developers of the Organizational Consultant, we had a number of alternatives: Make no change, modify the if–then rule, or change the size measure. Returning to the organization theory literature, we found the rule to be appropriate, but the size variable to be too coarse. The rule was modified to incorporate two components, the skill and education level of the employees and their number. Consequently, a size indicator has been developed: the number of employees multiplied by a skill and education index. This size indicator is based on theory (Robbins, 1990; Scott, 1987), with the result that the Organizational Consultant gives more appropriate and reasoned recommendations. This change was checked for the set of test cases discussed earlier.

Over a wide range of organizations described by students, a matrix recommendation seemed reasonable to them; however, the Organizational Consultant rarely suggested this design. We directly examined the knowledge-base rules and found the problem to be in the domain variables. A number of contingency factors that lead to a matrix recommendation were not in the domain. A changing environment, a nonroutine technology, nondivisible technology, and diverse products and markets call for a good deal of coordination and information processing, which can be realized in a matrix organization structure (Galbraith, 1974). These variables and the rules mapping their values into design variables values were added and the matrix structure recommendation gap was filled.

What is the Organizational Consultant's domain of applicability? The executive student organizations covered a broad range of organizations and provided a test. We found that the Organizational Consultant provided appropriate recommendations for the following:

- A 10-person software development company. The executive student owner gained insight about the simple and ad hoc organizational design alternatives.
- A 300-person manufacturing plant. The plant had been organized functionally for many years, but was being changed to a product or divisional organization. The Organizational Consultant made the same recommendation. Further, it provided detailed reasons — more than previously offered by the management.
- A large chemical company. The 5,000-person company had been organized by function for many years. New competitive realities suggested a need to consider a change. Again, the reasons given by Organizational Consultant were helpful.
- A 3,000-person software firm. The firm is a simple organization run by a single individual. Numerous potential problems were suggested by Organizational Consultant.
- A 300-person consulting firm. Its current matrix structure seemed very appropriate, despite a simple structure recommendation. This case was one of the supporting cases for the matrix change discussed previously.
- A small research and development laboratory. Its matrix structure did not work well. The Organizational Consultant offered the manager insights on the problem, and suggested a reasoned change.
- A university office. This small, nonprofit university department had grown over the years into a mixed complex structure. Numerous potential problems from the Organizational Consultant were, indeed, real. The recommendations were accepted by the executive student as reasonable.

These executive student organizations are diverse. The Organizational Consultant offered new insights, made reasonable recommendations in each case, and generally performed well.

The expert system can, as already described, operate with unknown information. This allowed us to run the system for each domain variable individually. For example, we input information that only relates to environment and then checked that the recommendations were in alignment with the coarse rules from the environment models. Similar runs were done for each of the contingency factors. With this process, flaws in the knowledge base and its basis models were detected and corrected. Marginal changes were checked to make sure that they were consistent with the changed portion of the system.

The Turing Test

The Turing Test has been put forward as one method to examine computers and their programs. Blanning (1984, p. 283; quoted on p. 311 in McGraw

& Harbison-Briggs, 1989) wrote, "System Validation is ideally accomplished by means of a Turing Test." A Turing Test suggests that an expert should not be able to determine whether a solution has been generated by the computer or another human expert. Briefly, the computer behaves as an expert. Clearly, this result is very difficult to obtain, even in a limited domain, and it will remain an unobtainable ideal. But is it really an ideal? The answer is that it is not.

Consider the Turing Test from a user's viewpoint. If the user has a Turing Test program, then the user need not understand the real problems and issues. The user could rely on the program as a black box genius; the computer can replace the human. Indeed, the human can be rather ignorant about the problem domain. Here, the user is the amateur, who not only needs help but is replaced by the computer for all intents and purposes. We suggest this is seldom the role of the computer program, or expert system, in management. Except for the most trivial of situations, managers are unwilling to turn the decision over to the computer. Indeed, managers want help, understanding, and an appreciation of trade-offs and their implications. Managers want help in their own decisions. They want intelligent decision support, not black boxes. So the goal for managerial expert systems is to help users (and, frequently, experts themselves) obtain better decisions and better understanding. With this different goal, we suggest that managerial knowledge-base expert systems have different criteria for validity. The system should be:

- Systematic: The expert system must use selected data from the real situation, and analyze it systematically to yield solutions or recommendations.
- Intuitive: The recommendation(s) must seem intuitively reasonable to the user.
- Instructive: The recommendation must broaden the domain of consideration, suggest new alternatives, and offer different insights on the issues than the user might otherwise generate.

An expert system that meets these criteria will help the manager, who assumes responsibility for choices. The manager wants more than an answer. The manager wants to develop a better understanding and intuition for the job. An expert system that meets the Turing Test ideal is not only unattainable, but undesirable. The manager wants help, understanding, and insight, not only expert answers.

In brief, the Turing Test is irrelevant, not because it may be an unattainable ideal, but because it is not what managers want and need. It is not what the experts who wrote it want either; their goal is to write even better systems and not ones that capture their knowledge at a sole point in time. They want help, understanding, and intuition, that is, decision support. The implications for expert system development suggest that we begin with the user, not the machine. The appropriate criteria will emerge rather naturally. We want a systematic approach that is instructive and intuitive.

Generalizations on Validation of Managerial Expert Systems

Our validation approach includes a number of methods. This is similar to the concept of triangulation (McGrath et al., 1982). This idea is that no one method is sufficient, so the validity question should be addressed from many viewpoints. We began with the careful development of a prototype, and we continue to test it in cases and with executives, experts, and executive students. The users and the cases were chosen to span a broad range of organizations to test the domain of applicability and the appropriateness of the recommendation within the domain. In modifying the Organizational Consultant, we always return to the theory for support. Bad results in designs made by the system are not by themselves enough of a logical basis to make a change. The development process is guided by theory, but the incompleteness of the theory also forces us to reconsider and develop the theory. The elements of our validation approach are:

Apply the theory.   The prototype is theory based. Use-triggered expert system changes should not be singular and ad hoc, but theory based. (Non-theory-based changes can be endless, and without foundation or reason.)

Use a variety of methods.   Seek a variety of users and situations.

Use practitioners, students, and experts for evaluation.   Validation is instructive to all users and must meet the tests of reasonableness and be intuitive appealing.

Return to the theoretical paradigms by partial analyses of incomplete data.

When applied, these maxims yield recommendations which are intuitive and instructive to the user.

In brief, our goal is to develop an expert system as a decision support system for the design of organizations. It must be theory based and operationally tested to be valid. Our approach focuses on qualitative, in-depth analysis of specific consultation episodes. Through this analysis, our understanding of what the Organizational Consultant can do, as well as should do, grows; with that understanding, we also gain insight into the organizational design process itself, and into what we, as organizational theorists, can do and should do to enhance the theory of organizational design.

REFERENCES

Baligh, H., & Burton, R. M. (1981). Describing and designing organization structures and processes. *International Journal of Policy Analysis and Information Systems, 5*(4), 251–266.

Baligh, H., Burton, R. M., & Obel, B. (1987). Design of organizational structures: An expert system method. In J.-L. Roos (Ed.), *Economics and artificial intelligence* (pp. 177–182). Oxford, UK: Pergamon.

Baligh, H., Burton, R. M., & Obel, B. (1990). Devising expert systems in organization theory: The organizational consultant. In M. Masuch (Ed.), *Organization, management, and expert systems* (pp. 35–57). Berlin: Walter de Gruyter.

Baligh, H., Burton, R. M., & Obel, B. (1993). *Creating the theory for a usable organization designing expert system.* Working Paper, Fuqua School of Business, Duke University, Durham, NC.

Berry, D. C., & Hart, A. E. (1990). Evaluating expert systems. *Expert Systems, 7*(4), 199–207.

Blanning, R. W. (1984). Knowledge acquisition and system validation in expert systems for management. *Human Systems Management, 4,* 280–285.

Burton, R. M., & Obel, B. (1984). *Designing efficient organizations: Modelling and experimentation.* Amsterdam: North Holland.

Campbell, D. T., & Stanley, J. C. (1963). *Experimental and quasi-experimental designs for research.* Chicago: Rand McNally.

Chadha, S. R., Mazlack, L. J., & Pick, R. A. (1991). Using existing knowledge sources (cases) to build an expert system. *Expert Systems, 8*(1), 3–10.

Cook, T. D., & Campbell, D. T. (1976). The design and conduct of quasi-experiments and true experiments in field settings. In M. D. Dunnette (Ed.), *Handbook of industrial and organizational psychology* (pp. 223–326). Chicago: Rand McNally.

Davis, R. (1984). Amplifying expertise with expert systems. In P. H. Winston & K. A. Prendergast (Eds.), *The A.I. business* (pp. 17–40). Cambridge, MA: MIT Press.

Duncan, R. B. (1979). What is the right organization structure? *Organizational Dynamics,* Winter, 59–79.

Feldman, D. C., & Arnold, H. J. (1983). *Managing individual and group behavior in organizations.* New York: McGraw-Hill.

Galbraith, J. R. (1974). Organization design: An information processing view. *Interfaces, 4*(3), 28–36.

Hayes-Roth, F., Waterman, D., & Lenat, D. (1983). *Building expert systems.* Reading, MA: Addison-Wesley.

McGrath, J. E., Martin, J., & Kulka, R. A. (1982). *Judgement calls in research.* Beverly Hills, CA: Sage.

McGraw, K. L., & Harbison-Briggs, K. (1989). *Knowledge acquisition: Principles and guidelines.* Englewood Cliffs, NJ: Prentice-Hall.

Miles, R. E., & Snow, C. C. (1978). *Organizational strategy, structure, and process.* New York: McGraw-Hill.

O'Leary, D. E. (1988). Methods of validating expert systems. *Interfaces, 18,* 72–79.

Perrow, C. (1967). A framework for the comparative analysis of organizations. *American Sociological Review, 32*(2), 194–208.

Preece, A. D. (1990). Towards a methodology for evaluating expert systems. *Expert Systems, 7*(4), 215–223.

Robbins, S. P. (1990). *Organization theory: Structure, design, and applications.* Englewood Cliffs, NJ: Prentice-Hall.

Scott, W. R. (1987). *Organizations, natural and open systems.* Englewood Cliffs, NJ: Prentice-Hall.

9

Computer Simulations of Organizations as Experiential Learning Systems: Implications for Organization Theory

Theresa K. Lant
New York University

Historically, the use of computer simulations has remained outside the mainstream of research methods used to study organizations. Computer simulations are often perceived as a tool for analytical modeling, viewed as artificial, simplistic, technical, difficult to understand, and of limited contribution to the field. Lately, however, a trend has emerged toward using simulations more frequently for theory-building organizations research. The field of organization theory has begun to recognize that our theories of organizing need to become more longitudinal and evolutionary in nature. However, there is a lack of sufficient theory development in this area because of the difficulty of theorizing about complex phenomena over time. It is difficult to explicate how organizational processes unfold over time in different contexts to yield various organizational outcomes. The unfolding of these processes can be observed, however, in a computer simulation. A computer simulation can take a complex set of assumptions, simulate a set of organizational processes, and represent the implications of these processes for organizational outcomes. Behavioral computer simulations, which model the procedures, processes, and decision rules used by a system (Crecine, 1969), have played an important, if limited, role in organizational theory development (Cohen & Cyert, 1965).

The purpose of this chapter is threefold. In the first section, I discuss the benefits of using computer simulation as a modeling technique in the so-called *behavioral* field of organization theory. In the second section, I discuss the reasearch that has been conducted in one particular conceptual area of organizational theory, *organizational learning;* this area has experienced a significant amount of theory development that has benefited from the use of computer simulations. This section reviews and comments on simulations of organizations as goal-directed, routine-guided, experiential learning systems. The contributions of this work to organization theory are discussed. In the third section, I discuss how work based on computer simulations can be communicated effectively to the larger organizational theory audience. I hope to demonstrate that organizational research based on computer simulations can be made accessible and relevant to a wide audience of organizational theorists.

WHY USE SIMULATIONS IN ORGANIZATION THEORY?

As the field of organization theory progresses, there is a need to increase the sophistication of our theories of organizing. Many organizational theories are fairly static in nature. Organizations, however, are not static entities. Rather, they are dynamic entities that can develop long histories of experience as they evolve over time. Thus, our theories of organizing must become more longitudinal and evolutionary. One reason for the lack of theory development about longitudinal and evolutionary processes of organizing may be the difficulty of theorizing about such complex phenomena. The evolutionary nature of organizational processes makes deriving the implications of any longitudinal theory of organizations quite complex. It is difficult to explicate how the processes unfold over time in different contexts to yield various organizational outcomes. The unfolding of these processes can be observed, however, in a computer simulation. The researcher is able to control all the variables under consideration, manipulate them to uncover their effects on dependent variables over time, examine all possible combinations and interactions of variables, and examine the dynamic effects of the variables (Mezias & Glynn, in press; Whicker & Sigelman, 1991). Thus, the development of longitudinal theories can be enhanced through the use of simulations. The real value of simulation for organization theory is that it provides a means of deriving implications of our theories that we might not be able to do using more common research methods. Further, simulations are dynamic, allowing the researcher to develop more realistic models, rather than static models, and avoid the shortcomings of equilibrium assumptions. Thus, this chapter proposes that computer simulations should be added enthusiastically to the organization theory tool kit.

EXAMPLES FROM ORGANIZATIONAL LEARNING THEORY

Organizational learning is one area of organization theory where computer simulations have been used widely and have contributed greatly to theory development. The roots of both organizational learning and the relevance of computer simulations for organizational theory can be found in Cyert and March's (1963) *Behavioral Theory of the Firm*. The basic assumptions behind organizational learning theory that they proposed are that organizations are target oriented, adapt incrementally to past experience, and engage in search and choice behavior that is guided by evolving routines. The learning process is assumed to function as follows. First, organizations set aspiration levels, or targets for performance. Aspiration levels are basically operating goals for the organization. These targets are themselves adaptive to experience; they increase when performance exceeds aspiration, and decrease when performance is below aspiration. Actual performance relative to these goals determines the organization's perception of success or failure. Second, performance outcomes relative to aspiration level influence the likelihood that the organization will change routines or other behavior. Change in behavior is more likely when performance is perceived as failing, and past actions are interpreted as having led to failure. When performance exceeds aspirations, change is unlikely. Such outcomes reinforce current behavior and routines. Third, organizations are boundedly rational; the acquisition and processing of information is costly, in terms of resources, time, and effort. Thus, search is routinized, sequential, and costly. Search processes are activated when performance falls below aspiration level. The search for alternatives will be problemistic; that is, a narrow search is conducted in the neighborhood of current behavior for modifications that can be made that will restore performance to the aspired level (Cyert & March, 1963; Lant & Mezias, 1992; Levitt & March, 1988).

Glynn, Milliken, and Lant (1992) contrast this *adaptive learning approach,* where the learning process is characterized by incremental adaptation by decision makers trying to uncover the nature of cause and effect relationships by adjusting their aspirations and behavior in response to experience, with a *knowledge development approach,* which focuses more on how knowledge is acquired and shared within an organization (Argyris & Schon, 1978; Jelinek, 1979). In this chapter, I focus primarily on work in the tradition of the adaptive learning approach. However, as simulations have become more sophisticated, researchers in the adaptive learning tradition have begun to delve into issues relevant to knowledge development, such as the development and institutionalization of beliefs within organizations (e.g., March, 1991). We may, in fact, see a merging of the two perspectives as research progresses on organizational learning.

The key processes of the adaptive learning approach are aspiration level formation and adaptation, adaptation of behavior and routines to performance or outcome feedback, and information search and use. Because these processes are guided by decision rules, they are fairly easy to translate into computer code, which itself includes a series of decision rules. By using simulation, we can create a large number of stylized organizations and watch them learn, take action, and perform over long periods of simulated time. Thus, by simulating organizations characterized by decision rules associated with experiential learning, we can explore the implications of experiential learning for organizational outcomes over time, for organizations with different structures or strategies, and under different environmental conditions. This dynamic property of simulations is very useful in furthering theory development for complex phenomena.

In computer simulations of organizational learning, however, the role of individual interpretations and beliefs is fairly limited. Many computer simulations treat organizations as unitary actors; cognitive processes such as setting aspiration levels, searching for information, making choices among alternatives, and learning are assumed to be characteristics of the organization, and are examined for their relationship to various organizational outcomes and patterns of behavior. As Glynn, Milliken, and Lant (1992) noted, although computer simulations "aptly describe the consequences of routine and rule-following over time, they do not capture fully either the complexities of organizational learning or the intraorganizational dynamics which underlie learning. This limitation seems to characterize both the theory and method" (p. 7). In most computer simulations of organizational learning, individual decision makers are present only implicitly (Masuch & LaPotin, 1989). This limitation is characteristic of the organizational learning literature in general, which has had difficulty in modeling the relationship between individual and organizational learning. The tendency to treat organizations as unitary learning entitities, or to treat individuals, groups, and organizations as equivalent, is not limited to the simulation work in this area, but is also characteristic of other theoretical and empirical work on learning (Lant, Milliken, & Batra, 1992). In fact, some of the first attempts to fill in the black box of how individual learning leads to organizational learning and vice versa have been based on computer simulation (Carley, 1992; Lounama & March, 1987; March, 1991). This type of theoretical progress is precisely what makes computer simulations so valuable.

Simulating Organizations as Experiential Learning Systems

In this section, I discuss several papers that use simulation to explore the implications of experiential learning for organizations. This section is divided into a discussion of simulations that have treated organizations as unitary actors, and those that have modeled organizations as consisting of individual actors within a structured environment. The contributions of these works to organizational learning theory are then assessed.

The discussion of these papers illustrates how computer simulations can be a flexible tool for developing theories of complex organizational phenomena. For each paper, I review the research question, the basic characteristics of the simulation that is used, the dependent (output) and independent (input) variables, and the key findings. We can see how this work has been critical to the development of theories about organizational learning. Simulations of organizational processes, such as learning, can yield compelling research implications and raise important research questions.

Organizations as Unitary Actors. The first simulations I discuss treat organizations as unitary actors. The issues of conflicts of interest and how individual learning relates to organizational learning are not modeled in these simulations. The papers are discussed in chronological order.

Levinthal and March (1981) examined the organizational implications of the simultaneous adaptation of search strategies, competencies, and aspirations under conditions of environmental instability and ambiguity. The simulated organizations in this study learn from their past experience. Such learning influences choices among search strategies, development of different competencies, and levels of aspiration. The impact of learning on these processes was shown to vary depending on the extent of environmental change and the extent of ambiguity in performance feedback. The authors argued that under conditions of environmental change and feedback ambiguity, basic learning routines can lead to superstitious beliefs.

This simulation models two types of search strategies. *Problemistic,* or *refinement,* search occurs when performance is below target, and emphasizes "relatively immediate refinements in the existing technology, greater efficiency, and discoveries in the near neighborhood of the present activities" (Levinthal & March, 1981, p. 309). *Slack,* or *innovative,* search occurs when performance exceeds target and slack accumulates in the organization. "By relaxing organizational controls, slack encourages search activities that cannot be justified in terms of their expected return for the organization" (Levinthal & March, 1981, p. 309). For both types of search, the organization samples a subset of alternatives, and if one of these alternatives represents an improvement over current practice, it is adopted. The outcomes of search depend on the size of the sample searched, the current practice, and the distributions of possible alternatives. The distribution of alternatives that an organization might discover is greater for innovative search than for refinement search. The larger the variance of the distribution of search, the more likely it is that a major, beneficial innovation will be discovered. The organization's performance is a function of the organization's technology or current practice, environmental characteristics, and the costs of refinement and innovation. There is uncertainty about the value of alternatives prior to their adoption. The efficiency of each search strategy (refinement or innovative) increases as the organization gains experience with each type of search. The organizations adapt their search expenditures and their search strategy based on the observed relationship between their past search level, their past search type, and their performance outcomes. The rate of learning or adaptation can vary.

The major implication of this study is that when performance signals are clear, or ambiguity is low, organizations learn to balance their levels of refinement and innovation pretty well, although not optimally. In stable environments, organizations perform better than their aspirations most of the time. This leads to an emphasis on innovative search, and increased efficiency at this type of search. Environmental uncertainty and change lead to more failure, and thus more refinement search, and more efficiency at this type of search. The authors concluded that performance outcomes generated by exogenous events influence choices of search strategies more than the relative efficacy of the two strategies. They also noted the strong path dependence of organizational experience. For instance, the luck of discovering a major successful innovation can lead to sequences of events that would not have otherwise occurred. Learning rates are also important: Learning quickly is an advantage when the process of interpreting signals is not prone to error. However, it is a disadvantage when signals are noisy and the interpretation of signals tends to be erroneous. Learning and adapting quickly can lead an organization to perpetuate a mistake, such as reducing expenditures on search, because such reductions were perceived to lead to improved performance. In actuality the performance outcome for that particular period may have had little to do with that period's search expenditure. Yet the organization forms a causal belief about a relationship that is spurious. The authors concluded that random or environmentally driven experiences of success and failure can lead to large and lasting changes in behavior. Such events can also lead to differentiation of organizations in essentially identical environments.

Lant and Mezias (1990) explored the implications of organizational learning processes for entrepreneurship in established organizations. The authors examined the effectiveness of different search routines for organizations that are faced with a fundamental restructuring of their environment. Organizations were modeled as having four core dimensions, with two choices on each dimension. The performance of organizations was determined by the fit of their characteristics with the environment. The likelihood of an organization changing its characteristics depends on its performance relative to its aspiration level, consistent with the adaptive learning perspective. Ambiguity was modeled as noise that interferes with accurate assessments of performance. The simulation created an ecology of organizations characterized by three different types of search strategies. The fixed type of organization does not search or change; it is structurally inert. The adaptive organization searches for information about the relationships between organizational characteristics and performance, and changes its characteristics based on this assessment. The imitative organization searches for the industry leader and determines the changes that are required to adopt the characteristics of this firm. The organizations in the simulated ecology were also characterized by either a high level of search activity or a low level of search activity. The simulation examined the performance, growth, and survival implications of the different search strategies and levels of search under conditions of environmental stability, environmental restructuring, low ambiguity, and high ambiguity.

The major conclusions of this paper were as follows. Under conditions of low ambiguity, adaptive firms outperform and grow larger than other firms. They are also not negatively affected by environmental change; they are able to quickly change to remain fit with the environment. Imitative firms are close behind, but they succumb to the follow-the-leader trap after a major change in the environment. They take longer to recover after an environmental shock because they continue to follow the largest firm in the population, which may no longer be the best performing firm. It takes a while for the new best performer to grow to be the largest in the population. Adaptive and imitative firms that have a high level of search activity end up significantly smaller than those with a low level of search activity. Thus, under conditions of low ambiguity, a high level of search is not necessary to maintain a good fit with the environment, and results in wasted resources.

Under conditions of high ambiguity, adaptive and imitative firms still perform better than fixed firms, but they both suffer from the environmental restructuring; imitative firms suffer significantly more and for a longer period of time than adaptive firms. This reflects, once again, the follow-the-leader trap. Adaptive firms and imitative firms tend to be smaller than fixed firms under ambiguity. Thus, they expend resources on searching and changing, but this costly activity may not consistently yield improved performance in an ambiguous environment. Adaptive firms suffer most from the cost of search in an ambiguous environment because they are most sensitive to the noise in the system. By imitating the largest firm in the population, imitative firms are less affected by noise in performance signals. Finally, high levels of search activity benefit adaptive and imitative firms following an environmental restructuring, but are not beneficial otherwise.

Lant and Mezias (1992) examined how patterns of organizational change are affected by environmental change, level of ambiguity, organizational size, search rules, propensity to change, and organizational performance. Specifically, this paper explored whether patterns of organizational stability and change consistent with a punctuated equilibrium perspective are the result of experiential learning rather than explicit managerial decisions.

Punctuated equilibrium models of change (Tushman & Romanelli, 1985) suggest that organizations are characterized by long periods of convergence or incremental change, punctuated by periods of reorientation, or fundamental change.

The model of organizational learning used in this simulation shares some characteristics with that of Lant and Mezias (1990). First, organizations are modeled as having four core dimensions. Second, the fit of an organization's characteristics with its environment determines its performance. Third, the likelihood of an organization changing its characteristics depends on its performance relative to aspiration level and a randomly assigned propensity to change. Fourth, ambiguity is modeled as noise that interferes with accurate assessments of performance. Fifth, the simulation creates an ecology of organizations characterized by three different types of search strategies: adaptive, imitative, and garbage can. The adaptive and imitative organizations have similar decision rules to those in Lant and Mezias (1990). Garbage can organizations search and change, but their changes are randomly associated with performance. Thus, searching and changing will not, on average, improve their fit with the environment and thus their performance. This simulation also models a founding search process for all firms. All firms search at founding, or intialization in the simulation, for the characteristics of the highest performing type of organization.

The patterns of change exhibited by the simulated organizations support the contention that managerial discretion is not necessary in order for firms to exhibit longer periods of convergence punctuated by fundamental reorganizations. They demonstrate that a learning model can account, to a large degree, for a punctuated equilibrium pattern of organizational change. The following results are patterns observed when there is no ambiguity in performance signals. The average number of changes that firms make declines over time during periods of environmental stability, and increases for a brief period following an environmental restructuring. Thus, the simple interaction of organizations that learn from experience with an environment that exhibits long periods of stability and occasional fundamental change produces a pattern of change predicted by punctuated equilibrium theorists. Adaptive firms are most responsive to environmental change; imitative firms respond, but only after the former industry leader is replaced, some time following the restructuring. Firms with high propensities to change (those that are more sensitive to performance feedback) make more changes than those with low propensities to change, on average, following initialization and environmental change; however, there is no difference in the level of change exhibited by these firms during periods of environmental stability. Level of performance does not impact the number of changes firms make during environmental change; however, poorly performing firms have a higher level of change than successful firms during environmental stability. Organizational size does affect level of organizational change during environmental change; small firms make more changes, on average, than large firms. The difference between large and small firms declines over time during environmental stability.

Observation of these learning organizations under conditions of ambiguity reveals several interesting patterns. Ambiguity tends to increase the average number of changes made by firms, but also makes them unresponsive to changes in the environment. Ambiguity also impacts the effects of competitive selection processes on the characteristics of firms in the population. Organizations with a high responsiveness to performance feedback tend to be selected out of the population during initial periods of environmental stability, regardless of the level of ambiguity. Thus, having a high sensitivity to performance signals when the environment is stable tends to increase organizational failure rates. However, following a major change in the environment, the number of firms with a high sensitivity to performance feedback increases in the low ambiguity condition. Thus, following an environmental restructuring, the average responsiveness to performance feedback in the population increases. This shift in selection pattern does not occur under conditions of ambiguity. Thus, being responsive to performance signals when these signals are clear helps firms respond quickly and accurately to environmental change. However, this responsiveness is not helpful when signals are not clear. These results highlight some important interactions between organizational learning, ambiguity, and environmental change.

Mezias and Glynn (1993) explored the effects of different search strategies on the level of organizational innovation and organizational resources. The authors predicted that deliberate strategies to increase the amount of innovation in organizations characterized by experiential learning would produce what they termed *paradoxes of innovation*. They argued that such deliberate strategies would not increase innovation levels. The basic characteristics of their model are the same as those of Levinthal and March (1981); they elaborated this model to examine the effects of different innovation strategies on the ultimate level of innovation in the organization. The search rules modeled in this simulation are as follows. The organization assesses the time since it has last adopted an innovation, the amount of search conducted previously, the success or failure of past search, and whether performance is above or below target, and determines the variance of the search process. As in the Levinthal and March (1981) model, organizations do two types of search—innovative and refinement. The resources they devote to searching, and what type of search they do, are affected by their experience. When an organization is successful at one type of search, it increases resources to this type of search. When performance is greater than aspiration, the firm does more innovative search. When performance is less than aspiration, the firm does more refinement search. Performance also affects the probability of changing (adopting an innovation), consistent with learning models.

The dependent variables in the simulation were the number of innovative changes made by organizations, the number of refinements to current technology, and firm resources. The key findings of this study were that "devoting more resources to search in the context of routine organizational functioning does not increase the level of innovation" (Mezias & Glynn, 1993, p. 91). Such increases in resources tend to increase the level of refinements of current technologies, rather than fundamental innovations. The level of innovation was increased, however, by increases in the variance of alternatives considered. The authors concluded that deliberate strategies used within routine-guided organizations can often have unintended consequences. In contrast, allowing variance in the adherence to routines can provide new and valuable opportunities for an organization.

Mezias and Lant (1994) explored the role of organizational level change in population dynamics. Specifically, the authors examined the conditions under which a significant proportion of firms using an imitation strategy will survive in populations of organizations consisting of imitating firms, which incur costs of search and change, and fixed firms, which do not incur costs of search and change. This research question is motivated by the claim of population ecologists (Hannan & Freeman, 1984) that adaptive efforts in a world of uncertainty are random with respect to future value. According to this assumption, organizations that expend resources searching and changing exhibit higher failure rates than fixed firms, and would eventually be selected out of the population.

The learning model by which imitative firms search and change is similar to that in Lant and Mezias (1992). Imitative and fixed firms are characterized by search rules as described in Lant and Mezias (1990). In this simulation, ambiguity during founding search is introduced. The environments within which the simulated firms operate are characterized by different levels of carrying capacity, the maximum number of firms that a given environment can support. The smaller the carrying capacity of the environment, the fewer the number of firms that will survive overall, and thus the higher the level of competition. The environments are also characterized by different levels of ambiguity, and different probabilities and magnitudes of environmental change. Imitative firms vary in terms of the cost of search and change. The effects of these environmental and organizational characteristics on the proportion of imitative firms that survive in the population are examined.

Their findings suggest that as the population reaches equilibrium, imitative firms make up approximately 20% of the population. These firms are helped by their ability to change following environmental change and when ambiguity in founding search has resulted in the adoption of inferior characteristics. This paper represents the first simulation in organization theory to model competition between organizations explicitly.

Structured Organization, Individual Decision Makers. This next set of simulations attempts to model some of the internal dynamics of learning organizations.

The simulation by Lounama and March (1987) made several unique contributions to the organizational learning literature. It was one of the first attempts to model the dynamics of mutual learning among different organizational members. It also broke new ground by incorporating ideas about attributional and interpretive biases into its model of learning. The authors explored the implications of biased mutual learning for organizational performance.

The model includes two key variables, a coordination control variable and a state variable, indicating a team member's belief about the strength of the interaction between two team members. The key organizational parameters are the team members' learning rates and the rules for adapting coordination rules based on experience. The key environmental parameter is noise in performance signals. Each team member decides on a level of personal effort such that the sum of the performance of the two members is maximized. Each member's performance depends on both members' effort — thus their own outcomes as well as the organization's outcomes are interdependent. There is no conflict of interest. Members modify their beliefs based on their experience. However, members exhibit common biases: They overestimate their own importance, and they attribute errors in their beliefs to the strength of the interaction of their efforts, rather than to themselves. The paper explored the impact on organizational performance when both team members and the coordinator learn and adapt simultaneously, first when performance feedback is unambiguous, and second, when it is ambiguous.

This simulation demonstrates that although learning can be a good process for improving organizational performance, "it can often be confounded by the effects of attributional biases on the part of members, by the interactions of simultaneous learning by the members and the coordinator, and by errors in perceiving or interpreting experience" (Lounama & March, 1987, p. 107). Even when performance outcomes are clear, the simultaneous learning of all parties can lead to mistakes that become larger over time. The coordinator or the members can misattribute a performance change to their own prior change in behavior, when it was in fact caused by another member's action. This superstitious learning leads to more changes in the direction of the prior change, and an eventual decline in performance. This highlights the difficulty of learning causal relationships when more than one variable changes at a time. Such errors are exacerbated when performance feedback includes random noise. The authors suggested several heuristics for improving the effectiveness of experiential learning in complex organizations. First, slow the rate of adaptation. That is, do not react too quickly when environmental signals are ambiguous or when interdependent actors are learning and adapting simultaneously. Second, reduce the simultaneity of changes. Only allow one actor to change behavior at a time. This will facilitate more accurate learning about cause and effect relationships. Third, scale the size of changes; they should be neither too big nor too small. Changes that are too small do not impact the system sufficiently to register a noticeable response. However, changes that are too large can yield poor results that perpetuate in time.

March (1991) explored the implications of adaptive learning for the allocation of resources to the exploitation, or refinement, of current activities and the exploration of new alternatives. A balance between these two activities is important for organizations, but it is a difficult trade-off to make. By exploring, an organization slows down the rate at which it gains competence in current activities. By exploiting, the organization gains competence, but this very competence makes experimentation a relatively unattractive alternative. The paper argued that adaptive learning processes create preferences for exploitation rather than exploration, because the gains from exploitation are certain, salient, and occur quickly. Potential gains from exploration are more risky and are not realized for long periods of time. Thus, adaptive learning will tend to drive out exploration. This can result in organizations being extremely competent at inferior technologies. An exclusive emphasis on exploitation yields short-term effectiveness, but long-term ineffectiveness. The paper explored this trade-off within the social context of a learning organization. Organizations store knowledge that they have learned from their members in the form of norms and routines. Conversely, organizational members are socialized to organizational beliefs, thus learning from the organization. This process is called mutual learning.

The characteristics of March's model of mutual learning are as follows. An external reality exists that is independent of beliefs about it. Individuals hold a set of beliefs about this reality, as does the organization. The beliefs of individuals and their organization may differ. Individuals modify their beliefs as they are socialized to the organization's beliefs. The organization also adapts in response to the beliefs of individuals, when these beliefs are a more accurate representation of reality than the organization's current beliefs. Both individuals and the organization start with no knowledge of reality, but learn about it over time. As individuals and the organization learn, their beliefs become more similar over time. An equilibrium is reached when all individuals and the organization share the same (but not necessarily accurate) beliefs. Within this model, March explored the impact of the rate of learning, the heterogeneity of learning rates, and personnel turnover.

With higher rates of learning, an equilibrium is reached sooner. However, slower rates of individual learning lead to greater knowledge at equilibrium, especially when the organization learns from individuals quickly. Thus, faster learning by individuals is not always desirable. Knowledge at equilibrium is increased even more if the learning rates of individuals within the organization vary; that is, there is some benefit to having a mix of both slow and fast learners. Slow learners do more exploration of alternatives and provide more variation of knowledge, and fast learners quickly learn from slow ones when this exploration discovers some improvement that can be made to organizational knowledge.

The impact of personnel turnover was explored as a means of introducing heterogeneity of knowledge into the organization. Turnover has a negative impact when the learning rates of individuals are slow. The knowledge at equilibrium decreases as turnover increases if individuals learn slowly. Thus, an organization of slow learners that experiences significant turnover is unable to do sufficient exploitation, and overall knowledge suffers. If individual learning is rapid, however, moderate amounts of turnover actually improve knowledge at equilibrium. Although individuals with higher tenure know more than newcomers, their knowledge is reflected in the beliefs of the organization. They have no more unique knowledge to add to organizational knowledge. Newcomers, even though they have less knowledge, on average, provide opportunities for exploration and increases in the variety of knowledge; there is a good chance that some of their unique knowledge may be useful to the organization.

When the reality that individuals and the organization are trying to understand exhibits turbulence, learning is more difficult. Learning in this instance is likely to result in less knowledge over time, as individuals and the organization converge on a set of beliefs while the reality they seek to understand is constantly changing. The relative value of exploitation and exploration changes under environmental turbulence; exploitation is less valuable if it improves knowledge about the wrong reality. This decline in accurate knowledge can be avoided with turnover, which brings new knowledge into the organization from which the organization can then learn.

Carley (1992) examined the impact of personnel turnover on organizational learning for organizations with different structures and tasks. Carley's model has the following characteristics: individuals and organizations base their decisions on their past experience. Organizational learning depends on the memories of individuals and their ability to learn. Organizations are characterized by disorder, such as the turnover and transfer of individuals. Organizations rarely face the exact same problem twice; problems are typically complex and require the knowldege of more than one individual. In the hierarchical structure, decision makers are organized by chain of command; decision makers at different levels have access to different types of information, and the final decision is made at the top of the hierarchy. In the team structure, decision makers act autonomously, have access to different information, and have equal voice in the final decision. Carley examined the impact of type of task, turnover, task complexity, and experience on the performance and rate of learning of both hierarchies and teams.

Carley's key findings were that teams generally learn better and faster than hierarchies, but that hierarchies are less affected by high turnover rates. Hierarchies preserve institutional knowledge in the face of turnover, and so are less affected by turnover. Teams are also more severely affected when new individuals do not have appropriate experience for their task.

Lessons from Simulating Experiential Learning Systems

Taken together, these simulations raise some intriguing possibilities and suggest some possible lessons about organizations that learn experientially.

The Impact of Ambiguity. Several of the simulations suggest that experiential learning is a fairly sensible process when signals from the environment and about performance feedback are clear. Under conditions of clarity there is a degree of validity in the perceived causal linkage between actions and outcomes. When feedback is informative about this causal linkage, experiential learning is functional (Lant & Mezias, 1992; Levinthal & March, 1981). However, when either the environment or performance feedback are ambiguous, experiential learning can create significant problems. Such ambiguity calls into question the validity of the perceived link between organizational actions and outcomes, and makes trying to ascertain these linkages very costly. Lant and Mezias (1990) demonstrated how search under conditions of ambiguity becomes very costly, because the search process does not yield consistent improvements in performance. Further, experiential learning tends to be quite sensitive to noise in signals. Thus, under conditions of ambiguity, learning and responding to experience are often a wild goose chase (Lant & Mezias, 1990). Further, ambiguity makes organizations change too much as they respond to noisy, inaccurate information. In addition, they are less responsive to changes in the environment. For instance, Lant and Mezias (1992) demonstrated that organizations in an unambiguous context change in response to environmental change but have low rates of change otherwise; those in an ambiguous context keep changing constantly, but do not exhibit higher rates of change in response to an environmental change. Lounama and March (1987) showed that the difficulty that experiential learning systems have when more than one variable changes at a time is exacerbated under conditions of ambiguity. However, Mezias and Lant (1994) suggested that learning under ambiguity is sometimes better than no learning at all. They demonstrated that organizations that learn are able to correct mistakes caused by ambiguity. They are best able to do this when their decision rules are designed to be less sensitive to noise in performance signals, such as an imitative search rule.

The Impact of Environmental Change. The impact of environmental change varies depending on whether performance signals are clear or ambiguous, and on the decision rules of the organization. Organizations that learn from experience have difficulty responding to environmental change under conditions of ambiguity; it is difficult to learn what types of changes will be associated with improved performance. From the perspective of organizations as unitary actors, experiential learning works pretty well when the environment changes if the nature of these changes and their effect on the organization's performance are clear (Lant & Mezias, 1992). However, from the perspective of mutual learning (March, 1991), learning in the presence of environmental turbulence is difficult, even without ambiguity. Ironically, "environmental change makes adaptation essential, but it also makes learning from experience difficult" (March, 1991, p. 80). Once the mutual learning process between individuals and the organization reaches a stable equilibrium, and socialized individuals cannot unlearn old lessons and learn new ones (Hedberg, 1981), then adaptation to environmental change will be difficult. By integrating this idea with Levinthal and March (1981) we can see how this rigidity might happen. Levinthal and March suggested that environmental change leads to more experiences of failure, which in turn leads to an emphasis on refinement rather than exploration. Refinement search is narrow and yields fewer alternatives that might be adopted in response to environmental change. This is one way in which environmental change can lead to rigidity. Lant and Mezias (1990, 1992) argued, however, that experiences of failure will lead to a higher level of organizational change than will experiences of success. If both perspectives have validity, then this suggests that, under unambiguous conditions, environmental change will lead to more change, but alternatives are chosen from a narrow set; change will be incremental rather than fundamental. This point leads to the next issue, which is the value of maintaining variability of information in the organization.

The Value of Variance. Mezias and Glynn (1993) noted that intentional strategies pursued by organizations that are governed by routine learning often have unintended consequences, and that unintended strategies often provide the most value. Specifically, they concluded that increasing resources in order to encourage innovation has the effect of encouraging only refinements in current practice, rather than fundamental innovation. Innovation is increased, however, if there is loose adherence to organizational routines. In other words, by loosely coupling behavior to routines, the actual variance of behavior increases, and this provides a pool of potentially beneficial innovations. March (1991) came to a similar conclusion: By maintaining some level of variance in the knowledge base of the organization (rather than everyone sharing the same beliefs and knowledge), opportunities to learn new, and potentially helpful, information result in greater knowledge in the organization in the long run. The issues discussed next, learning rates and turnover, are two methods of maintaining variance in organizational knowledge.

Learning Fast or Learning Slow?   Conventional wisdom suggests that it is better to be a fast learner than a slow learner. However, Levinthal and March (1981) and March (1991) highlighted the risks of learning quickly and the advantages of learning slowly. From the perspective of the organization as a unitary actor, learning quickly can be problematic when signals are ambiguous or when the apparent causal relationship between organizational action and outcomes is spurious. In these instances, the organization may learn an inaccurate lesson, or engage in superstitious learning. If it learns and adapts quickly to this inaccurate information, it is likely to perpetuate the initial mistake. An organization that learns more slowly, however, may wait for multiple signals before adapting, and thus is less likely to change based on a single, erroneous piece of information. Lant and Mezias (1992) also illustrated that responding quickly to performance signals is selected against (increases failure rates) in ambiguous environments.

From a mutual learning perspective, slow learning is a means of maintaining variance in organizational knowledge and thus organizational exploration. This perspective suggests that although it is beneficial for the organization to learn quickly from its members, the organization benefits if some members are themselves slow to learn the routines and beliefs of the organization.

Benefits and Risks of Turnover.   Turnover of organizational members is another means of maintaining variability in organizational knowledge. New members have not yet been socialized by the organization, and provide some amount of unique knowledge from which the organization can learn. However, there is an interaction between the rate of learning and turnover. If individuals learn slowly and turnover is high, the organization will suffer from having too much variance and not enough shared competence. Turnover can be beneficial when individuals and the organization learn quickly; thus, the organization quickly learns from the newcomers, and the newcomers, in turn, quickly increase their competence with organizational routines. These findings imply that if an organization's members tend to be slow learners, it is best to limit the amount of turnover that occurs. However, if there is a majority of fast learners in the organization, turnover is beneficial. Carley (1992) suggested that the impact of turnover also depends on the structure of decision making in the organization. Carley found that hierarchies are less affected by turnover than teams; this is because hierarchies institutionalize their knowledge, whereas teams maintain knowledge only in their members. However, teams learn better and more quickly than hierarchies. Integrating these findings with those of March (1991) raises an interesting implication. Hierarchies are slow to learn and immune from turnover. Teams learn quickly, but are significantly affected by turnover. Thus, from March's (1991) findings, turnover is probably beneficial for hierarchies, but should be limited in teams. Is it possible that the characteristics of each provide different, but effective, means of balancing refinement and exploration? Perhaps these structures have evolved in organizations because of these adaptive features. It would be worthwhile to examine the performance of these two decision making structures, with different rates of learning and turnover, under conditions of environmental change and ambiguity.

COMMUNICATING SIMULATION-BASED RESEARCH TO AN ORGANIZATION THEORY AUDIENCE

I have often had the same reaction as my organization theory colleagues when reading research based on computer simulations. The topic may be very interesting, but the paper is so loaded with formulas and notation that halfway through I forget the point of the study. Although simulation can be a flexible tool for developing theories of complex organizational phenomena, it is often viewed as making overly simplistic assumptions, and as being overly technical and difficult to understand. I am reminded of the *Harvard Business Review* cartoon in which a corporate CEO, standing in his penthouse office, sends his vice-president down to the lobby with the instructions to go look at the art and then tell him what it means. Mathematics, like art, has elegance, beauty, and conveys a lot of meaning. However, all forms of communication require interpretation, and these forms of communication require certain skills in order to make these interpretations. Organization theorists are typically not trained to develop these particular skills. The bulk of our work is based on verbal theory and quantitative empirical analysis (as opposed to quantitative theory, such as simulation, or qualitative empirical analysis). Thus, one of the critical challenges faced by simulation researchers who model organizational dynamics is how to enhance the interpretation of their work by the broader population of organization theorists. Some research based on simulation methodology has had a significant impact on organization theory, such as Cohen, March, and Olsen's (1972) garbage can model and Nelson and Winter's (1982) book on evolutionary theory. Organizational learning theory is another area where simulation has made a significant contribution. It is striking that most of the learning simulations discussed in this chapter have appeared in mainstream organization theory and strategic management journals, but have been virtually the only simulations appearing in these journals. What lessons can be learned from these simulations that have had an impact on organizational theory? One approach is to determine which characteristics make simulation studies more acceptable to organization theorists.

I next suggest a number of attributes that I believe increase the likelihood of simulation research having a significant impact on the field of organization theory. A key feature of any research that enhances its potential impact is whether it is theoretically interesting. If the theory is compelling, then even those who cannot follow the particulars of the method will come away with the essential meaning of the work. It is also important to communicate clearly about the purpose of the simulation. Simulations can be used for a variety of reasons, including theory building and policy planning. Simulations in organization theory are used typically for theory building. It is important to communicate to the reader that although simulations are quantitative, they are not empirical. Those not familiar with the method might assume that the "data" provided by the simulation were generated from empirical research. Having reasonable assumptions, parameter values, and algorithms, given what we know about organizations, is also important. A simulation will be more memorable to the extent that it has interesting and relevant input and output variables; that is, the dependent and independent variables should be of interest to organization theorists. It helps to keep research questions simple and straightforward. Elaborate simulations of entire systems are impressive, but are often overwhelming to the reader. The simulation should be able to address relatively straightforward theoretical questions that we can not examine easily in other settings.

Keep in mind that the organizations researcher is interested in the implications of your work, rather than its technical sophistication. Emphasize what the model and results mean for organizations and organization theory, not the "bells and whistles" of the model. All fields develop their own specialized language. Speaking the language of organization theory in simulation studies will help the theorist comprehend and accept the work. For those who are trained primarily as modelers or are from a different field with a different language, it sometimes helps to team up with a co-author from organization theory who does not do simulation work primarily. Such collaboration can help with many of these points. Finally, educate the reader about the use of simulations in behavioral research; many readers are uncertain about the purpose of simulations and why a behavioral scientist would want to do them.

CONCLUSIONS

The value of simulation research for organization theory in general can be demonstrated by the progress that has been made in modeling organizations as experiential learning systems, and by the influence of these simulations on empirical research. Many of the lessons drawn from these simulations are reflected in the research questions being addressed in empirical work. For instance, much empirical work on organizational adaptation and change is concerned with the how organizations learn in different environmental contexts, such as those characterized by environmental turbulence, environmental jolts, ambiguity, or uncertainty (Lant et al., 1992; Meyer, 1982; Meyer, Brooks, & Goes, 1990; Virany, Tushman, & Romanelli, 1992). The value of variance has appeared in the strategic management literature as a call for increased demographic diversity or heterogeneity in top management teams; such diversity is seen as a means to facilitate learning and responsiveness to the environment (Bantel & Jackson, 1989; Lant et al., 1992; Milliken & Lant, 1991; Murray, 1989; Wiersema & Bantel, 1992). Top management turnover has been explored as one means of introducing such diversity (Milliken & Lant, 1991). The implications of employee turnover for organizational learning have been explored as well. One stream of research explores the impact of employee turnover on organizational learning curves (Argote, Beckman, & Epple, 1990; Argote, Epple, Devadas, & Murphy, 1990; Devadas & Argote, 1992).

It is difficult to determine the extent to which empirical research has been influenced by simulation or vice versa. Clearly, the themes of environmental uncertainty, environmental change, and top management turnover have a long history in the organizations literature. However, some of the lessons derived from the simulations, such as the interaction of environmental change and ambiguity and the interaction of turnover and variance, are reflected in much of the more recent research on organizational learning, change, and adaptation. This is encouraging, because only recently have a significant number of simulations of organizational learning systems appeared in mainstream organizational and strategic management journals. Clearly, there are still theoretical ideas that have been generated by the experiential learning simulations that have not yet been reflected in empirical research. This fact is a primary reason for this chapter, to encourage integration across different approaches to studying organizations.

ACKNOWLEDGMENTS

The author would like to thank the participants of the TIMS Workshop on Mathematical Organization Theory for their comments, Steve Mezias for suggestions, and Kathleen Carley and Mike Prietula for their editorial assistance.

REFERENCES

Argote, L., Beckman, S., & Epple, D. (1990). The persistence and transfer of learning in industrial settings. *Management Science, 36,* 140–154.

Argote, L., Epple, D., Devadas, R., & Murphy, K. (1990, October). *The acquisition and depreciation of knowledge in manufacturing: Turnover and the learning curve.* Paper presented at ORSA/TIMS, Philadelphia.

Argyris, C., & Schon, D. (1978). *Organizational learning.* Reading, MA: Addison-Wesley.

Bantel, K. A., & Jackson, S. E. (1989). Top management and innovations in banking: Does the composition of the top team make a difference? *Strategic Management Journal, 10,* 107–124.

Carley, K. (1992). Organizational learning and personnel turnover. *Organization Science, 3,* 20–46.

Cohen, K. J., & Cyert, R. M. (1965). Simulation of organizational behavior. In J. G. March (Ed.), *Handbook of organizations* (pp. 305–354). Chicago: Rand McNally.

Cohen, M. D., March, J. G., & Olsen, J. P. (1972). A garbage can model of organizational choice. *Administrative Science Quarterly, 17,* 1–25.

Crecine, J. P. (1969). A computer simulation of municipal budgeting. Chicago: Rand McNally.

Cyert, R. M., & March, J. G. (1963). *A behavioral theory of the firm.* Englewood Cliffs, NJ: Prentice-Hall.

Devadas, R., & Argote, L. (1992). *Learning and depreciation in work groups: The effects of turnover and group structure.* Working paper, Graduate School of Industrial Administration, Carnegie Mellon University.

Glynn, M. A., Milliken, F. J., & Lant, T. K. (1992, August). *Learning about organizational learning theory: An umbrella of organizing processes.* Paper presented at the 1992 Academy of Management meetings, Las Vegas, NV.

Hannan, M. T., & Freeman, J. (1984). Structural inertia and organizational change. *American Sociological Review, 49,* 149–164.

Hedberg, B. (1981). How organizations learn and unlearn. In P. C. Nystrom & W. H. Starbuck (Eds.), *Handbook of organization design* (Vol. 1, pp. 3–27). Oxford, UK: Oxford University Press.

Jelinek, M. (1979). *Institutionalizing innovations: A study of organizational learning systems.* New York: Praeger.

Lant, T. K., & Mezias, S. J. (1990). Managing discontinuous change: A simulation study of organizational learning and entrepreneurial strategies. *Strategic Management Journal, 11,* 147-179.

Lant, T. K., & Mezias, S. J. (1992). An organizational learning model of convergence and reorientation. *Organization Science, 3,* 47-71.

Lant, T. K., Milliken, F. J., & Batra, B. (1992). The role of managerial learning and interpretation in strategic persistence and reorientation: An empirical exploration. *Strategic Management Journal, 13,* 585-608.

Levinthal, D. A., & March, J. G. (1981). A model of adaptive organizational search. *Journal of Economic Behavior and Organization, 2,* 307-333.

Levitt, B., & March, J. G. (1988). Organizational learning. *Annual Review of Sociology, 14,* 319-340.

Lounama, P. H., & March, J. G. (1987). Adaptive coordination of a learning team. *Management Science, 33,* 107-123.

March, J. G. (1991). Exploration and exploitation in organizational learning. *Organization Science, 2,* 71-87.

Masuch, M., & LaPotin, P. (1989). Beyond garbage cans: An AI model of organizational choice. *Administrative Science Quarterly, 34,* 38-67.

Meyer, A. (1982). Adapting to environmental jolts. *Administrative Science Quarterly, 27,* 515-537.

Meyer, A., Brooks, G., & Goes, J. (1990). Environmental jolts and industry revolutions: Organizational responses to discontinuous change. *Strategic Management Journal, 11,* 93-110.

Mezias, J. G., & Glynn, M. A. (in press). Using computer simulations to understand the management of technology: Applications for theory development. *Technology Studies.*

Mezias, J. G., & Glynn, M. A. (1993). The three faces of corporate renewal: Institution, revolution, and evolution. *Strategic Management Journal, 14,* 77-101.

Mezias, S. J., & Lant, T. K. (1994). Mimetic learning and the evolution of organizational populations. In J. A. C. Baum & J. V. Singh (Eds.), *Evolutionary dynamics of organizations* (pp. 179-198). Oxford, UK: Oxford University Press.

Milliken, F. J., & Lant, T. K. (1991). In J. Dutton, A. Huff, & P. Shrivastava (Eds.), *Advances in strategic management,* (Vol. 7, pp. 125-152). Greenwich, CT: JAI Press.

Murray, A. I. (1989). Top management group heterogeneity and firm performance. *Strategic Management Journal, 10,* 125-141.

Nelson, R. R., & Winter, S. G. (1982). *An evolutionary theory of economic change.* Boston: Belknap Press.

Tushman, M. L., & Romanelli, E. (1985). Organizational evolution: A metamorphosis model of convergence and reorientation. In L. L. Cummings & B. M. Staw (Eds.), *Research in organizational behavior* (Vol. 7, pp. 171-222). Greenwich, CT: JAI Press.

Virany, B., Tushman, M., & Romanelli, E. (1992). Executive succession and organization outcomes in a turbulent environment: An organization learning approach. *Organization Science, 3,* 72-91.

Whicker, M. L., & Sigelman, L. (1991). *Computer simulation applications: An introduction.* Newbury Park, CA: Sage.

Wiersema, M. F., & Bantel, K. A. (1992). Top management team demography and corporate strategic change. *Academy of Management Journal, 35,* 91-121.

10

Social Dilemmas and Fluid Organizations

Natalie S. Glance
Bernardo A. Huberman
Xerox Palo Alto Research Center

Collective action problems pose difficult quandaries for communities, be they social, economic, or organizational. Consider a group that wants to attain a common goal, such as cleaner air, better working conditions, or the elimination of poverty. Members of the group may be tempted to benefit from the common good without contributing to its production when the gain for collaborating is less than the cost.

There is a long history of interest in social dilemmas of this type in political science (R. Hardin, 1982; Schelling, 1978). G. Hardin coined the phrase "the tragedy of the commons" to reflect the fate of the human species if it fails to successfully resolve the social dilemma of limiting population growth (G. Hardin, 1968). Furthermore, Olson argued that the logic of collective action implies that only small groups can successfully provide themselves with a common good (Olson, 1965). Others, from Smith (1937) to Taylor (1976, 1987), have taken the problem of social dilemmas as central to the justification of the existence of the state. In economics and sociology, the study of social dilemmas sheds light on, for example, the adoption of new technologies (Friedman, 1990) and the mobilization of political movements (Oliver & Marwell, 1988).

Many of these theories agree about how difficult it is for a large group to provide itself with a collective good. Upper limits on the size of a group beyond which resolution of the social dilemma is not possible have been derived (Bendor & Mookherjee, 1987; Glance & Huberman, 1993). It has been shown that the possibilities for cooperation increase when the group is composed of individuals with a diversity of interests, abilities, and incentives (Oliver & Marwell, 1988; Huberman & Glance, 1993). More significantly, Bendor and Mookherjee recently demonstrated that the level of cooperation depends on the structure of the group (Bendor & Mookherjee, 1987). In particular, they showed that federated structures with a central monitoring office can support a high level of cooperation.

The recognition that the structure of interactions in a group need not be uniform is an important extension of previous research on social dilemmas. It opens up the possibility that large structured groups may be able to achieve cooperation in situations where unstructured groups cannot. In addition, the structure of the group need not be fixed over time. One may then ask, how does the dynamics of cooperation evolve in structured groups? Additionally, how will the fluidity of the structure affect the possibility for overall cooperation? In this chapter, we explore these avenues, extending our previous theory of the dynamics of cooperation in flat, structureless groups (Glance & Huberman, 1993) and relying on computer simulations to illustrate the complex behavior of fluid groups.

We assume that in a large group, the interdependency, or strength of connection, among different individuals can vary, and that these connections determine the inherent structure, or topology, of the group. What is meant by "connection" between individuals depends on the good produced or the goal pursued. Environmental movements, social action, such as civil rights, the Resistance in World War II, and student demonstrations provide examples of structure emerging from patterns of interdependencies. Typically, such movements are organized into local cadres, which are then mobilized into larger regional groups, themselves part of a larger whole.

The complex interactions in social networks have been studied in depth by organizational theorists and sociologists alike to better understand group behavior (Barnes, 1954; Bott, 1955; Burt, 1980; Granovetter, 1973; Hartigan, 1967; Knipscheer & Antonucci, 1990; Leinhardt, 1977; Scott, 1992; Srinivas & Béteille, 1964). The structure of the groups just described, however, reveals a hierarchy of interactions, although other topologies are also possible. Note that through the examples given we have purposefully attempted to separate the notion of rank from a hierarchical structure. Instead, the emphasis is on the topology of the interactions and the clustering of individuals at various levels of interaction. Because the advantages of hierarchies in facilitating the spread of information and control are already well known (Arrow, 1974), in this chapter we examine how a hierarchical structure facilitates group cooperation without any centralized control. We show that groups with hierarchical structure can more easily achieve cooperation than their counterparts with no structure, mostly because their size is effectively smaller.

Hierarchies are also shown to have strict size limits beyond which cooperation is not possible without changing the incentive structure.

However, these limits can be greatly stretched if structural changes are allowed. This quality of a group, the ease with which connections between individuals can be strengthened or weakened, the readiness with which clusters can be formed or broken up, we call *fluidity*. The concept of fluidity also has a precedent in the social sciences; for example, Srinivas and Béteille (1964) stated that "a network even when viewed from the standpoint of a single individual has a dynamic character. New relations are forged, and old ones discarded or modified." We find that fluid groups are significantly more able to achieve cooperation than those with fixed hierarchical structures. Individuals change their connections, or "move" within the hierarchy, causing a global restructuring of the hierarchy to one more able to achieve cooperation.

In tandem with fluidity, potential loss of effectiveness of a group must be considered. By effectiveness, we mean how productive a given organization is in obtaining an overall utility over time. Individual actions in changing connections, whether by moving to a different town or by switching to a different department in a corporation, if permitted, may lead to a decrease in the effectiveness with which the group can produce the common good. Thus, in considering the possibility of enhancing cooperation by increasing fluidity, the impact on effectiveness must considered. We find that for many hierarchical groups there will be an optimal range of fluidity.

In the next section, we introduce our dynamical model of social dilemmas for intentional agents with expectations and beliefs. Following that, we expand on the notion of structure in decentralized groups and develop the concept of a hierarchy of interactions. We then extend our dynamical theory of collective action to include hierarchical groups. Next we present the results of computer experiments that show that, in terms of their ability to sustain high levels of cooperation over time, hierarchical structures are superior to flat groups and fluid hierarchies perform better than fixed ones. The trade-off between fluidity and effectiveness is also examined. The final section is reserved for conclusions.

SOCIAL DILEMMAS

In a general social dilemma, a group of people attempts to obtain a common good in the absence of central authority. Each individual has two choices: either to contribute to the common good, or to shirk and free ride on the work of others. The payoffs are structured so that the incentives in the game mirror those present in social dilemmas. All individuals share equally in the common good, regardless of their actions. However, each person that cooperates increases the amount of the common good by a fixed amount, but receives only a fraction of that amount in return. Because the cost of cooperating is greater than the marginal benefit, the individual defects. Now the dilemma rears its ugly head: Each individual faces the same choice; thus all defect and the common good is not produced at all. The individually rational strategy of weighing costs against benefits results in an inferior outcome—no common good is produced.

However, the logic behind the decision to cooperate or not changes when the interaction is ongoing, because future expected utility gains will join present ones in influencing the rational individual's decision. In particular, individual expectations concerning the future evolution of the game can play a significant role in each member's decisions. The importance given the future depends on how long the individuals expect the interaction to last. If they expect the game to end soon, then, rationally, future expected returns should be discounted heavily with respect to known immediate returns. On the other hand, if the interaction is likely to continue for a long time, then members may be wise to discount the future only slightly and make choices that maximize their returns in the long run. Notice that making present choices that depend on the future is rational only if, and to the extent that, a member believes its choices influence the decisions others make.

One may then ask the following questions about situations of this kind: If agents make decisions on whether or not to cooperate on the basis of imperfect information about group activity, and incorporate expectations on how their decision will affect other agents, then how will the evolution of cooperation proceed? In particular, how will the structure and fluidity of a group affect the dynamics?

To study the evolution of social cooperation, we borrow methods from statistical thermodynamics, a branch of physics (van Kampen, 1981). This field attempts to derive the macroscopic properties of matter (such as liquid vs. solid, metal vs. insulator) from knowledge of the underlying interactions among the constituent atoms and molecules. In the context of social dilemmas, we adapt this methodology to study the aggregate behavior of a group composed of intentional individuals confronted with social choices. This allows us to apply results from theoretical physics to the study of the dynamics of group cooperation.

Our mathematical treatment of the collective action problem is presented later, in the section entitled The Economics of Free Riding. There, we state the benefits and costs to the individual associated with the two actions of cooperation and defection, that is, *contributing* or not to the social good. The problem thus posed is referred to in the literature as the n-person Prisoner's Dilemma (Bendor & Mookherjee, 1987; R. Hardin, 1971; Taylor; 1987). We then allow beliefs and expectations about other individuals' actions in the future to influence each member's perception of which action, cooperation or defection, will benefit it most in the long run. Using these preferences functions, we apply the stability function formalism (Ceccatto

& Huberman, 1989) to provide an understanding of the dynamics of cooperation in the case of groups with no organizational structure. We conclude that the emergence of cooperation among individuals can take place in a sudden and unexpected fashion. This finding will be useful when examining the possibility for cooperation in fluid organizations.

However, readers may want to merely peruse or skip the mathematical treatment entirely on first reading, because overemphasis on its technical aspects may detract from the main thrust of this chapter: the heightened ability of fluid organizations faced with a social dilemma to achieve cooperation over time.

In the next section, we address the various topological structures of organizations. In addition, we begin to formalize the notion of fluidity in organizational structure. These topics are central to our study of cooperation in organizations.

THE TOPOLOGY OF ORGANIZATIONS

Organizational theorists study group structure in order to elucidate the nature and working of the firm. In firms, there is generally an informal structure that emerges from the pattern of affective ties among participants, as well as a formal one imposed from above (Scott, 1992). In our study, we are interested in the former type, the network of activities and interactions that link individuals in a group, commonly known as the sociometric structure.

A school of sociologists and social psychologists also regards the social structure of a group as elemental to understanding group behavior. The approach, called *social network analysis*, began with Barnes' (1954) and Bott's (1955) first attempts to use the relationship of the linkages in a network to interpret social action, and has gained momentum in the previous decade (Knipscheer & Antonucci, 1990). From the microview of individual interdependencies emerges a global perspective on social structures.

Thus, organizational structure in social groups can spontaneously emerge from the interactions of group members. In contrast with its typical usage in sociology, we use the notion of *group* in a loose sense, defining it as the community affected by a particular problem or situation. There are a number of different general types of structural topologies: flat, or structureless, hierarchical, matrix, circular, linear, and many others. In this chapter we restrict ourselves to the first two topologies.

In addition to its topology, an organizational structure can also be described by the amount of fluidity it exhibits. Fluidity encompasses such features as how flexible the structure is, and how readily individuals can locally modify structure by changing the strength of their interaction with others.

Consider, as a concrete example, the social problem of limiting air pollution. This is a problem that on one level the whole world faces and must solve collectively. The common good is clean air with a minimum of pollution, not only to make living conditions better today, but, more importantly, to ensure that the world remains hospitable to life in the future. Clean air is a common good because everyone benefits from it independently of other individual's efforts to limit pollution.

In this example, the impact of pollution depends partially on relative geographical locations. That is, neglecting prevailing winds and currents, a person is more bothered when her neighbor burns his compost pile than when someone across town does the same. Similarly, the cumulative effect of everyone in town driving their cars to the popular bookstore (instead of bicycling) affects a local resident much more than someone else who lives miles away. Of course, some individuals' sphere of influence will range much further than others'. This dilution of impact with distance can be represented as a hierarchy of interactions that reveals itself in the unraveling of layer upon layer: neighborhood, town, county, state, world. The effect of one individual's actions on another depends on how many layers apart they are.

Within this hierarchical structure there is some fluidity. Although people are constrained by their resources and personal ties, they can often choose to move to a new location to escape a neighbor's radio or a textile company's fumes.

We now quantify the notion of many levels of clustering within a group. For a group with a hierarchy of connection strengths among the members, the organizational structure can be represented graphically by a tree, as in Fig. 10.1. The technique of representing the interdependencies in social networks by hierarchical clustering in treelike structures dates from the work of Hartigan (1967), and more recently, Burt (1980). The level of interaction between two individuals can be read directly from the tree. Tightly clustered individuals share an ancestor node one level up in the tree. Those more loosely coupled may be connected two levels up. In general, interaction strength is indicated by the number of levels to a common ancestor node. Thus the tree gives a visual description of the amount and extent of clustering in the group. Note that this interpretation of hierarchy as a pattern of interdependencies is divorced from any notion of rank within the group.

A second more general way to describe the pattern of interactions among individual members of a group is to define the matrix of interdependencies between them. Define A to be the matrix of interactions; then a_{ij} is the strength of interaction between individual i and j. This formalism permits

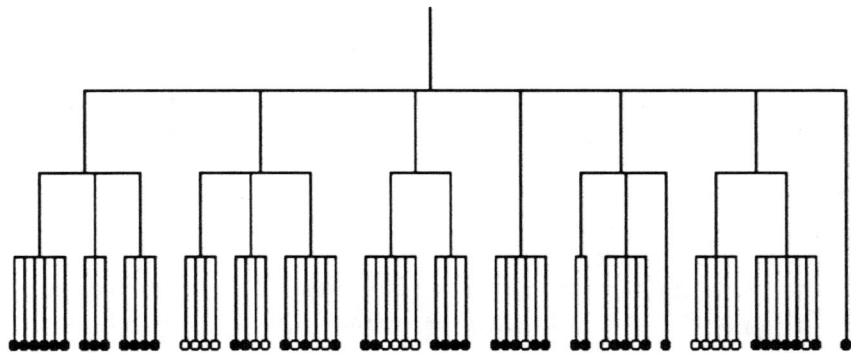

FIG. 10.1. A hierarchical organization can be visualized as a tree. The tree reveals the structure of the whole: Each branching represents a subdivision of the higher level. The nodes at the lowest level represent individuals, filled circles mark cooperators, and open circles mark defectors. One can read directly from the tree the number of layers of the organization separating any two individuals by simply counting nodes backward up the tree from each individual until a common ancestor is reached. This number determines the distance between two individuals. The larger the distance between them, the less their actions will affect each other.

generalization to many other topologies of group structure apart from hierarchical ones.

From this formalism it is easy to determine the extent of influence on any particular individual by the rest of the group. We call the cumulative influence perceived by individual i the rescaled quantity,

$$\tilde{n}_i = \sum a_{ij} \tag{1}$$

In a flat group, one in which all influences are equal, $\mathbf{A}$ would be filled with 1's, and in a group of size n, the rescaled size $\tilde{n}_i = n$ for all i. In a hierarchical structure, the components a_{ij} decrease with the number of levels separating i and j. One way to scale the strength of interaction with distance in the tree is to let

$$a_{ij} = \frac{1}{a^{d(i,j)}} \tag{2}$$

where $d(i,j)$ is the number of levels separating i and j [$d(i,j) = 0$ for members of the same cluster] and a is the scaling factor. With this scaling, a cluster of size a one level distant from individual i is equivalent, from i's point of view, to one agent in the same cluster as i. The rescaled size then becomes

$$\tilde{n}_i = \sum_j \frac{1}{a^{d(i,j)}} \tag{3}$$

Along with social structure comes the notion of fluidity. In a fixed structure the pattern of interactions remains fixed in time. This need not be the case. In the example tying relative geographical positions to influence, the pattern of interactions changes slightly every time someone moves to a new locale, and more significantly when whole groups dissolve and re-form. In a corporation, for example, employees may have some leeway to switch departments or even to move between regional branches. More importantly, the sum of small local changes in the structure of a group can result in broad restructurings over time.

The ease with which such moves can be accomplished reveals the amount of fluidity in the group structure. The notion of fluidity actually consists of two elements. One is how easily individuals can move within the structure, and the second, how easily they can break away on their own, thereby extending the structure. These moves are restructurings in the sense that they change the pattern of interactions. Breaking away can range from moving to a secluded area to branching off to start a new work group to founding a new company. In many structured groups there will be costs associated with both moving within the structure and breaking away. The higher the costs, the less fluid the structure will be, as individuals must anticipate a clear advantage to themselves before moving or breaking away.

In the section entitled Structures for Cooperation, we see how fluid hierarchical structures increase the ability of large groups faced with a social dilemma to achieve sustained levels of cooperation. But first we develop our dynamical model of the behavior of groups faced with a social dilemma in the next section. Specifically, we give theoretical predictions for the evolution of cooperation in flat groups. As these results are mostly pertinent to understanding the behavior of flat groups and have been summarized in Social Dilemmas, the material in this section may be skipped without greatly obstructing the flow of our argument.

THE ECONOMICS OF FREE RIDING

In our model of social dilemmas, each individual in the group can either contribute to the production of the good (cooperate), or not (defect). Although no individual can directly observe the effort of another, each member observes instead the collective output and can deduce overall group participation using knowledge of individual and group production functions. We also introduce an amount of uncertainty into the relation between members' efforts and group performance. There are many possible causes for this uncertainty (Bendor & Mookherjee, 1987); for example, a member may try but fail to contribute due to unforeseen obstacles. Alternatively, another type of uncertainty might arise due to individuals with bounded rationality occasionally making suboptimal decisions (Selten, 1975; Simon, 1969). In any case, we treat here only idiosyncratic disturbances or errors, which are assumed to be purely uncorrelated.

Consequently, we assume that a group member intending to participate does so successfully with probability p, and one meaning to defect actually cooperates with probability $1 - p$. Let k_i denote whether member i intends to cooperate ($k_i = 1$) or defect ($k_i = 0$), and let k_i' denote whether member i is cooperating or defecting in effect. Then, extending the terminology of the previous section, the rescaled number of members cooperating, from the point of view of individual i, is

$$\tilde{n}_i^c = \sum_j \frac{k_j'}{a^{d(i,j)}} \tag{4}$$

In a simple but general limit, collective benefits increase linearly in the contributions of the members, at a rate b per cooperating member. Each contributing individual bears a personal cost c. Then the utility at time t for member i is

$$U_i(t) = \frac{b}{\tilde{n}_i} \tilde{n}_i^c(t) - ck_i \tag{5}$$

Using its knowledge of the functional form of the utility, each individual can deduce the rescaled number effectively cooperating at some time t by inverting Equation 5. This estimation will differ from the actual intended amount of cooperation, due to uncertainty. We also define $\tilde{f}_i^c(t)$ to denote the fraction, $\tilde{n}_i^c(t) / \tilde{n}_i$, effectively cooperating at time t.

When all members contribute successfully, each receives net benefits $b\tilde{n}_i / \tilde{n}_i - c = b - c$. The production of the collective good is a social dilemma when

$$b > c > \frac{b}{\tilde{n}_i} \tag{6}$$

for all i. Thus, although the good of all is maximized when everyone cooperates ($b - c > 0$), the dominant strategy in the one-shot game is to defect since the additional gain of personal participation is less than the private cost ($b/\tilde{n}_i - c < 0$).

We now proceed to elaborate on how expectations about the future affect individuals engaged in ongoing collective action as they make the decision whether or not to contribute.

Expectations

The time scale of the interaction is set by the rate α at which members of the group reexamine their choices. Information about the level of cooperation is deduced from individual utility accrued in the past, and can be delayed by an interval τ. Along with expectations about the future, the two parameters α and $\tilde{f}_i^c$ determine how individuals believe the level of cooperation will evolve in time.

For simplicity we assume all members of the group share a common rationality in their method of forming expectations. Specifically, all members expect the game to be of finite duration H, the horizon length. Thus, future returns expected at a time t' from the present are discounted at a rate $e^{-t'/H}$ with respect to immediate expected returns. Second, each member expects that their choice of action, when reflected in the net benefits received by the others, will influence future levels of cooperation. Because, however, the decision of one individual affects another's return only $\pm b/\tilde{n}_i$, each member perceives that its influence decreases as the rescaled group size increases. Furthermore, individual changes in strategy are believed to be most effective in encouraging similar behavior when levels of cooperation are high. We postulate that these two effects compound so that each member expects its decision to cooperate or defect to encourage an overall growth or decay in the level of cooperation at a rate proportional to the ratio $\tilde{f}_i^c / \tilde{n}_i$. Roughly, then, a member expects its cooperative (defecting) action to stimulate an additional $\tilde{f}_i^c / \tilde{n}_i$ amount of cooperation (defection) during each subsequent time period.[1]

Putting it all together, member i perceives the advantage of cooperating over defecting at time t to be the net benefit

$$\Delta \hat{B}_i(t) = H(b - c) - \frac{Hb(\tilde{n}_i - 1)}{\tilde{n}_i + H\alpha \tilde{f}_i^c (t - \tau)} \tag{7}$$

as derived explicitly in (Glance et al., 1992). The functional form for $\tilde{f}_i^c (t + t')$ used in the calculation has the qualitative behavior already described: Its initial rate of change has magnitude $\alpha \tilde{f}_i^c / \tilde{n}_i$ and it approaches 1 (0) asymptotically in time if i is cooperating (defecting). Member i cooperates when the net benefit $\Delta \hat{B}_i (t)$ is positive, basing its decision on the fraction of the group it perceives to have cooperated at a time τ in the past, $\tilde{f}_i^c(t - \tau)$. These criteria reduce to the following condition for cooperation at time t:

$$\tilde{f}_i^{crit} \cong \frac{1}{H\alpha} \left(\frac{\tilde{n}_i c - b}{b - c} \right) < \tilde{f}_i^c (t - \tau) \tag{8}$$

---

[1] Assigning a functional form to individual expectations, although somewhat arbitrary, is necessary to study dynamics. Variations on the same theme, however, can be seen to yield similar dynamics, provided that the rate at which similar behavior is expected to encourage similar behavior rises monotonically in the ratio $\tilde{f}_i^c / \tilde{n}_i$.

Equation 8 provides a full prescription of the stochastic evolution for the interaction. The members of the group each engage in conditional cooperation, cooperating when the fraction perceived as cooperating is greater than the critical amount, $\bar{f}_i^{crit}$, and defecting when the perceived fraction cooperating is less than $\bar{f}_i^{crit}$. Because of the nature of the individuals' expectations, this behavior emerges from individually rational choices. In this way, conditional cooperation is a rational strategy. Furthermore, conditional cooperation is a more general type of strategy than might be expected from the explicit specification of the individuals' beliefs. As a result, it holds for a wider range of models than considered here, once one allows for variation in the functional form of $\bar{f}_i^{crit}$.

Finally, from Equation 8 we can derive the rescaled size $\tilde{n}^*$ beyond which no individuals will choose to cooperate and consequently cooperation cannot be sustained. This is the case when $\bar{f}_i^{crit} = 1$, which gives

$$\tilde{n}^* = H\alpha \left(\frac{b}{c} - 1 \right) + \frac{b}{c} \qquad (9)$$

as the upper limit for the rescaled size beyond which cooperation will not be achieved. As is shown later, the smaller the rescaled size of the group, the larger the potential for sustained cooperation.

The Stability Function

We now examine the special case where the structure of influence within the group is completely flat. All actions have equal weight for all individuals in the group. Equation 8 is actually n-dimensional for a group of size n with arbitrary structure. But for a flat group, it collapses down to one dependent variable and it becomes tractable to analysis. We apply the stability function formalism to study the dynamics of cooperation in the group. By applying this method we are able to demonstrate that cooperation (or defection) can persist in flat groups for very long times even when defection (or cooperation) is the overall equilibrium. In the analysis that follows, then, we drop the subscript i, and talk of group size instead of rescaled group size, and number/fraction of agents cooperating instead of rescaled number/fraction cooperating. The results of this analysis should also provide insight into the behavior of fluid organizations obtained by computer simulation that is presented in the next section.

The stability function Ω can be constructed from knowledge of the density-dependent utilities for cooperation and defection. This function has the important property that its local minima give the equilibria of the system as the most probable configurations of the system. Depending on the complexity of the function, several equilibria can exist, with the overall global minimum coinciding with the long-term final state of the system.

The equilibrium probability distribution $P_e(f^c)$ can be shown to be given by

$$P_e = C \exp[-n\Omega(f^c)] \tag{10}$$

where the stability function Ω for our model of ongoing collective action is given by

$$\Omega(f^c) = \int_0^{f^c} df'[f' - \rho_c(f')] \tag{11}$$

in terms of the mean probability $\rho_c(f^c)$ that cooperation is preferred. Thus, the optimal configuration corresponds to the value of f^c at which Ω reaches its global minimum.

Within this formalism it is easy to study the dynamics of fluctuations away from these minima. First, consider the case where there is a single equilibrium (which can be either cooperative or defecting). Fluctuations away from this state relax back exponentially fast to the equilibrium point, with a characteristic time of the order of $1/\alpha$, which is the average evaluation time for the individuals. Second, a more interesting case occurs when there are multiple equilibria, with the global minimum of the function denoting the long-term final state of the system. This is illustrated schematically in Fig. 10.2.

If the system is initially in an equilibrium that corresponds to the global minimum (e.g., state A), fluctuations away from this state will relax back exponentially fast to that state. But if the system is initially trapped in a metastable state (state B), that is, a minimum that is not the global one, the

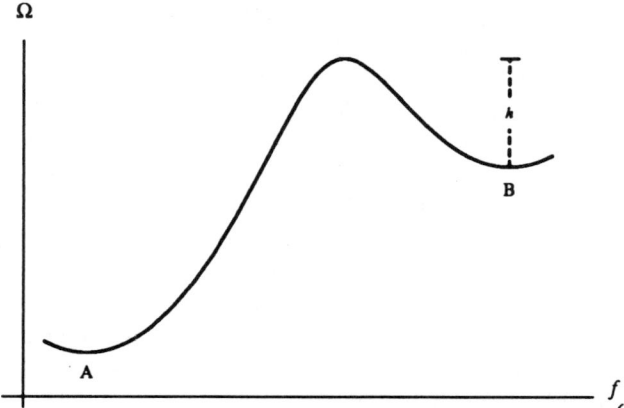

FIG. 10.2. Schematic sketch of the optimality function Ω versus f^c, the fraction of agents cooperation. The global minimum is at A, local minimum at B; h is the barrier height separating state B from A.

dynamics away from this state are both more complicated and interesting. As shown in Ceccatto & Huberman (1989), within a short time scale, fluctuations away from the local minimum relax back to it, but within a long time scale, a giant fluctuation can take place in which a large fraction of the agents switches strategies, pushing the system over the barrier maximum. Once the critical mass required for a giant fluctuation is reached, the remaining agents in the group rapidly switch into the new strategy that corresponds to the overall equilibrium and the system slides into its long-term state.

The relative depths of A and B depend on f^{crit}: For $0.5 < f^{crit} < 1$ defection is the global equilibrium and cooperation is metastable, whereas for $f^{crit} < 0.5$ the reverse holds. The exact relations depend upon the amount of uncertainty. Thus, the smaller the size of the group, the longer mutual cooperation can be sustained. Computer simulations of the evolution of cooperation in structured groups show that these relations hold in general — hierarchies with small rescaled size are better able to sustain cooperation.

The time scale over which the nucleation of a giant fluctuation occurs is exponential in the number of agents. However, when such transitions take place, they do so very rapidly — the total time it takes for all agents to do the crossing is logarithmic in the number of agents. Because the logarithm of a large number is very small when compared to an exponential of the same number, the theory predicts that nothing much happens for a long time, but when it does, the transition occurs very rapidly.

The process of escaping from the metastable state depends on the amount of imperfect knowledge that individuals have about the state of the system, in other words, on what other agents are doing. In the absence of imperfect knowledge the system would always stay in the local minimum downhill from the initial conditions, because small excursions away from it by a few agents would reduce their utility. It is only in the case of imperfect knowledge that many individuals can change their behavior. This is because in evaluating the number of members cooperating, imperfect knowledge amounts to occasional large errors in the individual's estimation of the actual number cooperating.

STRUCTURES FOR COOPERATION

We have shown that there is a clear upper limit to the size of a group that can support cooperation. Next we examine how this limit can be stretched by a hierarchically structured group whose members are able to move freely within the group. First we present the limitations of flat groups and groups with fixed structures. Then we show to what extent these limitations can be overcome by fluid groups. Finally, we discuss the possible trade-off between fluidity and effectiveness in organizations.

Flat Groups

Results of Monte Carlo simulations conducted in asynchronous fashion confirm the theoretical predictions for structureless groups obtained using the stability function formalism. Each individual decides whether to cooperate or defect based on the criterion given in Equation 8 that the perceived fraction cooperating, f^c, must be greater than a critical fraction, f^{crit}. Uncertainty enters because these decisions are based on perceived levels of cooperation, which differ from the actual attempted amount of cooperation.

As shown earlier, there is a critical group size beyond which cooperation will not be sustained. There is also a range of group sizes below the critical size for which the system has two equilibrium points, one with most of the group defecting, the other with most members cooperating.

In Fig. 10.3(a), the evolution of the system is shown for a group of size 16 whose horizon length is such that the critical size for cooperation is less than 16. The system begins in the metastable overall cooperation state and remains there for a very long time. Defection is the global equilibrium, however, and eventually, the transition to defection occurs. In Fig. 10.3(b), the horizon length is such that the critical size is greater than 16. In this case, the only equilibrium point is overall defection; accordingly, the onset of defection is swift for a group initially cooperating.

Fixed Structures

Imagine now that the pattern of interactions among the 16 individuals depicts a group broken down into four clusters of four agents each. If the

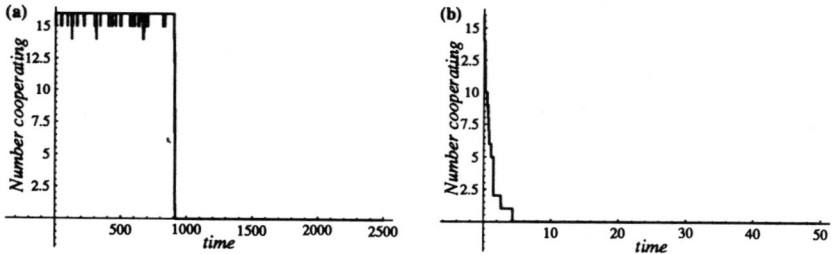

FIG. 10.3.   The evolution of cooperation is shown here for a structureless group of size $n = 16$. The benefit for cooperating, b, is 2.5, the cost, c, is 1, the probability p that agent cooperates successfully is .95, the reevaluation rate α is 1, and the delay τ is also 1. (a) Given these parameters, the horizon length is set at 12.0 to provide an example in which cooperation is the metastable equilibrium and defection, the global equilibrium. Indeed, the group cooperates for a very long time, over 900 time steps. The outbreak of defection is sudden and unpredictable, occurring at widely different times in numerous simulations of the same system. (b) Here the horizon length is set to 8.9; defection becomes the only equilibrium state for the system. As predicted by the theory, the group relaxes exponentially quickly to the defecting state.

amount of interdependency between agents scales down by a factor of $a = 4$ for each level in the hierarchy separating two individuals, then the rescaled size (Equation 3) of the group is $\bar{n} = 4 + 12/4 = 7$ for all the agents (symmetric structure). If only because the rescaled group size is smaller, cooperation can be sustained under more severe conditions for a hierarchical group than for a flat one.

More interestingly, an enclave of cooperation within the hierarchy can initiate a widespread transition to cooperation within the entire organization. The mechanism that explains this cascade to cooperation results from the clustering of agents and cannot occur in a flat group. The cascading phenomenon is more vivid in hierarchies with several layers; consider, for example, a group of 27 agents structured as in Fig. 10.4(a). In this case, the rescaled size $\bar{n} = 3 + 6/3 + 18/3^2 = 7$ for all the agents. Filled circles at the lowest level represent cooperating agents, and open circles are defecting agents. Individuals in different parts of the organization will observe widely differing amounts of cooperation. Those in the leftmost cluster see a fraction of about 3/7 cooperating, whereas agents one level away see 1/7 cooperating and agents two levels away see a fraction 0.33/7 cooperating. So if $1 / 7 < f^{crit} < 3 / 7$, the agents in the leftmost cluster can sustain cooperation almost indefinitely among the three of them despite the fact that the rest of the organization is defecting. On the other hand, although agents one level away may be defecting initially, for certain parameter choices, cooperation may actually be the long-term stable state for those clusters in the presence of uncertainty. If these agents in the clusters one level away start cooperating, they may then trigger the onset of cooperation in the clusters two levels away from the initial cooperators. Figure 10.4 shows four snapshots in time of a group of 27 agents exhibiting this sequence of behavior over time.

However, as with flat groups, groups with fixed structures easily grow beyond the bounds within which cooperation is sustainable. In the case mentioned earlier of 16 individuals broken down into four clusters, when the rescaled size is larger than $\bar{n}^*$, the group rapidly evolves into its equilibrium state of overall defection. But even when the rescaled size is less than $\bar{n}^*$, cooperation will be metastable in the sense that the agents may remain cooperating for a very long time but eventually a transition to overall defection will occur. Before and after snapshots that exemplify this abrupt transition are shown in Fig. 10.5.

Fluid Structures

In fluid structures, individual agents are able "move" within the organization. The way in which this might occur depends on what determines the structure, be it geographical location in the world or type of work within a

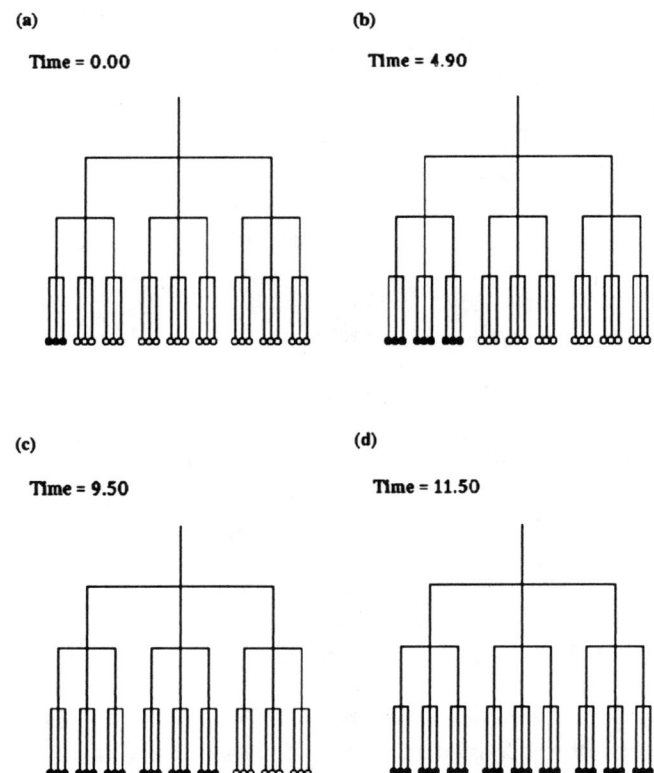

FIG. 10.4. Overall cooperation in a hierarchically structured group can be initiated by the actions of a few agents clustered together. These agents reinforce each other and at the same time can spur agents one level further removed from them to begin cooperating. In turn, this increase in cooperation can spur cooperation in agents even further removed in the structure. In this example, the structure is fixed: The three-level hierarchy consists of three large clusters, each subsuming three clusters of three agents each. The parameters in this example were set to $H = 10.0$, $b = 2.5$, $c = 1$, $p = 0.97$, $\alpha = 1$, and $\tau = 0$.

company. The amount of fluidity in an organization is variable. It depends on two factors: (a) the ease with which an individual can switch between two clusters, and (b) how readily agents break away to form clusters of their own. Globally, the sum of individual moves between clusters translates into a mixing and merging of the agents into larger clusters. On the other hand, the local decisions made by individuals to break away and start new clusters expand the structure by decreasing the extent of clustering.

In our simulations, agents regularly reevaluate the situation. Previously, they had only one choice to make: whether to cooperate or defect. In fluid organizations, they must also evaluate how satisfied they are with their location within the structure. However, the agents are assumed to evaluate only one of these two choices at any given decision point.

Time = 273.00   Time = 280.50

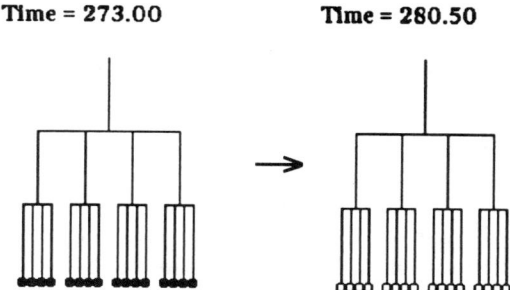

FIG. 10.5. Snapshots taken for a group before and after the transition from overall cooperation to overall defection. The times of the snapshots are shown to demonstrate the rapidity of the transition. The group's fixed hierarchical structure is unable to sustain cooperation indefinitely because the rescaled size $\bar{n} = 7$ is larger than the limiting size for cooperation, in this case, $\bar{n}^* = 4.42$. The parameters in this example were set to $H = 4.75$, $b = 2.5$, $c = 1$, $p = 0.9$, $\alpha = 1$, and $\tau = 0$.

Individuals make their decision to cooperate or defect according to the long-term benefit they expect to obtain, as before. In order to evaluate their position in the structure, an individual compares the long-term payoff it expects if it stays put with the long-term payoff it expects if it moves to another location, chosen randomly. In these calculations, the agent's strategy in response to the social dilemma remains the same, be it cooperation or defection. In order to determine the payoff it expects to obtain by moving, the individual must have access to the world as seen by the individual whose position it is evaluating. That is, if individual i wants to evaluate the position of individual j, i needs to know $\bar{n}_j$ and $\bar{n}$ as well as $\bar{n}_i$ and $\bar{n}_i^c$. This additional information is not required by individuals in groups whose structure is fixed. Thus, the validity of this model of fluid organizations is limited by the extent to which this information is available.

In addition, there might be a barrier to moving, either because there is a cost associated with it, or because the agents are risk-averse. So, for example, an individual might move only if it perceives the move to increase its expected payoff by a certain percentage, which we shall refer to as the moving barrier.

When evaluating its position, the individual also considers the possibility of breaking away to form a cluster of its own. The agent will do so if it perceives the payoff for either staying put or moving to be small enough that it feels it has nothing to lose by taking a chance and starting its own cluster. The agent can only break away one level at a time, so from a cluster of several agents, it may break away to form a cluster on its own one level distant from its parent cluster. The next time this same individual reevaluates its position, it can then break away an additional layer distant from its parent cluster, if no other agent has come to join it in its new cluster. In this way an agent can break away many levels from its original cluster.

How easily agents are tempted to break away determines the break away threshold. We give these thresholds as a fraction of the maximum possible payoff over time. Higher thresholds indicate that an individual is more likely to be unsatisfied with both its present position and the alternatives and thus will tend to break away.

Computer experiments implementing this notion of fluid organizations reveal a myriad of complex behavior. Through local moves and break-aways, the organization can often restructure itself either to recover from outbreaks of defection or to overcome an initial bias to defection in the group. A series of snapshots over time for a group of size 16 are shown in Fig. 10.6. Initially, the group is divided into four clusters of four defecting agents each—this represents an extreme condition and is thus a good test of

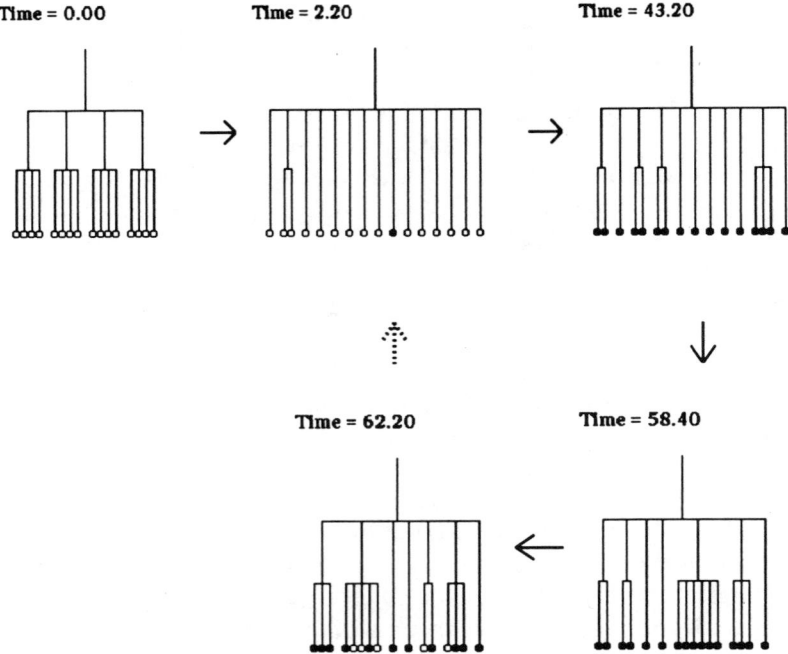

FIG. 10.6. This figure highlights the ability of fluid groups to recover from overall defection among its members. Initially all members of the group, divided into four clusters of four agents each, are defecting. The next snapshot in time shows that almost all of the agents have broken away on their own. In this dispersed structure, agents are much more likely to switch to a cooperative strategy, and indeed, by the next snapshot shown, all individuals are cooperating. Because of uncertainty, however, agents will occasionally switch between clusters. Eventually, a cluster grows large enough that a transition to defection begins within that cluster. At the same time, individuals will be moving away to escape the defectors. We see these processes happening in the fifth snapshot. At this point, more and more agents will break away on their own, and a similar cycle begins again. The parameters in this example were set to $H = 4.75$, $b = 2.5$, $c = 1$, $p = 0.9$, $\alpha = 1$, and $\tau = 0$, as in the previous figure.

the group's ability to overcome defection. A later snapshot shows that most of the agents have broken away on their own. This restructuring enables the global switchover to cooperation, because the rescaled size is now small enough that cooperation is the global equilibrium for the system, were the structure to remain fixed. Fixed it is not, however, and over time, the now mostly cooperating agents cluster back together again, moving toward clusters where they perceive the amount of cooperation to be highest. Eventually, one or more clusters will grow too large to support cooperation indefinitely, creating the potential for an outbreak of defection. Each outbreak is quelled by a process similar to that responsible for the initial recovery. Cycles of this type have been observed to appear frequently in the lifetime of the simulated organization.

Effectiveness Versus Fluidity

In a very fluid organization, individuals break away often, thus founding new clusters, and move between clusters very readily. On the other hand, these actions rarely occur in a group with little fluidity in its structure. In the example of a fluid organization given earlier, the amount of fluidity of movement was set to an intermediate amount: The moving barrier was set at 15% and the breakaway threshold was 45% of the maximum possible payoff.

Observations of many simulations at various levels of fluidity and for differing values of horizon length point to the following conclusions. High breakaway thresholds mean that individuals tolerate little deviation from the maximum available payoff and often break away in search of "greener pastures." Because breaking away is the primary mechanism that allows a group to recover from bouts of defection, a greater tendency to break away is favorable in this sense. However, higher breakaway thresholds also cause the structure to become very dilute and disconnected. In the extreme case, agents will tend to always want to be on their own, as in the second snapshot of Fig. 10.6. On the other hand, large moving barriers inhibit the clustering of agents and cause the structure to vary little over time. Thus, large moving barriers help stabilize the structure. If the group is cooperating, its structure may then remain relatively fixed over time. Coupled with high breakaway thresholds, large moving barriers mean that a cooperating system may be frozen into a structure with a very small amount of clustering.

In general, the combination of ease of breaking away and difficulty of moving between clusters enables the highest levels of cooperation. However, this yields the counterintuitive result of cooperating dis-organizations! That is, agents are all cooperating, but on their own.

The reason this seems counterintuitive is because, thus far, the effectiveness of the organization has not been considered. By effectiveness, we mean how productive a given organization is in obtaining an overall utility over time. This is revealed by how well an organization achieves its goals. It seems reasonable to assume that there is an optimal degree of clustering for which an organization operates most effectively. The ideal amount of clustering for a particular organization will depend on the type of good the group is attempting to provide itself with and how this good is produced. Determining the optimal amount of clustering for a given type of organization is beyond the scope of this chapter; however, we can say something about the range of fluidity that allows an organization to be most effective, given an optimal level.

To factor in effectiveness, we must modify the production function of the common good (Equation 5) to reflect increased performance at optimal clustering levels. One way to do this is to posit that the benefit to the group for a cooperative action depends on the amount of clustering. To this end, we introduce a variable

$$\tilde{n}^{clust} = \frac{1}{n} \sum_i \tilde{n}_i \tag{12}$$

that indicates the average amount of clustering within the structure and postulate that the benefits of cooperation are highest when the amount of clustering is equal to the optimal amount $\tilde{n}^{opt}$ and falls off to either side. Qualitatively, then, the revised individual utility function looks like

$$U_i(t) = b \exp\left[-(\tilde{n}^{opt} - \tilde{n}^{clust})^2 / n^2\right] \frac{\tilde{n}_i^c(t)}{\tilde{n}_i} - ck_i \tag{13}$$

The subsequent analysis in the prior section still holds by replacing b with $b' = b \exp[-(\tilde{n}^{opt} - \tilde{n}^{clust})^2 / n^2]$. Specifically, the collective action problem remains an n-person Prisoner's Dilemma as long as

$$b' > c > \frac{b'}{c} \tag{14}$$

for all possible reconfigurations of the structure.

The interplay between fluidity and effectiveness is best observed when the critical rescaled size falls inside a certain regime. Within this regime, the critical size is such that high levels of clustering cause the group to be unstable to defection while low levels allow to group to recover. To measure effectiveness, we keep track of the average actual payoff over time for varying amounts of fluidity, given a fixed optimal average amount of clustering. Once again, we consider a group of 16 agents, with a hierarchical structure two levels deep. The ideal amount of clustering is set at

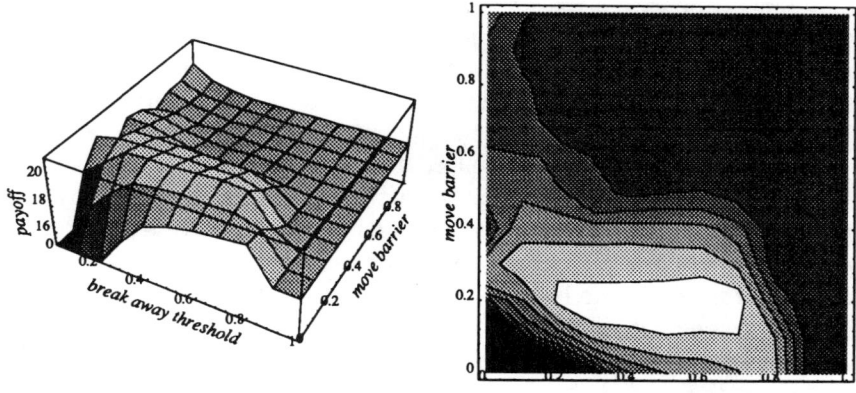

FIG. 10.7. Effectiveness versus fluidity in an evolving hierarchy of 16 agents. (a) Total actual payoff to the group, averaged over thousands of time steps, is plotted as a function of the breakaway threshold and move barrier. High breakaway thresholds and low move barriers correspond to high amounts of fluidity in the structure of the organization. (b) The contour plot is given to highlight the gradient of the functional dependence of payoff on fluidity. In this example, the optimal amount of clustering is taken to be $\tilde{n}^{clust} = 10$, a level corresponding to the clustering of the group into two large subgroups. These results show that there is a range in the amount of fluidity at which this organization operates most effectively. The other parameter values in this example are $H = 8$, $b = 2.5$, $c = 1$, $p = 0.95$, $\alpha = 1$, and $\tau = 0$.

$\tilde{n}^{clust} = 10$. Such a high level of clustering occurs when the agents break up into two large clusters. Figure 10.7 shows that there is indeed a range in the amount of fluidity at which the organization operates most effectively. Systems operating within this range of fluidity may cooperate less over time than those with less fluidity, but compensate by having higher levels of clustering.

DISCUSSION

The study of social dilemmas provides insight into a central issue of social behavior: how global cooperation among individuals confronted with conflicting choices can be secured. In recent work, we have shown that cooperative behavior in a social setting can be spontaneously generated, provided that the groups are small and diverse in composition, and that their constituents have long outlooks. Furthermore, the emergence of cooperation takes place in an unexpected fashion, appearing suddenly and unpredictably after a long period of stasis.

In this chapter, we showed that fluid organizations display levels of cooperation that are higher than those found in groups that either are unorganized or have a fixed social structure. By moving within the group structure, individuals cause restructurings that facilitate cooperation. Computer experiments simulating fluid organizations faced with a social dilemma reveal a myriad of complex behavior that results from the interplay between individual strategies and structural changes.

In our model of ongoing collective action, intentional agents make choices that depend on their individual preferences, expectations, and beliefs, as well as on incomplete knowledge of the past. Because of the nature of individuals' expectations, a strategy of conditional cooperation emerges from individually rational choices. According to this strategy, an agent will cooperate when the fraction of the group perceived as cooperating exceeds a critical threshold.

Because the critical threshold grows with group size, beyond a certain size, cooperation is no longer possible in flat, structureless groups. However, decentralized groups are often characterized by a distinct social structure that emerges from the pattern of interdependencies among individuals. Clustering in a social structure effectively decreases the size of the group as each individual cares most about the behavior of his or her own cluster. Accordingly, we showed how cooperation is a more likely outcome for hierarchically structured groups. In addition, isolated clusters of cooperation can survive and even trigger a cascade of cooperation throughout the rest of the organization.

The potential for cooperative solutions to social dilemmas increases further if groups allow for structural changes. In a fluid structure, the pattern of interdependencies can vary widely over time, because the sum of small local changes in the structure of a group results in broad restructurings. We found that fluid groups show much higher levels of cooperation over time. Significantly, fluid organizations can display long cycles of sustained cooperation interrupted by short bursts of fluidity. The levels of cooperation sustained over time depend on the amount of fluidity in the organization as well as the breadth and extent of the organization.

The advantages of fluidity must be balanced against possible losses of effectiveness for an organization. The production function for a social good will depend on the tightness or looseness of clustering, and possibly on the stability of the social structure. The form of the production function is not known a priori; however, given an optimal level of clustering for a particular good, we illustrate that there is an ideal range of fluidity.

Although our results are predicated on the assumption of hierarchical structures, we expect them to generalize to less constrained forms of social networks. Any types of structure that exhibit clustering should qualitatively behave like the hierarchies studied herein. Whether or not this is the case, the effect of the structure and fluidity of social networks on social behavior remains an interesting theoretical avenue to explore, both within and outside the study of social dilemmas.

REFERENCES

Arrow, K. J. (1974). *The limits of organization.* New York: W. W. Norton.

Barnes, J. A. (1954). Class and committees in a Norwegian Island parish. *Human Relations, 7,* 39–58.

Bendor, J., & Mookherjee, D. (1987). Institutional stucture and the logic of ongoing collective action. *American Political Science Review, 81*(1), 129–154.

Bott, E. (1955). Urban families: Conjugal roles and social networks. *Human Relations, 8,* 345–383.

Burt, R. S. (1980). Models of network structure. *Annual Review of Sociology, 6,* 79–141.

Ceccatto, H. A., & Huberman, B. A. (1989). Persistence of nonoptimal strategies. *Proc. Natl. Acad. Sci. USA, 86,* 3443–3446.

Friedman, D. D. (1990). *Price theory.* Cincinnati, OH: South-Western Publishing.

Glance, N. S., & Huberman, B. A. (1993). The outbreak of cooperation. *Journal of Mathematical Sociology, 17*(4), 281–302.

Granovetter, M. S. (1973). The strength of weak ties. *American Journal of Sociology, 78,* 1360–1380.

Hardin, G. (1968). The tragedy of the commons. *Science, 162,* 1243–1248.

Hardin, R. (1971). Collective action as an agreeable *n*-prisoners' dilemma. *Behavioral Science, 16*(5), 472–481.

Hardin, R. (1982). *Collective action.* Baltimore: Johns Hopkins University Press.

Hartigan, J. A. (1967). Representation of similarity matrices by trees. *Journal of the American Statistical Association, 62,* 1140–1158.

Huberman, B. A., & Glance, N. S. (1993). Diversity and collective action. In H. Haken & A. Mikhailov (Eds.), *Interdisciplinary approaches to complex nonlinear phenomena* (pp. 44–64). New York: Springer.

Knipscheer, C. P. M., & Antonucci, T. C. (Eds.). (1990). *Social network research: Substantive issues and methodological questions.* Amsterdam: Swets and Zeitlinger.

Leinhardt, S. (Ed.). (1977). *Social networks: A developing paradigm.* New York: Academic Press.

Oliver , P. E., & Marwell, G. (1988). The paradox of group size in collective action: A theory of the critical mass. *American Sociological Review, 53,* 1–8.

Olson, M. (1965). *The logic of collective action.* Cambridge, MA: Harvard University Press.

Schelling, T. C. (1978). *Micromotives and macrobehavior.* New York: W. W. Norton.

Scott, W. R. (1992). *Organizations: Rational, natural, and open systems.* Englewood Cliffs, NJ: Prentice-Hall.

Selten, R. (1975). Re-examination of the perfectness concept for equilibirium points in extensive games. *International Journal of Game Theory, 4,* 25–55.

Simon, H. (1969). *The sciences of the artificial.* Cambridge, MA: Massachusetts Institute of Technology.

Smith, A. (1937). *The wealth of nations.* New York: Random House.

Srinivas, M. M., & Béteille, A. (1964). Networks in Indian social structure. *Man, 64,* 165–168.

Taylor, M. (1976). *Anarchy and cooperation.* New York: Wiley.

Taylor, M. (1987). *The possibility of cooperation.* Cambridge, UK: Cambridge University Press.

van Kampen, N. G. (1981). *Stochastic processes in physics and chemistry.* Amsterdam: North-Holland.

11

Human and Artificially Intelligent Traders in Computer Double Auctions

Dhananjay K. Gode
University of Rochester

Shyam Sunder
Carnegie Mellon University

Why study artificial intelligence in computer-simulated competitive markets? Our study is an attempt to identify those performance characteristics of double auctions[1] that are consequences of their structure, from those that result from behavior of participating traders. The longer term goal of this effort is to understand the linkage between individual decisions in market settings on one hand, and aggregate market behavior on the other. Artificial intelligence (AI) appears to be a promising tool to study this linkage.

In this chapter, we report on three matched sets of computerized double auctions among buyers and sellers with exogenously given redemption value and cost schedules. Each set includes three auctions of six periods each as follows:

1. An auction involving human traders.
2. An auction involving artificially intelligent (i.e., program or AI) traders designed by the human traders who participated in the human trader auctions.
3. An auction involving "zero-intelligence" (ZI) computer traders.

---

[1]Double auction is a form of market organization in which buyers as well as sellers can make and accept public proposals. Buyer proposals, called bids, are made for a specified price and quantity. Similarly, seller proposals are called offers or asks. All proposals can be improved upon by any trader. Acceptance of a proposal by another trader results in a transaction. Each transaction is final; there is no recontracting.

The first auction in each set involved 13 human traders and was no different from thousands of other auctions that have already been reported in the literature. The participants in these auctions were then asked (after being presented with an introduction to trading in double auction and to the programming environment) to write and submit a computer program to trade on their behalf. The programs were submitted before their writers had the knowledge of the market parameters, and were debugged with the help of researchers. The second auction in each set was populated by these 13 AI or program traders.

Finally, zero-intelligence (ZI) computer buyers randomly generated a bid that was uniformly distributed between the redemption value of the unit the buyer wished to trade and the current bid, provided that the former exceeded the latter. Redemption value limit prevented these buyers from trading at a loss; the current bid limit prevented them from generating futile bids. Aside from these two limits, these programs made no other use of information, and did not learn either within a period of trading, or across periods. The ZI computer sellers are defined analogously, generating random asks that are uniformly distributed between cost of the current unit at the lower end and the current ask at the upper end.

The ZI traders make no explicit attempt to maximize their profits from trading; they only avoid money-losing trades. They submit a bid (or ask) every time they are prompted to do so, and thus, on occasion, even bid against themselves. They do not observe the market prices of the current or the past periods. They do not use the bid–ask data except to avoid making futile bids. They have no memory and do not alter their behavior in light of experience. Performance characteristics of a trading institution that is populated by ZI traders can properly be attributed to the institution itself, and not to the rationality or maximizing behavior of the participating traders. We use the performance characteristics of double-auction markets populated with ZI traders as the datum against which the performance of markets with intelligent traders—whether human or artificial—can be compared; see Gode and Sunder (1992, 1993a, 1993b) for further work on this topic.

TRADING ENVIRONMENT

At the beginning of each period, every buyer was endowed with a right to buy up to a specified number of units (one in each transaction) at any price between $0 and $200. The redemption value of each unit was guaranteed to be no greater than the redemption value of the preceding unit. Also at the beginning of each period, sellers were endowed with a right to sell up to a specified number of units (one in each transaction) at any price between $0 and $200. The cost of each unit was guaranteed to be no less than the cost of the preceding unit. Traders could (but rarely did, except when they made occasional keyboard errors) enter into money-losing trades. To engage motivation, realized profits of student traders entered into their course grade as a percentage of the equilibrium profit.

The trading screen used in Carnegie Mellon University's (CMU) MARKET-2001 computer double auction is shown in Fig. 11.1. All programs are written in Borland's Turbo Pascal. Most of the upper half of the screen is taken up by a dynamic real-time point graph of bid and offer prices punctuated by vertical lines that indicate that a bid–ask sequence has been terminated and another one started by conclusion of a transaction. On the computer screen, bids appear in white, asks in cyan, and transaction lines in green on a blue screen. The bid, ask, or the transaction line on the screen of the traders who generated it appears in red. The first column on the right-hand side of the bid–ask screen shows the redemption values for buyers and unit costs for sellers, with a red cursor highlighting the value or cost of the current unit being traded. As the trader enters into transactions, the prices of these transactions appear in the right-hand column against the value or cost of the corresponding unit. The lower left window of the trading screen shows a line graph of transaction prices. This is followed by an accounting and timer window in the middle, and a scrolling ticker window to the right.

CMU's double auction program executes crossing bids and offers at the price of the earlier of the two quotes. Bids and offers remain valid only until a transaction occurs, at which time they become void if not executed.

The program trading interface transfers control to the trading program (which is actually a Turbo Pascal procedure) whenever it is not processing

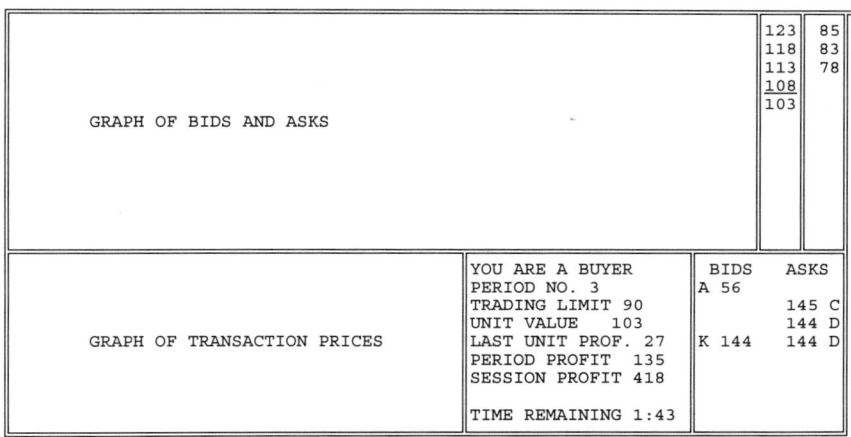

FIG. 11.1. Trading screen of Market 2001.

input from the trading program or from the central control (see Fig. 11.2 for system description). The trading program can respond by choosing one of three possible actions. If the program is assigned the role of a buyer, it can submit a bid at a specified price, or submit a "take" of the outstanding ask, or submit "no action." Similarly, if the program is assigned the role of a seller, it may choose to submit an ask at a specified price, or a "sell" to an outstanding bid, or submit "no action." The trading program has access to individual information (such as redemption values or costs, number of units it can trade, accounting information about profits) and market information

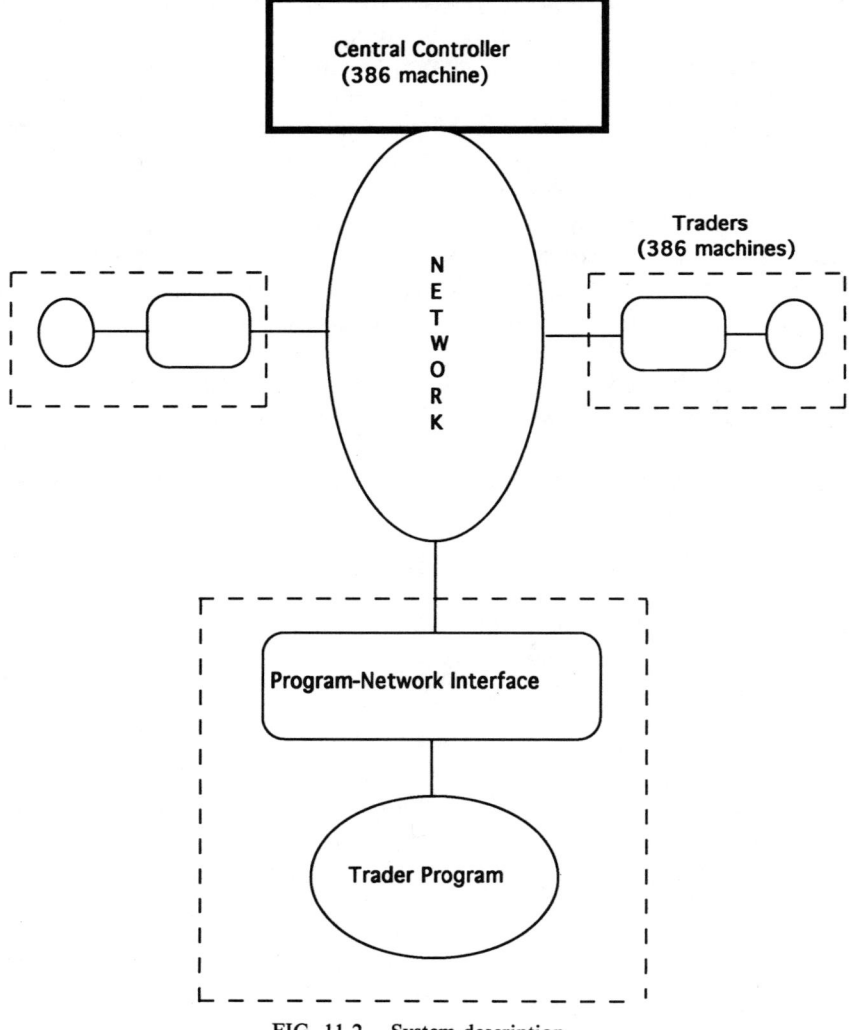

FIG. 11.2.   System description.

(such as prices, bids, offers, identities of traders taking various actions, time labels attached to various actions, and current time). In addition, the trading programs can utilize some packaged procedures that help retrieve the past data and compute summary statistics. Details of these variables and programming tools are given in Appendix A.

DECISION RULES AND TRADING PROGRAMS

The 13 trading programs whose performance is reported in this chapter used a variety of trading strategies. The programs are relatively short (150 lines of Pascal code on average) but not always simple in their logic. In Appendix B we provide a flavor of the range of the logical structure of the buyer programs. An analogous description could be prepared for the structure of the seller programs.

DESIGN OF EXPERIMENTS

Table 11.1 shows the buyer redemption values and seller costs for each of the four markets. Also shown are the equilibrium price, equilibrium volume, and equilibrium profits for buyers and sellers in each market. We used the same four sets of parameters for human, program, and ZI trader markets. The only difference was that in the first two human trader markets, there were seven buyers and six sellers; in all other human and in all program and ZI markets, there were six buyers and seven sellers. Parameters were chosen to yield a broad range of equilibrium prices (from $69 in Market 2 to $170 in Market 4) and volumes (from 6 in Market 3 to 28 in Market 1). In all cases, the equilibrium price was unique. All markets were run for six periods of 8 to 4 min each for human traders and 2 min for program and ZI traders (see Friedman & Sunder, 1994, for design of economics experiments).

RESULTS AND ANALYSIS

Prices

The three panels of Fig. 11.3 show the transaction price charts for Market 1 operated with human, program, and ZI traders, respectively. Figures 11.4, 11.5, and 11.6 provide similar charts for the other three markets. After some initial uncertainty, the prices in human trader markets quickly converge to the neighborhood of the equilibrium price in all instances.

TABLE 11.1
Design of Markets

Unit #1	1	2	3	4	5	6	7	8	9	10	Human	P	Q	π	πT	Program	P	Q	π	πT
Buyer values	102	97	92	87	82	77					Manual 1	82	28	50	1070	Auto 1	82	28	50	1070
Seller costs	34	46	58	70	82	94					7B, 6S			120		6B, 7S			120	
Buyer values	117	105	93	81	69	57					Manual 2	69	28	120	1140	Auto 2	69	28	120	1140
Seller costs	49	54	59	64	69	74					7B, 6S			50		6B, 7S			50	
Buyer values	133	95	90								Manual 3	95	6	38	263	Auto 3	95	6	38	263
Seller costs	90	95	100								B6, S7			5		6B, 7S			5	
Buyer values	180	175	170	165	160						Manual 4	170	12	15	860	Auto 4	170	12	15	860
Seller costs	90	140	170	190	199						B6, S7			110		6B, 7S			110	

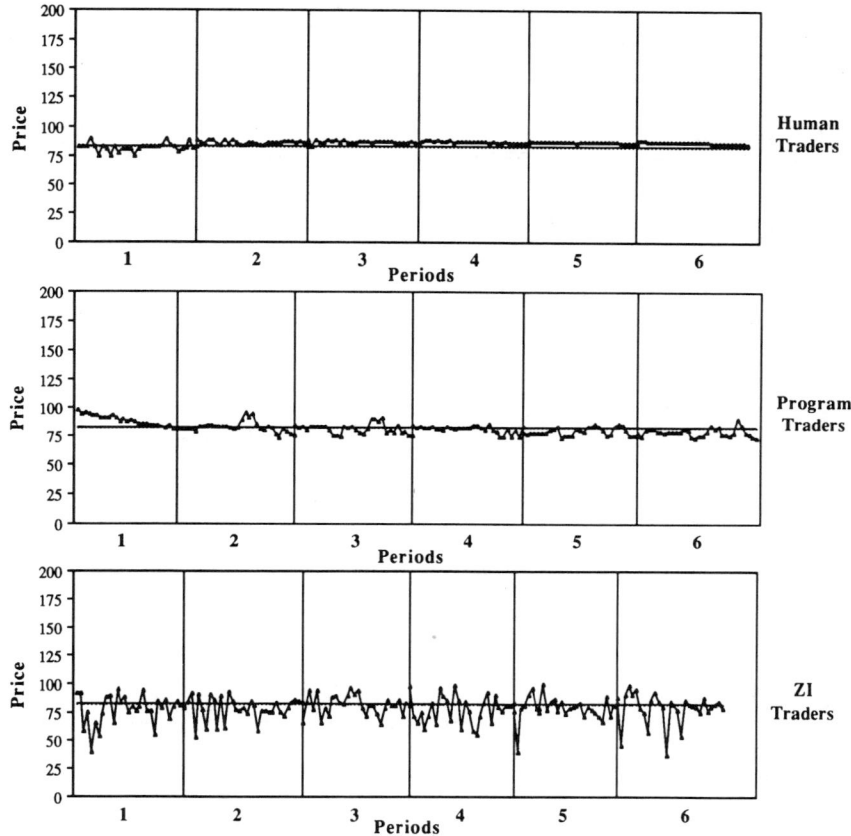

FIG. 11.3.   Transaction prices, Market 1.

These markets are characterized by the remarkable stability of price and volume.

In comparison, the prices in program trader (AI) markets are not as stable as in the human trader markets, but are more stable than in the ZI markets. The approach to equilibrium prices in AI markets is slower than in the human trader markets but faster than in the ZI markets. Even the ZI market prices converge to the neighborhood of equilibrium in the last few transactions. However, the ZI markets are characterized by persistent volatility of price within all periods and across all periods. This should not be surprising because, unlike the human traders and AI traders, ZI traders have no ability either to observe or to learn from the market phenomena. Their behavior is statistically identical across all periods of a market.

Late, but eventual, convergence of ZI markets to the neighborhood of equilibrium prices is particularly noteworthy. In these markets this convergence does not take place because the traders try to maximize their profits, nor because they learn and remember the market prices — by construction,

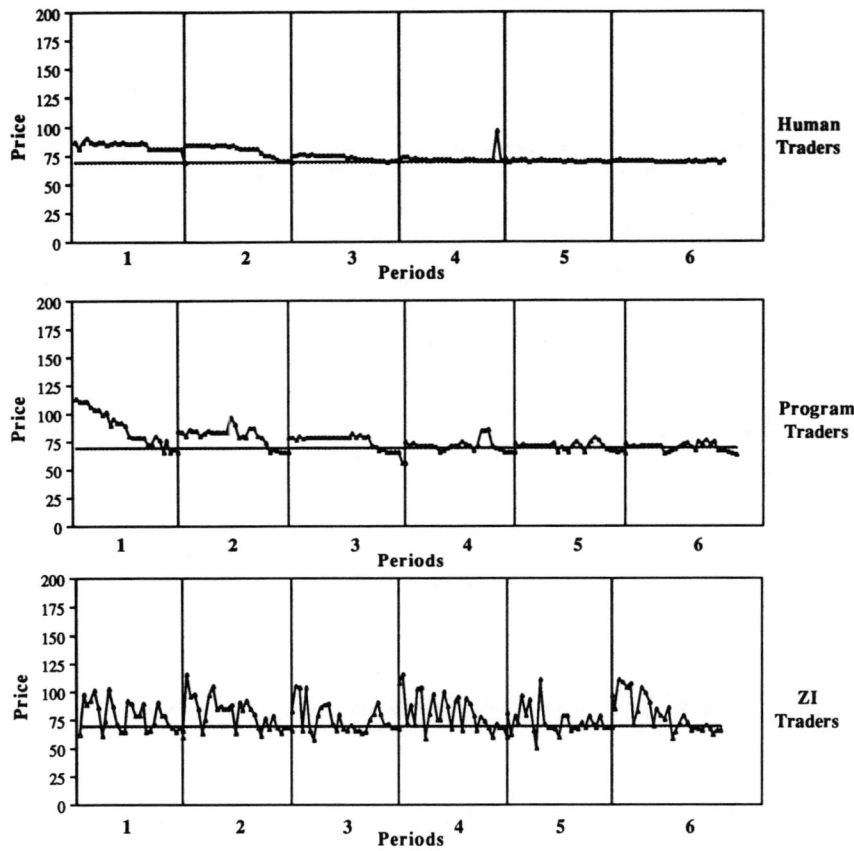

FIG. 11.4. Transaction prices, Market 2.

ZI traders are incapable of such behavior. It happens simply because the higher valued units in the hands of the buyers and the lower cost units in the hands of the sellers are exhausted first. In later parts of each trading period, the units traded have redemption values only slightly higher than their cost to the sellers. This tightening of the range in which profitable transactions are feasible funnels the transaction prices toward equilibrium in the later part of each period. It follows, then, that if the difference between the cost and value of the last units traded is large, the ZI markets will not converge as precisely to the equilibrium level.

Bids and Offers

Figures 11.7–11.10 show the average number of bids and offers made by various traders per completed transaction in the market. Human trader

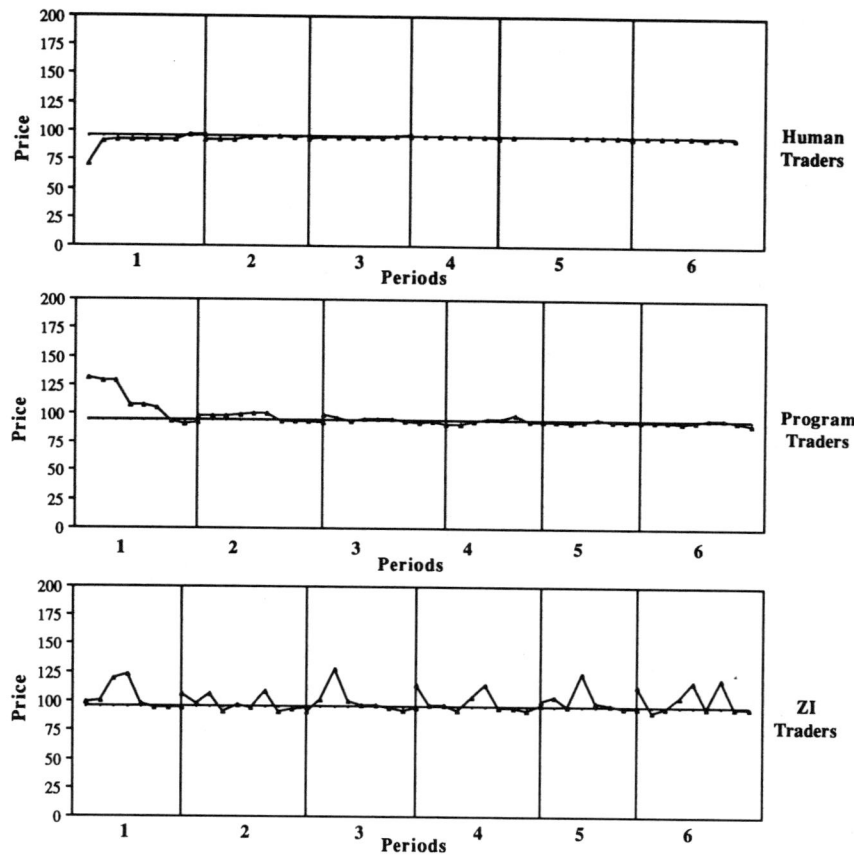

FIG. 11.5.   Transaction prices, Market 3.

markets are especially efficient in executing their trades with a minimum amount of activity and effort as measured by the bids and offers. This number remains in the neighborhood of 4–5 for human trader markets. The AI markets, on the other hand, are particularly inefficient in utilizing bids and offers because they seem to need approximately 15 bids and offers to consummate a transaction. The ZI markets are surprisingly more efficient than AI markets in this respect, using only 8–10 messages per transaction.

Bids and asks per transaction can be taken as a measure of how efficiently the communications resources of the market environment are utilized by the traders. Markets with intelligent traders (human and program) become generally more efficient in utilizing communications as they gain experience from trading in earlier periods. Without any capacity to learn, the ZI traders show no such tendency.

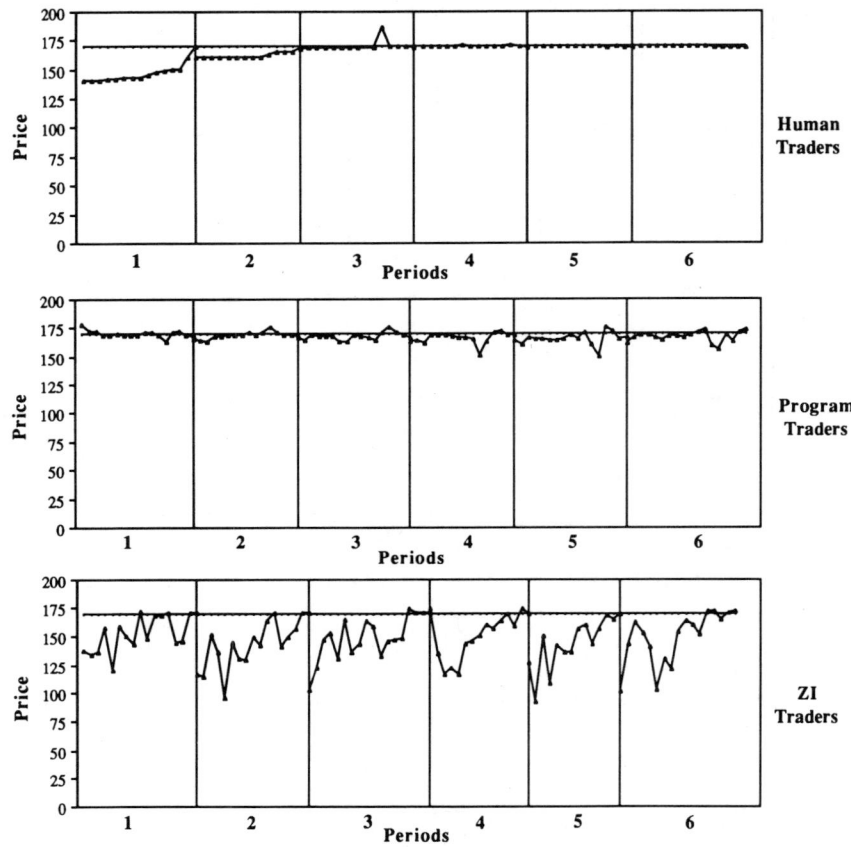

FIG. 11.6. Transaction prices, Market 4.

In the market environment reported here, communications were available for free. The only cost incurred by the traders was the cost of entering the message into the system. This entry cost, given the limitations of the keyboard entry, may be higher for the human traders than for program traders, and may explain the behavior observed in these markets. If the traders were charged a price for entering each bid or ask, perhaps a better measure of the economic trade-offs in utilizing the communication resources of the market environment could be developed.

Distribution of Profits and Efficiency

Figures 11.11–11.14 show the efficiency of Markets 1–4 plotted against the cross-sectional coefficient of variation of individual profits of traders.

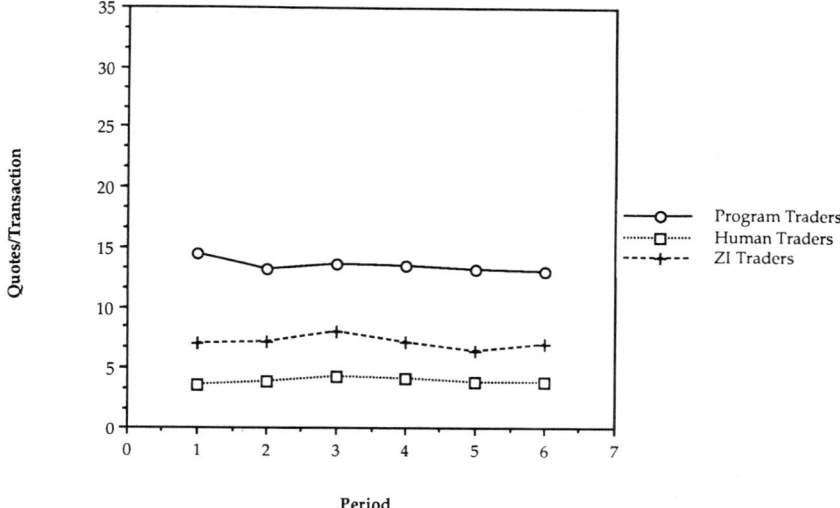

FIG. 11.7.   Bids and offers per transaction, Market 1.

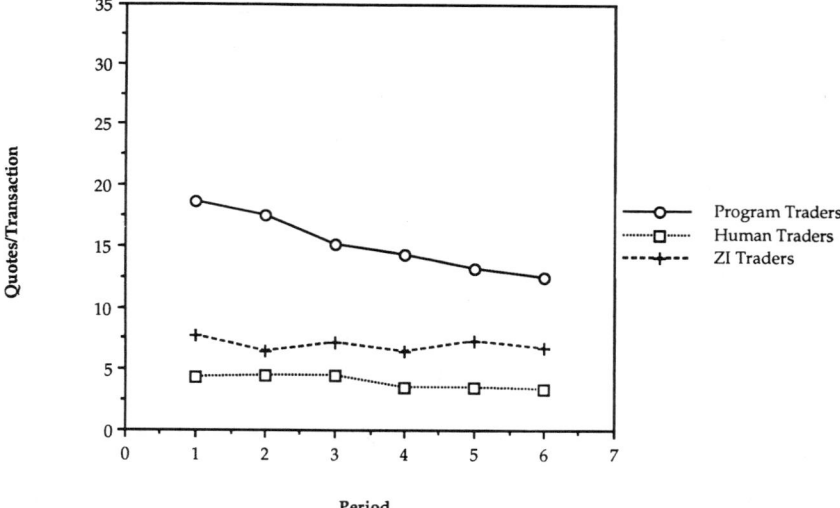

FIG. 11.8.   Bids and offers per transaction, Market 2.

Efficiency is the total profit of all traders divided by the sum of consumer and producer surplus for the market. Because the equilibrium profits for buyers and sellers are often quite different in these markets, the coefficient of variation (sample standard deviation divided by sample mean) was computed separately for the buyers and for the sellers, and the mean of those two numbers is presented here as the profit coefficient of variation.

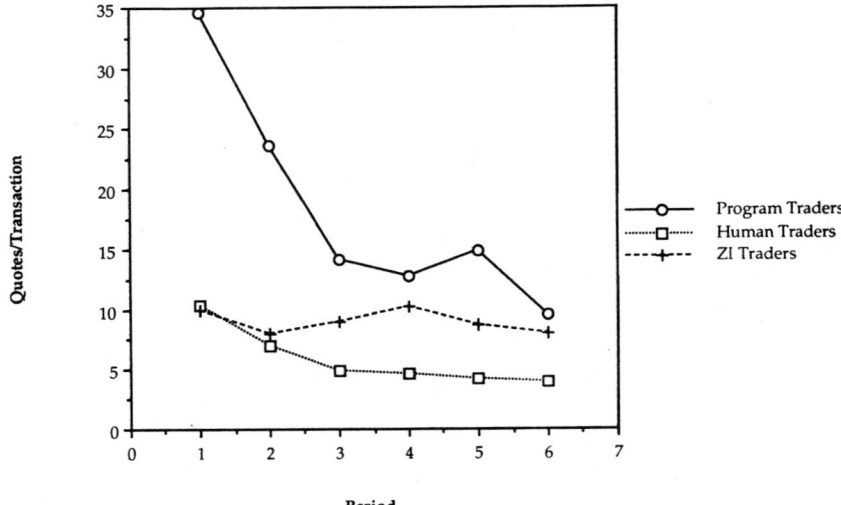

FIG. 11.9.   Bids and offers per transaction, Market 3.

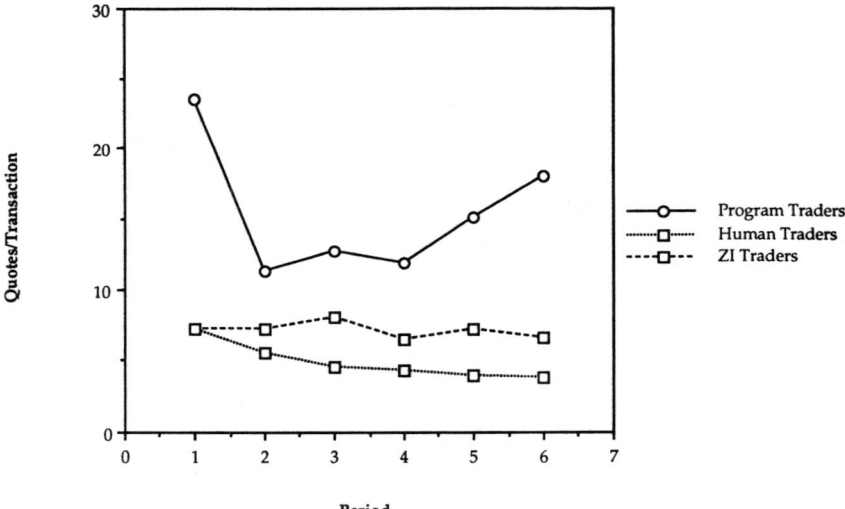

FIG. 11.10.   Bids and offers per transaction, Market 4.

The efficiency of human trader markets (shown by hollow squares on the charts) is 100% in most periods with occasional shortfall of 1 or 2 percentage points, mostly in the first period of the markets. Efficiency of the AI markets (shown by hollow circles on the charts) is very close to 100%, but generally falls 1 or 2 percentage points short of the efficiency of the human trader markets. The same is true of the efficiency of the ZI

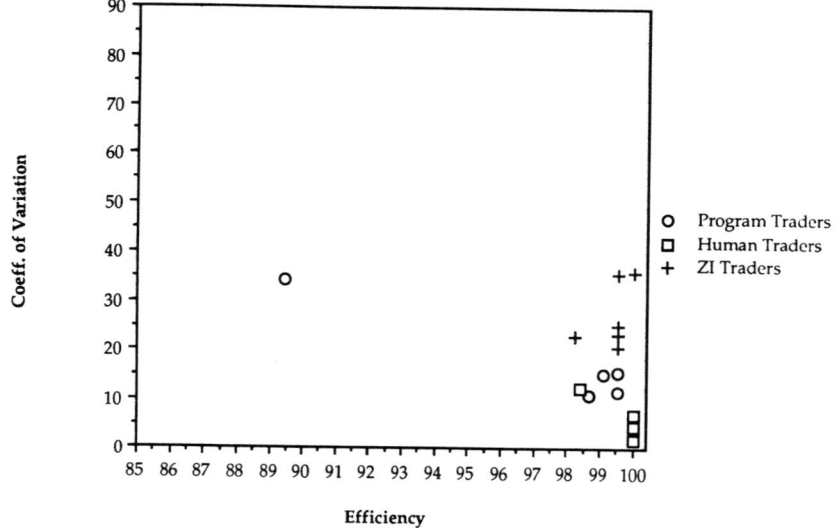

FIG. 11.11.   Efficiency versus profit coefficient of variation, Market 1.

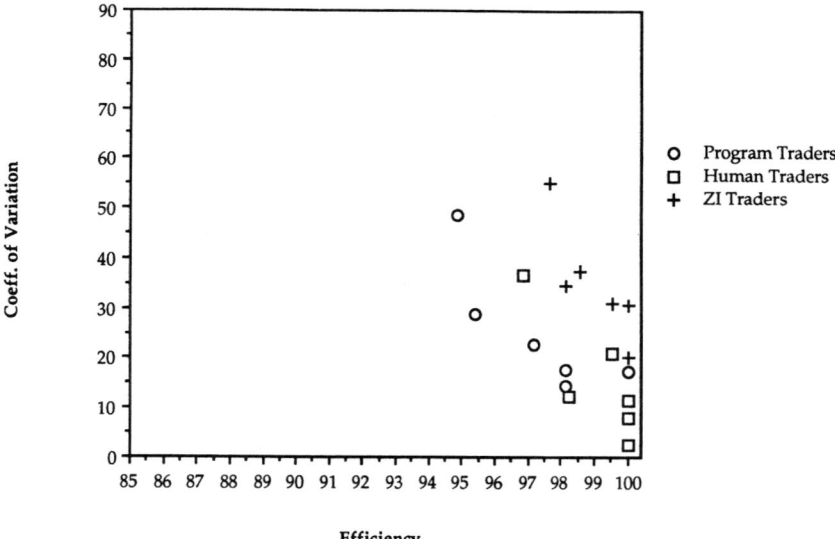

FIG. 11.12.   Efficiency versus profit coefficient of variation, Market 2.

markets—they too are virtually 100% efficient, and almost indistinguish-able from the human markets by efficiency criterion.

Although there are no significant differences in the ability of the human, AI, and ZI markets to exploit the total surplus in these double auction markets, there are significant differences in the way this total surplus is

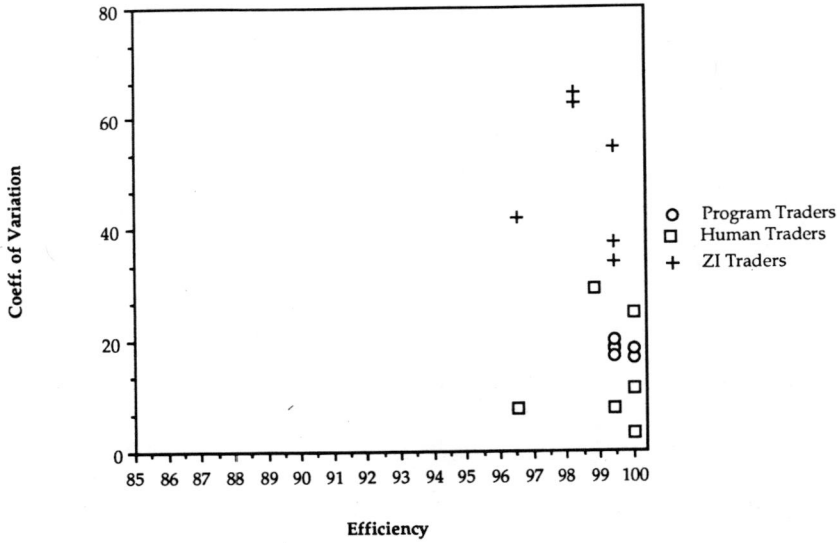

FIG. 11.13. Efficiency versus profit coefficient of variation, Market 3.

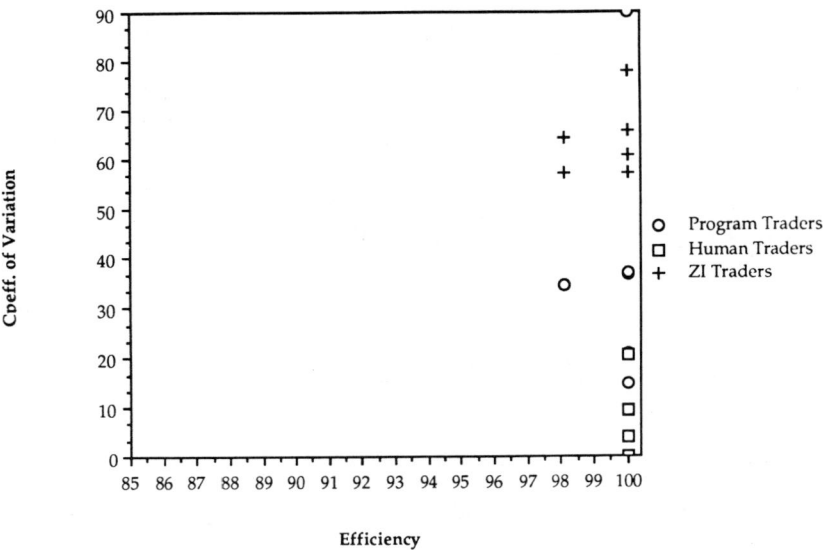

FIG. 11.14. Efficiency versus profit coefficient of variation, Market 4.

distributed among the individual traders. The profit coefficient of variation is the lowest for the human trader markets.[2] In AI markets, profits were less evenly distributed, and this dispersion was the highest in the ZI markets. It is easy to distinguish the degree of intelligence in the markets by the dispersion of individual profits but not by the magnitude of total profits.

CONCLUSIONS

In double auctions with a unique equilibrium price, relatively simple AI traders can achieve convergence to equilibrium price and virtually 100% efficiency. Indeed, little intelligence is necessary for achieving either of these two goals. Markets populated by zero-intelligence traders that make no attempt to maximize profits, and have no power to observe, learn, or remember do almost as well in efficiency and converge to the proximity of equilibrium price, although not as rapidly or as smoothly as the markets with human and AI traders.

Double auction markets populated by human traders do, however, exhibit more efficient utilization of the communications resources of market environment by executing transactions with fewer bids and asks per transaction. They also exhibit superiority in more even distribution of profits across traders as compared to markets with AI and ZI traders.

The ability of the double auctions to yield virtually 100% of the surplus to ZI traders suggests that this ability may be a consequence of the structure of the double auction itself, and is possibly independent of the trader behavior (or capability). The ability of traders to observe, remember, and learn does not seem to affect the efficiency of the simple double auctions we have examined so far with artificially intelligent (and unintelligent) traders. We already know that in certain double auctions, human traders significantly improve their ability to exploit surplus upon replication and experience (see Plott & Sunder, 1982, 1988). Much more work would be needed to delineate boundaries between those performance characteristics of double auctions that arise from their structure and those that arise from the purposive human or artificially intelligent behavior.

These preliminary results leave us with two other tentative thoughts. First, in experimental economics literature, percentage of the surplus exploited has often been used as an index of learning and rationality of subjects, as well as of attainment of control in an experimental economy. Such inferences may not be appropriate for market mechanisms that yield

---

[2]An occasional large value of this coefficient in human markets occurred because a keyboard error by a trader caused a transaction to take place at a price far removed from the equilibrium and adjacent transaction prices.

all their surplus to zero-intelligence traders. Second, if it is true that surplus exploitation is a property of double (and perhaps other kinds of) auctions independent of individual behavior, the behavioral critique of the rationality assumptions of economics may need a reexamination.

ACKNOWLEDGMENTS

Earlier drafts of this chapter were presented at the meetings of the Economic Science Association and the Institute of Management Sciences' Workshop on Mathematical Organizational Theory. We have benefited from many comments received at these and other presentations. Financial support of this work from Margaret and Richard M. Cyert Family Funds and Information Networking Institute is gratefully acknowledged.

APPENDIX A
LIST OF INFORMATION VARIABLES AND TOOLS
AVAILABLE TO PROGRAM TRADERS

This appendix describes the variables as a segment of a Pascal program presented to the students; it can be read by the trader programs to get information about the market activity and status, and about their own performance and status.

Const

| MaxPeriod = 10 | The maximum number of periods in a session. |
| MaxTrade = 75 | The upper limit of the number of individual buyer's or seller's trades that the system is designed to handle. |

Var

Myid	char	Terminal_ID of your computer (may take values from 'A' to 'Q').
ControllerID	char	Terminal_ID of the central system, normally set to 'M.'
Asker	char	Terminal_ID of the player making the current ask.
CurrentAsk	longint	Current asking price at the local system.
Bidder	char	Terminal_ID of the player making the current bid.
CurrentBid	longint	Current bidding price at the local system.

CurrentTransNo	integer	= n when the nth unit is being transacted in the market. For the first transaction number it is 1, and it is incremented by 1 each time a transaction occurs in the market. Remember this variable counts the number of units in the market as a whole and not the number of your transactions. See rcount.
Rcount	integer	= n where you are bidding or asking for your nth unit, after having transacted n-1 units. Remember this is your personal transaction count.
Info.TradeLimit	integer	This indicates the maximum number of units you can buy (if you are a buyer) or sell (if you are a seller). Please remember that Info.TradeLimit − Rcount +1 is the number of units remaining in your hand.
Buyer	boolean	"TRUE" if you are a buyer.
Seller	boolean	"TRUE" if you are a seller.
LocalRejectFlag	boolean	This is set to "TRUE" if your previous request was rejected locally.
ControllerReject-Flag	boolean	This is set to "TRUE" if your last request was rejected by the central system (controller).
remainmin	integer	Number of minutes remaining in the current period.
remainsec	integer	Number of seconds remaining in the current period.
RemainTotSec	longint	Total seconds remaining in the period.
PeriodTotSec	longint	Total seconds in the period.
Info.PeriodCount	integer	This variable stores the current period number. This is set to 1 at the start of the first period and incremented by 1 at the beginning of every period.
Info.PeriodMinutes	integer	This indicates the length of each period in minutes. It is set at the beginning of every session.
Info.TradeCount	array	[1..MaxPeriod] of integer. This indicates the number of trades you had during each period—that is, Info.TradeCount[1] is the number of trades you had in the first

		period, Info.TradeCount[2] is the number of trades you had in the second period.
Info.RpriceArray	array	[1..MaxTrade] of longint. This array holds your values or costs depending on whether you are a buyer or seller respectively. Info.RpriceArray[rcount] gives the value or cost of the unit that you are currently supposed to trade.
Info.TotalProfit	longint	This variable stores the profits made by you since the beginning of the session.
Info.PeriodProfit-Array	array	[1..MaxPeriod] of longint. Stores the profit for each period.
LastTransProfit	longint	Profit made in the previous transaction.
LastBidTime	integer	Time at which the last bid was made.
LastAskTime	integer	Time at which the last ask was made.

In addition to the variables just listed, the following Pascal procedures are also available to the program traders:

1. Access.

    Procedure Access(Period_no, Trans_no:longint; var Error: integer)

This procedure helps locate the pointer for the data file (the transactions file) where bids, asks, and transactions data are stored. It requires two inputs—period number and transaction number. A call to the procedure positions the file pointer in the transactions file (which is maintained on disk) to the record where the data for the specified transaction is stored. The procedure also returns an error code with specified interpretations.

2. PeriodSummary. The structure of the Pascal record is as follows:

```
PeriodSummaryRecType = record
OpeningPrice:        longint;
ClosingPrice:        longint;
Maximum:             longint;
Minimum:             longint;
Mean:                longint;
StdDeviation:        longint;
MaxTrans_no:         integer;
MinTrans_no:         integer;
NoOfTransactions:    integer;
MaximumBid:          longint;
```

```
MinimumAsk:        longint;
LastUnacceptedBid: longint;
LastUnacceptedAsk: longint;
end;
```

```
PeriodSummaryArrayType = array[1 .. MaxPeriod] of PeriodSum-
maryRecType; { MaxPeriods = 10}
PeriodSummaryArray: PeriodSummaryArrayType;
```

3. TransactionSummary.

```
TransactionSummaryRecType = record
Price:             longint;
OpeningBid:        longint;
OpeningAsk:        longint;
AverageBid:        longint;
AverageAsk:        longint;
NumberOfBids:      integer;
NumberOfAsks:      integer;
TimeTaken:         integer;
end;
```

```
TransactionSummaryArrayType = array   [1..MaxTransactions]   of
TransactionSummaryRecType;
TransactionSummaryArray: TransactionSummaryArrayType;
```

To access the Transaction summary of the past period, one has to call the Procedure *TransactionSummary* but the structure of the call is very different.
This procedure should be used to get information about only the past periods.

```
Procedure TransactionSummary(Period_no, Trans_no: integer;
   var Error: integer;
   var TransactionSummaryRec: TransactionSummaryRecType);
      Error: = 1 Invalid Period Number;
      Error: = 2 Invalid Transaction Number;
```

All the bids and asks for the current transaction are also stored in the memory in an array of the following format.

```
BidAskRecord = record
Trans_Type: char;
```

  Price: longint;
  end;

  BidAskArrayType = array[1..MaxBidAsks] of BidAskRecord;
  BidAskArray: BidAskArrayType;

4. LastAccess

  Procedure LastAccess(Period_no: longint; var Error: integer);

  This procedure is similar to Access except that it positions the pointer to the last activity record of the specified period.

5. ReadTransaction

  Procedure ReadTransaction(PeriodNo, TransNo: longint;
   var Error: integer;
   var Trans_rec: Trans_Rec_Type);

  This procedure is similar to Access except that in addition to positioning the pointer, it also reads the record into Trans_rec.

APPENDIX B
STRUCTURE OF BUYER PROGRAMS

This section gives a short list of the trading decisions made by the programs, and the decision criteria employed by these programs.

Opening Strategy

 1. Whether to open the bidding or not.
 2. If yes then at what price?
  a. What are the variables on which opening price is based?
  b. How do these variables change with
   i. time and/or
   ii. number of transactions
   iii. across periods?

  Possible bidding strategies include bidding at previous period's minimum bid/transaction price minus some multiple of standard deviation. In the first period, current period mean and standard deviation could be used. Some traders decided to wait for a specified number of transactions in the market before opening the bidding.

Bidding Strategy

There are three major decisions to be made in the case of bidding:

1. When to bid:
   i.   Only when someone else has bid.
   ii. Only when a new ask has come in.
   iii. When either i or ii is true.
   iv. When a significant amount of time has passed since the last bid or ask.
   v.   Very little time is left in the period.
2. Bidding increment: Most programs used a very small increment (it is safe!). Most popular number is an increment of 1 (the minimum possible in this programming environment). Other strategies included:
   i.   Increment depends on the difference between the current bid and the trader's value for the current unit. It could either be
        A. A fraction of the difference. This causes the current bid to approach the trader's value asymptotically.
        B. A step function with the size of the steps changing at fixed points.
   ii. Increment is a random number in a small range.
   iii. Increment depends on the difference between the current ask and current bid.
3. When to stop bidding, that is, what is the upper limit on the bids?
   i.   Dependent on (mostly a fixed multiple of) the last transaction price.
   ii. Dependent on the mean transaction price of the previous period plus some multiple of the standard deviation of transaction prices in the previous period.
   iii. The maximum transaction price of the previous period (or the maximum bid of the previous period in case the last event of the period was not a transaction.)
   iv. Mean of the last n transactions plus a multiple of their standard deviation.
   v.   The closing price of the previous period.
   vi. Value of the unit to the buyer.

Take Strategy

1. When a fixed amount of profit can be made, that is, value minus current ask is greater than a fixed number.

2. Current ask less than a fixed percentage of the value.
3. Current ask less than the minimum price of the previous period.
4. Current ask less than mean price minus a multiple of its standard deviation.
5. Current ask less than the last transaction price minus a fixed number.

Urgent Strategy

The traders included a period end strategy to make any profit possible when very little time is left in the period. They were willing to bid against themselves and were also willing to raise the bid to their value.

REFERENCES

Friedman, D., & Sunder, S. (1994). *Experimental methods: A primer for economists.* New York: Cambridge University Press.

Gode, D. K., & Sunder, S. (1992). *What makes markets efficient?* Working paper, Graduate School of Industrial Administration, Carnegie Mellon University.

Gode, D. K., & Sunder, S. (1993a). Allocative efficiency of markets with zero intelligence traders: Market as a partial substitute for individual rationality. *Journal of Political Economy, 101*(1), 119–137.

Gode, D. K., & Sunder S. (1993b). Lower bounds for efficiency of surplus extraction in double auctions. In I. D. Friedman & J. Rust (Eds.), *The double auction market: Institutions, theories, and laboratory evidence* (pp. 199–219). Santa Fe Institute Studies in the Sciences of Complexity. New York: Addison-Wesley.

Plott, C. R., & Sunder, S. (1982). Efficiency of controlled security markets with insider information: An application of rational expectation models. *Journal of Political Economy, 90*(4), 663–698.

Plott, C. R., & Sunder, S. (1988). Rational expectations and the aggregation of diverse information in laboratory security markets. *Econometrica 56*(5), 1085–1118.

12

Team Coordination Under Individual and Team Goals

Ping Shi
Peter B. Luh
David L. Kleinman
University of Connecticut

The need to consider human decision-making behavior in system design has been demonstrated repeatedly by problems in military Command and Control (Vaughan, 1990), accidents in air traffic control (Perry, 1991), and emergency management (Brehmer, 1988). Systems may be designed in optimal ways to meet certain criteria, but they may still fail to perform in the expected ways because of the involvement of human decision makers (DMs), whose performance is constrained by their bounded rationality, judgment biases, and various cognitive limitations. Among these salient human characteristics are peoples' individual goals, which are defined here as the objectives toward which DMs direct their efforts. Unfortunately, human DMs' individual goals are not necessarily congruent with the nominal/design goal.

It has long been recognized that goals affect human decision-making processes and system performance. Research in behavioral science, social psychology, organizational decision making, and so forth, has mostly focused on topics such as types of goals and effects of goal settings. Generally, four types of goal settings have been studied: individual, team, individual plus team, and no specific goal (i.e., do your best). Results show that having a team goal, or a team plus individual goal, can result in performance that is better than having individual goals or having no goal (Likert, 1967). It is argued that under a team goal or individual plus team goal, better cooperation enhances performance.

The research results on the effects of goal settings show that goals play a significant role in regulating human action at both the individual and team/organization levels. The studies also suggest that goals influence performance by varying the effort, persistence, and task strategy (Earley & Northcraft, 1989). Different goals can "facilitate or hinder performance, depending on whether the motivation and strategy they produce are appropriate for the problem at hand" (Terence & William, 1990).

The preceding findings were obtained in studies where individuals worked on their own tasks in static environments. In many distributed decision-making problems, however, decision-making and/or task-processing functions are distributed over several physically separated DMs, each specializing in one kind of activity, which has to be conducted with a limited amount of resource. Moreover, tasks (jobs to do) often arrive randomly with only a limited time available for their processing. To achieve good performance, the DMs must coordinate their resources, information, and actions in what is generally a dynamic and uncertain environment. Under different goals, the DMs may have different preferences on which task(s) to process, and, perforce, their coordination strategies will change as the specific goals change. Understanding how different goals affect team performance and coordination is the ultimate objective of our research.

This chapter utilizes a normative-descriptive approach (Kleinman, Luh, Pattipati, & Serfaty, 1992), combining empirical and analytic efforts, to examine the effects of different goals in a distributed dynamic task processing context. In the Reward Structure (REST) experiment, which is conducted within a controlled laboratory environment, team versus individual goals are operationalized through team versus individual reward structures. Under a team reward structure, the DMs are rewarded based on team performance, and are thus motivated by a team goal. Under an individual reward structure, they are rewarded based on their individual performances, and are thus motivated by their individual goals. In the experiment, human decision-making and coordination processes are examined with respect to *reward structure* (team versus individual), *task requirement* (sequential versus parallel), and *resource availability* (low versus high). Specifically, the following issues are addressed:

1. How do different goals affect a team's decision-making and coordination processes within a dynamic environment?
2. Under different reward structures, how do DMs adapt their strategies to task-processing requirements that impose different coordination demands?

In the modeling phase of this study, normative and normative-descriptive models are developed and validated to represent human decision-making and coordination processes within the task-processing environment.

The chapter is organized as follows. We first describe the experiment context, the independent variables manipulated, and dependent variables collected. We next present the experimental results, and discuss their implications. Normative (or prescriptive) models are formulated for the decision problem, and their solutions are described. Finally, normative-descriptive models are presented that include observed human biases and limitations, and that are shown to replicate quite well the experimental data over all conditions.

THE REWARD STRUCTURE EXPERIMENT

Experiment Setup

Using the distributed simulation facility developed by Kleinman and Song (1990), a synthetic task processing environment is created for a team of two DMs as shown in Fig. 12.1. Tasks, which symbolize generic "things-to-do," arrive randomly with different values and limited time available for their processing. To create a rich task environment that allows for observing shifts in team processing behavior, two generic types of tasks are used. An individual task (IT) has one operation and requires only one DM's processing. A team task (TT) has two operations and requires both DMs to process it either sequentially or in parallel. Each task has specified attributes: value, processing responsibility by DM, resource requirements, processing time, and processing deadline (or time remaining).

In the experiment, each DM sits at his or her respective workstation and sees tasks "arrive" at the top of the workstation screen with their attributes indicated by size, icon shape, and color. Icons with triangular shapes are

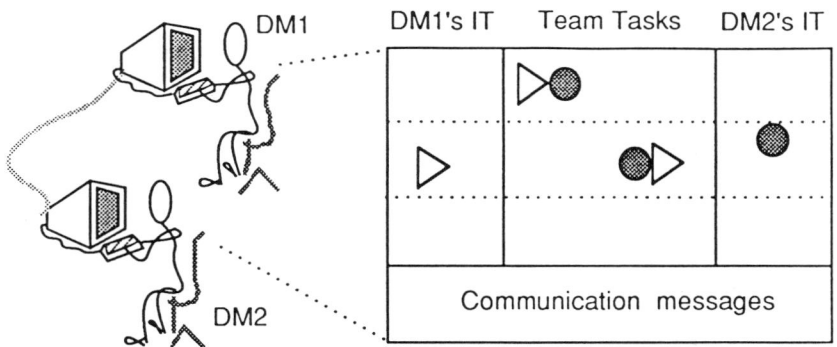

FIG. 12.1.   Experiment set-up.

tasks/operations under DM1's responsibility, and icons with round shapes indicate tasks/operations under DM2's responsibility. A team task is denoted by two connected icons of different shape. Whenever a task or an operation is available for a specific DM to process, or has already been processed by a DM, the icon color will be changed to visually inform both DMs. As time elapses, the tasks move down toward a perimeter (symbolizing a deadline). In order to earn the value of a task, the task must be completely processed by its deadline.

Each DM has a limited amount of renewable resource with which to process tasks and/or operations. To process an IT, a DM must allocate the required amount of resource for a fixed period of time. To process a sequential TT, the DMs must process the task in a specified order as indicated by the task icon, and only when the first operation is finished can the second operation be started. For a parallel TT, both DMs have to allocate their resources concurrently for a given period of time. With limited resources, a DM has to decide which tasks to process and when.

The DMs must also dynamically coordinate their activities. Coordination is facilitated by the centralized information displayed on the screens (i.e., both DMs see the same picture) and the computer-mediated communication channel. Through formated communication messages, the DMs can inform or ask each other what task(s) they are doing now, and what they plan to do next.

Experiment Design

Independent Variables

The experiment manipulated three independent variables: reward structure, task requirement, and resource availability. The information structure, communication structure, and team size were fixed. Other factors affecting decision making and coordination, such as time pressure and personal characteristics, were either predefined or smoothed out statistically by using data from a number of teams and subjects. The independent variables were operationalized as follows.

Reward Structure. Under a *team* reward structure, the accumulated value of all processed tasks is shared equally by the two DMs, irrespective of who processed what. The chance of conflict, that is, disagreement between the DMs' decisions on task processing, is small because good team performance implies good individual performance. The two DMs are thus motivated by a common team goal. Under an individual reward structure, a DM receives the full value of any of his or her processed ITs, and a prespecified, unequal portion of the value of a processed TT. The motivation for unequal distribution of value is that often DMs have different expertise for processing different operations of TTs, and that they would obtain a reward commensurate with their expertise under an individual reward structure. The DMs have to coordinate on TTs, but may have different preferences on specific tasks so as to maximize their individual rewards. Under the two different reward structures, the DMs are expected to behave differently in selecting tasks and in allocating resources to maximize their rewards gained.

Task Requirement. The two task requirements were designed to be balanced in terms of DMs' effort on task processing so that the experimental results would be comparable. In the *parallel* condition, a mix of parallel tasks and ITs arrive randomly. A parallel task requires both DMs to allocate their resources simultaneously for a given period of time (processing time T_r). As processing cannot be started until the resources from both DMs are allocated, asynchronous or noncooperative resource allocation to a parallel team task will result in unproductive tie-up of resources by DMs. The DMs are thus highly interdependent on processing team tasks. In the sequential condition, sequential tasks and ITs are presented to the DMs. A sequential task must be processed by the two DMs in a specific sequence, and a DM can only start processing his or her operation once it is available. Each operation takes one processing time unit (T_r). Without a synchronization requirement the DMs are not as interdependent as they are under the parallel condition. In either condition, a DM's effort to process a team task is equivalent in terms of processing time required and the amount of resource allocated. However, the DMs may adopt different task strategies to manage different levels of interdependency as the task processing requirement changes.

Resource Availability. Resource availability is manipulated by varying the number of resource units owned by each DM. As resource availability changes, DMs are expected to change their resource allocation strategies to achieve the best possible performance. Scarcity of resources can be viewed as a team stressor. With limited resources, more mental effort is needed to evaluate the best allocation; with rich resources, a "process everything" strategy can be used effectively.

A Mental-Model-Based Hypothesis

It is generally recognized that a DM makes decisions based on his or her mental model (Hastie, 1991)—a mental representation of the situational environment and of other DMs' behaviors and likely actions. If a DM held an accurate mental model it would represent the decision-making environment with little uncertainty, and possible conflicts with other DMs would be minimized and easily resolved. (Here conflict refers to the disagreement among DMs as to their decisions on interdependent activities.) However, conflict is bound to arise because DMs, motivated by different goals and constrained by various limitations and biases, are likely to perceive the environment differently. The DMs' uncertainty about their decision-making environment and their conflicts in task processing may lead to failures in team coordination.

In the REST experiment, different reward structures give the DMs different objectives for decision making and coordination, whereas different task-processing requirements provide different situational environments. Under a team reward structure, the DMs, motivated by a common team goal, should have a common interest in task processing. They are likely to have less uncertainty about each other's future decisions and less conflict, indicative of the DMs' more precise mental models of each other. With a precise mental representation of the other DM's behavior, a DM's decisions can be made in a coordinated manner with one's teammate without explicit information exchange. Under an individual reward structure, however, the DMs have their own interests with regard to task processing. The DMs are likely to have different and inaccurate mental representations of each other's possible decisions. These discrepancies in DMs' mental models will inevitably breed uncertainty and conflict in decision making, and hence result in the need to increase communications to reduce uncertainty.

Parameter Value Selection

Experimental parameter values should be carefully selected to ensure proper scenario complexity, and to avoid extreme team behaviors such as concentrating only on TTs or only on ITs. Several parameter values were preselected based on experiences from previous experiments. The ITs and the TTs, which are either sequential team tasks or parallel team tasks, arrive according to a Poisson process. The arrival probabilities of TTs and ITs are approximately equal. All tasks have the same initial time available, $T_a = 120$ sec, and all operations have the same processing time, $T_r = 30$ sec. The amount of resource owned by each DM is either two or three units, corresponding to low and high levels of resource availability, respectively.

Task value serves as an incentive for coordination. In the experiment, each operation of a TT requires one unit of resource, and each IT requires two units of resource. Task values were chosen to be 10 points for each TT, and 8 points for each IT. This corresponds to 4 points for each unit of a resource required, and 2 extra points as an incentive for coordinating. Under an individual reward structure, the 10 points of a successfully processed TT are distributed to the DMs in a 7:3 ratio. For 50% of the TTs DM1 could receive 7 points, whereas for the other 50% DM2 could receive 7 points. (In the experiment these TTs were distinguished by showing their relative icon sizes in a 7:3 or a 3:7 ratio.) Under a team reward structure, the value of any successfully processed task is divided equally between the two DMs no matter who processed what.

Given these parameters, a bulk service queuing system with finite buffer size (Kleinrock, 1975) was used to model task processing so that an appropriate work-load environment could be obtained. From the model results, an overall task arrival rate of six tasks per minute was selected.

Dependent Variables

As in previous studies on human decision making (Kleinman et al., 1992) our dependent variables are classified into three categories: performance, decision strategy, and coordination strategy. The major variables are described next.

Performance Measures. The major performance measure is *reward per DM,* defined as the ratio of total task value obtained by a DM to the total task value (one's individual tasks plus their share of team tasks) presented to the DM in a trial.

Decision Strategy Measures. This category of measures reflects general strategy in task processing. *Cooperation index* is defined as the percentage of total reward obtained from TTs. *(Average) slack time* is a task's deadline minus its completion time. *(Average) latency* is the time of first action on a task minus its arrival time.

Coordination Measures. Team coordination is reflected in both task processing and communication. *Coordination failure* is defined as the ratio of started but unfinished TTs to the total number of TTs processed, indicating failed coordination attempts. Coordination failure happens when the first operation was done (under sequential task requirement) or the first unit of resource was allocated (under parallel task requirement), and the second DM did not have enough time, resource, nor desire to cooperate on this team task. *The number of messages per team task* reflects explicit coordination effort.

Experiment Procedure

The formal experiment implemented a full factorial design across the three independent variables with three replications ($2 \times 2 \times 2 \times 3$). It was conducted with eight teams of two subjects each, drawn from graduate and undergraduate students at the University of Connecticut. Before the formal experiment, the subjects were trained for 10–12 hrs under all conditions using task arrival scenarios/patterns that were statistically equivalent to those they would face in the actual experiment. The experiment was then conducted in different sequences for different teams. Each subject/team did 24 trials, each lasting 15 min. During each session, which generally consisted of several trials, the subjects were only exposed to conditions within a specific reward structure. This was to minimize any confusion as to what their specific goal or goals were. Before each trial, the subjects received a card indicating the experimental conditions for that trial.

Individual and team goals were operationalized by establishing two bonus pools. One was for the individual reward structure, and the other was for the team reward structure. Under an individual reward structure, the DMs were evaluated based on their individual performance, and the three best subjects shared the individual reward bonus pool. Conversely, under a team reward structure the DMs were evaluated based on the team performance, and the three best teams shared the team reward bonus pool. A potential concern was that the subjects might form coalitions under the individual reward structure and redistribute the bonuses after the experiment. To ensure that the reward structures accurately reflected team goal and individual goals, the 16 subjects were randomly grouped into eight teams. For each trial, the subjects were regrouped so that there were no two subjects who would see each other more than twice under the same experiment condition. Hence, the teams were always formed by different team members, and undesired coalitions were not observed.

EXPERIMENTAL RESULTS

The experimental results presented in this section include: (a) the one-way effects of reward structure and task requirement on team decision making and coordination, and (b) interactions between reward structure and task requirement. The first-order effects of resource availability and interactions between reward structure and resource availability are not discussed here, but may be found in a master's thesis work (Shi, 1993).

Effects of Reward Structure

It is hypothesized that DMs hold different perceptions (mental models) of their environment under different reward structures. This should lead to different preferences regarding task types, and different coordination patterns. The experimental results show that reward structure did significantly affect team performance and coordination.

General Performance.   Analysis showed that the team reward structure yielded higher reward per DM (64.7%) than did the individual reward structure (60.9%) with $p < .001$. The percentage of tasks processed was also significantly affected ($p < .002$) and displayed the same pattern as the reward per DM: 61.1% and 59.5% for team and individual cases, respectively. The changes in reward and percentage of tasks processed were largely related to coordination effectiveness. Coordination failure (percentage of started but unfinished TTs) was 2.5 in the team case but was 8.6 in the individual case ($p < .001$). The high failure under an individual reward structure indicates that coordination is less effective, coincident with lower rewards and fewer tasks processed.

Coordination Measures.   Under different reward structures, coordination strategies and coordination activities were significantly different, as shown in Table 12.1. A shorter latency (the time of first action on a task minus its arrival time) on TTs indicates that team tasks drew earlier attention from the DMs, implying that the DMs had a higher willingness to cooperate. A higher cooperation index (the percentage of total reward obtained from processing TTs) under a team reward structure shows higher coordination effectiveness. Under a team reward structure, the DMs started their actions on TTs earlier, processed more TTs, and coordinated more implicitly (i.e., without the need for overt communications) than they did under an individual reward structure. The results suggest that DMs' better performance under a team reward structure was not simply because more tasks were processed, but as shown in Table 12.1, was also caused by the DMs' attitudes toward cooperation, patterns of task processing, and communication/coordination activities.

Interpretation of Results

Under a team reward structure, the DMs shared a common interest in task processing. They thus had a better anticipation of each other's likely actions. There was less uncertainty and conflict in the DMs' interdependent task processing activities as evidenced by the coordination failure measure. The DMs therefore had less need to communicate, could coordinate more

TABLE 12.1
Coordination Measures for Reward Structure

Measures	Team	Individual	p Value
Latency	34.8	38.5	$< .005$
Cooperation Index (%)	81.4	66.7	$< .001$
Message per TT	0.08	0.17	$< .001$

effectively, and could perform better. Under an individual reward structure, however, the DMs had different preferences in processing tasks as motivated by their individual goals. It is difficult for one DM to have an accurate mental representation of the other DM's behavior and of the environment. This resulted in a higher level of coordination uncertainty and communication needs.

In summary, these analyses suggest that the team reward structure facilitates implicit yet effective coordination, and better performance. Under an individual reward structure, the DMs could not achieve the same performance although they coordinated explicitly. There were increased levels of coordination uncertainty and conflict.

Effects of Task Requirement

Overall, task requirements did not significantly affect performance. Significant effects, however, were observed in the team's process measures for decision strategies and coordination activities under different task requirements. The results in Table 12.2 show that under the parallel task requirement, the DMs processed more team tasks, had fewer coordination failures, and coordinated more explicitly than they did under the sequential task requirement.

Under the sequential task requirement, a DM could start processing his or her operations once those operations were available. The DMs were not forced to process the same team task at the same time and thus had flexibility in their resource utilization. The DMs therefore did not concentrate only on processing TTs, which resulted in lower cooperation index and higher coordination failure as shown in Table 12.2. Furthermore, given the centralized information structure, each DM knew when a specific task or operation was available, under processing, or finished. Therefore, they could coordinate on team tasks implicitly.

Under the parallel task requirement, the DMs had to synchronize their resource allocation actions in order to start processing a TT. Asynchronized or poorly coordinated resource allocation actions on TTs led to the DMs' wasted effort as evidenced by coordination failures. To optimize their resource utilization, the DMs need to synchronize their actions on TTs. The

TABLE 12.2
Coordination Measures for Task Processing Requirement

Measures	Sequential	Parallel	p Value
Cooperation Index (%)	70.9	77.3	< .001
Percent Coordination Failure	11.0	7.2	< .001
Message per TT	0.03	0.23	< .001

centralized information structure could only provide the DMs with "after-event" information, that is, displaying TT status changes after a resource allocation event happened. To assure more effective and prompt processing, the DMs cooperated explicitly by sending formatted messages. Coordination failure was therefore largely reduced, which led to a higher cooperation index as shown in Table 12.2.

Interpretation of Results

The preceding analysis indicates that a parallel team task processing environment is more interdependent. The DMs have to synchronize their actions on resource allocation, which makes explicit coordination necessary. On the other hand, sequential team task processing is relatively independent. The DMs therefore could utilize implicit coordination mechanisms under a centralized information structure. With these results, the hypothesis that more explicit coordination behavior will be expected within a more interdependent task environment is validated.

Interaction Between Reward Structure and Task Requirements

The decision-making and coordination processes are directly related to the goal(s) the DMs strive to optimize and the nature of tasks to be processed. As the reward structure and the task-processing requirements change, the DMs may need to adapt their coordination strategies accordingly in order to achieve their goals.

Task Processing. Figure 12.2(a) shows the interaction between reward structure and task requirements on the percentage of tasks processed.

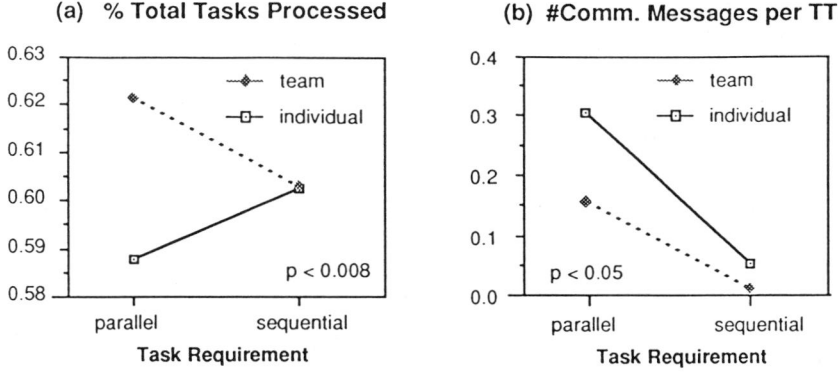

FIG. 12.2. Task-processing and communication measures.

Under the parallel task requirement, the team reward structure surpassed the individual reward structure in percentage of tasks processed by a large amount. Under the sequential task requirement, however, the two reward structures resulted in about the same percentage of tasks processed. In the parallel case, a team reward structure had an advantage over an individual reward structure as it reduced the coordination uncertainty and conflict caused by high interdependency on task processing. In the sequential case, there was less coordination uncertainty due in large part to low interdependency on task processing and the centralized information display. The DMs knew exactly when an operation was under processing or when the processing had been completed. It was therefore possible for the DM responsible for the second operation to plan his or her resource with sufficient lead time. The two reward structures thus did not exhibit much difference.

Communication. Figure 12.2(b) shows the interaction effect on the number of communication messages per TT. In the parallel case, a team reward structure greatly reduced the number of communication messages as compared to an individual reward structure. A team reward structure, providing the DMs with more accurate mental representation of the environment, reduced the uncertainty and conflict associated with the high interdependency in task processing. It thus largely decreased DMs' communication needs. Under a sequential task requirement, however, the result shows that different reward structures had only a minor effect. In this case, lower interdependency on task processing between the DMs made communication less important. The DMs thus communicated little under both reward structures. Adequate task processing was achieved using implicit coordination in conjunction with centralized displayed information.

THE NORMATIVE MODEL

The purpose of developing a normative model is to provide a baseline for the task-processing problem, and to identify human DMs' cognitive limitations and biases. The normative solutions shed light on optimal team behavior, such as performance achievable, and partitions of effort on different types of tasks.

The problem formulated for the REST experiment is very difficult to solve in view of its long time horizon and its dynamic and random task features. Research on human behavior has indicated that humans are either incapable or unwilling to project the effects of a decision far into the future because of their cognitive limitations, such as myopic behavior (options are evaluated based on a short planning horizon) and limited short-term memory (only a small group of facts is used to make a decision; Simon,

1982). It has also been shown that a very long planning horizon is unnecessary if *optimal* performance is not intended (Hernandez-Lerma & Lasserre, 1990). It is therefore assumed in our model that decisions on task processing are based on arrived tasks only. The dynamic problem is thus solved in a "moving window" fashion, that is, one snapshot at a time. A snapshot is taken by a DM at his or her decision epochs, that is, when a new task arrives or when resources are released.

In this section, the one-snapshot problem is formulated as a decision tree for the team reward structure, and as a Nash game tree for the individual reward structure. The models capture all of the key experimental ingredients, including the two reward structures, two task processing requirements (sequential and parallel), and two levels of resource availability (low and high). The decision tree model is first developed for the sequential task condition and then for the parallel task condition. The Nash game tree model is then developed in a similar manner.

The Decision Tree Model

Under the team reward structure, the two DMs, motivated by a common team goal, are expected to coordinate their task processing to maximize the team reward. The decision tree contains both DMs' decision choices, from which the team rewards are obtained. Because DM1 and DM2's decision-making roles are symmetric, and all of the operations require the same amount of time, the tree is also symmetric with respect to DM1 and DM2, and the two DMs act in turn. Two DMs' consecutive decision epochs comprise a *level* of the tree.

Decision Tree with Sequential Task Processing Requirement

Under the sequential task processing requirement, each DM is responsible for processing two types of tasks: ITs and sequential TTs. For a sequential TT, the second operation cannot be started until the first operation is finished (operation precedence constraints). The number of resource units used by each DM cannot exceed the number available to him or her at any time (resource capacity constraints). The construction of a decision tree is thus subject to the operation precedence constraints and resource capacity constraints.

Construction of a Decision Tree. In the decision tree, each decision choice, that is, the task-processing action, is expressed as a node. A node is valid only if it satisfies the operation precedence constraints and resource capacity constraints. Starting from the root node, the depth-first approach (Horowitz & Sahni, 1984) is adopted to expand the decision tree until all the leaf nodes, that is, termination nodes, are reached. At each leaf node the team reward is calculated based on both DMs' decisions leading to the leaf node. The branch that yields the maximum team reward is selected as the solution.

To better explain the construction of a decision tree, consider the scenario shown in Fig. 12.3. In this example, DM1's operations are denoted as triangles and DM2's operations are denoted as circles. Each horizontal zone separated by dashed lines represents a time period T_r needed for the processing of one operation.

The decision tree with level $n = 3$ is constructed as shown in Fig. 12.4. For simplicity, each DM owns one unit of resource, and each operation requires one unit of resource. It is assumed that a TT is worth 10 points and an IT 4 points for the team. The team reward associated with the two DMs' specific decision sequences are provided inside the parentheses of leaf nodes.

Attractiveness Measure.   Constructing and solving a complete decision tree will become very difficult as the number of tasks increase. In actuality, because of myopic behavior and limited short-term memory, a DM will not look many steps ahead in making a decision. The *attractiveness measure* (AM) is therefore introduced to estimate the value of a "future" decision at the mth level of a tree (m is a parameter to be selected, and $m < n$, the number of levels of the tree). The AM of a future decision is defined as the difference between the *potential gain* (i.e., reward to be earned if this decision is exercised) and *potential loss* (lost opportunities because of resource commitment to this decision), and reflects the *attractiveness* of selecting this decision (Pattipati, Kleinman, & Ephrath, 1983). The AM of this decision can then be combined with values obtained from the first $m - 1$

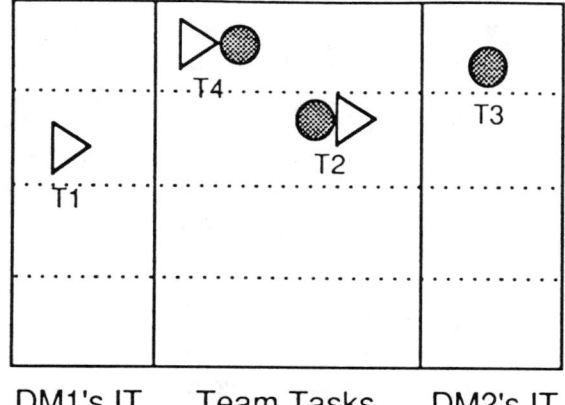

DM1's IT   Team Tasks   DM2's IT

FIG. 12.3.   An illustrative scenario.

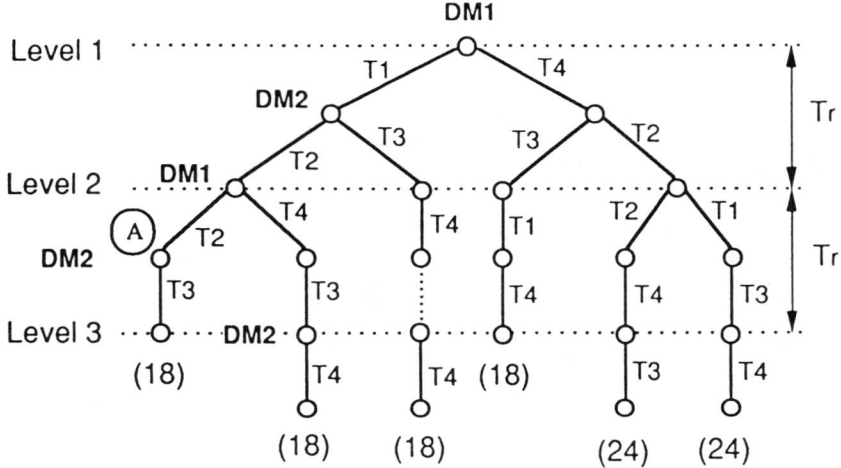

FIG. 12.4.   Complete decision tree for a sequential task requirement.

levels of the tree (representing values gained from immediate and near term decisions) to obtain the total reward for these *m* decisions, or decision path.

The AM for acting on operation *j* of task *i* [abbreviated as operation (i,j)], $M_{ij}(t)$, is given by

$$M_{ij}(t) = v_{ij} - \sum_{k \neq i} v_{kj} \tag{1}$$

where v_{ij} is the potential value (which can be earned only if the task is finished before the deadline) of operation (i,j) under consideration, and v_{kj} is the value of operation (k,j) that will be lost because of processing (i,j).

To illustrate how the AM is calculated, consider node A, the node representing DM1's Level 2 decision at the leftmost branch of the decision tree shown in Fig. 12.4. At node A, task T4 will be lost by the time DM1 finishes task T2. The AM of processing T2 is thus calculated as $M_{21} = v_{21} - v_{41} = 5 - 5 = 0$.

Construction of a Decision Tree with AM.   Employing the AM, a smaller and more manageable decision tree is constructed using the following steps:

1. A DM forms an *m*-level decision tree based on options available to both DMs subject to operation precedence constraints and resource capacity constraints.
2. The reward of each leaf node is computed by adding the AM (M_{ij}) of the DM's last decision to the values of the first (m-1) levels using a recursive calculation.

Figure 12.5 shows the decision tree for $m = 2$ corresponding to the example in Fig. 12.3. To illustrate how the outcomes are calculated, consider node A, the leaf node of the first branch. The team reward at node A is $V + M_2 = v_1 + v_{21} - v_{41} = 4 + 5 - 5 = 4$.

The solution to the decision tree is obtained by searching for the maximum team reward among the leaf nodes. For the decision tree in Fig. 12.5, the solution is 16, corresponding to the branch T4–T2–T2, which is shown as a thicker line.

Decision Tree with Parallel Task-Processing Requirement

Under a parallel task-processing requirement, each DM is responsible for processing ITs and parallel TTs. To process a parallel TT, both DMs need to allocate their resources at the same time (operation synchronization constraints). The DMs' unsynchronized actions on a TT are therefore not considered in constructing a tree. For example, if a node represents the processing of a TT by DM1, and DM2 has not yet allocated resource on this TT, then the only child node is the processing of the same TT by DM2. To construct the decision tree, the depth first approach is again used in a manner similar to the sequential case. For the example just considered, the decision tree is constructed in Fig. 12.6.

Considering human DMs' cognitive limitations, the decision tree is simplified with AM as described before. For the example considered, the simplified tree is shown in Fig. 12.7, and the solution is indicated by the thicker branches (T1–T3–T2) with value 18.

The Game Tree Model

Under an individual reward structure, the interrelated task processing responsibility of the two DMs and their different preferences on tasks may result in disagreement on which set of tasks to process and which task to

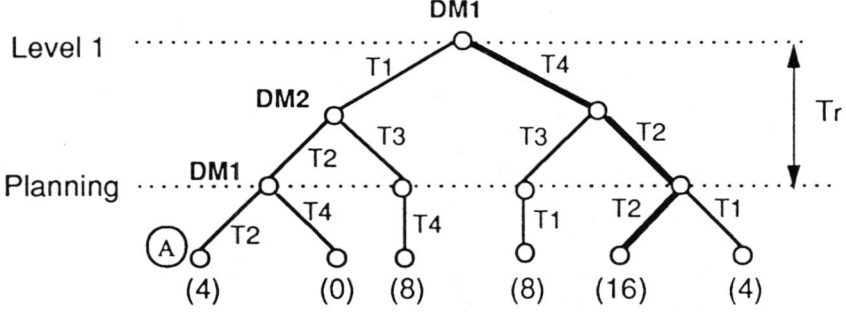

FIG. 12.5.   Simplified decision tree for a sequential task requirement.

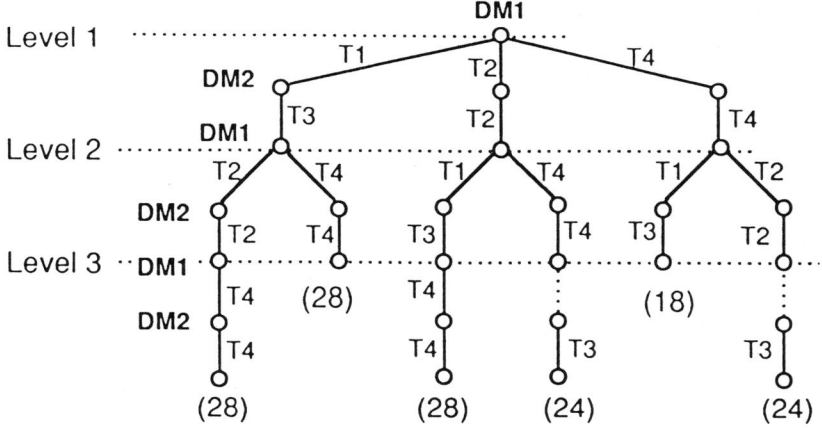

FIG. 12.6. Complete decision tree for a parallel task requirement.

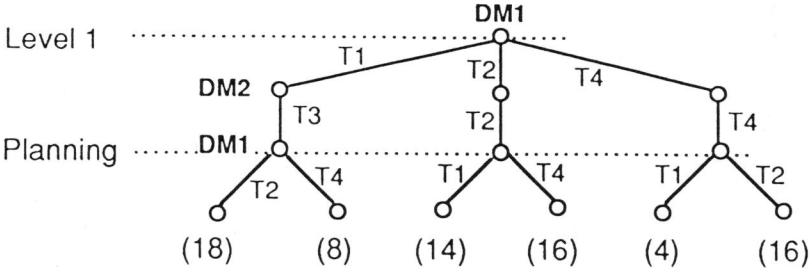

FIG. 12.7. Simplified decision tree for a parallel task requirement.

process first. This problem can be formulated as a Nash game, that is, a noncooperative game where each DM pursues his own interests.

The game tree is constructed in a manner similar to the construction of a decision tree. The outcome of the game tree, however, is different from that of a decision tree because the solution considered is a Nash equilibrium where no DM can improve his or her outcome by unilaterally altering his or her decisions.

Considering the example from Fig. 12.3, Fig. 12.8 shows the game tree under the sequential task processing requirement. All of the parameters follow those of Fig. 12.4 except that the first operation of a TT is worth 7 points, the second operation 3 points. This gives incentive to the DMs to process TTs and creates conflicts between the DMs. The rewards to the two DMs are provided at leaf nodes in the form of (v_1, v_2) where v_1 indicates DM1's reward and v_2 indicates DM2's reward.

A game tree can be simplified by applying AM following the same procedure described before. To solve the simplified game tree, an algorithm

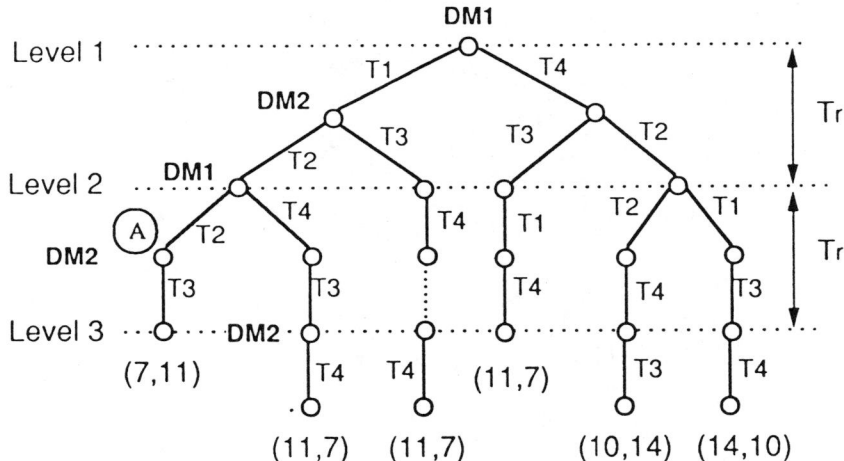

FIG. 12.8.   Complete game tree for a sequential task requirement.

developed in a study of game theory (Basar & Olsder, 1982) is adopted. Starting from the leaf nodes, a series of single-act Nash games are solved backward in time, similar to the backward induction procedure of dynamic programming. One or multiple Nash equilibria for the entire problem are then obtained by concatenating the equilibrium of single-act Nash games. Mathematically, any Nash equilibrium found is a solution to the problem. For simplicity, the model takes the first Nash equilibrium found as the solution.

For the example considered, the simplified game tree under the sequential task processing requirement is depicted in Fig. 12.9. DM1's reward at node A can be obtained as $V + M_{21} = v_{11} + v_{22} - v_{41} = 3 + 4 - 7 = 0$. It is obvious to DM1 that DM2's only choice for the next step is T3. Task T4 will be lost because there would not be enough time left once T3 is completed. DM2's reward from DM1's perspective is thus calculated as

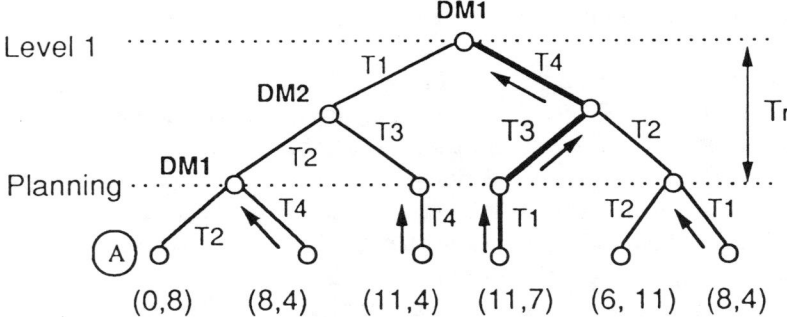

FIG. 12.9.   Simplified game tree for a sequential task requirement.

$V + M_{22} = v_{21} + v_{31} - v_{41} = 7 + 4 - 3 = 8$. The Nash solution in this case is (11,7), corresponding to the branch T4–T2–T1.

The game trees under the parallel task processing condition can be constructed and solved similarly.

Model Results

The preceding models were applied to solve the actual REST experimental cases across the three independent variables, including reward structure, task requirement, and resource availability ($2 \times 2 \times 2 = 8$ cases). The models were tested extensively with different numbers of levels m included in the simplified decision/game trees. Comparing model and experimental results, m was selected to be 3 to ensure that the models had better performance than did the human DMs. Although a normative model is of interest in its own right, the reason for its development is to have it serve as the first step toward a normative-descriptive model that replicates actual human team performance and strategy measures.

NORMATIVE-DESCRIPTIVE MODEL

Normative-descriptive models are developed in this section for teams with individual or team reward structures. A normative-descriptive model can be viewed as the solution to a constrained optimization problem, in which human biases and limitations (descriptive factors) are incorporated to constrain the optimization so as to bring model predictions in line with observed human decision-making behaviors. In implementing this process, experimental results are compared to model predicted results, and descriptive factors are added to models to reduce the differences.

Phase I: Preliminary Normative-Descriptive Model

On average, the normative model as developed in the previous section had significantly better performance than did human DMs, with higher reward per DM (69.6% for the model vs. 62.8% for human DMs), higher percentage of tasks processed (75.2% vs. 60.3%), and longer slack time (41.4 sec vs. 29 sec), and so forth. This is because the model assumes that DMs have the capability to make and implement decisions promptly, and uses a longer planning horizon than a human might have. Compared to the humans in the experiment, the model implementation ignored the following factors:

1. Human DMs usually had a time delay in making and implementing decisions (realizing the change of task and resource status, reading the messages, entering instructions to the computer, etc.).
2. The model solved the decision-making problem using a three-stage planning horizon. Human DMs, however, might not plan as many steps ahead, given the multitask dynamic environment and their limited information-processing capability.

The human DMs' limitations noted in (1) and (2) are recognized as humans' operational time delay and short-term planning horizon, respectively—two descriptive factors that reduce performance globally. In building the phase 1 normative-descriptive (ND1) models, the focus was to bring model and data performance results into agreement. In the models, a t_m-second delay was added to each operation's processing time in order to mimic the operational time delay. The limited short-term planning horizon of humans was emulated mathematically in both game and decision tree models by reducing the number of steps (m) that the models look into the future. After extensive testing, t_m was selected as 5 sec and m as 2 to bring model performance into agreement with the experiment results. The results of the ensuing ND1 models are shown in Table 12.3.

Phase II: Modeling Descriptive Factors That Affect Strategies

Table 12.3 shows that the model solutions are close to experimental results in performance and timing measures. Consistent discrepancies, however, surface as the results are examined in term of task-processing strategy (percentage of different types of tasks processed). Under the individual reward structure the model is processing more TTs than the humans; under the team reward structure the model is processing significantly less TTs than the humans. These discrepancies indicate that, relative to normative models, the human DMs *overvalue* TTs in the team reward conditions, and *devalue* TTs (or *overvalue* ITs) under an individual reward structure. This can be viewed as an "overdriven by goal" phenomenon in which DMs are

TABLE 12.3
Model–Data Comparison (Phase I)

	Reward		% Task Processed		Slack Time		% TT Processed	
	Team	Individual	Team	Individual	Team	Individual	Team	Individual
Data	64.7	60.9	61.2	59.5	31.8	26.1	75.7	59.8
Model	64.6	62.1	62.8	60.5	35.7	30.1	66.2	62.1

pushed or driven by their operational goal(s) in determining the importance of different types of tasks. This "overdriven by goal" bias makes DMs deviate from strategies that ensue from normative models—overall performance is not necessarily changed, but the mix of tasks processed can be quite different.

The models were modified to include this bias by associating a subjective "weight" to TT values. Specifically, a TT value is multiplied by a factor of .9 under an individual reward structure, and is multiplied by a factor of 1.2 under a team reward structure (i.e., the models devalue TTs by 10% under an individual reward structure, and overvalue TTs by 20% under a team reward structure). These weights were selected based on a tuning process for a good fit between model predictions and experimental results.

After incorporating the descriptive factors, the models were again applied to solve all experimental cases across the three independent variables. The model solutions closely match the empirical data across the major measures. Table 12.4 shows the model-data comparison in terms of three measures averaged across different conditions.

The model solutions also match empirical data in terms of DMs' task processing pattern. Such pattern matching indicates that the model adequately replicates human decision making in task-processing strategies, as well as in team performance.

More importantly, the resulting phase II models (ND2) accurately replicate human behavior in the REST experiment for major dependent variables on a case-by-case basis, and thus exhibit the same effects of the independent variables as did the experimental results. Figure 12.10 shows the model-data comparison for three major measures. In the figure, the cases are coded by a three-character string XYZ with $X = T$ or I (team vs. individual reward structures), $Y = S$ or P (sequential vs. parallel task requirements), and $Z = L$ or H (low vs. high resource levels).

Overall, the consistent model-data matchings shown in Fig. 12.10 led to the conclusion that the DMs' "overdriven by goal" bias was the major contributor to the model-data mismatches on task processing strategies. This can be seen especially in the %TT Processed measure, where the ND2 model results are in much closer agreement with the data than are the ND1 results. By incorporating all the descriptors identified, the models capture

TABLE 12.4
Model-Data Comparison (Phase II)

	Reward		% Task Processed		Slack Time		% TT Processed	
	Team	Individual	Team	Individual	Team	Individual	Team	Individual
Data	64.7	60.9	61.2	59.5	31.8	26.1	75.7	59.8
Model	63.7	61.6	60.7	60.6	33.6	30.0	74.4	60.2

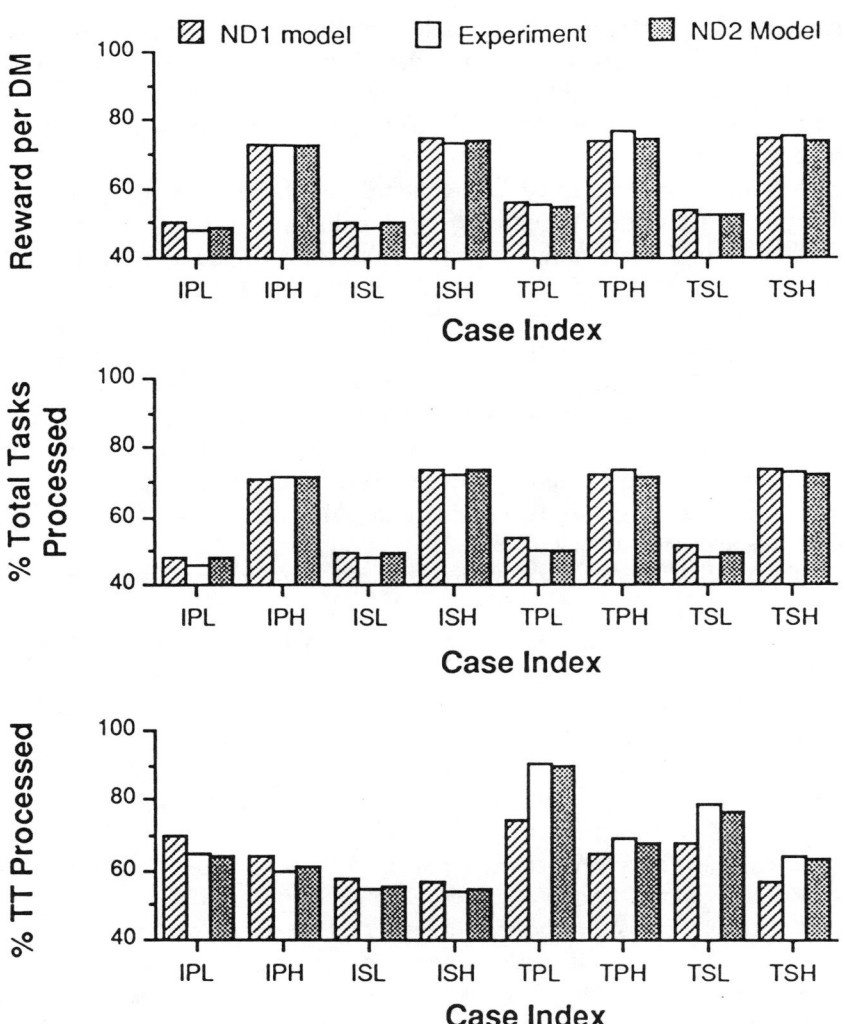

FIG. 12.10   Case-by-case model–data comparisons.

the essence of human decision making and reflect the actual human decision-making biases for the problem considered.

IMPLICATIONS AND CONCLUSIONS

The normative-descriptive modeling approach is a framework that brings together how humans actually behave and how they should behave. By being able to identify human/team biases that impact overall system performance, and thus generate models that yield realistic predictions of actual human behavior, this approach provides a tool that ultimately can be used to suggest design modifications to enhance organization performance. In using the normative-descriptive approach to investigate the effects of team versus individual goals (as operationalized via the imposed reward structures) on human team coordination and decision making, this chapter has made the following contributions.

Motivated by allocation problems in distributed decision-making systems, an experiment was designed and operationalized to study the effects of team versus individual goals on human team coordination. The main empirical findings show that different goals produce significant changes in DMs' decision strategies (e.g., their priority for different task types) and coordination processes (e.g., communication), as measured by a rich set of dependent variables. Moreover, significant interactions between reward structure and task processing requirement have been found. In a broad sense, the major findings and their implications are:

1. The current effort examined the effects of a pure team goal versus pure individual goals on team performance and coordination. The results of our study show that a team goal is superior to individual goals in terms of performance and coordination. A team/organization goal and individual-/local goals usually coexist in real-world systems. Goal integration—that is, the congruence between the local goals of team members and the global goals of the team itself—has been a ubiquitous problem in organizational design. Our findings provide a step in this direction for future research.

2. The finding that a team reward structure is more beneficial (than a local reward structure) for environments having strong interdependent task processing requirements suggests that a team/organization goal should be fostered in such cases. When tasks are structured to be less interdependent, individual goals (which are often better understood by humans) are likely to suffice for achieving near-optimal team performance.

The mathematical models that were developed for the dynamic multitask processing problem emulated by the REST experiment included either a team goal or individual goals. In the model, a decision or game tree was constructed with a small number of decision levels supplemented by the use of attractiveness measures to capture the effects of future decisions. A difficult scheduling problem was thus simplified and solved efficiently, and so the modeling framework proved to be reasonable as a basis for a normative model of human decision making.

Finally, by comparing human data with the normative modeling results, "short-term planning horizon" and "overdriven by goal" phenomena were identified as the major factors that inhibited the teams from attaining "optimal" performance. The normative-descriptive models incorporating these human limitations and biases replicate major aspects of human decision-making and coordination processes, as observed within the constrained laboratory setting in which the experiment was conducted. It is our hypothesis that these phenomena are indigenous to human decision processes—a hypothesis to be tested in future experiments. Furthermore, the current study and major model–data results suggest that team members should be trained more positively in evaluating their individual/local tasks when they are given a specific team/organization goal.

ACKNOWLEDGMENTS

This work was supported by the National Science Foundation under grant IRI-8902755. The authors would like to thank Mr. Daniel Serfaty of ALPHATECH, Inc., Burlington, MA, for his valuable insights and comments on the experiment design, data analysis, and interpretation of experimental findings.

REFERENCES

Basar, T., & Olsder, G. J. (1982). *Dynamic noncooperative game theory.* New York: Academic Press.

Brehmer, B. (1988). Organization for decision-making in complex systems. In L. P. Goodstein, H. B. Andersen, & S. E. Olsen (Eds.), *Tasks, errors, and mental models* (pp. 116–127). London: Taylor & Francis.

Earley, P. C., & Northcraft, G. B. (1989). Goal setting, resource interdependence and conflict management. In M. A. Rahim (Ed.), *Managing Conflict* (pp. 161–170).

Hastie, R. (1991). A review from a High Place: The field of judgement and decision making as revealed in its current textbooks. *Psychological Review, 2*(3), 135–138.

Hernandez-Lerma, O., & Lasserre, J. B. (1990). Error bounds for rolling horizon policies in discrete-time markov control processes. *IEEE Transactions on Automatic Control, 35*(10), 1118–1124.

Kleinman, D. L., Luh, P. B., Pattipati, K. R., & Serfaty, D. (1992). Mathematical models of distributed decisionmaking. In R. W. Swezey & E. Salas (Eds.), *Teams: Their training and performance* (pp. 177–218). Norwood, NJ: Ablex.

Kleinman, D. L., & Song, A. (1990, June). A research paradigm for studying team decisionmaking and coordination. *Proceedings of the 1990 Command and Control Research Symposium, Monterey, CA, pp. 129–135.*

Kleinrock, L. (1975). *Queueing systems. Vol. I. Theory.* New York: Wiley.

Likert, R. (1967). *The human organization.* New York: McGraw-Hill.

Pattipati, K. R., Kleinman, D. L., & Ephrath, A. R. (1983). A dynamic decision model of human task selection performance. *IEEE Transactions on Systems, Man, and Cybernetics, 13*(2), 145–166.

Perry, T. A. (Ed.). (1991). Air traffic control: Improving the world's largest, most advanced system. *IEEE Spectrum, 28*(2), 22–36.

Simon, H. A. (1982). *Models of bounded rationality: behavioral economics and business organization.* Cambridge, MA: MIT Press.

Shi, P. (1993). *The effects of individual and team goals on team coordination.* Unpublished masters thesis, University of Connecticut, Department of Electrical and Systems Engineering.

Terence, R. M., & William, S. S. (1990). Individual and group goals when workers are interdependent: Effects on task strategies and performance. *Journal of Applied Psychology, 75*(2), 185–193.

Vaughan, W. S., Jr. (1990, June). Toward a science of command and control: Challenges of distributed decision making. *Proceedings of 1990 Symposium on Command and Control Research,* Monterey, CA, pp. 26–35.

13

A Decision Logic for Operational Risk Management

Giampiero E. G. Beroggi
Delft University of Technology

William A. Wallace
Rensselaer Polytechnic Institute

The potential for catastrophic events is inherent in every largescale operational system, such as nuclear power plants, chemical processing plants, public transportation, and freight transportation on land, water, and air. Risk management refers to preevent activities (prevention and mitigation) and postevent activities (response and recovery). These four activities are addressed by the risk management community both for strategic and for operational (or real-time) purposes.

Strategic risk management refers to the design of measures to prevent or mitigate potential accidents and their consequences — for example, the design and activation of emergency plans in cases of disruptions. However, strategic plans, such as preselected routes for hazardous material shipments or contingency plans for emergency response, are based on various assumptions about the hazards involved and the behavior of their environment. Unfortunately, unexpected events affecting hazards or their environment can cause disruptions to strategic plans, making them useless or even dangerous. For example, a brake failure in a truck carrying hazardous material can result in a catastrophic event, or the sudden change of weather conditions can make an oil spill contingency plan useless.

Operational risk management includes performing the activities designed to monitor and guide the prevention, mitigation, and response operations of large-scale systems in a real-time setting. Revision of planned activities must be performed under time pressure and usually with higher uncertainty than for strategic decision making. Unexpected events triggering operational risk management are called *real-time events* (RTE). They can refer to sudden environmental changes (e.g., snowstorms), unexpected malfunctions of technical parts (e.g., brake failures), and unanticipated changes in the system (e.g., traffic congestions).

Support for this operational decision making can be provided by either a centralized or decentralized organization structure. For example, response activities in a nuclear power plant or a chemical production plant are typically managed in decentralized fashion (on-site). On the other hand, prevention activities for hazardous material shipments and emergency response to transportation accidents are generally managed from centralized headquarters. Operational risk management (especially the decentralized approach) has only recently become an issue as a result of the commercialization of advanced communications and computing technologies.

Operational risk management begins with the activation of the strategically planned course of action. This can be the beginning of a shipment involving hazardous materials, the activation of contingency plans in response to an oil spill, or the initialization of an evacuation around a nuclear power plant. As long as these operations proceed as planned, operational risk management is a passive process; it consists of monitoring these activities and any occurrences that could threaten their successful completion. As soon as an unexpected event occurs that threatens the successful completion, operational risk management becomes active. The affected parts of the planned courses of action must be reevaluated and alternate courses of action need to be investigated. As soon as a decision has been made, either to continue on the planned course of action or to change to an alternate course of action, operational risk management goes back to the passive and reactive stage.

Operational risk management (ORM), diagrammed in Fig. 13.1, consists of three components:

1. The large-scale operational system (LSOP), which is expected to perform according to a strategically designed course of action (CA).
2. The unanticipated real-time events (RTE) that have an impact on the expected achievement of the planned course of action and that cannot be considered strategically.
3. The man–machine system that (a) monitors the LSOP as part of passive ORM, (b) assesses impacts of RTEs on the planned CA as part of active ORM, and (c) if necessary revises the CA as part of active ORM.

The focus of this chapter is on the active part of operational risk management—that is, the assessment of the impact of unexpected RTEs on

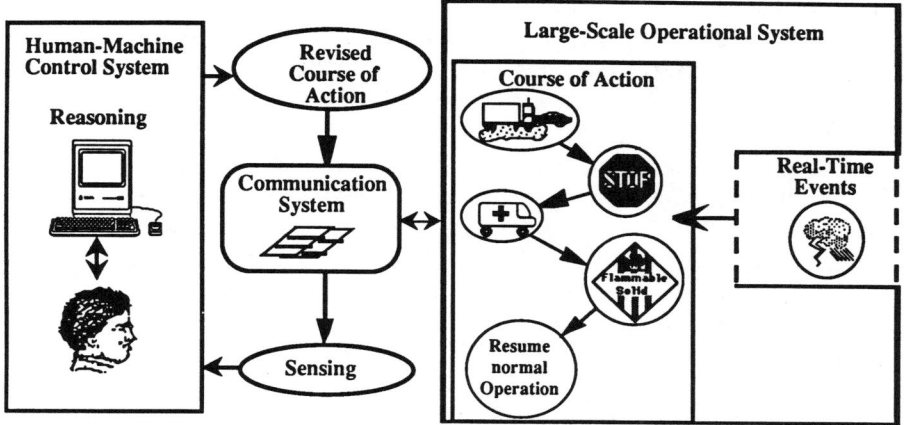

FIG. 13.1.   Conceptual model of operational risk management.

the planned course of action, the evaluation of alternative courses of action, and the decision process of choosing the optimal course of action for the time the RTE is active.

MODELING THE DECISION PROBLEM

An operational risk management plan consists of a set of concatenated decisions to take specific activities. Examples of activities in the case of transportation are driving on the road, loading a vehicle, and refueling the vehicle. Examples of activities in the case of emergency response are activating the response team, closing the harbor, and using dispersants. Each activity is preceded by a decision—that is, every specific activity has been chosen out of several possible activities. Let $D = \{d_1, \ldots, d_n\}$ be the set of all possible decisions in operational risk management, and $\Re$ a binary relation on D defines as $(\Re, D)$: $d_s \Re d_t = a_{st}$, stating that decision d_s leads to decision d_t by taking activity a_{st}.

Operational risk management is defined as a finite nonempty set $D = \{d_i\}$ of decisions together with a relation $\Re$ on D. The relation $\Re$ can be irreflexive ($\neg\, d_i \Re d_i$), is always transitive ($d_i \Re d_j \wedge d_j \Re d_k \rightarrow d_i \Re d_k$)), but is not necessarily symmetric ($d_i \Re d_j \rightarrow d_j \Re d_i$). Every relation $d_i \Re d_j$ stands for an activity a_{ij} as part of the operational measure. The activity a_{ij} is said to be *incident from* d_i and *incident to* d_j. Two subsets of D are fundamental: $S \in D$ is the set of decisions to start operational risk management and to begin with a strategically planned procedure (i.e., an RTE has been perceived), and $E \in D$ is the set of decisions to end operational risk management (e.g., a hazardous material shipment has reached its destination, or an emergency response has been successfully completed).

An operational risk management plan is called a *course of action* (CA). It consists of an ordered sequence of decisions and concomitant selected activities, for example, $CA = d_1, a_1, d_2, a_2, \ldots, a_{n-1}, d_n$, beginning with the decision $d_1 \in S$, stating that a RTE has occurred, and ending with the decision $d_n \in E$, stating that the objectives of the operation have been met, such that for $1 \le j < n$, a_j is incident from d_j and incident to d_{j+1}. Each activity in operational risk management is therefore proceeded by a decision to take this activity and leads to a new decision regarding the following activity. Therefore, decision d_i has been made to take activity a_{ij}, which leads itself to decision d_j.

A *subcourse of action* (SCA) is an ordered sequence of decisions and concomitant selected activities that does not necessarily contain elements out of S and E. A course of action $CA^{(k)}$ with k decisions and k-1 activities is said to be of order k (k-order CA). In terms of the decisions, it can be written in the following way: $CA = \{s_1, \ldots, d_i, \ldots, e_k\}$. In terms of the activities, it can be written as $CA = \{a_1, \ldots, a_j, \ldots, a_{k-1}\}$. The last decision, e_k, does not lead to a new activity but to the end of a satisfactory operation.

Two CAs are *decision-disjoint* if they do not have any decisions in common. Two CAs are *activity-disjoint* if they do not have any activities in common. An operational risk management problem is called *connected* if between any two decisions there is at least one SCA.

Theorem 1. Two decision-disjoint courses of action are activity-disjoint.

Proof. Case 1: a_{ij} is a common activity of CA_1 and CA_2. Let it be incident from d_i^1 and incident to d_j^1 of CA_1, and incident from d_i^2 and incident to d_j^2 of CA_2. It then follows that at least two decisions are common. Case 2: d_i is the only joint decision. In this case, no activity can be common.

An important class of connected operational risk management problems are those where all possible SCAs lead to different end decisions. These problems will be called *prestructured* ORM problems. In graph-theoretical terms this family of ORM is represented by trees.

Theorem 2. In a prestructured operational risk management (ORM) problem, there is only one SCA leading to the end of operational risk management.

Proof. Let SCA_1 and SCA_2 be two different SCAs, leading to the same end decision d_j. In order to be different (not unique), they need to merge somewhere (latest at d_{end}). The set of decisions from the start decision of SCA_1 to d_j and the set of decisions from the start decision of SCA_2 to d_j

form two new SCAs with common end decision. This, however, is not possible.

An important characteristic of an ORM problem is the number of feasible CAs. If the number of feasible CAs is small, then the ORM problem is said to be *sensitive* to RTEs; if it is large, it is said to be *stable*. In order to define a measure of stability for ORM, the *activity matrix* A is introduced. The element $a_{ij} \in A$ is 1 if $d_i \Re d_j$, and 0 otherwise — that is, if the decision d_i can be made to take activity a_{ij} that leads to decision d_j. Let

$$(a^k_{ij}) = \sum_{r=1}^{n} (a_{ir})^{k-1} a_{rj}$$

be the kth matrical product of the activity matrix, where $(a_{ij})^0 = 1$, and $(a_{ij})^1 = a_{ij}$.

Theorem 3. The element $(a_{ij})^k$ is the number of k-order SCAs from d_i to d_j. This is a well-known result from graph theory (Gibbons, 1989).

Proof. By definition, if $k = 1$, then $a_{ij} = 1$ if $d_i \Re d_j$, and 0 otherwise. Let's assume that the theorem holds for all powers smaller than k. Therefore, $(a_{ir})^{k-1}$ is the number of k-order SCAs from d_i to d_r, and $(a_{ir})^{k-1} a_{rj}$ the number of k-order SCAs with a_{rj} as last activity. The summation over all decisions incident to d_j gives the result.

Both for the strategic planning of CAs and for the revision of CAs when RTEs occur, one is interested not only in the feasible CAs but in the optimal CA. In order to compute the optimal CA, a preference structure must first be overlaid on the activities of the ORM task. The preference of activities, as well as the adjacency of decisions (i.e., the existence of activities), can be conditional or unconditional. Conditional preferences can depend on previous activities and decisions but also on state variables, such as weather and environmental conditions. A course of action is said to be affected by an RTE if the preference or existence of at least one activity is affected by the RTE.

In this following chapter, a preference structure is introduced to assess preferences of activities and revise them given an RTE. Thereafter, a procedure for reassessing preferences is given, and also an algorithm to compute optimal CAs, both for conditional and unconditional CAs. In the section entitled Finding and Revising Optimal Courses of Actions, a procedure for determining the affected activities and an algorithm for computing optimal courses of action is described.

PREFERENCE ALGEBRA AND REASONING LOGIC

The process of ORM can be generalized as one of assessing current conditions, identifying any potential for immediate change to those conditions, comparing both to a desired state, and if there is a gap, taking action to bring the present or future state into concordance with the desired state (Wallace, 1989). A change in the environment, a real-time event, affects the attributes of some activities. An example is a sudden temperature drop that causes a road surface to freeze and makes an initially safe shipment hazardous. The activity is "driving along that specific road segment" and the "temperature drop" causes a change in the risk attribute.

Changes in environment and conditions of the system can be anticipated or unexpected. In this context we address specifically the unanticipated events for which no actions have been planned strategically. Although RTEs seldom occur, the dispatcher must have quick and efficient support in reevaluation of the planned courses of action.

Although many approaches to strategic decision support are based on normative aspects (numerical measure and probabilistic reasoning), little attention is paid to heuristic aspects. In addition, normative models do not recognize the cognitive capabilities and limitations of humans for assessment and choice. However, this does not necessarily imply that normative models would not be able to consider these aspects.

Simon changed the focus of decision research by questioning the optimal decision model and showing that the human decision process is characterized by bounded rationality. This so-called *suboptimal behavior* considers the limited cognitive capabilities of the decision maker and the lack of complete relevant information (Simon, 1955).

Past research has shown that in unavoidable decision situations under time pressure, decision makers tend to make choices according to outstanding characteristics or even randomly (Belardo, Karwan, & Wallace, 1984; Janis & Mann, 1977). In addition to time pressure, the dynamics of the tasks and decisions for an operational control system require special attention. For example, the weather situation changes over unpredictable periods. A critical point is, therefore, the interaction of the human and the machine in this dynamic control system.

De Keyser (1987) stated that operators in an emergency situation rarely reason in a perfect deductive way but act as furious pattern matchers. Wagenaar and Groeneweg (1987) showed that people construct a hypothesis by looking only at the most salient symptoms, and thereby forget contrary evidence. Moray (1987) considered that the operator has a mental model of the system that consists of a set of quasi-independent subsystems that do not correspond a to a one-to-one mapping of the real system. Mancini (1987) therefore concluded that operator models have to take into account the cognitive aspects of human behavior. We do this by first structuring the cognitive assessment and decision-making process and then formulating cognitive assumptions about the human operator.

Once a real-time event is perceived and the affected CAs are identified, the operational manager (operator) must reevaluate those CAs and decide either to alter them to new CAs or to leave them because the impact of the RTE is not considered to be significant. Operational decision problems are in general complex, due to the high number of feasible CAs and their implicit representation. Therefore, CAs are not directly visible but must be constructed following the relations defined earlier for the specific problem. The evaluation of CAs can be done in two ways: (a) by assessing the impacts of the RTE on the attributes of the affected activities and then computing new optimal CAs with an appropriate algorithm, called *evaluation by attribute,* or (b) by constructing a few feasible CAs (e.g., using a simple heuristic) and comparing them to each other, called *evaluation by alternative.*

When evaluation by attribute is done, the operational manager might decide not to suggest the new optimal CAs to the on-site managers. One reason might be that the operator does not want a certain CA to be altered, although the choice model suggests to do so. In such a case, the operator might change the attributes of certain activities that seem not assessed properly. This iterative decision-making approach will be repeated until the new CAs are satisfactory to the operational manager or until the decision is made to evaluate CAs by alternative, ignoring the results of the decision model.

There are basically three different constellations possible for evaluation by attribute before the operator suggests a new CA to a on-site manager (Fig. 13.2):

1. The new CA determined by the decision model does not satisfy the operator and he or she chooses a different one (suboptimal behavior).

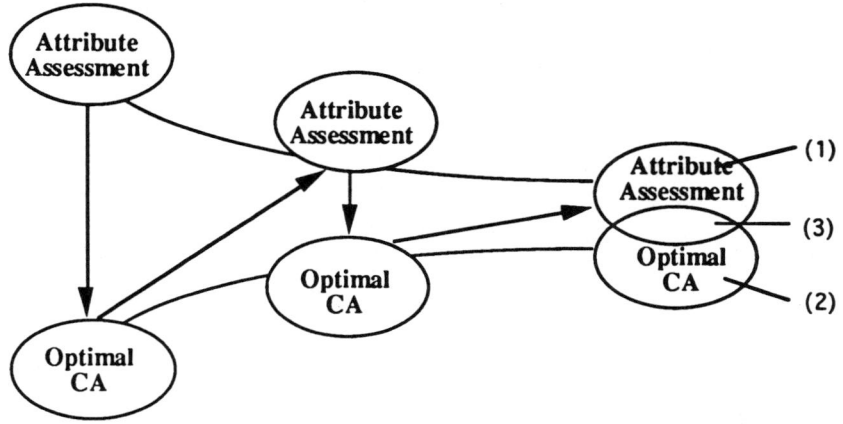

FIG. 13.2.   Iterative decision-making approach for evaluation by attribute.

2. The iterative reassessment of the attributes produced a satisfactory solution, but the assessment does not satisfy the operator (suboptimal behavior).

3. The assessment by the operator and the determined route by the decision model both satisfy the operator (optimal behavior).

Before an attempt is made to develop a model that considers the behavioral aspects of operational risk management, assumptions are presented about how an operational manager assesses and reasons about the variables of control. These cognitive assumptions define the assessment process and the reasoning logic for choice in an operational setting.

Cognitive Assumption 1.   Evaluation by Alternative. Empirical evidence showed that decision making by attribute is more accurate and requires less effort than decision making by alternative (Beroggi & Wallace, 1992). Therefore, the decision variables of finding an optimal course of action are the activities of the operational risk management problem.

Cognitive Assumption 2.   Measures for Assessment. Experienced operators stated that they prefer to assess risks (attribute with high uncertainty) to well-defined *preference classes* rather than relating them to a numerical scale (Beroggi & Wallace, 1992). Costs (attribute with low uncertainty) are assessed on numerical scales. The ordering function $\phi(a_{ij}|H)$: $a_{ij} \rightarrow \Pi^{(k)}$ assigns an activity a_{ij} to a preference class $\Pi^{(k)}$, given a *history* H. The assessment spectrum Π can therefore be defined as an ordered set using the relation $\Pi^{(k)} < \Pi^{(l)}$, which means "$\Pi^{(k)}$ is less preferred than $\Pi^{(l)}$": $\Pi = \Pi^{(1)} < \cdots < \Pi^{(n)}$. The class $\Pi^{(k)}$ is said to be "lower" than the class $\Pi^{(l)}$. These classes stand for attributes, such as Cost, High-Risk, and Low-Risk.

The history of preferences, H, reflects all the conditions under which this preference holds. These can be previously taken activities (*operational history*) or environmental conditions, such as weather, time, and so forth (*state history*). Time dependency is crucial in operational risk management of large-scale systems. It is characterized by two aspects: the location of the operation in space and the actual status of the operation. The preference for an activity as a function of its geographical location fluctuates in time. For example, the activity "driving by a school" may be safe at night but not during the day. Because the operator may not know the time of day the activity takes place, the preference must be expressed dynamically, even for the "normal" situation when no RTEs are present. We call this the *spatial aspect of time.*

In addition, the preference for an activity depends on its status. The preference for driving by a school during the day depends also on the number of students in the school and the day of week. In the "normal" case, this time dependency is taken into account in planning a route. But it might also be the situation where several real-time events already affect an activity. If an additional RTE affects this activity, the operator has to consider the whole situation, including the previous RTEs. We call this the *contextual aspect of time*. Therefore, if RTE_o is an ongoing real-time event and RTE_n is a new real-time event, the conditional preference assessment function for activity a_{ij} is $\phi(a_{ij}|RTE_o,RTE_n)$.

Cognitive Assumption 3. Insignificance of Entities (De Minimis). An operator assigns an ω-preference to an activity, knowing that a CA consisting of any number of ω-preferences is the most preferred CA; that is, entities with preferences ω can be neglected.

Cognitive Assumption 4. Avoidance of Activities. An operator assigns an α-preference to an activity, knowing that no CA can contain this entity; that is, the activity becomes unacceptable and any CA containing this activity is not feasible.

A preference structure for hazardous material transportation was the following: $\alpha <$ High-Risk $<$ Cost $<$ Low-Risk $< \omega$ (Beroggi & Wallace, 1992). The only activities were "driving along the various road segments." Every road segment was assigned a risk value out of $\{\alpha,$High-Risk, Low-Risk, $\omega\}$, and a cost value out of $\{\alpha,\{Cost\},\omega\}$. Given this assessment, optimal routes (courses of action) had to be computed. The preference of a course of action with n activities, given the preferences of all activities, π_{ij}, is defined as: $\pi_{CA} = \pi_{1,2} \oplus \cdots \oplus \pi_{n-1,n}$. In order to be able to compute optimal courses of action, or to compare two activities and "add" the preferences of two activities, a preference algebra must be introduced. The following preference algebra is a generalization of the preference algebra in Beroggi (1991).

The preference algebra is defined as a system $<\Pi, \prec, \approx, \oplus, \alpha, \omega>$. It consists of an infinite set of preferences $\pi_i \in \Pi$, two relations $\prec$ (preference) and $\approx$ (indifference) in the preference algebra, an operator $\oplus$ on couples of elements of Π, and two distinguished elements $\alpha, \omega \in \Pi$. The set Π is closed under the operator $\oplus$.

The preference α stands for activities that must be avoided, and the preference ω stands for activities that are of no concern. The set Π consists of any number of compound preferences.

For $\pi_i, \pi_j, \pi_k \in \Pi$, the operator $\oplus$ is monotone, $\pi_i \prec \pi_j$, $\pi_k \neq \alpha \rightarrow \pi_i \oplus \pi_k \prec \pi_j \oplus \pi_k$; holds also for $\approx$; is commutative, $\pi_i \oplus \pi_j \approx \pi_j \oplus \pi_i$; and is associative, $(\pi_i \oplus \pi_j) \oplus \pi_k \approx \pi_i \oplus (\pi_j \oplus \pi_k)$. The relation $\prec$ is irreflexive ($\neg \, \pi_i \prec \pi_i$), transitive ($\pi_k \prec \pi_i \wedge \pi_i \prec \pi_j \rightarrow \pi_k \prec \pi_j$), and asymmetric ($\pi_i \prec \pi_j \rightarrow \neg \, \pi_j \prec \pi_i$). The relation $\approx$ is reflexive ($\pi_i \approx \pi_i$), transitive ($\pi_k \approx \pi_i \wedge \pi_i \approx \pi_j \rightarrow \pi_k \approx \pi_j$), and symmetric ($\pi_i \approx \pi_j \rightarrow \pi_j \approx \pi_i$). Preference and indifference relations are complete ($\pi_i \prec \pi_j \vee \pi_j \prec \pi_i \vee \pi_i \approx \pi_j$).

This preference algebra allows the "addition" and the comparison of preferences of any two activities, subcourses of action, or any combination of them. In order to compare two preferences, the following theorem is introduced: $\pi \oplus \omega \approx \pi_i$; $\pi \in \Pi$.

Theorem 4. The more preferred of two subcourses of action is the one with the fewest number of elements in the lowest preference class (for ties, the next higher preference class is used). This can be written as: $p\pi_i \oplus \pi_j \quad q\pi_i \oplus \pi_k$; $\pi_i, \pi_j, \pi_k \in P$; $\pi_i \quad \pi_k$; $p, q \in N$; $p > q$.

Proof. It can be shown by induction that $k\omega \approx \omega$; $k \in N$. In addition, it can be shown that if $\pi_i \quad \pi_j$ and $\pi_m \quad \pi_n$, then $\pi_i \oplus \pi_m \quad \pi_j \rightarrow n\pi_i \quad \pi_j$; $\pi_i \quad \omega$, $\pi_i, \pi_j \in \Pi$, $n \in N\backslash 0$.

From this it follows: $\pi_i \quad \pi_k \rightarrow (p-q)\pi_i \quad \pi_k \rightarrow p\pi_i \quad q\pi_i \oplus \pi_k$. Case 1: $\pi_j \approx \omega \rightarrow p\pi_i \oplus \omega \approx p\pi_i \quad q\pi_i \oplus \pi_k$. Case 2: $\pi_j \quad \omega \rightarrow p\pi_i \oplus \pi_j \quad q\pi_i \oplus \pi_k \oplus \omega \approx q\pi_i \oplus \pi_k$.

This theorem has several important implications. It first states that there is no number of activities of a higher preference class that can be considered equivalent to one activity of a lower preference class. For the example of hazardous material transportation, it means that high-risk road segments must be avoided, regardless of the costs for rerouting. The theorem also allows comparison of any two activities or courses of action. The principle of comparison corresponds to the lexicographic ordering or choice by first difference in the preference classes.

FINDING AND REVISING OPTIMAL COURSES OF ACTION

Similar to the activity matrix A introduced in the second section, we introduce a preference matrix P. The element $\pi_{ij} \in P$ is the preference of activity a_{ij}. The activity matrix can therefore be redefined in terms of the preference matrix: The element $a_{ij} \in A$ is 1 if $\alpha \quad \pi_{ij}$, and 0 otherwise—that is, the activity a_{ij} is feasible if the preference is higher than α. By definition, α stands for activities that must be avoided, that is, activities that are not feasible. Figure 13.3 illustrates the tasks and decisions that an operator must address in operational risk management.

Operational risk management consists of an active and a passive part. It starts by activating a strategically planned course of action. In the case of emergency response, the course of action can be the evacuation of populated areas, the removal of oil on the sea, and the salvage of the vessel. In the case of transportation of hazardous materials, the courses of action are the vehicles driving along the transportation network. As long as no real-time events occur, the operator monitors the execution of these CAs

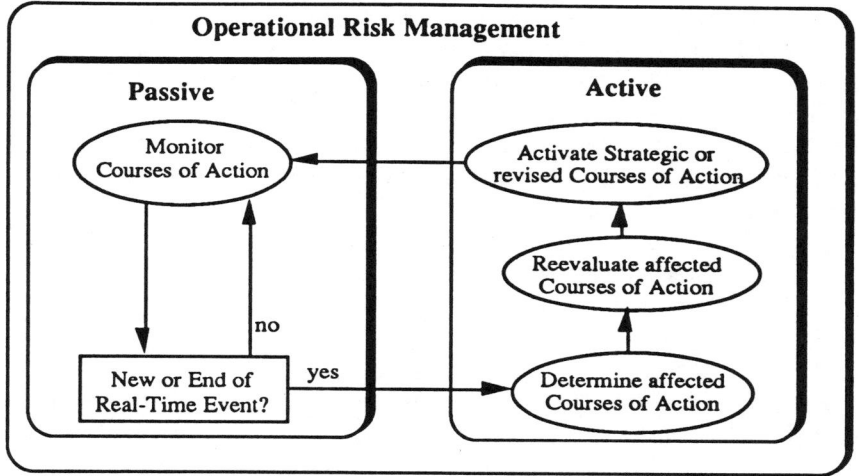

FIG. 13.3. Tasks and decisions in operational risk management.

passively. If an RTE occurs, however, ORM becomes active. The operator must determine which CAs are affected by the RTE. In the case of hazardous material transportation, the dispatcher must determine the vehicles that plan to drive through the area affected by a snowstorm.

As previously defined, a course of action is affected by an RTE if at least the preference of one activity is affected. After the affected CAs have been reevaluated—that is, the preferences of the affected activities have been reevaluated—new optimal CAs need to be determined. Then, these new CAs have to be implemented and ORM goes back to the passive stage.

Two procedures must be defined in this process: (a) how to determine the affected CAs, and (b) how to compute optimal CAs, given that all activities have assigned multiple conditional preference values. We first outline the procedure for finding the affected CAs. Every activity a_{ij} has assigned multiple preferences $\pi_{ij}^{(k)}$. These preferences can be conditional or not; that is, they can have a history, consisting of activity and/or state dependency. Let $\pi_{ij}^{(k)}(ah_{ij}^{(k)}, sh_{ij}^{(k)})$ be the k-th conditional preference of activity a_{ij}, where $ah_{ij}^{(k)}$ stands for the activity conditions (i.e., the preference holds if the mentioned activities have been taken previously), and $sh_{ij}^{(k)}$ for the state conditions (i.e., the preference holds if the mentioned states, referring to environmental conditions, time when the activity takes place, etc., hold). An RTE can affect state variables (e.g., weather) and/or activities. Every activity has a set of relevant state variables and relevant activities. If an activity or a state variable influences a preference of an activity, it is considered to be relevant. The affected activities are those that have at least one relevant activity or state variable affected by the RTE. The affected CAs are those that have at least one affected activity.

The affected CAs must then be reevaluated. This can be done, as mentioned previously, either by alternative or by attribute. Due to cognitive assumption 1, we limit our discussion to the construction of CAs by attributes. This requires that the impacts of the RTEs on the attributes of the CAs must first be assessed. This is usually done by revising the preferences for each affected activity one by one. After this reassessment, new optimal CAs must be computed.

The objective of the search problem for an optimal CA is to find the CA with the highest overall preference either from the beginning of the operation or from the activity that is going on at the moment an RTE happened. The decision variables are the activities. Based on the preference algebra, a mathematical description can be given.

Let n be the number of decisions of the ORM problem, π_{ij} the preference of activity a_{ij}. The x_{ij} terms are the decision variables, which are 1 if activity a_{ij} is chosen for the most preferred CA and 0 otherwise. Then, the mathematical formulation of the CA problem is the following:

$$\text{maximize:} \quad \bigoplus_{i=1} \bigoplus_{j=1} x_{ij}\pi_{ij} \tag{1}$$

subject to:

$$\Sigma_i x_{ij} - \Sigma_r x_{ri} = 1 \text{ (for } d_i \in S\text{), or } -1 \text{ (for } d_i \in E\text{),} \\ \text{or } 0 \text{ (for all other } d_i\text{)} \tag{2}$$

$$\alpha \prec x_{ij}\pi_{ij} \tag{3}$$

$$x_{ij} = 1 \text{ or } 0 \tag{4}$$

The objective function (Equation 1) states that the most preferred CA is the one with highest preference. The two summations over n are for the total ORM problem preference, where n is the number of decisions. Equations 2 through 4 define the space of feasible CAs. Equation 2 stands for connectivity of the CAs. Equation 3 states that no CA can contain an activity of α preference. Equation 4 states that the decision variables x_{ij} must be either 1 for when the activity a_{ij} is an element of the most preferred CA or 0 for when the activity a_{ij} is not chosen.

The algorithmic search for the optimal CA is different for ORM problems with conditional preferences and those with unconditional preferences.

Case 1: Unconditional Preferences.

Let P be the preference matrix for a specific ORM with n decisions, where π_{ij} is the preference of activity a_{ij}. Let $\pi_{ij}^{(k)} = \text{pref}\{\pi_{ij}^{(k-1)}, \pi_{ik}^{(k-1)} + \pi_{kj}^{(k-1)}\}$, where $\pi_{ij}^{(0)} = \pi_{ij}$, and $\text{pref}\{\pi_r, \pi_s\} = \pi_r$ for $\pi_r > \pi_s$.

Theorem 5. The most preferred CA from $d_i \in S$ to $d_j \in E$ is $\pi_{ij}^{(n)}$.

Proof (by induction, as known from graph theory (Gibbons, 1989). If $k = 0$ then $\pi_{ij}^{(k)}$ is the preference of taking only activity a_{ij}. Assuming that the statement also holds for $\pi_{ij}^{(k-1)}$ then $\pi_{ij}^{(k)}$ is the higher preference of $\pi_{ij}^{(k-1)}$ and $\pi_{ik}^{(k-1)} + \pi_{kj}^{(k-1)}$. According to the hypothesis of induction, $\pi_{ij}^{(k-1)}$ is the highest preference of the subcourse of action consisting only of decisions out of $\{d_i, \ldots, d_{k-1}\}$. However, if there is a more preferred path that uses also d_k as decision, then its preference must be $\pi_{ik}^{(k-1)} + \pi_{kj}^{(k-1)}$. After $\pi_{ij}^{(n)}$ has been constructed, every alternative has been examined and the theorem holds. As is well known from graph theory, this algorithm is of $O(n^3)$. A faster algorithm would be based on Dantzig's algorithm ($O(n^2)$) (Dantzig, 1975).

The approach with Dantzig's algorithm is the following. Assume that at some stage k in the computing process the preferences π_{OC_i} and the sequence of activities of the most preferred subcourse of action from the origin decision O to the decisions C_i are known, where $C_i \in C = \{C_1, \ldots, C_k\}$. The decisions in C are called closed decisions. Let $M_j \in M$ (set of adjacent decisions of C, $M_j \notin C$) with the preference $\pi_{C_iM_j}$ to take activity (C_i, M_j). The algorithm is the following:

1. *Initialize.* Choose (close) the origin decision O.
2. *Close node.* Choose and close (the preference to the origin decision is definitive) as the $(k + 1)$-th decision, M_j, where j satisfies $\alpha \quad \pi_{C_iM_j}$ and $\pi_{OC_i} \oplus \pi_{C_iM_j} \approx \max(\pi_{OC_i} \oplus \pi_{C_iM_r})$, where $i = 1,2, \ldots ,k$, $M_r \in C$. Ties are broken arbitrarily. In words, M_j is a direct successor of an already closed decision C_i. In addition, it has the highest preference to the origin decision among all the direct successors of all the closed decisions.
3. *Loop.* If the destination decision D is not in C, then go to (2), that is, if $M_j \neq D$, else stop. The preference to go from the origin decision to M_j is $\pi_{OC_i} \oplus \pi_{C_iM_j}$ and the most preferred subcourse of action is via C_i.

Case 2: Conditional Preferences

In an ORM problem with conditional preferences, every activity has assigned a set of conditional preferences. Some of these preferences have been assessed after an RTE has occurred. The kth conditional preference of activity a_{ij} is $\pi_{ij}^{(k)}|(ah_{ij}^{(k)}, sh_{ij}^{(k)})$, where $ah_{ij}^{(k)}$ stands for the activity conditions, and $sh_{ij}^{(k)}$ for the state conditions. Therefore, two activities can only be concatenated if they have the same history. In addition, we state explicitly that an activity can be taken only once in a CA. Thus, the algorithm must first search exclusively for all feasible CAs and then choose the one with the highest overall preference as the optimal one. Feasible CAs are constructed by concatenating exhaustively activities with common history.

In a predicate logic notation, we use the following two predicates:

activity(decision,decision)
course_of_action(decision,decision)

The clauses consist of all explicit activities and the definitions of a course of action:

activity(d_{ij},d_{jk})
course_of_action(d_x,d_y) if activity(d_x,d_y)
course_of_action(d_x,d_y) if activity(d_x,d_z) and course_of_action(d_z,d_y)

To find all feasible courses of action that are initiated by the decision d_{start} and that lead to the satisfactory operational condition d_{end}, the goal needs to be introduced:

course_of_action(d_{start},d_{end})

The optimal course of action among all the feasible courses of action is the one with the highest overall preference.

OPERATIONAL RISK MANAGEMENT WITH MULTIPLE OPERATORS

Operational risk management usually involves multiple operators from different locations. These can be chemical expert, response manager, vehicle dispatcher, and so forth. Due to advanced communications technology they can communicate with each other and download data about real-time events and the status of the operation (see Fig. 13.4). They all

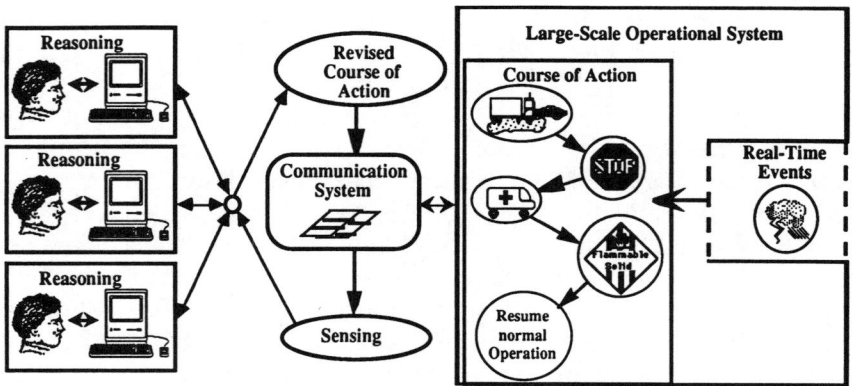

FIG. 13.4.   Conceptual model of operational risk management for multiple independent operators.

receive the same data from the large-scale operational system. In fact, everything that has been said about a single operator holds also for several operators. However, different operators process incoming data differently. Thus, the results of their analyses and the recommendations for changes in CAs are not expected to be identical.

Assuming that all operators make decision making by attribute, that is, they first assess the impacts of the RTEs on the attributes of the alternatives, discrepancies among the operators can be determined at two stages: (a) at the stage of assessment, and (b) at the stage of decision making (i.e., the recommendations in changing CAs).

The operators are assumed to work independently. Their statements are also assumed to be of equal importance; that is, there is no operator whose assessment or decisions are more important than the other operators' assessments and decisions. The ways assessments and choices by n operators can be handled is illustrated in Fig. 13.5. The assessments by n operators are first checked for feasibility (where feasibility needs still to be defined) — that is, to see if they all can be considered as feasible, although they are not all identical. If this is not the case, the assessments of some operators could be ignored and other operators could be asked to repeat their assessment. With the feasible assessments, a group assessment could be generated that will be used to determine the optimal course of action.

If such an aggregated group assessment is not desired, one could compute for each operator an optimal course of action based on the assessment. Then these multiple courses of action must be checked for feasibility (which also needs to be defined). If they are all feasible, the desired course of action could be computed. In the other case, reassessment must be done.

We now introduce a set of notations and definitions both at the level of assessment and at the level of decision making. Let's assume that an RTE requires the preferences of n activities to be reassessed and m courses of action to be revised.

Assessment

The assessment spectrum Π was introduced as consisting of several preference classes, some of them referring to attributes with high uncertainty (e.g., risks of taking an activity) and some of them referring to attributes with low uncertainty (e.g., costs of taking an activity): $\Pi = \Pi^{(1)} < \cdots < \Pi^{(n)}$. An example of a preference spectrum for hazardous material transportation is:

$$\alpha < \text{High-Risk} < \text{Transportation-Costs} < \text{Low-Risk} < \omega$$

Let us assume that the attribute classes for high-uncertainty attributes (in this example the two classes High-Risk and Low-Risk), as well as the classes

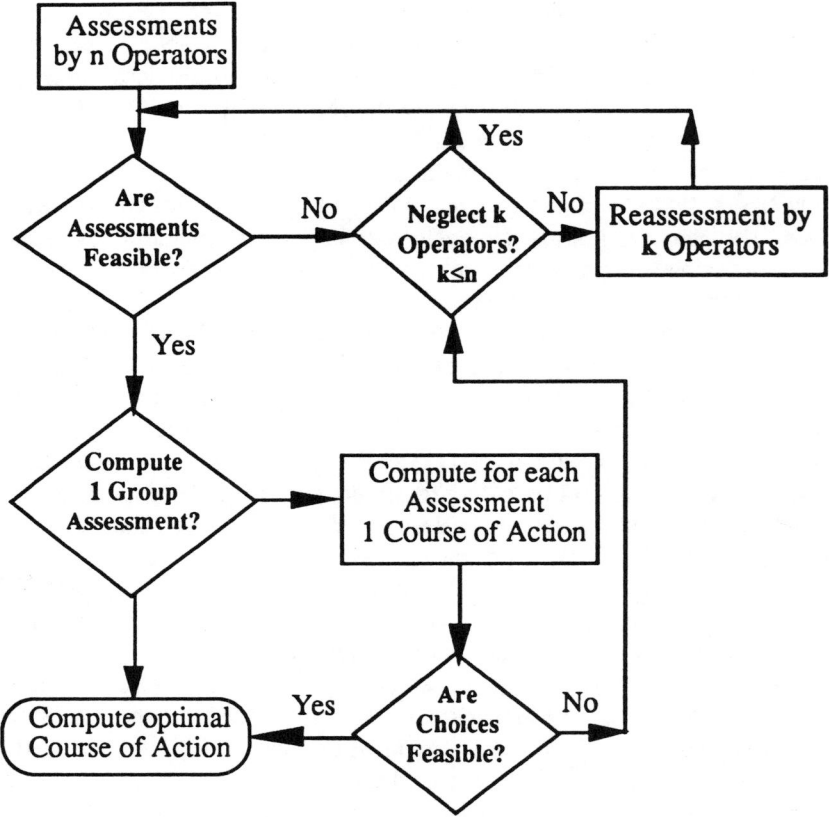

FIG. 13.5. Assessment and choice with multiple operators.

α and ω, consist of only one element, and the classes of low uncertainty of multiple elements. It is further assumed that an assessment is done properly if to every activity one element reflecting every attribute is assigned to it. For the example of hazardous material transportation, an assessment is proper if every activity has a risk element out of $\{\alpha$, High-Risk, Low-Risk, $\omega\}$ and a cost element out of $\{\alpha, \{\$\}, \omega\}$.

An RTE affects usually several activities. With k experts, the probability that all experts assess the risk value for one activity identically is therefore $4/4^k$. Because their assessment is independent, the probability of having m identical assessments out of n assessments (i.e., n activities), where $m \le n$, is binomially distributed, where $p = 4/4_k$:

$$p_m^{(n)} = \binom{n}{m} p^m (1-p)^{n-m}$$

We would of course not expect that all k operators agree on all n assessments. If, let us say, k-2 operators agree and 2 disagree in their assessment, the assessment would certainly be valuable. On the other hand, we know that with four risk classes and k experts, trunc$(k/4) + 1$ operators agree on at least one value.

An assessment by n operators is called *sufficient* if the majority of the operators trades off risks appropriately compared to another attribute class. For the assessment spectrum $\{\alpha$, High-Risk, Low-Risk, $\omega\}$, this implies that the assessment is sufficient if the majority of experts agrees on one of the two sets $\{\alpha$, High-Risk$\}$ or $\{$Low-Risk, $\omega\}$. The corresponding set is called the sufficient set.

An assessment is called *efficient* if it is sufficient and a majority of the operators choosing the sufficient set agree on one preference. Finally, an assessment is called *satisfactory* if a majority of operators agrees on one preference class.

Theorem 6. A satisfactory assessment is efficient.

Proof. Let $\Pi_<$ be the set of preference classes (e.g., α, High-Risk) of an attribute that are less preferred than the one class of another attribute X(e.g., Cost), and let $\Pi_>$ be the set of preference classes (e.g., Low-Risk, ω) of the same attribute that are more preferred than X. Let Π_i be the preference class that determined that the assessment is satisfactory; that is, by definition $|\Pi_i| > |\Pi_j|$, where $i \neq j$. Because $\Pi_i \in \Pi_<$ or $\Pi_i \in \Pi_>$, it follows that the assessment is efficient.

An RTE causes several activities to be reassessed. So far, we have only addressed how much multiple experts "agree" on the preference assessment of an activity. However, a measure needs to be introduced that accounts for the consistency in conservatism. An operator that assigns consistently lower preferences to activities than the other operators is called *conservative*. Being consistently conservative over all activities is acceptable, but if the group of operators has continuously different operators assigning low preferences to activities, the assessment is not consistent any more.

The assessment of m activities by n operators is called *consistent* if there is significant agreement between the rankings of the operators with respect to conservatism. This means that the ranking of the operators concerning conservatism should not change too often when multiple activities have to be reassessed. With n operators making q assessments, there are $\binom{4}{2}$ comparisons among the n experts. The significance of rank order can be expressed using Kendall's coefficient of concordance W (see Kendall & Gibbons, 1990, chapter 6):

$$W = \frac{12S}{q^2(n^3 - n)}, \text{ where } S = \sum_{i=1}^{n} \left[R_i - \frac{q(n+1)}{2} \right]^2$$

where R_i is the actual rank sum for each assessment. If all the operators are independent in their assessment, then any set of rankings is just as probable as any other set. The distribution of W in the $(n!)^q$ possible sets of ranks is given in Table 5 in Kendall and Gibbons (1990). If the hypothesis that all n operators have the same degree of conservatism is rejected, we can conclude that some operators are more conservative than the others; that is, there is no significant agreement between the assessment of the operators concerning their conservatism.

For a pairwise comparison of the operator's conservatism, we could use a nonparametric test, such as the Mann-Whitney test (Conover, 1980). In this case, one is interested in testing whether two operators have the same degree of conservatism against the hypothesis that one is more conservative than the other one. The values that the two operators obtained in q assessments are ranked. With the test statistic being $T = \Sigma_i R(X_i)$, or if there are many ties T minus the mean and divided by the standard deviation, the hypothesis of equal conservatism is tested. If it is rejected at some level of significance, we can conclude that one of the two operators is more conservative than the other one.

Another way to measure consistency among the operators' assessments is using a doubly stochastic transition matrix between different assessments as proposed in (Collins & Ruefli, 1992). The element p_{ij} in the transition matrix is the probability that an operator that was the ith most conservative operator for the assessment α will be the jth most conservative operator for the assessment $\alpha + 1$. If the operators are all equally conservative, this conditional probability of transition from ith rank to jth rank is $1/n$. The relative uncertainty of the n operator's q assessments, defined as the normalized conditional entropy, expresses the relative uncertainty of the assessment process. This is the relative uncertainty given the assessments of the operators compared to knowing only the number of operators.

Feasibility of assessment can now be defined in different ways. An assessment of q activities by n operators is *feasible* if the assessment of every activity is satisfactory and the q assessments by n experts are consistent. A less stringent definition of feasibility would be to replace "satisfactory" with "efficient."

Decision Making

When n experts assess m activities, they could agree in all n assessments. This assessment would be feasible by any definition and the computed CAs would also be identical. Assuming that they do not agree on all assessments, but the assessment is still feasible, the n CAs could be either identical or not, depending on the characteristics of the ORM problem. We introduce the following definitions.

Two alternatives, CA_i and CA_j, are called *indifferent* if they have the same overall preference: $\pi_{CA_i} \oplus \pi_{CA_j}$. They are called *congruent* if they consist of the same activities in the same sequence: $a_i^{(CA_2)} = a_i^{(CA_2)}$. They are called *analogous* if they are congruent but not indifferent. And, finally, they are called *identical* if they are congruent and indifferent.

The feasibility of CAs can also be defined at all four levels. The appropriate approach has to be determined considering the specific ORM problem.

CONCLUSIONS

In this chapter, decision logic for operational risk management has been proposed. It is based on a set of cognitive assumptions that have been assessed in an experimental setting with experienced operators. The operational risk management approach has been discussed for single and multiple operators acting under stress in an uncertain environment. An algorithm for revising optimal courses of action, based on a preference algebra, was discussed and a procedure for multiple operators was outlined.

There is no doubt that advanced communications and computing technologies will continue to have a major impact on the way operational risk management can be addressed. However, if in this highly interactive human–machine system new approaches are not based on the human's cognitive capabilities, operational risk management could increase the risks instead of mitigating them. One must also bear in mind that despite the potential for automation, large-scale operations will always require humans as decision makers. Therefore, research should also focus on the integration and not only on the automatization of decision-making processes.

In order to gain a clear understanding of the appropriateness of operational risk management approaches, empirical evidence must be gathered. This can be done by presenting prototype systems to experienced operators. In addition, this evidence should be substantiated in an experimental setting. For single operators and unconditional preferences we showed that the cognitive assumptions are significant. Further research should consequently focus on conditional preferences and multiple operators.

REFERENCES

Belardo, S., Karwan, K. R., & Wallace, W. A. (1984). Managing the response to disasters using microcomputers. *Interfaces, 14*(2), 29–39.

Beroggi, G. E. G. (1991). Modelling real-time decision making for hazardous material transportation. PhD dissertation. *Dissertation Abstracts International.* (University Microfilms No. 9202173).

Beroggi, G. E. G., & Wallace, W. A. (1992). *Operational control of the transportation of hazardous materials: An experimental assessment of alternative decision models.* Technical Report, Polyproject Risk & Safety. Zurich: Swiss Federal Institute of Technology.

Collins, J. M., & Ruefli, T. W. (1992). Strategic risk: An ordinal approach. *Management Science, 38*(12), 1707–1731.

Conover, W. J. (1980). *Practical nonparametric statistics.* New York: Wiley.

Dantzig, G. B. (1975). On the shortest route through a network. *Mathematical Association of America: Studies in Graph Theory, Part I,* 89–93.

DeKeyser, V. (1987). How can computer-based visual displays aid operators? *International Journal of Man-Machine Studies, 27,* 471–478.

Gibbons, A. (1989). *Algorithmic graph theory.* Cambridge: Cambridge University Press.

Janis, I. L., & Mann, L. (1977). *A psychological analysis of conflict, choice, & commitment.* New York: Free Press.

Kendall, M., & Gibbons, J. D. (1990). *Rank correlation methods.* New York: Oxford University Press.

Mancini, G. (1987). Commentary: Models of the decision maker in unforseen accidents. *International Journal of Man-Machine Studies, 27,* 631–639.

Moray, N. (1987). Intelligent aids, mental models, & the theory of machines. *International Journal of Man-Machine Studies, 27,* 619–629.

Simon, H. A. (1955). A behavioral model of rational choice. *Quarterly Journal of Economics, 69,* 99–118.

Wagenaar, W., & Groeneweg, J. (1987). Accidents at sea: Multiple causes & impossible consequences. *International Journal of Man-Machine Studies, 27,* 587–598.

Wallace, W. A. (1989) *Command & control: A team problem solving & decision making process.* Griffis AFB, NY: Rome Laboratory/COE.

Author Index

A

Allen, T. J., 90, *111*
Allison, G. T., 133, *158*
Altman, E., 59, 60, *86*
Anderson, C. R., 115, *158*
Anderson, J., 80, *86*
Anderson, P. A., 40, *54*, 78, *84*
Antonucci, T. C., 218, 220, *239*
Argote, L., 114, *158*, 213, *214*
Argyris, C., 197, *214*
Arnold, H. J., 181, 182, *193*
Arrow, K. J., 218, *239*
Arthur, W. B., 162, *176*
Ashby, W. R., xii, *xvi*
Axelrod, R., 21, 25, 26, *37*

B

Balanchandran, M., 3, *17*
Baligh, H. H., 80, *84,* 179, 183, *193*
Bantel, K. A., 213, *214*
Barnes, J. A., 218, 221, *239*
Baron, R. A., 41, *54*
Basar, T., 166, 167, *176,* 280, *286*
Bateman, T., 81, *84*
Batra, B., 198, 213, *215*
Baylor, G., 57, *86*
Beckman, S., 213, *214*

Beer, S., xii, *xvi*
Belardo, S., 294, *307*
Bendor, J., 217, 218, 220, 224, *239*
Beroggi, G. E. G., 296, 297, *307, 308*
Berry, D. C., 181, *193*
Bertsekas, D. P., 169, *176*
Beteille, A., 218, 219, *239*
Blalock, H., 58, *84*
Blanning, R. W., 181, 190, *193*
Bond, A. H., 162, *176*
Booker, L. B., 21, *37*
Bott, E., 218, 221, *239*
Bouwman, M., 80, *84*
Box, G., 11, 13, *17*
Boyd, B., 8, *18*
Bradshaw, G., 80, *85*
Brehmer, B., 263, *286*
Brooks, G., 213, *215*
Burgelman, R. A., 23, *37*
Burns, T., 90, *111*
Burt, R. S., 218, 222, *239*
Burton, R., 22, *37,* 80, *84,* 179, 183, *193*
Bushnell, L. G., 3, *17*

C

Cameron, K. S., 114, *158*
Campbell, D. T., 181, 182, *193*

Carley, K. M., xii, *xvi*, 3, 11, *17,* 39, 40, 43, 44, 52, *54,* 56, 57, 58, 60, 64, 70, 71, 74, 80, *84, 85, 86,* 113, 114, 115, 116, 117, 120, 121, 133, 134, 147, *158,* 198, 207, 211, *214*
Carroll, G. R., xii, *xvi*, 23, 36, *37*
Ceccatto, H. A., 220, 229, *239*
Chadha, S. R., 186, *193*
Chandler, A., 81, *85*
Charnes, A., 55, *85*
Chatman, J. A., 11, *18*
Chatterjee, K., 162, *176*
Child, J., 114, *158*
Christiansen, T., 16, *17*
Clancey, W. J., 3, *17,* 80, *85*
Cohen, G. P., 3, 13, *17*
Cohen, K. J., 195, *214*
Cohen, M. D., xii, *xvi*, 3, *17,* 39, *54,* 57, 58, 74, *85,* 212, *214*
Collins, J. M., 306, *308*
Conover, W. J., 306, *308*
Cook, T. D., 181, 182, *193*
Cooper, W., 55, *85*
Coyne, R. D., 3, *17*
Crecine, J. P., 195, *214*
Crowston, K., 11, *17, 18,* 36, *37,* 162, *177*
Cummings, L. L., 133, *158*
Cyert, R. M., xii, *xvi*, 20, *37,* 55, *85,* 195, 197, *214*

D

Daft, R., 56, *85*
Dantzig, G. B., 301, *308*
Daugherty, A. F., 166, 170, *176*
Davis, R., 182, *193*
DiMaggio, P., 22, *37*
DeKeyser, V., 294, *308*
Delbecq, S. L., 133, *158*
Devadas, R., 213, *214*
Donaldson, G., 81, *85*
Doreian, P., 100, *111*
Dow, G. K., 163, 164, 165, 166, *176*
Downs, A., 77, *85*
Drazin, R., 114, 115, *158*
Duncan, R. B., 183, *193*
Dym, C. L., 2, *18*

E

Earley, P. C., 264, *286*
Ehtamo, H., 162, 170, 174, *177*

Ephrath, A. R., 276, *286*
Epple, D., 114, *158,* 213, *214*

F

Fararo, T., 147, *158*
Feldman, D. C., 181, 182, *193*
Feldman, M., 57, *85*
Fischer, G. W., 40, *54,* 78, *84*
Fisher, F. M., 167, *176*
Fisk, S. T., xii, *xvi*
Fontana, W., 26, *37*
Forrester, J. W., xii, *xvi*
Freeman, J., 20, 24, 25, 26, 36, 37, *38,* 162, *176, 177,* 204, *214*
Friedell, M. F., 100, *111*
Friedman, D., 245, *262*
Friedman, D. D., 217, *239*
Friedman, J. W., 166, *176*
Fulk, J., 8, 9, *18*

G

Galbraith, C. S., 115, *158*
Galbraith, J. R., 4, 6, 10, 14, 15, 16, *18,* 189, *193*
Gero, J. S., 3, *17*
Gibbons, A., 301, *308*
Gibbons, J. D., 305, 306, *308*
Gioia, D., 55, *86*
Glance, N. S., 217, 218, *239*
Glasser, L., 162, *176*
Glazer, R., 55, *85*
Glueck, W., 81, *86*
Glynn, M. A., 196, 197, 198, 203, 204, 209, *214*
Gode, D. K., 242, *262*
Goes, J., 213, *215*
Goldberg, D. E., 21, *37*
Granovetter, M. S., 218, *239*
Groeneweg, J., 294, *308*
Guetzkow, H., 89, *111*

H

Haberstroh, C. J., xii, *xvi*
Hage, J., xii, *xvi*
Hämäläinen, R. P., 162, 170, 174, *177*
Hammond, K. R., 120, *158*
Hanada, M., 113, *158*
Hannan, M. T., 20, 24, 25, 26, 36, 37, *38,* 162, *176,* 204, *214*

Hansen, R. G., 176, *177*
Harary, F., 91, *111*
Harbison-Biggs, K., 181, 191, *193*
Hardin, G., 217, *239*
Hardin, R., 217, 220, *239*
Harrison, J. R., xii, *xvi*, 36, *37*
Hart, A. E., 181, *193*
Hartigan, J. A., 218, 222, *239*
Hastie, R., 267, *286*
Hayes-Roth, F., 181, *193*
Hedberg, B., 209, *214*
Heiner, R. A., 163, 174, 175, *177*
Hernandez-Lerma, O., 275, *286*
Hoffman, A. N., 98, 102, *111*
Holland, J. H., 21, 22, 23, 26, 34, *37*, 162, *177*
House, J. S., xii, *xvi*
Houskisson, R. E., 115, *158*
Huber, G., 55, 82, *85*
Huberman, B. A., 217, 218, 221, 229, *239*
Hunter, J., 11, 13, *17*
Hunter, W., 11, 13, *17*

J

Jablin, F. M., 77, *85*
Jackson, S. E., 213, *214*
Janis, I. L., 294, *308*
Jelinek, M., 197, *214*
Jin, Y., 2, *18*
Johnson, M. P. xii, *xvii*

K

Karwan, K. R., 294, *307*
Kendall, M., 305, 306, *308*
Kersten, G., 162, *176*
Kiesler, S., 11, *18*
Kjaer-Hansen, J., 3, 11, *17*, 39, 43, 44, 52, *54*, 56, 64, *85*
Kleinman, D. L., 3, *17*, 82, *87*, 264, 265, 269, 276, *286*
Kleinrock, L., 269, *286*
Knipscheer, C. P. M., 218, 220, *239*
Koza, J. R., 21, 25, *38*
Krackhardt, D., 81, *85*, 90, *111*, 113, 115, 116, 121, 122, 125, *158*
Kulka, R. A., 181, 192, *193*
Kumar, A., 115, *158*
Kunz, J. C., 3, *18*

L

Laird, J. E., 39, 43, *54*, 59, 60, 64, *85*, *86*, 162, *177*
Lane, D. A., 162, *177*
Langley, P., 80, *85*
Lant, T. K., 197, 198, 200, 201, 202, 204, 208, 209, 210, 213, *214*
LaPotin, P., xii, *xvii*, 3, 11, 13, *18*, 39, 42, *54*, 198, *215*
Lasserre, J. B., 275, *286*
Lawrence, P. R., 83, *85*, 114, 115, *158*
Leinhardt, S., 218, *239*
Lenat, D., 181, *193*
Levinthal, D. A., 199, 203, 208, 209, 210, *215*
Levitt, B., 197, *215*
Levitt, R. E., 2, 3, *18*
Likert, R., 263, *286*
Lin, Z., 57, 80, *85*, 114, 115, 116, 117, 120, 121, 125, 133, 147, *158*
Lincoln, J. R., 98, 102, *111*, 113, *158*
Long, R. J., 114, *158*
Lord, R., 55, *85*
Lorsch, J. W., 81, 83, *85*, 114, 115, *158*
Lounama, P. H., 198, 205, 209, *215*
Luh, P. B., 264, 269, *286*
Lumsden, C. J., 19, 37, *38*

M

Mackenzie, K. D., 102, *111*, 113, 115, 116, 121, 122, 125, *158*
Maher, K., 55, *85*
Malone, T. W., 11, *18*, 34, *38*, 113, 115, 116, 121, *158*, 162, *177*
Mancini, G., 294, *308*
Mann, L., 294, *308*
March, J. G., xii, *xvi*, 4, 13, 16, *18*, 20, *37*, 39, *54*, 55, 57, 58, 74, 77, 78, *85*, *86*, 133, *158*, 197, 198, 199, 203, 205, 206, 208, 209, 210, 211, 212, *214*
Marschak, J., 82, *86*
Martin, J., 191, 192, *193*
Marwell, G., 218, *239*
Mason, L., 9, 11, *18*
Masuch, M., xii, *xvii*, 3, 11, 13, *18*, 39, 42, *54*, 198, *215*
Maynard Smith, J., 175, *177*
Mazlack, L. J., 186, *193*
McBride, K., 113, *158*

McGrath, J. E., 181, 192, *193*
McGraw, K. L., 181, 192, *193*
McGuire, C. B., 82, *86*
McKelvey, B., 25, 34, *38*
Meyer, A., 213, *215*
Mezias, S. J., 196, 197, 200, 201, 202, 203, 204, 208, 209, 210, *215*
Michalewicz, Z., 24, *38*
Michels, R., 89, *111*
Miles, R. E., 187, *193*
Miller, J. H., 162, 165, 175, *177*
Milliken, F. J., 197, 198, 213, *214*
Mintzberg, H., 81, *86*
Mookherjee, D., 217, 218, 220, 224, *239*
Moray, N., 294, *308*
Moss, S., 162, *177*
Murphy, K., 213, *214*
Murray, A. I., 213, *215*

N

Nass, C. I., 9, 11, *18*
Nelson, R. R., 25, 34, *38,* 212, *215*
Neves, D., 80, *86*
Newell, A., 3, 11, *17,* 39, 43, 44, 52, *54,* 56, 57, 58, 59, 60, 64, 80, *85, 86, 87,* 162, *177*
Northcraft, G. B., 264, *286*

O

Obel, B., 22, *37,* 80, *84,* 179, 183, *193*
O'Leary, D. E., 181, 182, 183, *193*
Oliver, P. E., 218, *239*
Olsder, G. J., 280, *286*
Olsen, J. P., xii, *xvi,* 39, *54,* 57, 58, 74, 78, *85,* 133, *158,* 212, *214*
Olson, M., 217, *239*
O'Reilly, C. A., 11, *18*
Ostrom, T. M., 147, *158*
Ow, P. S., 115, *158*

P

Padgett, J. F., 40, *54*
Pattipati, K. R., 82, *87,* 264, 269, 276, *286*
Pentland, B. T., 36, *38*
Perrow, C., 58, *86,* 120, *158,* 183, *193*
Perry, T. A., 263, *286*
Pfeffer, J., 133, *158*
Pick, R. A., 186, *193*
Plott, C. R., 255, *262*

Porter, L. W., 77, *85*
Powell, W., 22, *37*
Preece, A. D., 181, *193*
Prietula, M., 3, 11, *17,* 39, 43, 44, 52, *54,* 56, 64, 80, *85, 86,* 115, *158*
Putnam, L. L. 77, *158*

R

Radford, A. D., 3, *17*
Radner, R., 55, 82, *86,* 163, *177*
Rae, J., 162, *177*
Robbins, S. P., 189, *193*
Roberts, K., 114, *159*
Roberts, K. A., 77, *85*
Romanelli, E., 20, 24, 25, 26, *38,* 202, 213, *215*
Romelaer, P., 57, *86*
Rosenbloom, P. S., 39, 43, *54,* 59, 60, 64, *85, 86,* 162, *177*
Rosenman, M. A., 3, *17*
Ruefli, T. W., 306, *308*

S

Sah, R. K., 163, *177*
Salancik, G. R., 133, *158*
Samuelson, W. F., 176, *177*
Schelling, T. C., 217, *239*
Schmerken, I., 20, *38*
Schon, D., 197, *214*
Scott, R. S., xi, *xvii*
Scott, W. R., 61, *86,* 113, 133, *158,* 189, *193,* 218, 221, *239*
Seashore, S. E., 113
Selten, R., 225, *239*
Serfarty, D., 3, *17,* 264, 269, *286*
Shakun, M. F., 162, *176*
Shapira, Z., 55, *86*
Shi, P., 270, *287*
Shortliffe, E., 80, *85*
Shrader, C. B., 98, 102, *111*
Shrivastava, P., 120, *158*
Shull, F. A., 133, *158*
Sigelman, L., 20, *38,* 196, *215*
Simon, H. A., 4, 7, 13, 16, *18,* 20, *38,* 40, 43, *54,* 55, 56, 57, 58, 60, 77, 80, *85, 86,* 89, 90, 93, *111,* 175, *177,* 225, *239,* 274, *287,* 294, *308*
Sims, H., 55, *86*
Singh, J. V., 19, 37, *38*
Smith, A., 217, *239*

Snow, C. C., 187, *193*
Snyder, N., 81, *86*
Song, A., 265, *286*
Sproull, L., 11, *18*
Srinivas, M. M., 218, 219, *239*
Stahl, D. O., 167, *177*
Stalker, G. M., 90, *111*
Stanley, J. C., 181, *193*
Staw, B., 80, *86*
Steckel, J., 55, *85*
Steinfeld, C., 9, *18*
Stelzner, M. C., 3, *18*
Stern, R. N., 90, *111*, 113, 116, 121, 125, *158*
Stiglitz, J. E., 163, *177*
Stinchcombe, A. L., 20, 36, *38*, 55, 80, *87*
Sunder, S., 242, 245, 255, *262*

T

Tancredi, L. R., 113, *158*
Tang, Z., 82, *87*
Tatum, C. B., 3, *18*
Taylor, M., xii, *xvii*, 217, 220, *239*
Terence, R. M., 264, *287*
Thompson, J. D., xiv, *xvii*, 4, *18*, 27, 34, *38*
Tsitsiklis, J. N., 169, *176*
Tushman, M. L., 202, 213, *215*

V

Van de Ven, A. H., 114, 115, *158*
van Kampen, N. G., 220, *239*

Vaughan, W. S., Jr., 263, *287*
Verhagen, H., 45, *54*
Verkama, M., 162, 170, 174, *177*
Virany, B., 213, *215*

W

Wagenaar, W., 294, *308*
Wallace, W. A., 294, 296, 297, *307, 308*
Waterman, D., 181, *193*
Weick, K., 81, *87*
Weingart, L., 80, 82, *86, 87*
Weissinger-Baylon, xii, *xvi*
Whicker, M. L., 20, *38*, 196, *215*
Wiersema, M. F., 213, *215*
Wilensky, R., 80, *87*
William, S. S., 264, *287*
Williams, M. D., 3, *18*
Williamson, O. E., 23, 25, *38*, 55, *87*
Wilson, R. J., 95, *111*
Winer, R., 55, *85*
Winter, S. G., 25, 34, *38*, 212, *215*
Woods, J., 113, *158*

Y

Yost, G., 59, 60, *86, 87*

Z

Zeithami, C., 81, *84*
Zytkow, J., 80, *85*

Subject Index

A

Actor, *see* agent
Adaptive agents, *see* Agent adaptation
Adaptive organizations, *see* organizational
  adaptation
Administrative theory, 55
Agent, 3, 4, 6, 10, 11, 13, 22, 23, 27,
  29–31, 34, 39, 40, 45, 50, 52–53,
  56–60, 62–67, 76–81, 267–268
  adaptation, 19–38, 55–87, 161–177, 197,
    205–208
  autonomous, 68
  beliefs, 206–207
  incentives, 217–219
  influence, 223
  knowledge, 57, 60, 64, 69, 70, 72, 79, 81,
    165–169, 197, 206–207, 229
  learning, 59–60, 63, 64, 76, 205–208
  preferences, 40–41, 64, 68, 179, 183, 264,
    293, 296–302
  reactive, 161, 165–169, 170–176
  relations among, 81, 97–102, 218–219,
    221, 238
  search, 64–70
  types of, 35
  unavailability, 134
  zero intelligence, 241–262
Ambiguity, 200–201, 204–206, 208–209

A

Artifact design, 2
Artificial intelligence, 1, 3, 11, 39
Authority relations, 93

B

Boundedly rational agent, 4, 7, 14, 40, 45,
  55–57, 60, 63, 64, 70, 72, 78–80, 84,
  175, 224–225, 263, 274, 294

C

Centralization, 10, 89, 183
Coalitions, 270
Cognition, 55–58, 61–64, 70, 79, 80, 84, 162
  situated, 71, 296–297
Cognitive capability, 41–42, 44, 64, 79, 263,
  268, 274, 294–298
Commitment, 41–42, 45
Communication, 4, 5, 6, 8, 9, 10, 13, 39,
  43–45, 50, 52, 53, 57, 59, 68–70, 250,
  268, 274
  breakdowns, 74, 77
  channels, 4, 134
  cost, 26
  network, *see* Communication, pattern
  pattern, 6, 24, 26, 40, 45, 64, 90
  technology, 1, 3, 8, 9, 10, 11, 19, 302
Competition, 19, 23, 205

Contingency theory, 10
Cooperation, 14, 23, 44, 45, 53, 161–162, 195–215
Coordination, 27, 29–34, 68, 72, 113, 161–162, 264, 269–271
Cost, 3, 113, 115, 121–122, 131–133, 197, 199, 208–209, 296
Crises, 67, 74, 76–78, 289–308
Culture, 81

D

Decision rules, 169–176, 195, 197–198, 209, 245
Decision tree, 275–278
Design, 14

E

Economic theory, 55
Emergent behavior, 58, 68
Emotion, 81
Enactment, 81
Environment, 20–27, 56–60, 134–146, 179, 183, 189, 199–201, 204–206, 208–209, 264, 273
Environmental change, see Environmental restructuring
Environmental restructuring, 19–20, 199–201, 208–209, 213
Experience, 6, 70, 72, 206
Experiential learning, 70–78, 197–198
Expertise, 11, 25, 40, 42, 45, 304

F

Formal organization, 97, 99
Formalization, 183

G

Game theory, 163, 166, 278–281
Graph connectivity, 95–97, 102, 115, 126, 128
Graph efficiency, 98–99, 102, 115, 123–124, 131–133
and performance, 135–146
Graph hierarchy, 97–98, 102, 115, 125–128, 131–133
and performance, 135–146
Graph least upper boundedness, 99–100, 102, 115, 126–127, 129, 131–133
and performance, 135–146

Graph theory, 91–93, 102
Group, 3, 221
flat, see Teams
performance, 224, 271
size, 230–231

H

Hierarchy, 10, 21, 23, 34, 45, 66, 71–73, 77, 78, 89–91, 113, 116–120, 218–219, 222, 231
and learning, 208, 211
and performance, 135–146
measure of, 93–102, 113, 124–128, 131–133

I

Imitative organizations, 201, 204
Individual connections, see Agent, relations among
Individuals, see Agent
Informal organization, 89–91, 94
Information condensation, 77
Information distortion, 77, 229
Information feedback, 71–72, 164
Information flow, 90
Information inaccuracy, 208
Information loss, 74, 134
Information processing, 4–6, 59–61, 163
Information redundancy, 73, 74
Information sharing, 82
Information technology, see Communication, technology
Information uncertainty, 167, 175, 199, 268, 271, 303–306
Innovation, 199–200, 203–204, 210
Institutional memory, see Organizational memory
Interaction, 81, 89, 166–169, 205, 218, 221–223, 238

L

Learning, see also Agent learning, Organizational learning
chunking, 63–70
experiential, 70–78, 205–209
mutual, 206, 209
rate, 199–200, 207, 210
superstitious, 205

M

Market, 34, 241–262
Matrix, 116–120, 189
Mental model, 56, 65–66, 69–71, 74, 81, 267–268

N

Negotiation, 68, 76, 80
Norms, 64, 68, 84, 206

O

Open Systems theory, 61
Organic organization, 90, 98
Organizational adaptation, 199–202, 204, 209, 213, 228–229
Organizational behavior, 55, 60, 68
Organizational beliefs, 206–207
Organizational climate, 42
Organizational constraints, 56–59
Organizational decision making, 39, 63, 68, 71, 162, 211, 291–293, 306–307
Organizational design, 2, 4, 14, 19, 57, 64, 72–78, 80, 83, 113, 115–120, 131, 183, 192
  measures of, 89–111, 113–159
Organizational effectiveness, 230–239, 271
Organizational efficiency, 99, 113, 122–124, 133, 249–255, 305
Organizational evolution, 20, 176, 195
Organizational experience, 199–200
Organizational fitness, 25, 36
Organizational form, see Organizational structure
Organizational learning, 39, 80, 195–215
Organizational memory, 73
Organizational opportunities, 56–59
Organizational performance, 10, 16, 25, 30, 42, 64, 68–71, 74, 76–78, 89, 113, 114, 133–134, 197, 199–205, 271–272
Organizational policies, 10
Organizational position, see Roles
Organizational reorganization, see Organizational transformation
Organizational size, 64, 68, 69, 179, 183, 187, 189, 202–203, 218–219
Organizational structure, 1–11, 23–25, 31, 36, 40–45, 68–78, 100, 116–120, 124–131, 134, 161, 166, 172–176, 179, 221

Organizational survival, 201
Organizational transformation, 179, 202, 236
Organizational type, 200–201

P

Planning, 68, 281–282, 289–291
Product, 4

Q

Quality, 3

R

Resource access structure, see Task, assignment
Resources, 19, 251–255, 267
Roles, 9, 59, 66, 68, 81
Routines, 34, 206, 209–210
Rule-based behavior, see also Decision rules 13, 34, 63–70, 241–245

S

Simulation
  expert system, 179–193
  genetic algorithms, 21–23, 162, 164–165, 176
  Monte Carlo, 13, 135–146, 229–238
  numerical, 16, 70–78, 101–102, 169–175, 245–255
  review relative to organizational learning, 195–215
  symbolic, 11, 16, 60, 63–70
Situated agents, 59, 65, 71
Skills, see Expertise
Social network, see Agent, relations among; Interaction; Organizational structure
Social situation, 57, 60–66, 68–70, 72, 74–79, 82
Specialization, 53, 54, 183
Strategy, 179, 183

T

Task, 1–13, 26, 27, 29–31, 40–47, 57–71, 74–83, 97, 135–146, 263–266
  assignment, 27–34, 36, 41, 64–68, 72–78, 83, 116–120, 134, 272–273

complexity, 10, 74
decomposition, *see* Task, assignment
interdependency, 2, 5, 10, 13, 27, 267,
    273, 303
overlap, 27–34
routine, 97
Team, 68, 71, 72, 77, 78, 116–120, 230–231,
    263, 273–274, 285–286
and learning, 208, 211
theory, 163

Technology, 179, 183, 188–189, 199, 204,
    206
Ties, *see* Agent, relations among
Training, 120, 135–146
Turing Test, 190–192
Turnover, 73–76, 134, 207, 210–211, 213

U

Uncertainty absorption, 77